Routledge Library Editions

THE BRITISH MONOPOLIES COMMISSION

ECONOMICS

Routledge Library Editions – Economics

INDUSTRIAL ECONOMICS
In 10 Volumes

I	Monopoly and Restrictive Practices	*Allen*
II	Effects of Mergers	*Cook*
III	Productivity and Economic Incentives	*Davison et al*
IV	An Economic Study of the City of London	*Dunning & Morgan*
V	Industry and the State	*Florence*
VI	The Logic of British and American Industry	*Florence*
VII	The Logic of Industrial Organization	*Florence*
VIII	The British Monopolies Commission	*Rowley*
IX	Studies in Industrial Organization	*Silverman*
X	Mergers and Acquisitions	*Young*

THE BRITISH MONOPOLIES COMMISSION

CHARLES K ROWLEY

Routledge
Taylor & Francis Group
LONDON AND NEW YORK

First published 1966 by Routledge

Published 2014 by Routledge

2 Park Square, Milton Park, Abingdon, Oxfordshire OX14 4RN
711 Third Avenue, New York, NY 10017

First issued in paperback 2014

Transferred to Digital Printing 2007

Routledge is an imprint of the Taylor & Francis Group, an informa business

British Library Cataloguing in Publication Data
A CIP catalogue record for this book
is available from the British Library

The British Monopolies Commission

ISBN 978-0-415-31349-0 (hbk)
ISBN 978-1-138-87863-1 (pbk)

Miniset: Industrial Economics

Series: Routledge Library Editions – Economics

THE BRITISH MONOPOLIES COMMISSION

CHARLES K. ROWLEY
BA, PhD
Department of Industrial Economics
The University of Nottingham

Routledge
Taylor & Francis Group
LONDON AND NEW YORK

FIRST PUBLISHED IN 1966

in 10 *on* 11 *point Plantin type*
BY SIMSON SHAND LTD
LONDON, HERTFORD AND HARLOW

TO THE MEMORY

OF MY FATHER

Author's Preface

This book grew out of a research project commenced in the Department of Industrial Economics at the University of Nottingham in 1961. The work of the Monopolies Commission appeared to provide valuable raw material for an analytical study of problems of monopoly supervision and control. At the same time, it appeared important that an appraisal should be undertaken of the administrative procedure of inquiry and report on economic problems, as typified by the Monopolies Commission. As a result, this book combines a detailed critical study of the Monopolies Commission itself, with an analysis of the economic issues involved in monopoly supervision and control.

My sincerest thanks are due to Professor S. R. Dennison, CBE, who provided invaluable assistance at a critical stage in the development of this book, who has read and commented upon early drafts of the entire work, and without whose kindly and sustained encouragement this book would not have been completed.

I would also like to thank Professor F. A. Wells, OBE, who read and commented upon early drafts of the book and who made available the finance required for accumulating case material. His assistance in improving the style and clarity of the text was invaluable.

Many others have generously contributed time and effort to this work. I would particularly thank Professor G. C. Allen, CBE, Professor T. Barna, D. Clark, A. Gabor, A. E. Hall, H. Levy, QC, W. Gilbert, CBE, K. M. Gwilliam and Professor J. H. B. Tew.

I am indebted to Margaret Aspden, my secretary, for the cheerful, efficient, and conscientious manner in which she typed and re-typed drafts of this work. The accuracy and speed with which the task was accomplished are most gratefully acknowledged.

I owe a personal debt to my wife for her unfailing support and encouragement, and for the active assistance she provided throughout the project.

C. K. ROWLEY
University of Kent at Canterbury
Canterbury
Kent

July 1965

Contents

AUTHOR'S PREFACE *page* 9

PART I THE HISTORICAL APPROACH

1. The Historical Background 1914–48 17
2. The Common Law Background 39

PART II THE MONOPOLIES COMMISSION

3. The Structure and Constitution of the Monopolies Commission 51
4. The Scope and Authority of the Monopolies Commission 61
5. The Investigating Procedure of the Monopolies Commission 81

PART III TRADE ASSOCIATION INQUIRIES

6. The Monopolies Commission and Price Agreements 109
7. Trade Associations and the Competitive Process 149
8. Trade Association Agreements and Barriers to Inter-Member Competition 161
9. Trade Association Agreements and Barriers to Independent Competition 171
10. The Trade Association and Public Policy 187

PART IV THE DOMINANT FIRM

11. The Dominant Firm and Oligopoly 193
12. The Dominant Firm and the Competitive Process 201
13. The Dominant Firm and Barriers to Independent Competition 215
14. Dominant Firm Activities and the Public Interest 235
15. The Dominant Firm and Public Policy 257

PART V STATISTICAL MEASURES OF ECONOMIC PERFORMANCE

16. Unit Production Costs and Prices 263
17. The Calculation of Rate of Return on Capital as a Public Interest Indicator 282
18. Rate of Return on Capital and the Public Interest 302

PART VI GOVERNMENT ACTION: ECONOMIC CONSEQUENCES

19. The Implementation of Monopolies Commission Recommendations 323
20. Economic Consequences of Monopolies Commission Reports 347

PART VII CONCLUSIONS AND RECOMMENDATIONS

21. The Monopolies Commission and Future Developments 371

APPENDICES

1. Members of the Monopolies Commission 1949–64 379
2. A Case Study of the Procedure of Inquiry—The Imperial Tobacco Company 381

CLASSIFIED BIBLIOGRAPHY 384

INDEX 389

Tables

1. Members of the Monopolies Commission 1948–53 *page* 52
2. The Time Period of Investigation 88
3. Monopolies Commission Official Annual Expenditures 91
4. The Nature and Extent of Expenditure by Investigated Bodies 91
5. Linoleum Products: Pence per Square Yard 265
6. Rubber Footwear Costs: December 1954 266
7. Metal Windows Production: Unit Costs 271
8. 25-watt Lamp Prices—International Comparisons 273
9. Total Match Costs per Gross 276
10. Ammonium Sulphate: Costs per Ton 277
11. Single Superphosphate: Cost per Metric Ton 280
12. Oxygen and Dissolved Acetylene Price Changes: Comparative Data 280
13. Measures Suggested and Accepted for Rate of Return on Capital Comparisons 306
14. Rate of Return on Capital Employed—Reference Fields 318
15. Calico Dress Print Prices 1957–62 353
16. BICC: Rate of Return on Turnover 1958–9 356
17. Sales of Matches in the United Kingdom 1953–62 359
18. The British Match Corporation: Match and Non-Match Activities 1959–63 361
19. BOC: Selected Statistics Relating to Annual Price Increases 1939–62 364

PART I

THE HISTORICAL APPROACH

History, a distillation of Rumour
Carlyle, *French Revolution*

Chapter One

THE HISTORICAL BACKGROUND 1914–48

In 1948 the British Labour Government produced the first legislation[1] for three centuries that dealt with market dominance by private enterprise organizations as a general matter for public supervision and control. Lack of earlier legislative activity in the field does not reflect, however, private and public apathy towards the issue of market dominance. This chapter provides an introduction to the most important relevant developments in attitudes and conditions that took place during the thirty years prior to the 1948 legislation.[2]

INTERNATIONAL TRADE—THE MOVEMENT TOWARDS PROTECTIONISM

For many years prior to the First World War Britain had pursued a general policy of free trade. Foreign commodities could cross British frontiers without encountering physical or financial obstruction[3] of any kind. This freedom provided keen competition for British producers in many fields.

During the First World War the British Government disrupted this general policy by the imposition of non-revenue duties on selected imports. This first interruption of a seventy-five year tradition—the McKenna duties, 1915—was designed less as an aid to British industry than as a means of limiting the use of shipping and of conserving foreign exchange. It is true that the McKenna duties were abolished in 1924 by a minority Labour Government which had been elected largely on the free trade issue. However, the duties were quickly reimposed by the Conservative Government in 1925. They were to remain in being until

[1] The Monopolies and Restrictive Practices (Inquiry and Control) Act 11 and 12, Geo. VI, c. 66.

[2] Those who desire to pursue their reading in this field beyond the confines of this chapter are referred to the classified bibliography.

[3] The minor revenue tariffs in existence were perfectly matched by excise duties on domestic commodities.

they were merged into the general tariff structure adopted at the outbreak of war in 1939.

The 1920s witnessed further limitations of British free trade policy. The British dyestuffs industry, sponsored by the Government after the war, was afforded protection by legislation in 1920. This legislation prohibited dyestuff importation save under licence. In 1921 heavy *ad valorem* import duties were introduced for a selected range of commodities by the 'Safeguarding of Industry' Act. Considered as temporary impositions initially, these duties became established with the passage of time. The range of commodities covered by the legislation was extended little by little. Eventually such clearly non-strategic commodities as gloves and gas mantles became subject to the legislation.

The British economy had suffered from economic depression throughout the 1920s. This depression had been exacerbated by the over-valuation of sterling in terms of foreign currencies when Britain returned to the Gold Standard in 1925. British depression in the 1920s contrasted sharply with the experience of most important industrial economies. However, the beginning of the 1930s witnessed the onset of international economic depression. This encouraged further nationalistic curtailment of international trade. A sequence of interrelated financial crises eventually resulted in a reluctant abandonment of the Gold Standard by Britain in 1931. Sterling immediately depreciated in value in relation to those currencies that remained on the Standard.

This depreciation afforded temporary relief to British producers from the competition of foreign commodities. It was evident, however, that a further British retreat from free trade policy would be forthcoming. The MacDonald Government had been returned in October 1931 with a very considerable protectionist majority. The anticipated movement towards British protectionism crystallized in February 1932 with the passing of the Import Duties Act. A general tariff at ten per cent *ad valorem* was imposed upon all imports save those specifically exempted.

This increase in protection placed Britain in a more powerful position to negotiate a reciprocal preference agreement with Commonwealth countries. The negotiations culminated in the Ottawa Agreement of 1932. This Agreement remains an important basis for the tariff system adopted by the British Government. In return for continued freedom of entry into the British market for all Dominion products, with the exception of meat, Britain obtained certain tariff concessions and increased preferences for British commodities in Dominion markets. In order to increase the preference afforded to Commonwealth imports the British Government imposed additional 'Ottawa' duties on a number of non-Commonwealth food imports. Such duties affected wheat, maize, butter, cheese and other dairy products.

The Ottawa Agreement represented the only British exception to a general establishment during the 1930s of a protectionist trading system. The protection afforded to British producers was primarily financial. Occasionally, however, tariff protection was fortified by the imposition of quantitative controls on imports. Steel and agricultural products were subjected in particular to the latter form of protection. In certain instances import protection was offered by the British Government as a specific inducement for the accomplishment of rationalization schemes.

The Second World War accelerated the progress of British protectionism. The total commitment of national resources for the war effort induced extensive import control by the British Government. Termination of hostilities did not involve, as it had in 1919, a rapid dismantling of import controls. The immediate background to the 1948 legislation was one of exchange control, quantitative controls over imports, and high *ad valorem* tariffs. Britain during the 1940s was a highly protectionist country by any standard.

The protectionist developments outlined above undoubtedly weakened public confidence in the automatic safeguards provided against the abuse of market power by firms and trade associations. During the early part of the twentieth century it had been commonly argued that British anti-trust legislation was rendered unnecessary by the existence of competing imports, especially where transportation costs comprised a small proportion of unit production costs. The progression of protectionist devices undermined the basis of this thesis, and contributed towards postwar suspicion of market dominance in Britain.

IMPACT OF THE TWO WORLD WARS[1]

The First World War had a profound effect upon the relationship between government and industry, and upon the organization of industry and trade. In December 1916 the Asquith Coalition Government collapsed and Lloyd George became Prime Minister. From that date controls of an extensive and detailed nature were established over the industrial sector. The Government also requisitioned a large amount of industrial property on a temporary basis. Selected controls included the issuing of building licences, limitations on plant capacity, output quotas, raw material allocations and regulations regarding working hours. Quality standards were imposed and publicly enforced and a rudimentary utility clothing scheme was introduced. Import and export licensing regulated the pattern of international trade. Price fixing and rationing became a feature of the domestic economy.

[1] A most useful reference book in this field is J. W. Grove, *Government and Industry in Britain*, Longmans, 1962.

A rapid expansion of the administrative organs of the Government was necessitated by this increase in public intervention in economic affairs. A large number of temporary civil servants were employed to this end providing many industrialists with first-hand experience of the machinery of government. Firms and representatives of industries were consulted on issues relating to public intervention; in certain instances firms themselves provided the means of supervision and collective discipline. Advisory committees were established in the majority of industries to facilitate public control over the economy.

It is not surprising, therefore, that the events of the First World War greatly stimulated the expansion and development of trade associations in the United Kingdom. A close working relationship was established between Ministers and trade associations during the war period and early postwar committees of inquiry emphasized the advantages of such co-operation, whilst encouraging the expansion of trade associations.

During the First World War three important national associations were established in the United Kingdom. The first to emerge, in 1915, was The National Union of Manufacturers, initially entitled The Association of British Manufacturers. This was closely followed in 1916 by the establishment of the Federation of British Industries which received particularly powerful support from firms in the Birmingham area. Until 1919 the Federation of British Industries concerned itself with union-employer relationships. In 1919 however, this function was transferred to a newly-constructed organization—The British Employers' Confederation. These three organizations were to play an important part in encouraging the consolidation and concentration of business activities in the United Kingdom.

Government intervention in the private sector was greater both in extent and in detail in the Second World War. Trade associations were empowered to act once again as agents of government in market allocation schemes, raw material rationing and price fixing. There were many more well-organized trade associations to undertake such responsibilities than had existed in 1916. Indeed, during the Second World War the staff of a number of trade associations comprised the entire staff of Government Control Organizations. Perhaps the most important such example is to be found in the Iron and Steel Control. More frequently, however, controls were staffed in part from the ranks of trade associations, in part from the ranks of senior company executives, and in part from the ranks of permanent civil servants.

Undoubtedly the close connections established between Government and trade associations during the war once again provided an impetus to the expansion of the latter kind of collective organization in this country. It has been estimated that rather more than seventy trade associations and federations were established between 1939 and 1945, whilst many of those already in existence experienced large membership increases and substantial expansion in the range of services provided to members.

Government wartime policies encouraged close relationships between independent companies. This development can be seen most clearly in the Export Group arrangements, and in the wartime concentration schemes for industries forced to release manpower for military purposes. Not unexpectedly, such soundly forged links provided a framework for outright financial merger or loose consultative relationships in the post-war period.

The immediate aftermath of the two World Wars differed considerably, both with regard to public attitudes and to government policy. Termination of hostilities in 1918 produced a powerful surge of opinion in favour of ending the wartime system of controls. Four days before the Armistice Mr Churchill[1] provided a foretaste of Government thoughts on the issue:

> Although it will undoubtedly be necessary for the Government of this country to intervene in industry and to control and regulate aspects of industry . . . our only object is to liberate the forces of industrial enterprise, to release the controls which have been found galling, to divest ourselves of responsibilities which the State has only accepted in this perilous emergency, and from which, in the overwhelming majority of cases, it had far better keep itself clear.

Five days after the Armistice *The Economist* took up the call for economic freedom:[2] 'The vital factor in procuring an abundance of productive employment is not raw materials but freedom; the first requisite of industry is the restoration of freedom.'

The Labour Party was deeply concerned, it is true, by fears of profiteering on the part of private enterprise unshackled from public controls. It was committed politically in any event to an expansion of state economic interference. Its fears accounted for little, however, in the face of the united wishes of its political rivals and of British industrial interests.

The programme for abolition of controls was spread formally over a three-year time period. In fact a large number of controls had disappeared within six months, whilst the majority had been dismantled by the late summer of 1919. In August 1919 a Profiteering Act was legislated making it an offence punishable by fine or imprisonment to make, on selling any article, an unreasonable profit. During the eighteen

[1] Report of the War Cabinet for 1918. (Quoted by A. C. Pigou, *Aspects of British Economic History*, 1918–25, p. 121.)

[2] November 16, 1918.

months of the Act's existence 1,800 profiteering committees were established; they accomplished virtually nothing. The prevailing post-war attitude towards profiteering was one of complacency.[1]

The end of the Second World War, in contrast, coincided with a much greater public interest in the maintenance of government controls. The 1945 General Election swept the Labour Party into office with a substantial Parliamentary majority for the first time in its history. The Labour Government was committed to an extensive programme of public ownership and control of the means of production. Controls were maintained over investment expenditure, and the location of industry, whilst import and export controls were manipulated as instruments of public policy. Government agencies engaged in State trading of food and raw materials, and even by 1951 Government Departments purchased approximately one-half by value of all imported commodities. Throughout the reconstruction period such wartime restrictions as exchange control, building and construction licensing, price controls and rationing were maintained. There was no attempt at allowing free market forces to reimpose their discipline over economic activity.

The experience of the inter-war years, particularly with regard to employment, had left its mark upon the major British political parties. In particular there was a firm resolve to prevent the outbreak of widespread unemployment. This resolve was publicly expressed in the Coalition Government's White Paper on Employment Policy published in 1944.[2] In pledging the responsibility of government to maintain a high and stable level of employment the publication emphasized the corresponding need to check the abuse of market power that might arise under such conditions:

> There has been in recent years a growing tendency towards combines and towards agreements, both national and international, by which manufacturers have sought to control prices and outputs, to divide markets and to fix conditions of sale. Such agreements do not necessarily operate against the public interest; but the power to do so is there.[3]

The Coalition Government pledged itself to seek powers to inform itself of the extent and effectiveness of restrictive agreements and combinations. Appropriate powers would be sought to check practices operating to the advantage of sectional producing interests but working to the detriment of the country as a whole. This was an early indication of impending postwar legislation in the field of monopoly control.

[1] A. J. Youngson, *The British Economy*, 1920–57, p. 225. 'Free trade was still felt to provide protection from oppressive monopolistic policies. And there were more urgent things to do.'

[2] Cmnd. 6527.

[3] ibid., paragraph 54.

THE DEVELOPMENT OF RESTRICTIVE PRACTICES

The period 1914–48 was notable for the establishment and expansion of restrictive practices in the United Kingdom. The majority of such developments were privately inspired, stemming from the mutual requirements of independent business units. In addition, however, a powerful stimulus was received intermittently from successive governments, anxious to stumble upon a solution to the major economic problems of structural imbalance and depression. It is true that active state participation in the establishment of restrictive practices in Britain was but a pale shadow of 'New Deal' activities in North America. Nevertheless it should not be completely ignored as a factor in the cartelization and rationalization process.

The chronic depression of many British industries during the 1920s and 1930s—especially severe in the staple pre-war export industries—provided a strong motive for the establishment of restrictive agreements. The primary objectives of such agreements were the maintenance or re-establishment of satisfactory price levels, and the elimination of excess capacity by joint action. It was by no means easy to effect such aims under depressed conditions. This difficulty is reflected in the large numbers of trade associations that mushroomed and disappeared during the inter-war years. Two important abortive attempts at cartelization during the 1920s are to be found in the American Cotton Yarn Association in the cotton spinning industry and in the Five Counties Scheme in coal-mining. During the 1920s the existence of free trade limited significantly the ability of trade associations to raise prices.

The worsening of the depression in 1931 and the abandonment by Britain of the Gold Standard[1] culminated in extensive trade protection for United Kingdom producers. This removed an important constraint upon the activities of trade associations. Attempts were made through associations to rationalize production by means of price agreements, market sharing schemes, entry limitations, and elimination of excess capacity. The historical chapters of many of the Monopolies Commission reports provide a wealth of data illustrating such developments. An interesting and representative example relates to calico printing.[2]

Calico printing had been involved inevitably in the severe contraction of trade that occurred in the cotton industry following the First World War. Between 1921 and 1927 exports by yardage of printed cotton piece goods averaged merely 50 per cent of average export yardage for 1910–13.

[1] See J. Grove, op. cit., p. 45. 'The Departure from Free Trade in 1932 has been called a stroke of fate rather than an act of policy.'

[2] See *The Report on the Process of Calico Printing*.

Despite this contraction the Federation of Calico Printers succeeded in maintaining a minimum price scheme until 1928. With a further worsening of trading conditions after 1928 the Federation experienced increasing difficulty in preserving full observance of its minimum prices. Firms began to classify given quality prints in lower grades for price determination within the List system. In 1932, following widespread non-observance of the prices listed, the Federation formally abandoned its price management functions. Between 1932 and 1939 the Federation functioned as a representative organization for the trade with responsibilities for most matters of common interest other than prices. Members intermittently pressed for more detailed organization. In 1936 the Federation placed before the Board of Trade a scheme recommending the control of calico printing for a period of fifteen years by a Calico Printing Board. Under this scheme licences would be granted to existing firms and quotas would be allocated on the basis of past performance. A pooling system would ensure that fines were extracted for over-fulfilling quotas, whilst corresponding compensation would be paid for underfulfilment. New entry would not be permitted except where outside firms purchased existing quotas or obtained express permission from the Board.

The President of the Board of Trade[1] refused to recommend the scheme to Parliament. He suggested, however, that the entire cotton industry might put forward a reorganization scheme. This suggestion met with approval from the industry. The Federation of Calico Printers took part in the negotiations which culminated in The Cotton Industry (Reorganization) Act of 1939. The outbreak of war resulted in the Act's suspension. The Act was subsequently repealed.

The experiences of the calico printing industry are reflected by most associations which attempt to maintain or to establish restrictive agreements under depressed conditions. It is not surprising to find associations requesting the state to provide legal sanctions for their agreements in order to limit the extent of non-compliance by members. In a number of instances during the 1930s governments acceded to such pressure. Indeed upon occasion governments pressed restrictive agreements upon unco-operative firms.

In 1930 the minority Labour Government[2] legislated to stimulate amalgamation and co-operation in the British coal-mining industry. Further action relating to the industry was taken in 1936 by the legal establishment of central selling arrangements designed to extend pro-

[1] Mr Walter Runciman.

[2] With Liberal Party support. See H. Wilson, *New Deal for Coal*, p. 21. 'In fact its [Labour Party's] powers were weakened by the fact that its majority depended on Liberal support and this support was not forthcoming for any vigorous policy.'

ducer control over the market for coal. The legislation was not notably successful.

In 1936 The Spindles Act provided statutory authority for a reorganization of cotton spinners designed to eliminate surplus spindleage. In 1939 the Cotton Industry (Reorganization) Act empowered spinners to fix minimum prices for cotton yarn. The intervention of war frustrated the application of this latter legislation.

Throughout the 1930s the Government utilized the Import Duties Advisory Committee initially to press iron and steel producers into the British Iron and Steel Federation, and subsequently to encourage this body to organize iron and steel production on a centralized basis. The Government persuaded the Federation to enter into agreement with the European Steel Cartel for the regulation of steel imports into the United Kingdom. In 1935 the Government introduced import licensing for steel, designed to reinforce the international agreements negotiated by the Federation. Subsequently British iron and steel prices were determined largely by the Federation in close association for this purpose with the Import Duties Advisory Committee. Steel import duties during the late 1930s were in the region of 50 per cent *ad valorem*.

Government intervention of this kind during the inter-war period was largely confined to providing a legal framework for restrictive practices. The administration of restrictive practices was usually left in the hands of the producers and suppliers.

Such was the interest of Government in the rationalization developments in British industry during the 1930s that one section of political thought pressed for a General Enabling Act. Legislation of this kind would have authorised all industries which so desired to extend restrictive arrangements under government supervision. Lord Melchett's Industrial Reconstruction League pressed particularly strongly for such action. But the general political response was lukewarm, in certain instances hostile. The entire process resembled too closely the Corporative State system which had been established in Italy under Mussolini. At the same time the suggestion was suspect on economic grounds. It would tend to maintain in production inefficient, high cost units. Additionally, most businessmen feared public interference in the affairs of private enterprise. Where the Government had sponsored restrictive activities industrial reaction had been far from one of universal enthusiasm. Any study of the operation of legislation in the coal industry will quickly illustrate the antipathy that could be aroused.

The Government did not confine its intervention during the 1930s solely to instances of specific legislation. In 1935 The Finance Act contained a provision that levies payable by firms under approved schemes for compensating firms that had reduced capacity should be allowed as business expenses in assessing profit. Thus the general financial policy of Government supported the rationalization process. A detailed analysis of events during the 1930s would scarcely justify the conclusion, however, that the Government was successful in its policy. The joint impact of severe depression and business resistance to rationalization—not unconnected—largely frustrated legislative activity in the field.[1]

The economic climate had changed radically in Britain by 1945. Full employment and inflationary pressure had replaced the depressed conditions of the 1930s. It is not surprising therefore that public attitudes towards restrictive arrangements hardened and that fears of the abuse of market power became more widespread. The Government largely mirrored the change of attitude of the general public. Questions were frequently raised in the House of Commons regarding the activities of trade associations and dominant firms. The prevailing attitude of the Government was not condemnatory. It favoured a pragmatic approach to the suspected problems of market dominance. The Government itself was not entirely consistent in this respect. Legislation in 1947 provided various agricultural marketing boards with cartel powers for their respective products. Government controls and licences formed an important basis for the operation by trade associations of restrictive arrangements. This dichotomy did not pass unnoticed by the critics of the Labour Government.

BUSINESS CONCENTRATION AND THE DOMINANT FIRM

The development of restrictive practices during the period 1914–48 tended to overshadow a separate but important tendency—the increasing size and market power of the industrial firm. Size of itself does not always denote market dominance. A firm may expand vertically, backwards and forwards and laterally as well as horizontally. Horizontal expansion by the firm may no more than maintain its proportion of a rapidly expanding market. The inter-war period was typified by each of these forms of development. It was undoubtedly typified by an increase in industrial concentration as defined by most writers in this field.

A firm may expand internally or it may expand through integration. Both aspects of growth were once again apparent during the inter-war period. There is not space in this brief review to examine the genesis and pattern of growth of the industrial unit. It may be useful, however, to review a number of state actions during the period which undoubtedly influenced the process of expansion of the business unit.

During the inter-war period the governments of the day retained a

[1] The commonly held theory that *kartelle sind kinder der Not* is scarcely substantiated by the findings of the Monopolies Commission. The difficulties of the 1930s resulted in the suspension of many activities of trade associations in this country.

largely paternalistic interest over developments within the business unit. In general the State encouraged the expansion in size of the firm. The Government made use of fiscal policy to this end. The Trade Facilities Act, 1921, empowered the Treasury to underwrite loans made to private firms from private sources provided that the loans were raised for aims that would promote employment. This facility encouraged the provision of expansion finance to firms. In 1926 the Government allowed the remission of stamp duties on capital issues made consequent upon an amalgamation. In addition the banks, in close association with the Bank of England, were encouraged to assist rationalization schemes involving amalgamation.

Government policy encouraged an extension of business concentration during the inter-war period, both by stimulating the internal development of the firm and by supporting integration. The latter process proceeded apace in particular sectors. In 1925 The Distillers Company was established by amalgamation, in 1927 The British Match Corporation, and in 1926 the most important private amalgamation of the inter-war period produced Imperial Chemical Industries. This last-mentioned organization was the product of the fusion of Brunner-Mond, Nobel Industries, United Alkali, and The British Dyestuffs Corporation. Imperial Chemical Industries provided a powerful multi-product organization, with common control over chemicals, dyestuffs, explosives, and non-ferrous metal interests in the United Kingdom. Instances of rapid concentration in relatively prosperous industries are fairly frequent even in the 1930s. Examples include motor car assembly, rayon production, aluminium production, electrical equipment production and soap production. The motives behind concentration in these sectors were more commonly related to scale and economic efficiency than to defensive rationalization.

During the inter-war period the Government pursued a predominantly permissive policy towards amalgamation and concentration. There were isolated instances, however, of more positive intervention. In 1921 an Act was legislated, designed to rationalize the railway system. Over 100 companies were merged to form four separate railway units. In 1924 the Government established The Imperial Airways Company as a monopolistic unit in air transportation. Such examples of direct State interference during the inter-war period to encourage concentration are sporadic and rare.

The end of war in 1945 brought extensive changes in the institutional environment of business enterprise. The early postwar years clearly demonstrated the trend towards larger-scale enterprise. The movement was scarcely recognized by 1948 to be a major problem for public policy. Nevertheless sufficient concern had been generated to persuade the Government of the need to provide for supervision of the dominant firm as well as the trade association. A more positive interest in the activities of dominant firms by the state was to be delayed for a further decade.

COMMITTEES OF INQUIRY AND THE OFFICIAL REPORTS

During the inter-war period a number of official inquiries were conducted into the structure and performance of British industry. It is worth while to examine the reports of the more important committees. They provide a useful mirror of public opinion and in certain instances they were instrumental in shaping public attitudes towards the issues upon which they were instructed to report.

Two important committees[1] were established shortly after peace had been negotiated in 1918. A conflict of viewpoints provided a background to their institution. Public hostility towards suspected wartime profiteering on the part of organized industries, and fears at the rapid expansion of restrictive arrangements, undoubtedly influenced the Government. On the other hand there was widespread recognition that large-scale enterprise and powerful marketing organizations had served Germany well under wartime conditions. It was felt in certain sectors that British export performance might be improved by facilitating developments of a similar nature in this country. The Government considered that a public examination of these issues would be beneficial.

The later inter-war industrial inquiry examined in this section[2] was initiated against a rather different background. During the 1920s the British economy failed to achieve the dynamism that had been anticipated in the first flush of postwar optimism. A failure of leading British industries to retain their pre-war position in export markets resulted in a certain structural imbalance, a high level of unemployment, and major problems of retrenchment and reconstruction. The onset of international depression during the 1930s intensified these problems. The later inquiry must be viewed against this backcloth, and in the light of cogent public requests for a national rationalization policy. The committee of inquiry was instituted in 1924 by Ramsay MacDonald. It made its final report in 1929. The terms of reference under which this committee operated emphasized the importance of the export trade to the well-being of the British economy. In the late 1920s a further committee was established to investigate the economic effects of resale price maintenance.[3]

The two inquiries effected in the immediate postwar period substantiated the belief that trade associations had expanded both in number

[1] The Committee on Commercial and Industrial Policy After the War, Cd. 9035 (1918), and The Committee on Trusts, Cd. 9236 (1919).

[2] The Committee on Industry and Trade, Cmnd. 3282.

[3] The Committee on Restraint of Trade, HMSO, 1931.

and in influence during the 1914–18 war. The committees were convinced that one reason for this expansion was the desire to restrict competition and to control prices. Both committees were loth to condemn these developments on dogmatic grounds. Indeed, The Committee on Commercial and Industrial Policy After the War recommended a rapid development of trade associations in British industry. The Committee considered that combination for marketing, especially in the export field, was not only desirable, but also inevitable. It suggested that the Government should encourage developments of this kind.

The Balfour Committee[1] subsequently confirmed the factual conclusions of earlier inquiries. It demonstrated in an impressive manner the strong tendency towards an increase both in the size of the average industrial unit and towards the association of legally independent units. The Committee noted that such developments were not limited to producers; they were equally common within the distributive trades. The Committee emphasized once more the potential economic advantages of specialization from internal expansion or close co-operation. It chastised British firms for lagging behind other countries in these developments. There is no evidence within these official reports of any general hostility towards the accelerating process of market concentration and to the regulation of competitive activity.

This does not mean that these committees were unaware of the potential misuse of positions of market dominance by firms and trade associations. The Committee on Trusts explicitly accepted the need to provide safeguards for the public against high prices and output limitation. The fears of the early postwar committees found their public expression in the Profiteering Acts of 1919. Those who obtained unreasonable profits committed an offence under the legislation, punishable by fine or by imprisonment.[2]

A number of British firms subsequently complained to the Balfour Committee of unfair use of economic power by dominant organizations and suggested that organizations suspected of anti-social behaviour should be subjected to public investigation.

The inter-war committees of inquiry were aware of the desire for supervisory machinery for dominant organizations. The Committee on Commercial and Industrial Policy recommended that all international combines to which British firms were party should be registered with the Board of Trade. All other agreements between British companies should be granted legal sanction if they were registered in similar manner. The Board of Trade should be empowered to demand con-

[1] The Committee on Industry and Trade, 1929. Cmnd. 3282.

[2] In total 202 prosecutions resulted in total fines and costs of £2,241. 'The Act was not business as the controls had been but window-dressing.' (A. C. Pigou, op. cit., p. 130.)

fidential information necessary for examining the nature, extent and activities of industrial combinations. The Committee considered that appropriate publicity would usually provide ample protection for the general public.

The Committee on Trusts was prepared for a more radical change in public policy towards market dominance. The Committee recommended the establishment of a tribunal similar in construction to those existing in North America and in certain British colonies. Members of the tribunal would be appointed by the President of the Board of Trade. The tribunal would not be responsible for initiating investigations. The Board of Trade, working from complaints received, would be responsible for preliminary inquiries. If it considered that a prima facie case existed that activity contrary to the public interest was taking place, the Board might refer individual cases to the tribunal for investigation and report.[1]

In many ways this recommendation foreshadowed the 1948 legislation and the creation of the Monopolies Commission. The tribunal would have been empowered to obtain evidence, to inspect documents and to cross-examine witnesses. The tribunal would also have acted in an advisory capacity. Remedial action stemming from its recommendations would have rested with the Board of Trade.[2]

The Balfour Committee, however, retreated from the position adopted by the Committee on Trusts. The Balfour Committee relied heavily upon publicity as a public safeguard against abuse of economic power. It recommended that a public authority, or tribunal, should be established, vested with the power to investigate complaints. The reports of this tribunal should be published. Rectifying action against abuses, however, would not meet with general acceptance. No doubt the deteriorating economic climate influenced the Balfour Committee into adopting a more malleable attitude towards market dominance than that of earlier committees of inquiry.

After the Second World War, a number of official committees were appointed to investigate industries in which restrictive practices were known, or widely suspected, to exist. The periodic publications of these committees helped to keep alive the issue of market dominance. They provided fuel for Members of Parliament advocating the quick introduction of legislation in the field of monopoly and restrictive practices.

The Working Party on the Cotton Industry[3] was established in

[1] See A. J. Youngson, op. cit., p. 225. '*The Economist* did not regard the Report as a very startling document—"a modern postscript to the standard works on the subject" (June 7, 1919)—and despite its belief that the nation was currently submitting to a "yoke imposed by bureaucratic bunglers" it approved the Majority recommendations.'

[2] A minority section of The Committee on Trusts was prepared for more radical intervention by the Government, including where necessary the State or municipal ownership of offending business units.

[3] HMSO, 1946.

October 1945 to examine the structure and performance of the cotton industry. Its report in 1946 stressed the difficult problems of readjustment which confronted the industry. The Committee recommended that a Central Body should be created for the cotton industry—The Cotton Council. The Council would serve as a medium through which members of the industry might communicate with the Government. The Council might also prepare plans for a uniform costing system and uniformity of production records for the industry.[1] It might introduce a continuous study of distribution techniques within the industry. Quite clearly these recommendations, if implemented, would create the climate for a tightly-knit set of restrictive arrangements within the cotton industry.

The Central Price Regulation Committee[2] reported in 1946 on the prices of radio valves. In many ways it was one of the least satisfying official reports published between 1945 and 1948. Nevertheless, it exposed a wide range of restrictive practices in the valve industry. The valve industry, by way of contrast with cotton, was undergoing fairly rapid expansion. The industry had become conditioned to a high pace of technical development, involving frequent product changes. Nine of the twelve firms in the valve industry were members of the British Radio Valve Manufacturers' Association. Association members accounted for a large majority of United Kingdom valve production.

The Committee found two clearly distinct markets for radio valves in Britain. Valves for new radio sets constituted one market, whilst replacement valves formed the second market. The replacement market was less predictable than the initial equipment market. Replacement production involved manufacturers in relatively low turnovers of obsolete valves required by owners of old-fashioned radio sets. Under such conditions it is not surprising that price discrimination existed in the valve industry. The Association members individually established prices for initial equipment valves which were sold to set-manufacturers included on the Association White List. Keen competition for this market resulted in valve prices that did not fully cover the factory cost of production. Association members were able to recoup initial equipment losses by charging much higher prices in the replacement market, under a price agreement. The higher prices in the latter market more than reflected differences in unit production costs.

This system carried considerable advantages for Association members. Public demand for new radio sets at that time was price elastic. Under such conditions a low price for valves encouraged a high level of radio

[1] G. C. Allen has suggested (Ed. Chamberlin, *Monopoly and Competition and their Regulations*, London, 1954), p. 104. 'The Development Councils which were set up after the war were an outcome of this line of thought.'

[2] HMSO, 1946.

set sales. The greater the number of sets in the public's possession, the larger would be the quantity of replacement valves demanded at each price. The replacement market, too, was far less resistant to price increases.

The Committee refused to consider the public interest implications of this form of price discrimination. It pleaded that the practice was evident in many industries in the United Kingdom. Nevertheless the report fanned the flame of public dissatisfaction at the existing regulation of market dominance.

The fforde Committee[1] was appointed in December 1945 to review the financial structure of the cement industry, and to report upon its price structure. The report of the Committee outlined a welter of restrictive arrangements indulged in by members of the industry. All manufacturers of Portland cement in the United Kingdom were members of the Cement Makers' Federation. The Federation organized a minimum price scheme. Minimum prices were fixed in accordance with a basing point system which discriminated in favour of consumers distant from the manufacturing centres. This system was reinforced by a market sharing agreement together with exclusive dealing and deferred rebate arrangements.

The fforde Committee was favourably impressed by the structure of the cement industry and by the activities of the Federation. It accepted the policy of subsidizing distant consumers, whilst suggesting that a more satisfactory costing system should be installed. It recommended that the Federation's price schedules should be submitted to an independent body which should develop consultative relationships with the Federation. The Committee concluded that the restrictive arrangements in cement raised entry barriers for outside firms. This was not a significant fault of the arrangements in the Committee's opinion for[2] 'there are arguments against the existence of independent producers who obtain the advantages which follow from the existence of the Federation without conforming to the obligations imposed by membership of it'.

The Committee noted with satisfaction that profits within the industry had not been excessive in 1945—indeed the rate of return on capital in that year had only averaged 6½ per cent. This factor played a significant role in inducing a favourable conclusion on the price system in operation. The Committee could find no evidence that the Federation had abused its position by limiting output. The report made no recommendations regarding Government action. The complacency of the report did not serve to allay completely public unease at the range of restrictive practices encountered in the industry.

In July 1946 the Simon Committee[3] was established by the Ministry of Works to examine 'the organization and methods of distribution of

[1] HMSO, 1947. [2] op. cit., p. 22. [3] HMSO, 1948.

building materials and components with particular reference to cost and efficiency', and to make recommendations. The report of this Committee in 1948 was the most important of all early postwar reports in inflaming public hostility towards restrictive practices.[1] The Committee was precluded by its terms of reference from investigating manufacturing except insofar as manufacturing activities impinged upon distribution. Nevertheless the Commission noted that the various sanctions exercised by manufacturers eliminated active competition in many sectors of the reference field. Absence of restrictive arrangement between manufacturer and distributor clearly did not imply necessarily that the former exercised no control over the latter:[2] 'the absence of an agreement may mean that the manufacturers' association is for one reason or another strong enough to dictate its terms without resorting to the use of such an instrument'.

The Committee spoke freely in its report of the widespread use of restrictive practices in the building materials industry:[3]

> It may be fairly said that in this field monopoly, quasi monopoly, and restrictive practices have reigned almost unchallenged for many years. These arrangements, whether embodied in formal agreements between manufacturers and merchants, in tacit agreements or in analogous arrangements, and whether or not the merchant is a party to them, permeate virtually the whole field.

The Committee concluded that such arrangements did not operate in the national interest. In particular they encouraged high prices, wide distributive margins, excessive provision of services, and an unduly low rate of technical development in the industry. In reaching these conclusions the Committee had considered comparative data relating to the efficiency of North American counterparts of the British industry. The Committee was most impressed by conditions in that country in the absence of restrictive practices. Two members of the Committee visited the United States of America to obtain first-hand impressions.

The Simon Committee recommended immediate Government action designed to control distributors' margins in the building materials and components sector. This recommendation was seen as a short-term measure. In the longer-term the Committee stressed the need to destroy restrictive practices. In this respect action seemed desirable on a more extensive scale than that of the reference industry alone. The Simon Committee recommended legislation which would provide for specific inquiries into selected industries by a body empowered to obtain information, and authorized to make orders prohibiting certain practices. On

[1] Two members of the Committee—Sir Arnold Plant and R. Yeabsley—subsequently joined The Monopolies Commission.

[2] op. cit., p. 20. [3] ibid., p. 50.

the assumption that legislation of this kind would be forthcoming, the Committee refrained from recommending special legislation for its own reference field. The report foreshadowed legislation in the form of the 1948 Act. It is notable that the building industry and related sectors featured among the early references to the Monopolies Commission.

The tenor of the early postwar reports clearly favoured a pragmatic system of inquiry into market dominance conditions. The committees emphasized the special circumstances of their own reference fields in formulating their conclusions. They were extremely reluctant to generalize upon their specific findings. The Simon Committee report in particular directly foreshadowed the approach of Parliament to the problems of market dominance. The reports became inflammable political material during the debates over the 1948 legislation.

ATTITUDES OF THE POLITICAL PARTIES

The practical reflection of political viewpoints towards market dominance during the inter-war years has been examined already. In the last analysis one must assess the policies of any political party by what it does rather than by what it states it would have liked to do, or by reference to selected speeches of its representatives. Nevertheless conditions of government may obstruct a party in the furtherance of its aims. A short analysis is provided therefore of the expressed attitudes of the major political parties towards market dominance between 1914 and 1939.

The Liberal Party

The Liberal Party, by tradition, was an ardent believer in the value of free competition under a private enterprise system. The development of the combination movement, and the trend towards rationalization in Britain during the inter-war period, therefore, provided the Liberal Party with an intellectual challenge. The Party responded to this challenge, not by rejecting rationalization and combination, but by serious attempts to recommend changes in the environment of business enterprise, in order to evolve new safeguards for the public.

The main recommendations and conclusions drawn by the Liberal Party were clearly and forcibly expounded in the Liberal Report, entitled: 'Britain's Industrial Future'.[1] The Report accepted fully that 'instinctive public distrust of monopolies is well founded, because it is competition which has passed on to the consuming public, in the form of low prices, the results of industrial and economic progress'.[2]

Realistically, however, the inquiry concluded that under modern conditions, based on heavy capitalization of firms and mass production tech-

[1] London, 1928. [2] ibid., p. 459.

niques, the old-fashioned form of competition, comprising many firms each with no influence over price, was outmoded and wasteful.[1] Under modern conditions some degree of monopoly power was inevitable, indeed often desirable in a large number of industries.

In many instances monopoly powers were vulnerable to concerted action of the part on consumers, and in such cases adequate publicity must play a vital role in canalizing corporate action into channels compatible with the wishes of the consumer. The Report recommended, therefore, that large companies—those controlling more than 50 per cent of the supply of a product within Great Britain—should be registered as Public Corporations; such Corporations should thenceforth be subjected to particularly stringent publicity provisions. They should be open to inspection by the Board of Trade, who should have the powers to report upon its findings. The Board should be obliged to publish, periodically, relevant details regarding the rate of profit on capital and on turnover, and should report on other matters including the market dominance of the organization and any agreements upon prices or output entered into by the organization. Where the evidence compiled by the Board of Trade indicated, in the mind of the President, a prima facie case that the public interest was being injuriously affected, the President should refer the Corporation to a 'trust tribunal' similar in constitution and powers to that envisaged by the majority Report of the Committee on Trusts. On the basis of the findings of this tribunal, the Board should make recommendations for Government action, even to the extent of recommending price control.

Trade associations, also, were not exempted from analysis and recommendation in the Liberal Report. The report pursued the policy of advocating publicity. Trade associations covering more than 50 per cent of a trade or industry, should, it was suggested, be incorporated and be subjected to publicity regulations and an investigation procedure similar to that advocated for the Public Corporation. The Report fully accepted the potential advantages of strongly organized trade associations in British industry. The Committee did not want desirable rationalization to be obstructed by recalcitrant minorities: 'We recommend that, in special cases and subject to special safeguards, an Incorporated Trade Association should be allowed to apply for the Association rules to be enforced throughout the industry.'

The theme of the Liberal Report was adopted by the Liberal Party in

[1] ibid., pp. 93–4. 'In modern conditions a tendency towards some degree of monopoly in an increasing number of industries is . . . inevitable and even quite often desirable in the interests of efficiency. It is, therefore, no longer useful to treat trusts, cartels, combinations, holding companies and trade associations as inexpedient abnormalities in the economic system to be prevented, checked and harried.'

its Manifesto in 1928. The policy was purposeful and practical, perhaps the most sensible party programme relating to the field that emerged during the period in question. However, it coincided with the decline of the Liberal Party in Britain. The Party did assist the minority Labour Government to draft the Coal Mines Act, 1930, but in general the policies of the Liberals were associated by the two major political parties with the past rather than the present, and the impact of its rationalization policy was thereby weakened and dissipated.

The Labour Party

The Labour Party, of course, was in no way ideologically committed to a system of free competition within a capitalist framework. Indeed, by ideology the Party leant heavily to a belief in public ownership and control of the means of production and distribution, and one might therefore have anticipated strong party enthusiasm for nationalization during the inter-war years. Two factors prevented the emergence of such radical proposals from the main body of the Party at this time. In the first place, the Labour Party at no time obtained a majority of seats in the House of Commons during the inter-war period. The 1930 administration was dependent upon the support of the Liberal Party—a Party opposed solidly to nationalization save under exceptional circumstances. In the second place, the Labour Party was more concerned during the inter-war period with other serious social ills such as unemployment, poverty, and health, than with the problem of monopoly policy.

One example of Labour thinking on monopoly policy is indicated by the proposals of the Parliamentary Committee of the Trades Union Congress,[1] published in 1921. In order of priority proposals for dealing with monopoly were put forward:

(1) The extension of public ownership, at the national and the local level as the case might warrant.
(2) The encouragement and extension of voluntary co-operation.
(3) Public regulation of the economy.

The Committee recommended the creation of a permanent Costings Department, empowered to conduct surveys of industry and trade in Britain. This Department, responsible to the Board of Trade, should publish statistical data at regular intervals, relating to costs, profits and prices. In addition, a Consumer's Council should be instituted, which would consider the statistical evidence provided by the Department, and make appropriate recommendations to the Government concerning further action. One suggestion was that each monopolistic organization, once examined, should be allowed a specified annual dividend payment and additions to this dividend should be conditional upon lowering

[1] Final Report of the Cost of Living (London, 1921), pp. 199, et seq.

prices; thus the consumer would obtain his share of increased efficiency.[1]

In practice, the Labour Party appears to have accepted the need for some form of 'rationalization' policy in seriously depressed industries. The Coal Mines Act, which encouraged and enforced price fixing in the coal industry, was the brainchild of the Labour administration. As a safeguard, however, the Coal Mines Reorganization Commission was established to perform a supervisory role within the industry. The tendency of the Labour administration to favour rationalization disturbed certain of its supporters. Despite such opposition during the 1930s, the Labour Party adopted platforms strongly favouring the rationalization of certain primary and other depressed industries. The Party leaders were careful to recommend adequate safeguards to prevent the interests of labour and the consumer from being cast into jeopardy. In general, however, the Labour Party marked time on the problem of monopoly control; it was busy formulating policy in other fields.

The Conservative Party

The Conservative Party throughout the inter-war period—most especially during the years of the Great Depression—fully accepted the need for a retreat from the rigours of cut-throat competition. Although the Conservative Party was opposed, in general, to interference in the free enterprise system, it accepted the need for government assistance in maintaining and expanding price supports, output restriction and allocation among firms, and the elimination of surplus capacity upon an administrative basis. Indeed, as we have noted, the National Government, largely composed of Conservatives, was extremely busy during the 1930s devising systems for the encouragement of concentration and restrictive practices.[2]

The position of the Party, in respect to rationalization, was clearly expounded by the President of the Board of Trade in the House of Commons in May 1929:

> We must have rationalization. It is necessary for efficiency and it inevitably involves the creation of larger units and the making of agreements. . . . In practically every industry not only in this country but elsewhere the productive capacity of plant is far in excess of either national or world demand. No one is likely to put forward a scheme of rationalization with a view to raising prices or curtailing production.[3]

[1] See P. Guenault and J. F. Jackson, *The Control of Monopoly in the UK*, Longmans, 1960, p. 21. 'Such an idea was not entirely original for sliding scales of this kind had been used in Britain since 1855 as a means of regulating the profits and prices of certain public utilities, notably gas companies, and it had been adopted, though not widely, in the United States for similar purposes.'

[2] e.g. in agriculture, transport, iron and steel industries.

[3] Sir P. Cunliffe-Lister, *Proceedings in the House of Commons*, vol. 227, col. 1978.

The Conservative Party, during the 1930s, clearly recognized the weakness of free competition as a solution to industrial malaise. The pragmatic background of the Party in this respect allowed it considerable flexibility in formulating policies; it is evident that the National Government at that time was far more concerned with the problem of industrial organization than was its major political opponent.

GENERAL CONCLUSIONS

During the inter-war period the rationalization movement achieved far less than had been anticipated. Many schemes mushroomed, only to disappear. Government sponsorship and encouragement was usually insufficient to maintain restrictive arrangements through the worst part of the depression. Those arrangements that survived and operated effectively did so less because rationalization lowered unit production costs than because consolidation augmented producer control over the price level. During the inter-war years public attitudes towards rationalization underwent a transformation. In 1919 rationalization had been advocated as an instrument for raising efficiency and lowering unit costs of production and marketing—the early committees of inquiry cited German cartelization developments in glowing terms. However, with the onset of depression rationalization was proposed to strengthen producers' efforts at price fixing and market allocations. Its success was evaluated more by its effectiveness in improving the financial position of the firm than by its effectiveness in lowering costs of production. In this change in public opinion the Governments of the day played a leading part—an interesting example of preoccupation with surplus capacity and uneconomic prices at that time.

Following the Second World War changes in the economic climate, harnessed to the reaction against the failure of inter-war rationalization as an instrument of income stabilization, were reflected in a more suspicious attitude towards market dominance. The Government, armed with Keynesian instruments, was more confident of its ability to maintain income levels. In the belief that this problem could be controlled, attention reverted to the problem of resource allocation.[1] Contemporary literature suggested that market imperfections impeded the efficient allocation of resources. Public opinion emphasized the need to supervise the activities of large firms and restrictive trade associations. The major political parties responded in their election platforms by promising appropriate legislation. When the Labour Government entered office in 1945 the only obstacle to early legislation in the field appeared to be the crowded Parliamentary programme. In 1948 the political pledge was honoured.

[1] Attention also centred upon techniques designed to maintain a high rate of economic growth.

Chapter Two

THE COMMON LAW BACKGROUND

INTRODUCTION

The common law interpretation of agreements in restraint of competition has not been fully consistent through time. The courts have displayed increasing legal tolerance for such agreements[1] since the seventeenth century. The dominant firm, meanwhile, has been completely unfettered in its activities by court action other than that generally prescribed to prevent fraud, mistake, wilful termination of contract, etc.[2]

This chapter attempts to trace the common law development of the two important civil remedies available to damaged third parties or unwilling parties to agreements restraining competition—action in contract under the law of restraint of trade, and action in the law of tort alleging actionable conspiracy.

TRADE COMBINATIONS AND THE LAW OF RESTRAINT OF TRADE

There are, of course, enumerable forms of contract in restraint of trade. The basic, and perhaps the simplest, form of such contract is that between two or more parties which limits competition between them, or which obstructs the possibility of competition on the part of third parties.

The civil courts in England have not maintained a consistent policy throughout the past 400 years towards contracts in restraint of trade. Early cases during the Tudor period indicate a marked antipathy from the courts towards such contracts. In one early judgment, 'to prohibit or

[1] W. Friedmann (ed.), *Anti-trust Laws* (London, 1956), p. 346. 'The policy of the civil courts towards agreements in restraint of trade has evolved from one of suppression up to the seventeenth century, through partial recognition in the eighteenth century, to near-abstention in the nineteenth and twentieth centuries.'

[2] P. Guenault and J. M. Jackson, op. cit., p. 11. 'The position of the single-firm monopolist was in fact strengthened by the legal protection afforded to inventions and improvements by the Patents Acts. . . .'

restrain any person to use a lawful trade at any time, or at any place', was considered to militate 'against the benefit of the Commonwealth'.[1] Soon, however, it became obvious that the Commonwealth need not necessarily suffer whenever the vendor to goodwill bound himself not to compete against the purchaser for a specified period of time. Thus it was concluded in 1613[2] that 'a man cannot binde one, that he shall not use his trade generally . . . but for a time certain, a man may well be bound, and restrained from using of his trade'.

Throughout the seventeenth century the courts continuously relaxed their condemnation of contracts in restraint of trade. In 1711 the basic foundations for modern law in this field were laid by judgments in the case of Mitchell v. Reynolds.[3]

The defendant, in this case, had assigned to the plaintiff the lease of a bakehouse in Liquorpond Street, Holborn, for a period of five years. For the duration of this lease the defendant entered into a bond of £50 that he would not practise as a baker in the parish. In the subsequent case the defendant pleaded that the bond was illegal since it prevented him from practising as a baker, a trade for which he was fully qualified. The court, led by Lord Macclesfield, held that the bond was legally binding:

> In all restraints of trade, where nothing more appears, the law presumes them bad; but if the circumstances are set forth, that presumption is excluded, and the court is to judge of those circumstances, and to determine accordingly; and if upon them it appears to be a just and honest contract, it ought to be maintained.[4]

Lord Macclesfield contended that general restraints, among others, were void and unenforceable as 'being of no benefit to either party, and only oppressive'. It is unfair, however, to interpret his distinction between general and partial restraints of trade as being a rigid one. Underlying his judgment was the importance placed upon the reasonableness rather than the form of the contract.[5] In particular Lord Macclesfield would have admitted readily that improvements in the transport and communications network would render a rigid distinction between general and limited restraints inconsistent with commercial reality. Successive court judgments for the subsequent 200 years nevertheless insisted upon a rigidly literal interpretation of Macclesfield's judgment.[6]

[1] Colgate v. Bachelor (1596). Cr. Elizabeth 872.

[2] Rogers v. Parry (1613). Bulst, 136. [3] (1711) 1 Peere Wms. 181. [4] ibid., p. 191.

[5] Cheshire and Fifoot, *Law of Contract*, Butterworth, London, 1956, p. 311. 'The true significance of this passage, no doubt, was that everything must turn upon whether the contract was reasonable and fair.'

[6] The history of these judgments is chronicled in the judgment of Bowen, L.J., in 'Maxim Nordenfelt Guns and Ammunition Co v. Nordenfelt' (1893), 1, Ch. 630, p. 662.

The presumption was enforced that general restraints were, without exception, void; whereas partial restraints were prima facie valid and, if reasonable, could be enforced.

The first break in this long line of judgments came in the Nordenfelt case of 1894.[1] The defendant in this case, Nordenfelt, was a manufacturer of quick-firing guns and other implements of war. He sold this business to the plaintiff company for £287,500, covenanting in return that he would not 'for twenty-five years, engage . . . either directly or indirectly in the trade or business of a manufacturer of guns, gun mountings, or carriages, gunpowder explosives or ammunition (or in any business competing or liable to compete in any way with that for the time being carried on by the company)'. Nordenfelt reserved to himself the right to deal in explosives other than gunpowder, in torpedoes, or submarine boats, and in metal castings or forgings. A number of years later, notwithstanding his covenant, the defendant recommenced manufacture of guns and ammunition. The plaintiffs sought an injunction to restrain him from this task.

There can be no doubt that the restraint was general—the company's business extended throughout the world. Nevertheless, the House of Lords decided that this was insufficient proof that the covenant was void and unenforceable. The court considered that the final clause[2] of the covenant was unreasonable and therefore void. Since this clause was distinct from the covenant, however, it could be severed without jeopardizing the rest of the agreement. The court decided that the rest of the contract was reasonable, and therefore enforceable. During the judgment Lord Macnaghten eschewed the distinction between general and partial restraints. He argued that both partial and general restraints were prima facie void but, if proved to be reasonable, must be considered valid. This did not meet with the approval of his fellow Judges. In any event the ratio decidendi of the case was confined to the validity of a general restraint. The *obiter dicta* comments of Lord Macnaghten could not bind future courts. The Macnaghten contention regarding partial restraints was not in fact upheld by the courts until the House of Lords' decision in Mason v. Provident Clothing and Supply Co Ltd, in 1913.[3]

The modern position of the law relating to contracts in restraint of trade, as laid down in the Nordenfelt case, and subsequently amended and expanded, may be expounded fairly briefly:

(1) All restraints of trade, in the absence of special justifying circumstances, are contrary to public policy, and therefore void.

[1] Nordenfelt v. Maxim Nordenfelt Guns, etc. (1894), A.C. 535.
[2] Bracketed above.
[3] (1913) A.C. 724.

(2) Whether special circumstances justify the contract is a question of law to be decided by the judge in the light of facts determined by the jury.
(3) A restraint may only be justified if it is reasonable as between the parties and, in addition, is in the interest of the public.
(4) Onus of proof of reasonableness between the parties rests on the party so alleging; the onus, once this has been proved, of proving the restraint still injurious to public policy rests with the party so alleging. Legal authorities have pointed out that 'if once the Court is satisfied that the restraint is reasonable as between the parties, the onus will be no light one'.[1]

In the first instance, therefore, an acceptable restraint must form part of an agreement which is reasonable to all parties. The test of reasonableness is the same for both parties, and the Court has stated that 'as long as the restraint to which he subjects himself is no wider than is required for the adequate protection of the person in whose favour it is created, it is in his (i.e. the covenanter's) interest to be able to bind himself for the sake of the indirect advantages he may obtain by so doing'. The Court refuses in such cases to consider the adequacy of the consideration received in return for the restricting covenant. In practice the courts have placed far more emphasis upon the agreement being reasonable inter partes than upon its being reasonable in public policy.

There have been very few cases where restraints held to be reasonable inter partes have nevertheless been voided on grounds of public policy. Although the law explicitly states that public policy should be considered as well as the interests of the parties, the former 'is invariably brushed aside with the observation that only in exceptional circumstances what is reasonable between the parties is not also reasonable towards the public'.[2]

In part this situation has resulted from the eventual victory of freedom of contract over freedom of trade, following a long and fundamental conflict in the courts.[3] In part it results from the unwillingness of the

[1] Lord Parker in Att. General for Australia v. Adelaide Steamship Co Ltd (1913), A.C. per. 781.

[2] W. Friedmann, *Law and Social Change in Contemporary Britain*, London, 1951, p. 126.

[3] Wilberforce, Campbell and Elles, *Restrictive Trade Practices and Monopolies*, Sweet and Maxwell, London, 1957, p. 53. 'On the one hand the right of every member of the community to carry on any trade or business he chooses, and in such a manner as he thinks most desirable in his own interests, with a corresponding obligation not to interfere with another's freedom; and on the other hand the freedom to contract, which implies the freedom to combine with some against others, and the freedom to contract in restraint of freedom.' See also Lord Parker, Att. General of Australia v. Adelaide Steamship Co Ltd, op. cit., who commented in detail upon this conflict.

courts to enter into arguments of political economy in discussing agreements in restraint of trade.[1] While evidence of the circumstances surrounding a contract may be given, the ability of the courts to place sufficient weight on public interest issues is greatly weakened by the rule that no evidence is admissible on the actual or probable economic consequences of the agreement under examination.[2]

It is not, however, completely true to suggest that the judiciary is not influenced by changing political and economic attitudes. In particular Benthamite thinking influenced the courts in favour of freedom of contract as did the strength of *laissez-faire* doctrines in general during the nineteenth century. Active Government participation in the rationalization movement of the 1930s further encouraged the courts to emphasize the importance of private interests rather than those of public policy, or rather to consider the two as being identical.

The 1948 legislation occurred at a time when the law of restraint of trade could not be considered of value as a weapon against restrictive agreements.[3] The courts had upheld the legal sanctity by this time of agreements relating to tenders, exclusive dealing, pre-auction bidding, output and market sharing, resale price maintenance, and prices.

It is true that 'public policy' still had to be considered, and that this was a flexible concept,[4] but there was much unrest and dissatisfaction at the existing health of the law in the face of more prosperous economic conditions.[5] Even where an agreement was voided it could be retained as long as those concerned were prepared to honour it. The voiding of such a contract did not render it illegal.

The 1948 Act itself made no direct impact upon the common law. The Monopolies Commission was established as an extra-judicial organization possessed solely of advisory powers. It is of course conceivable that the Commission's reports published between 1950–6 may influence the courts in their interpretation of public policy. There is no evidence available to support this contention.

[1] W. Friedmann (ed.), *Anti-trust Laws*, p. 351. 'As is almost universally agreed among lawyers in England, the complex politico-economic considerations in monopoly cases mark a natural limit of the judicial function.'

[2] See Lord Finlay in Crown Milling Co v. The King (1927), A.C. 394. See also J. B. Heath, 'Not Enough Competition?', Hobart Paper II, p. 22.

[3] P. Guenault and J. M. Jackson, op. cit., p. 15. 'The attitude of the courts in practice had rendered the common law and the doctrine of the restraint of trade quite useless as a public safeguard against the abuse of monopoly power.'

[4] A. Guest and Anson, *Law of Contract*, Oxford, 1959, p. 308. 'The judges have wisely retained the power to make private rights subserve the general good.'

[5] W. Friedmann, op. cit., p. 129. 'It has recently been pointed out . . . that the whole law on this subject needs reconsideration in the light of modern conditions.'

The 1956 Act, of course, established a system of judicial evaluation for certain contracts in restraint of trade. This was much more directly related to the common law situation. Authorities still argue however that 'public policy' may be distinguished from 'public interest', and therefore that decisions of the Restrictive Practices Court may not be mirrored in common law suits.[1] At present there have been no test cases in this field of common law. Common law remedies for contracts in restraint of trade are rarely sought at present. A recent decision may encourage an expansion in the number of cases involving a plea of restraint of trade.

The case in question was decided in the Chancery Division of the High Court on March 29, 1965.[2] Mr Justice Buckley ruled that a 'solus' agreement between Petrofina (Great Britain) and Mr Headley Martin of Motorways Filling Station, Chesterfield, was unenforceable because it was in restraint of trade and contrary to the public interest. This is a case of special interest since the report of the Monopolies Commission relating to the solus site system has been lodged with the Board of Trade awaiting publication for some time.

Petrofina's action claiming an injunction to restrain the defendant from selling motor fuel and other petroleum products other than those of the plaintiff company was dismissed with costs. Petrofina also wished to prevent the defendant from selling his garage without first offering it to themselves.

'Mr Martin had acted in complete disregard of the terms of the "solus" agreement, but while it may not have been admirable conduct it was legitimate, as the agreement was not legally binding, constituting a restraint of trade and being contrary to the public interest.'[3]

The Judge ordered that an injunction granted earlier, preventing the plaintiff from selling the station, be continued pending the lodging of an appeal.

This case may be instrumental in producing a wave of cases in the field of restraint of trade. If this is so it will be interesting to compare the results of the common law decisions in this field, with the conclusions and recommendation of the Monopolies Commission and Restrictive Practices Court.

[1] Wilberforce, Campbell and Elles, op. cit., p. 109. 'It is not impossible that an agreement which has been held by the Restrictive Practices Court to be not contrary to the public interest, might still be held contrary to public policy, as being unreasonable between the parties. . . .'

[2] *Financial Times*, March 30, 1965, p. 22.

[3] Mr Justice Buckley, ibid., p. 22.

TRADE COMBINATIONS AND TORTIOUS CONSPIRACY

Actionable conspiracy in the law of tort was an unknown process of law before the late nineteenth century. Prior to this period trade conspiracies were challenged in the criminal courts on the ground that they were indictable conspiracies. A definition of indictable conspiracy was presented by Justice Fitzgerald in 1887:[1]

> Conspiracy has been aptly described as divisible into three heads: (i) where the end to be obtained is in itself a crime; (ii) where the object is lawful but the means to be resorted to are unlawful; (iii) and where the object is to do an injury to a third party or to a class, so if the wrong were effected by a single individual it would be a wrong but not a 'crime'.

Early in the nineteenth century the courts were under heavy pressure from trade conspirators to recognize the legal sanctity of their agreements. The courts proved much more willing to sanctify businessmen's trading agreements than to allow agreements among workers. This dichotomy remained until trade union protection by Parliament eliminated its possibility.

The decision of the House of Lords in the Mogul case in 1892[2] signified the removal of criminal conspiracy as an effective weapon against trade agreements. The case in question was brought against a number of ship-owners who had formed an Association designed to secure an exclusive carrying trade and thereby to improve their shipping rates. Secondary agreements provided extensive support for this prime purpose of the Association. The plaintiffs were ship-owners excluded from the agreement, whose trading interests were damaged by the agreements. The House of Lords upheld the high court decision in favour of the Association. It decided that the defendants had not transgressed the line distinguishing reasonable and legitimate selfishness from wrongful and malicious conspiracy. Lord Esher's dissent in the Court of Appeal sounded the final cry at the disappearance of criminal conspiracy as a remedy for damaged traders. The wording of the judgments left little future hope for a reinstatement of the process by future court decisions.[3]

Tortious cases relating to conspiracy appear to have become im-

[1] R. v. Parnell (1887), 14 Cox c.c. 508–13.

[2] Mogul Steamship Co v. McGregor, A.C. 25.

[3] e.g. Bowen, L.J., 'A man is bound not to use his property so as to infringe upon another's right . . . *sic utere tuo ut alienum non laedas*. . . . But there is surely no doctrine of law which compels him to use his property in a way that judges and juries may consider reasonable; if there is no such fetter upon the use of property . . . why should there be any such fetter on trade.'

portant following the Mogul case and the process was probably accepted finally by the courts in 1901.[1]

Actionable conspiracy was the centre of a very important case in 1925, Sorrell v. Smith.[2] This case involved a threat by the agents of the publishers of London daily newspapers to withdraw supplies of newspapers from certain newsagents unless they terminated certain agreements. The agents of the publishers were sued in tort by W. H. Smith for a restraining injunction against their contemplated action. The case is important because in his judgment Viscount Cave laid down the basic principles governing the law of tortious conspiracy:[3]

(i) A combination of two or more persons wilfully to injure a man in his trade is unlawful and, if it results in damage to him, is actionable.

(ii) If the real purpose of the combination is, not to injure another, but to forward or defend the trade of those who enter into it, then no wrong is committed and no action will lie, although damage to another ensues.

This criterion of actionable conspiracy could only mean that the possibility of successful action was slight. It is true that a successful action might lie where the purpose of the combination was the making of an empty display of power, or injuring for malice's sake alone, but 'in practice, the net result of the law of civil conspiracy . . . is one of acquiescence in a wide range of commercial practices which reduce the degree of competition in industry and trade'.[4]

The law enunciated in Sorrell v. Smith was fully endorsed, indeed broadened, in 1948 by judgments in the Crofter case.[5] Production of Harris Tweed cloth is an industry centred upon the Isles of Lewis, off the Scottish coast. At one time all yarn woven on the island was hand-spun from wool by the crofters of Lewis, the entire operation being located on the island. By 1930, however, yarn was less economically produced by hand than by machines. Many of the weavers on the island began to import yarn from the mainland. Despite this development, five mill-owners on the island continued to use yarn spun by hand by the local crofters. In so doing they accepted a commercial disadvantage in relation to those importing yarn. The weaver-employees of these five mills were members of the Transport and General Workers' Union, which demanded higher wages for its workers. The mill-owners rejected the claim on the ground of the competition from mills using cheap imported yarn. As a result union officials placed an embargo upon imported yarn. Lewis dockers refused to handle the yarn, thereby damag-

[1] In Quinn v. Leathem (1901), A.C. 495.
[2] (1925) A.C. 700, 701, 712. [3] ibid.
[4] W. Friedmann (ed.), op. cit., p. 360.
[5] Crofter Hand Woven Harris Tweed Co v. Veitch (1942), A.C. 435, 439.

ing the trading interests of the seven small producers of tweed relying upon imported yarn. Since the union officials were sued by these owners in their individual capacities the case did not involve any point under the Trade Disputes Act of 1906.

The House of Lords gave judgment for the defendant union officials. The court held that in such a case, where more than one motive was discernible, the predominant motive should be decisive. In the Crofter case the Judges submitted that the predominant objective of the respondents, in placing the embargo on yarn imports, was to benefit their trade union members by preventing the emergence of unregulated competition. 'A combination with such an object is the legitimate promotion of the interests of the combiners.'[1]

It is now well-established, therefore, that in an action for conspiracy the defendants need only demonstrate that their predominant motive in combining was to protect or to promote legitimate trading interests, and their case is assured.[2]

One critic of legal developments has powerfully demonstrated the lengths to which the courts have committed themselves in the Crofter Case:

> Now we discover new freedoms. Businessmen seeking to advance their private trade interests may not only combine with each other, but also bring their workers into the scheme, and promise them part of the swag. . . . Now we know that they may use not only their own workers, but workers in any other industry who happen to belong to the same union. . . . The householder who prefers Danish bacon to British may find that, at the behest of British farmers, the agricultural workers have persuaded the transport workers not to take him to his office, the laundry workers not to wash his clothes, the shop assistants not to sell to him, and so on, provided that they all belong to the same general union.[3]

CONCLUSION

The value of common law remedies in restraint of trade and in actionable conspiracy has been gradually and continuously reduced during the past 400 years. The years of depression between the wars influenced

[1] ibid., see Viscount Simon: He argued that evidence of malevolence need not lead to a case for conspiracy; the pursuit of a legitimate practical objective could not be vitiated by glee at the discomfiture of one's adversary since such glee could not affect the practical result. 'It is not consequence that matters, but purpose.'

[2] W. Friedmann (ed.), op. cit., 'the tort of conspiracy has probably been buried by the decision in the Harris Tweed Case'.

[3] W. A. Lewis, *Overhead Costs*, Allen & Unwin, London, 1951.

politicians, economists, businessmen and the judiciary in their open encouragement of the rationalization process. Under changed post-war conditions the judiciary has shown itself to be least well-equipped for a flexible reversal of its inter-war attitudes.

The weakness of the common law in relation to trade combination provided further fuel for those determined to obtain appropriate legislation in the immediate postwar period.

PART II

THE MONOPOLIES COMMISSION

'Who was it? A friend? A good man? Someone who sympathized? Someone who wanted to help? Was it one person only? Or were they all there? Was help at hand? Were there some arguments in his favour that had been overlooked? Of course there must be. Logic is doubtless unshakeable, but it cannot withstand a man who wants to go on living. Where was the Judge whom he had never seen? Where was the High Court, to which he had never penetrated?'

F. Kafka, *The Trial*, p. 250

Chapter Three

THE STRUCTURE AND CONSTITUTION OF THE MONOPOLIES COMMISSION

THE COMMISSIONERS

The Labour Government established the Monopolies and Restrictive Practices Commission by Act of Parliament in 1948.[1] The Act placed the Commission under the general supervision of the Board of Trade, as the Department of State most suited to the supervision of industry and commerce. The Board of Trade was responsible for the appointment of Commissioners, and for deciding the industrial and professional backgrounds most suited for membership of the Commission. The Board of Trade was responsible for deciding whether Commissioners should be appointed on a full-time or a part-time basis.

The Act limited the number of Commissioners to not less than four, nor more than ten; the actual number appointed was left to the discretion of the Board of Trade. Commissioners were to be appointed for terms of office varying between three and seven years, but the Act provided for possible extensions, with an upper limit of twelve years as the maximum period of office for any individual member. Commissioners could resign at any time by offering notice in writing. The Board of Trade could dismiss any member who proved 'unfit to continue in office or incapable of performing his duties under this Act'.[2]

In making its appointments the Board of Trade was authorized to select one member as Chairman. In any instance of voting equality at a meeting the Chairman would have the casting vote.

The Commission itself, once constituted, could decide upon the quorum required for the performance of its duties, always providing that such quorum should be not less than two-thirds of the Commissioners. This provision prevented members from using separate panel systems of examination to expedite the completion of their inquiries.

The salaries and other remuneration payable to Commissioners were

[1] op. cit.
[2] ibid., S.I. (3) (b and c).

to be determined by the Board of Trade, subject to approval by the Treasury. Finance would be provided through Parliament.

THE APPOINTMENT OF MEMBERS 1948–53

The Government recognized the paramount importance of ensuring that the Commission, from the outset, should meet with the respect and general acceptance of industrialists and the public at large. Respect and authority, in the case of the Commission, seemed to depend upon a wide range of experience on the part of members, 'including some first-hand knowledge of the current problems of the business community'.[1] The enclosed table demonstrates the varied backgrounds of the Commissioners appointed during the early years of the Monopolies Commission's existence.

TABLE I

Members of the Commission 1948–53*

Sir Archibald Carter, GCMG, KCB, KCIE (Chairman)	Seconded Civil Servant
Professor G. C. Allen, MCom, PhD	Academic Economist
C. N. Gallie, Esq	Trade Union Official and Company Director
I. C. Hill, Esq	Industrialist
Sir H. L. Saunders, FCGI, BSc (Eng)	Seconded Civil Servant
Gordon Stott, Esq, QC	Barrister
The Hon Josiah Wedgwood, BSc	Industrialist
Sir R. Yeabsley, CBE, FCA, FSAA	Accountant
F. Grant, Esq, MC, QC	Barrister
Mrs J. Robinson, MA	Academic Economist

* A full list of Commissioners, together with information relating to their period of office, is provided in an appendix.

In 1953 the former President of the Board of Trade, Mr Harold Wilson, stated[2] that he would not have contemplated the appointment of any Commissioner connected in any way with a monopoly firm or with an industry containing a trade association which exercised restrictive powers. He would have refused to appoint anyone with a grievance against a monopoly or a cartel. He wished to guard against damaging the reputation of the Commission by an unwary appointment. It is interesting to note that a later President, Peter Thorneycroft, refused to give such an undertaking when pressed in the House of Commons.[3]

[1] See Sixth Report of Select Committee on Estimates, 1952–3, p. V. 'In making appointments, the Board of Trade have attempted to select persons of such varied outlook and experience as are required for the work of the Commission.'

[2] Proceedings in the House of Commons, July 10, 1953, at col. 1603.

[3] Proceedings in the House of Commons, July 17, 1953, at cols. 2427–9.

Until 1953, only the Chairman and one other Commissioner held full-time appointments as members of the Commission.[1] The remaining members operated on a part-time basis, continuing to practise their outside professions. Commissioners holding office ranged in number from eight to ten during this period; two resignations took place in 1952.[2] Initially the periods of appointment ranged from three to five years, with, of course, the possibility of subsequent extension of office. The dates of appointment were staggered, as were terms of appointment, to provide for continuity in membership insofar as this was dependent upon the lagged retirement of members. There is little indication that any of the political parties were dissatisfied with the calibre of appointments or with the terms of office adopted by the Board of Trade during the early period of the Commission's activities.

CHANGES IN THE CONSTITUTION OF THE COMMISSION—1953

During 1953 discussions took place in Parliament concerning the structure of the Commission. A Parliamentary Committee[3] reported on the subject to the House of Commons. Consequential legislation followed in the shape of the Monopolies and Restrictive Practices Commission Act, 1953.[4]

The Government was determined that Commissioners of the very highest calibre should be appointed; prior to 1953 insecurity in tenure of office had handicapped the making of such appointments. The new legislation provided[5] that senior appointments—the Chairman, and up to three Deputy Chairmen of the Commission—should be permanent and pensionable. A maximum age limit of seventy years was established for these offices, with provision for extension of office at the discretion of the Board of Trade. Any Commissioner could resign at any time by giving notice in writing, and could be removed by the Board of Trade 'if in the opinion of the Board he becomes incapable of performing his duties as such or on the ground of misbehaviour'. The increased superannuation expenses resulting from the Act would be paid out of moneys provided by Parliament.

The Government desired to accelerate the pace of the Commission's work. To this end the legislation extended the maximum statutory number of Commissioners to twenty-five, and laid down that at least five Commissioners must be assigned to each inquiry. This development had been strongly recommended by the Committee on Estimates.

[1] Sir Archibald Carter and Sir H. Saunders respectively.
[2] F. Grant, QC, and Mrs Joan Robinson.
[3] Sixth Report from the Select Committee on Estimates—Session 1952–3.
[4] 1 and 2 Eliz. 2, c. 51.
[5] ibid., Schedule I.

In point of fact, in the period between the passing of the 1953 Act and legislation in 1956 the number of Commissioners gradually rose to sixteen and stabilized at that level. During the same period the Commission was organized into two panels of eight and nine Commissioners respectively. The Chairman participated in the work of each panel, thereby providing a degree of co-ordination. This system of panels undoubtedly extended the number of inquiries that the Commission could handle at any time. The acceleration of the Commission's work resulted in a more rapid accumulation of the important empirical data required for further legislation of a more specific nature.

RECONSTITUTION OF THE MONOPOLIES COMMISSION—1956

The 1956 Restrictive Trade Practices Act[1] abolished the Monopolies and Restrictive Practices Commission, and established a new Monopolies Commission.[2] All Commissioners holding office in 1956 were immediately dismissed. They were eligible for appointment to the new body. The statutory maximum number of Commissioners was lowered from twenty-five to ten, and the Commission was no longer allowed to exercise its functions in separate panels.[3] No deputy chairmen could be appointed after 1956.

In the event, a number of ex-Commissioners were appointed to the Monopolies Commission for varying periods of office. Since 1956 Commissioners have fluctuated around nine in number whilst resignations and new appointments have been made from time to time. The former Chairman of the Commission[4] was not appointed after 1956, although the present Chairman,[5] like his predecessor, possesses legal qualifications.

FULL OR PART-TIME COMMISSIONERS

Throughout the entire existence of the Monopolies Commission, the Board of Trade has appointed very few full-time members. The Chairman has always, naturally, been full-time but only on rare occasions has he had any full-time colleague. This has been conscious policy on the part of the Government. It was strongly felt that a full-time, professional Commission might become rigid and short-sighted in its approach.[6]

[1] 4 and 5 Eliz. 2, c. 68. [2] ibid., section 28 and section 29.

[3] In the view of Government the 1956 legislation had reduced the scope of the Monopolies Commission to a very great extent.

[4] D. Cairns, QC. [5] H. Levy, QC.

[6] Sixth Report from the Select Committee on Estimates, 1952–3, p. 8. Sir A. Carter. 'There is no doubt at all that it would go much faster with a smaller Commission, all the members of which were whole time. But I think they would tend to become rather professional "ring" hunters, so to speak.'

Moreover the willingness of industry to co-operate with the Commission was deemed rightly or wrongly to be dependent upon its having practising industrialists as Commissioners.

There is little doubt that the inclusion of part-time Commissioners on such a large scale has retarded the completion of inquiries. The full Commission is able to meet only once a fortnight to discuss the progress of its inquiries and to formulate conclusions during the public interest stage of the inquiry. The difficulty becomes most apparent during the later stages of an inquiry, when the burden of work inevitably shifts from the staff to the Commissioners. A number of part-time Commissioners admit this weakness but argue the compensating advantages of part-time members in retaining contact with the business environment and with their respective professions.

The Select Committee reporting in 1953 concluded that the Commission should retain its existing structure in this respect, but considered that the experience of the full-time members should be as wide as possible. This view finds support from the business community. A representative of one large company stated that some of the part-time members of the Commission were very able and versatile, showed considerable insight into industrial problems, and maintained a balanced outlook. The same could not be said for the full-time members and staff of the Monopolies Commission.

The Chairman of the Monopolies Commission emphasized the impossibility of obtaining the full-time services of businessmen and professional people eminent in their respective fields. The Franks Committee Report on 'Administrative Tribunals and Enquiries'[1] was quite adamant 'in rejecting any suggestion that, in general, tribunal service should become whole-time or salaried. Such a change would, we think, impair many valuable features of the system.'[2]

The balance of current opinion supports the need to appoint a greater proportion of full-time Commissioners. Such Commissioners should be drawn largely from the professions. Businessmen should be appointed largely on a part-time basis, thereby retaining contact with dynamic developments affecting the structure and environment of business enterprise. It is more likely that part-time businessmen will retain the co-operation of those under investigation than would those who were seen to desert completely their former habitat. Where the appointment of full-time members of sufficiently high calibre proves impossible, attempts might be made to operate a system of temporary secondment for minimum periods of three years.[3] In this event it might prove difficult to preserve the independence of the Monopolies Commission.

[1] Cmnd. 218, July 1957.

[2] ibid., p. 13.

[3] On the pattern established by the National Economic Development Council.

THE NATURE AND CALIBRE OF COMMISSIONERS

The Board of Trade has attempted to make appointments to the Commission of persons chosen in part for their varied backgrounds. In recent years the Chairman has been legally qualified, although the first Chairman was a Civil Servant. The Franks Committee underlined the importance of the quality of chairmanship, and commented that 'there has been substantial agreement among witnesses that any rate the majority of chairmen of tribunals should have legal qualifications'.[1]

A number of companies expressed criticism regarding the experience of the Commissioners. One industrial representative pointed out that in certain respects it was unfortunate that the chairman of the Commission should be a lawyer, since much of the Commission's work involved economic, accountancy and business matters and the Report was primarily an economic one. However, it was unthinkable that the chairman of a quasi judicial body such as the Commission should not be legally qualified. Another criticized the lack of practical industrialists on the Commission. He pointed out that the majority recommendation on one major issue had been made entirely by the non-industrialist members of the Commission. 'A study of the names of the majority reveals at once that none had had practical business experience.' This complaint was reiterated by yet another executive who commented that 'we shared the feelings of a number of other industries at the time that the inclusion of businessmen in the Monopolies Commission meant that the points made would be more readily assimilated and understood'.

A number of industrialists were extremely critical of the calibre of the Commissioners responsible for their respective inquiries. In particular they had been angered by the attitudes of Commissioners at their two formal meetings with the Monopolies Commission. They felt that the questions asked were lacking in penetration, and that many of the Commissioners had not prepared their briefs efficiently. A spirit of apathy and boredom was apparent throughout the meetings.

On the other hand five organizations expressed complete satisfaction both with the calibre and the background of members and also in the quality of the final Reports. It is noticeable that companies best known for their high quality management were critical, in the main, of the calibre of the Commissioners.[2]

The Board of Trade has failed to make sufficient impact in its appointments to the Monopolies Commission. The Commission should be composed of members with widespread reputations—people of similar stature to those appointed to the National Economic Development

[1] op. cit., p. 12.

[2] Albeit, some of the smaller organizations had not been very closely concerned in the inquiries.

Council. Many existing members are thorough, efficient and highly talented. They are not well-known, especially outside their specialist fields. The Monopolies Commission can scarcely aspire to a position of real significance unless the nature of its membership is transformed.

There are major problems of course in such a radical departure from the existing structure of the Monopolies Commission. Salaries would have to be raised substantially. During the early years of the Act the Chairman received £5,000 per annum. A figure of £25,000 per annum would not be excessive for obtaining a first-rate Chairman; appropriate upward adjustments at all other levels would then be possible.

Equally important is the prestige of the Commission. The Government must elevate the status of the Commission to the highest level. This would encourage those most gifted to offer their services, especially those at present hesitant 'to betray their fellow-industrialists'. In part, prestige in Britain is closely correlated to salary, in part to the political prestige accorded to the organization.

These recommendations would go far to providing the Board with a choice of highly gifted potential Commissioners. It would not guarantee enthusiasm and vitality. In part this must be imposed from above. The Board of Trade has failed in recent years to provide the Commission with a real sense of mission.

THE STAFF OF THE MONOPOLIES COMMISSION

The 1948 legislation made the Monopolies Commission responsible for appointing its Secretary and staff. The Secretarial appointment was subject to the approval of the Board of Trade. The appointment of remaining staff was subject to the joint consent of the Board of Trade and the Treasury.

In practice the Commission has been served by secretaries with a legal background, seconded from the Board of Trade. The numbers and composition of staff have varied with the scope and size of the Commission itself. In December 1949 staff with the Commission numbered thirty-seven, four of whom held the equivalent rank of Principal in the Civil Service. There was a statistician and an accountant on the staff. An economist was obtained for a special period of three months only. The staff numbered, at that stage, twelve officers of executive class, the remainder being typists, clerical officers, and clerical assistants. Staff numbers slowly increased during the early years reaching fifty-five by 1952, but the 1953 Act stimulated a rapid increase. In 1954 staff numbered 100, but fell swiftly, following the passage of the 1956 Act. In 1962 the staff of the Monopolies Commission had fallen to thirty-seven in number.

Calibre and Training of Staff

It is clear that a predominantly part-time Commission must rely substantially upon its staff for discriminating and incisive reporting back. The quality and organization of the staff will tend to set the tone for the entire inquiry.

The staff of the Monopolies Commission work under the immediate control of an assistant secretary. The staff are organized into separate panels, each conducting a specific inquiry, or a part of one inquiry. Each team is controlled by a principal. One or two principals are attached to any one inquiry. The Monopolies Commission has tended to entrust the more complex inquiries to its most experienced principals. The Select Committee on Estimates 1952–3[1] provided an insight into the operations of the Commission's staff. At that time about two-thirds of the staff were appointed by the Commission; the remainder were seconded Civil Servants.[2] Staff appointed directly were usually subjected to contract terms of one month's notice. The Commission felt at that time that the nature of the work and the restricted prospects of promotion in so small an organization made it prudent to retain a good deal of flexibility in the term of staff appointments; this did not rule out the possibility that many of its staff would serve for lengthy periods.

Most of the companies and trade associations subjected to inquiry were critical of the staff of the Monopolies Commission. They considered that the staff were poorly qualified for the task in hand, and in particular that they were deficient in knowledge of economics, statistics and commerce. Lack of expertise and of experience in business activities resulted in a considerable waste of time for the companies involved in an inquiry. The staff refused to make use of modern technical equipment to speed the pace of inquiry. In particular they declined consistently to have Minutes photographed; in place of this they laboriously typed out each Minute, and in certain instances they copied them by longhand methods. Companies found themselves involved in detailed correcting of the factual material obtained by the Commission's staff, and found themselves enveloped in details of company operations that could not conceivably be of any relevance to the inquiry. A number of staff had been young and enthusiastic, but their enthusiasm had led them into pursuit of every issue that was discovered, irrespective often of its relevance for the inquiry. In particular, the Commission's staff annoyed those under investigation by demanding documents relating to events which had occurred sixty years or more before the date of the inquiry. One trade association complained of prejudice on the part of the staff,

[1] op. cit.

[2] See Guenault and Jackson, op. cit., p. 58. 'This ability to draw upon the Civil Service for staff did at least permit the Commission to start work quickly with a solid nucleus of experienced personnel.'

but with this exception those investigated do not complain of biased treatment. On the other hand, few trade associations, and even fewer companies, were prepared to praise the efficiency of the Commission's staff and its procedure of inquiry.

The staff should not be held fully responsible for the dissatisfaction of those investigated. At times the staff work under severe pressure, and they do not receive detailed guidance from the Commissioners during the early stages of an inquiry. The Commissioners themselves must bear partial responsibility for untidy inquiries.

One Commissioner suggested that staff appointed during the late 1940s had been highly qualified and enthusiastic. This was inevitable in the light of early postwar ambitions for the Monopolies Commission. In later years, however, enthusiasm for the work of the Commission had declined. A few of the most able staff had departed, and it had been difficult to obtain equivalent replacements. The Monopolies Commission was outside the normal run of Civil Service promotion, and could scarcely expect to obtain the more ambitious young Civil Servants. Nevertheless, he had always been impressed by the quality of his staff, especially of the accountants. He accepted some responsibility for the undisciplined approach of the staff, admitting that the Commissioners were frequently guilty of providing inadequate instructions. He agreed that the speed and effectiveness of inquiry would have improved if staff had been recruited with commercial and economics training.

The Secretary of the Monopolies Commission, Mr Gilbert, CBE, provided full support for his staff. He admitted that staff appointments had been affected by the keen competition that existed for highly qualified people, but felt that the Commission had been very successful in its staff appointments. He admitted that economists had been appointed by the Commission purely by chance. The Chairman of the Commission, Mr Levy, QC, argued that his staff were fully trained in the technique of inquiry most appropriate for a Monopolies Commission investigation, and that they were particularly disciplined with regard to relevance. Staff were always aware that a line of inquiry might expose unsuspected facts relevant to the inquiry. Probing must remain an essential part of the staff's functions.

Evidence relating to the calibre and the efficiency of the Commission's staff is conflicting. Nevertheless, there does seem to be ample cause for concern. Criticisms have been levelled at the staff of the Commission not only by those subjected to examination, but also by a few Commissioners. Clearly, a reappraisal is required of the nature of the staff's duties, and of the qualifications necessary for affecting such duties.

The work of the Monopolies Commission has clearly become more important in recent years, not only in the view of Parliament, but also in the view of the general public. Government powers relating to action on reports of the Commission are being extended. There can be no excuse for imposing upon the Monopolies Commission poorly qualified staff. The Commission's work is one of complex research and analysis. Graduate qualifications in various branches of the social sciences must be well represented on its staff. This will involve a complete reassessment of the salary structure of the Monopolies Commission. An example exists in the National Economic Development Council. It is extremely dangerous to conduct important inquiries on a shoe-string budget. If the reports of the Monopolies Commission are to be considered of sufficient consequence to warrant Government action, then companies have every right to expect that the body will be staffed with people who measure up to the task required.

Chapter Four

THE SCOPE AND AUTHORITY OF THE MONOPOLIES COMMISSION

A. THE LEGISLATIVE FRAMEWORK

Powers of Initiating an Inquiry

The Monopolies Commission has no power to initiate an inquiry.[1] In this respect the powers of the Commission are far more limited than the powers of the United States Federal Trade Commission.

The Commission inquires into and reports upon references issued by the Board of Trade. The Board of Trade acts 'as the co-ordinating department for all the governmental departments',[2] and may refer cases to the Commission where it appears to them that 'conditions to which the Act applies prevail'.[3] Within this field the Board of Trade has an unfettered freedom of choice.

The Board receives a large number of complaints relating to activities which might fall within the scope of the Act both from the general public and from interested organizations.

The Board of Trade is not limited to such complaints when making its references;[4] it has not considered it necessary in practice to give preference to complaints in its decisions. References suggested to the Board in communications from the general public are not always those which appear to the Board to be of the greatest significance, either in themselves or as representative examples of restrictive practices. The Board has made a practice of consulting other Government depart-

[1] Section 2 of the 1948 Act. This would not debar the Commission from making informal suggestions to the Board of Trade. 'I imagine if there was something which we really thought important, we should find informal ways of passing it to the Board of Trade for consideration. But we have not so far found that necessary. The Board of Trade has kept us very busily employed.' Sir A. Carter, Chairman of the Commission. Minutes of Evidence taken before Sub-Committee 'F' of Select Committee on Estimates, 1953, at question 121.

[2] Dame Alix Kilroy, Manchester School, 1954, p. 41.

[3] Section 2 of the 1948 Act.

[4] Much of the following detail has been extracted from The Annual Reports of the Board of Trade.

ments concerned with trade and industry prior to finalizing its list of references.

The Board of Trade has been influenced occasionally by the recommendations of Government committees of inquiry. For example, the report of the Simon Committee[1] was largely instrumental in persuading the Board of Trade to make an early reference relating to builders' castings. The Board may pay regard from time to time to public debate over a product or a process.

The 1948 legislation obliged the Board of Trade to publish an annual report of the work of the Monopolies Commission. The report must contain 'a review in such detail as the Board think fit of the suggestions and requests (not being frivolous) which have been made to the Board for the reference of any particular matter to the Commission under the provisions of this Act'.[2] The Board of Trade itself must decide whether or not any suggestion warrants inclusion in the annual report. The Board must state the source of any complaint or suggestion where it is made by 'representative groups' as defined in the 1948 legislation.

At first the Board of Trade provided the Commission with a number of references all at the same time. It was intended to allow the Commission to plan its work schedule well ahead. The Monopolies Commission is free to pursue its inquiries in any order it selects, irrespective of the order in which references are made.

The early references were selected 'to cover a wide range of different types of allegedly restrictive practices so that the Commission's first reports should enable a considerable section of industry to look at its trading practices in the light of authoritative judgments'. The Board also wished the Commission to cover several different types of industry in the early years. The following statement of the Board's aims provides a useful summary:

> The Board's general aim, in choosing references from the large number of possible cases for investigation, is to build up a programme of study which will enable the Commission to bring under review, in the early years of their work, representative examples of all the common types of restrictive practice and monopolistic influence in British industry. For the time being, therefore, the choice is being directed chiefly to subjects which may be expected to break new ground.[3]

Various criteria have been adopted by the Board of Trade during the sixteen years of the Act's existence in determining the priority of references. Criteria have included the size of the trade concerned, the im-

[1] op. cit.

[2] Section 16 (2 and 3) of the 1948 Act.

[3] Annual Report of The Board of Trade, 1950, p. 5.

portance of the trade in the national economy, the volume and nature of representations received, the prospect of obtaining conclusions of wider application, and the prospect of obtaining an indication of the value of further inquiries into similar problems. The pneumatic tyres reference is an interesting example of a combination of motives:

> Take the case of pneumatic tyres, I should say that considerations which led to the choice of that industry were, perhaps, twofold. The first is, of course, it is a very important industry. Tyres enter into the cost of all kinds of things; motor cars, aeroplanes, heavy tractors, and so on. The second is that it is an industry where there does appear to be a considerable lack of competition owing to price fixing, and what are loosely called 'rings' and the whole apparatus of discounts, lists, and so on.[1]

The Board of Trade initially wished to use the Commission in such a manner that a 'coherent and authoritative body of guidance on monopolistic conditions and restrictive practices within the scope of the Act may be built up as quickly as possible'.[2] Another factor relevant to the selection of early references was the future possibility of making a Section 15 reference to the Commission.[3] In later times the Board has paid more attention to the importance of the referred industry than to the range and variety of practices known or suspected to exist.

The Board of Trade may frame its references in various ways. It may ask for a factual report whether the conditions do apply and, if so, in what manner and to what extent, and what practices are operated as a result of, or for the preservation of, such conditions.[4]

The Board may further request a report whether the conditions and practices operate or are likely to operate against the public interest.[5] Alternatively the Board may require the Commission to state where the conditions do apply, what are the effects of a specified selection of the practices upon the public interest.[6]

The Board of Trade may vary any reference at any time[7] although it

[1] Mr Hill in answer to Question 229 of Select Committee on Estimates, 1953.

[2] Annual Report of The Board of Trade, 1948, p. 6.

[3] Infra.

[4] Section 6 (1) (a) of the 1948 Act. In fact all the references with the exception of 'The supply of various semi-manufacturers of copper and copper-based alloys, and exports of such products from the United Kingdom' have required fulfilment of both Section 6 (1) (a) and Section 6 (1) (b) of the Act. This restricted reference was subsequently extended to cover 6 (1) (b). Following the passing of legislation in 1956 the reference on electronic valves and cathode ray tubes was completed on a factual basis only.

[5] Section 6 (1) (b) of the 1948 Act.

[6] Section 6 (2) of the 1948 Act.

[7] Section 6 (4) of the 1948 Act. It has made use of this clause upon occasion.

is not allowed to change a public interest reference into a report solely upon the facts.[1] On the other hand the Board has full powers to alter a factual reference into a public interest reference.[2] The Board of Trade must publish each reference and each reference variation in such a manner as will best bring it to the notice of affected persons.[3]

Market Dominance—Some Problems of Definition

All legislation aimed at the supervision and control of market dominance is complicated by the need to define the concept. This definitional problem has afflicted legislation in North America, and has excited the attention of most economists working in the field of anti-trust.

The term 'monopoly' springs from Greek origins, and literally translates as 'a single seller'. Strictly the term monopoly has no place in a capitalistic society. The existence of a monopolist would signify that one organization had total command over the entire income of the community, irrespective of the price that it decided to charge for its products. The situation would be mirrored by a demand curve in the shape of a rectangular hyperbola. It is clear that it is not this phenomenon that legislation is designed to control.

More commonly the term 'monopoly' is loosely used to denote any single seller of the whole supply of a particular commodity. This definition corresponds closely to the classical Cournot-Marshall definition of monopoly. A definition of this kind involves a number of complications. It is not easy to define 'a commodity', when product differentiation is widespread. Attempts to define 'the market' by reference to 'a gap in the chain of substitutes' are less confusing in principle than they are in practice. Efforts at defining 'the firm' are far from simple in a country increasingly characterized by the financial group and the investment trust.[4]

It is not possible to evade the problem by falling back upon some conventional formula. For the definition of an industry varies with the purpose underlying the definition. It is a weakness in the 1948 legislation that no attempt was made to produce a definition of market dominance relating to variations in the cross-elasticity of demand between products.

[1] Section 6 (4) of the Act. The case of the variation in the reference on electronic valves and the cathode ray tubes is a special exception to this rule.

[2] e.g. The reference on semi-manufactures of copper and copper-based alloys. Infra.

[3] Details of all references and reference variations are disclosed in The Annual Reports of The Board of Trade, as prescribed under the 1948 Act.

[4] Readers who wish to pursue reading relating to this problem are advised to examine the following references: R. Triffin, *Monopolistic Competition and General Equilibrium Theory*, Harvard, 1941; H. Edwards, *Competition and Monopoly in the British Soap Industry*, Oxford, 1962; J. M. Clark, *Competition as a Dynamic Process*, Brookings, 1961.

Later sections demonstrate the practical problems that have resulted from a neglect of this important criterion.

Those responsible for the 1948 legislation clearly recognized the existence of a definitional problem. They largely evaded the issue by resorting to an arbitrary criterion of market dominance. It is significant that the term 'monopoly' was not used in the 1948 Act except in the title and in the preamble.

In the event the Government decided that conditions of the Act should apply with respect to the supply[1] and processing of goods when at least one third of all the goods supplied or processed[2] in the United Kingdom or in any substantial part of the United Kingdom were supplied or processed by or to any person, or two or more persons being inter-connected bodies corporate.[3] This definition was intended to cover the dominant firm.

The conditions were to apply on similar terms to restrictive agreements between firms, whether oral or written, tacit or overt. In such instances the conditions would appear to prevail 'if the parties to a restrictive agreement or arrangement supply at least one third of the goods in question, even though the agreement or arrangement itself affects the supply of less than one-third of the goods'.[4]

Furthermore, the 1948 Act extended to the supply or processing of goods where two or more firms 'so conduct their respective affairs as in any way to prevent or restrict competition'[5] and where such firms accounted for at least one-third of the goods supplied or processed in the UK of that description. This 'seems to be wide enough to cover so-called oligopoly conditions in which each of a small number of firms may in its own interest eschew the more severe methods of competition (e.g. price competition) without there being any overt or covert agreement or arrangement among the firms'.[6] In part this clause was designed to overcome the difficulty faced by guardians of US anti-trust laws when confronted by 'twilight zone' situations of open-price filing or oligopoly.[7]

[1] The term 'supply' was extended to cover supply by way of lease, or hire, and in relation to buildings or structures, included their construction for another person. Section 20, sub-section 1.

[2] References concerning the application of a process do not include instances where the process is applied by the owner of the goods or his servants. Section 4 (3). Such a case, however, would presumably not be of real importance.

[3] Section 20 (2) of the Act defines 'inter-connected bodies corporate' in the manner relating to S. 154 of the Companies Act of 1948. This would cover a holding company and its subsidiaries as defined in this latter Act.

[4] W. Friedmann (ed.), *The Anti-Trust Laws*, p. 365.

[5] Section 3 (2), 'any two or more persons who, whether voluntarily or not, and whether by agreement or arrangement or not, so conduct their respective affairs as in any way to prevent or restrict competition. . . .'

[6] W. Friedmann (ed.), op. cit., p. 366.

[7] e.g. The notorious Gary dinner parties in the American steel industry.

The scope of the Act extended to exports of goods of any description from the United Kingdom. In respect of exports the conditions applied where one firm, or a group of firms operating within an agreement, or otherwise in restriction of competition, produced or processed at least one third of all such goods produced or processed in the United Kingdom. It is feasible for a firm to be caught by the export clause whilst exporting merely five per cent of total exports of a particular commodity, as long as it produced at least one third of the entire United Kingdom production of that commodity. An export reference may be made separately, or in conjunction with a production or process reference; it may be made in relation to all exports of the products or in relation to specific export markets.[1]

Conditions apply throughout where goods or processes of a particular description are not supplied in the United Kingdom, in any substantial part thereof, or in specified export markets.[2]

The Board of Trade and the Monopolies Commission are jointly responsible for determining the measurement of market share accounted for by firms or associations of firms.[3] A large range of criteria has been used in the various inquiries.[4] The Monopolies Commission has been most careful to explain the use of particular types of measurement.[5] In practice the Monopolies Commission has played the dominant role in selecting measurement criteria. This is desirable since the practical problems of measurement are clearer and more pertinent to the Commission than to the Board of Trade.

Fulfilment by a reference of the conditions of the 1948 Act depends to a large extent upon the exact wording of the reference, and in particular upon the manner in which 'a substantial part of the United Kingdom' is interpreted both by the Board of Trade and by the Monopolies Commission. For instance by defining a referred commodity as a 'Ford Popular' motor car there is no doubt that the Board of Trade could catch the Ford Motor Company under the 1948 legislation. Equally, by confining the supply area for evening newspapers to Nottingham the *Evening Post* would be caught by the Act. Lack of precision in relation to these possibilities created genuine concern during the early stages of the Act's existence. The Royal Commission on the Press[6] commented upon the

[1] To date export references have been made only in conjunction with domestic references. In all cases they have been general to all exports irrespective of their respective overseas markets.

[2] Section 3 (1) (b); Section 4 (1) (b) of the Act.

[3] Section 20 (3).

[4] To date the following criteria have been used: value, weight, cubic capacity, yardage, number of units, numbers employed.

[5] e.g. (a) 'Report on the Supply and Export of Pneumatic Tyres', at para. 447. 'Supply and production of tyres are better measured by value than by units because of the wide range of tyres and sizes.'

[6] The Royal Commission on the Press, 1947–9, Cmnd. 7700, pp. 162–3.

problem, displaying anxiety lest areas of the size of Devon and Cornwall or extensive conurbations should be exempt from the Act, thereby freeing local monopolies of the press from investigation and control. These fears seem to have been unfounded in practice. Two references limited geographically to particular regions within the United Kingdom have been made[1] and were reported upon by the Monopolies Commission without difficulty. The Board of Trade has not attempted to make any 'trick' reference designed to bring a particular company within the scope of the Act. There is little likelihood of such an attempt being made at a time when the Government is most anxious to preserve the good name of the legislation.

Organizations Exempted from the 1948 *Legislation*

Certain kinds of organization and a number of specified practices were excluded from the scope of the 1948 Act. The most obvious exemptions were firms and associations accounting for less than one-third of their respective markets. However dominant such organizations might be they need not fear an inquiry from the Monopolies Commission.

The Act does not extend to sectors in which the conditions present are expressly authorized by or under any enactment, other than enactments relating to patents and trade marks. This excludes, among other sectors, the nationalized industries.[2] In addition it would exclude such statutory bodies as the Agricultural Marketing Boards established by legislation in 1931, 1932 and 1949. In practice the clause has not been construed to exclude firms or industries whose structure and practices may have been influenced by official intervention and licensing techniques.[3]

During any inquiry the Commission must take no account of the effect of 'practices as to the workers to be employed or not to be employed by them or as to the remuneration, conditions of employment, hours of work or working conditions of workers, or any class of workers, so employed . . .'[4] Thus if any agreement negotiated with trade unions resulted in restriction of competition the conditions of the Act would

[1] The Report on the Supply of Building in the Greater London Area, 1954, H.C.P. 264, and The Report on the Supply of Sand and Gravel in Central Scotland, 1956, H.C.P. 222.

[2] This exemption incensed many members of the Conservative Party during discussion of the Bill in the House of Commons. Nevertheless, the exemption has not been remedied during the long period in which the Conservatives were in power. The nationalized industries have been subject to investigation from time to time by *ad hoc* Government committees, and are by statute accountable to Parliament for their activities.

[3] This is apparent in reading most of the early Reports of the Commission on industries subjected to detailed Government interference: e.g. The Report on the Supply of Cast Iron Rainwater Goods, 1951, H.C.P. 136.

[4] Sections 3 (2), 4 (2), 4 (4) of the 1948 Act.

not apply in the absence of other completely independent conditions.

The Act consistently refers to the supply, processing and exporting of *goods*.[1] Services are not mentioned in the Act at all.[2] Services are excluded also from the definitional clause,[3] which interpreted the term goods as encompassing buildings, ships, and aircraft. It is quite clear that the supply of labour services is entirely outside the scope of the 1948 legislation.

The supply of services, irrespective of the concentration in supply, must be presumed outside the scope of the Act, except where the service is provided to a good, or is intimately bound up with the supply, processing or exports of goods. Thus distributive services are caught insofar as they deal in goods.[4] Service trades such as hairdressing, cinemas, insurance companies, indeed the banking and financial sector as a whole, are not covered by the Act.

There is little excuse for the exclusion of service trades. The omission is serious and places outside the scope of the legislation the activities of building societies, insurance companies, joint stock, and merchant banks.[5] The growing importance of institutional investment in Britain underlines the urgency for a broadening of the 1948 Act to include this form of economic activity. The Bow Group[6] recently emphasized the importance of such an extension of legislation:

> One limitation of the Act . . . is the complete exclusion of services from its provisions. Of course measures to deal with them would be complicated and would involve the special problems of country bus routes and the political headaches of controlling nationalized industries and trade union monopolies but it is hard to see why hotels and insurance, for instance, should not be dealt with in the same way as brewing and building.

Further support was forthcoming from another Conservative publication concerned with the problem of market dominance: 'The Act of 1948 applies only to goods and processes; we recommend that it should apply also to commercial services.'[7]

[1] Section 3–5 inclusive of the 1948 Act.

[2] It is, perhaps, significant that the Board of Trade, in its Annual Report for 1949, mentioned 'Boot and Shoe Repairing' as a '*service trade*' potential reference.

[3] Section 20 (i).

[4] Distributive sectors have been examined in the majority of Commission inquiries: e.g. Report on the Supply of Cast Iron Rainwater Goods and Report on the Supply of Imported Timber.

[5] These are the main sources of 'monopoly capitalism' in the eyes of the Socialist countries.

[6] The Bow Group, *Monopolies and Mergers*, p. 42.

[7] Conservative Political Centre, *Monopoly and the Public Interest*, p. 28.

Consequent upon these reports the Conservative Government produced a White Paper proposing legislation in the field. This legislation was frustrated by the change of government in October 1964. The Labour Government have recently introduced a Bill into the House of Commons concerning the Monopolies Commission. Both these developments are examined critically in the concluding chapter of this book.

The Section 15 'General' Reference

The initial draft of the 1948 Monopolies Bill did not provide for a general inquiry into a specified range of practices. This omission reflected a strong feeling in Parliament in favour of an empirical rather than a dogmatic approach to problems of market dominance.[1] The case study system was considered to provide the best safeguard against the intrusion of dogma. The early draft of the Bill directed the Monopolies Commission to inform the Board of Trade of any important information that it might obtain.[2] Mr Wilson intimated in the House of Commons that the Commission might provide a report upon a common practice where it was conducting an inquiry into two or three industries in which such a practice existed.[3]

At the instigation of a Labour back-bencher a new Section was inserted into the Bill at the Report Stage. Section 15 empowered the Board 'at any time [to] require the Commission to submit to them a report on the general effect on the public interest of practices of a specified class, being practices which in the opinion of the Board are commonly adopted as a result of, or for the purpose of preserving, conditions to which the Act applies'.

This Amendment met with hostility and mistrust from the Conservative Opposition. It was considered that the clause 'ran counter to the empirical spirit of the Bill'.[4] These fears were not entirely dissipated by the proviso made by the President of the Board of Trade that 'the Board shall not require a report under this subsection on the general effect of practices of any class unless they are satisfied that the practices of that class have been dealt with, in relation to goods of particular descriptions, by previous reports of the Commission'.[5]

During the Debate over the Amendment the chief Conservative spokesman on the Bill, David Maxwell-Fyfe, extracted from Mr Wilson

[1] Nobody expected that the Monopolies Commission would approach the problem of market dominance without viewpoints of any kind. But an empirical approach was strongly desired. See Dame Alix Kilroy, *The Tasks and Methods of the Monopolies Commission*, Manchester School, January 1954, p. 61.

[2] Section 2 (2) of the 1948 legislation.

[3] Proceedings of the House of Commons, Standing Committee B, June 3, 1948, col. 187.

[4] P.E.P., May 1, 1953, p. 196.

[5] Proviso to Section 15.

a pledge that no report would be requested during the early stages of the Commission's existence under Section 15. It was considered that the Commission should first obtain experience through specific industry inquiries.

In fact two references only have been made to date under Section 15. The first general reference culminated in the Collective Discrimination Report of 1955. The second such reference was made in June 1955,[1] covering the practices of common prices and level tendering. The 1956 legislation, however, resulted in the cancellation of this latter reference.

The Section 12 'Follow-up' Reference

Once the Monopolies Commission has completed a report the Board of Trade may refer to the Commission, at any time, the question whether and to what extent the parties have complied with a Commission recommendation or with the decision of the competent authority under the Act. Such a reference cannot be laid relating to compliance with any Order made by the competent authority. To date only one Section 12 reference has been made; this concerned the supply of imported timber.[2] The lack of Section 12 references, in the face of repeated complaints from third parties, has been a serious weakness of government action under the Act. The difficulties imposed upon firms by such references would scarcely outweigh the beneficial demonstration effect upon firms who are parties to undertakings with the government.

The Restrictive Trade Practices Act, 1956—Implications for the Monopolies Commission

The Restrictive Trade Practices Act, 1956,[3] severely reduced the scope of the Monopolies Commission. The Act established a Restrictive Practices Court, and provided for the judicial review of registrable agreements[4] relating to the supply and processing of goods. In addition the Act prohibited the collective enforcement of resale price maintenance[5] whilst providing for individual enforcement of resale prices through the law courts.

The Act provided that conditions formerly covered by the 1948 Act, but which thereafter were catered for by Part I of the 1956 Act, should no longer be the concern of the Monopolies Commission. The newly-

[1] Proceedings in the House of Commons, June 16, 1955, col. 729.

[2] The Report was laid before Parliament in 1958.

[3] 4 and 5, Eliz. 2, c. 68.

[4] The agreements subjected to registration and to examination are defined in Sections 6, 7 and 8 of the Act. They may be defined briefly as collective agreements on prices or other terms and conditions, collective agreements involving discrimination between persons, market sharing, or restrictions on production and processing.

[5] Section 24 of the 1956 Act.

constituted Monopolies Commission would henceforth concern itself with the following conditions:

1. Where one concern, or group of related concerns, is responsible for at least one third of the supply, processing or (in the case where exports are the subject of a reference) production of the goods in question in the United Kingdom.

2. Where two or more concerns, together responsible for at least one third of the supply or processing or exports of goods defined, so conduct their affairs other than by means of a registrable agreement, as to prevent or restrict competition. This clause again covers conscious or perhaps even unconscious parallelism of action, including for instance the open-price filing systems substituted for many price-fixing agreements registrable under the 1956 Act.[1]

3. Where there are agreements or arrangements preventing or restricting the export, or competition in relation to export of goods from the UK generally, or the supply of goods to any particular market for UK goods and these agreements or arrangements are operative as respects one third of all the goods of such description produced in the UK. Such agreements, relating exclusively to exports, are exempted from registration obligations with the Registrar.[2] Such agreements are registrable with the Board of Trade and may be referred by the Board to the Monopolies Commission.[3]

4. The Board of Trade may still refer to the Monopolies Commission a Section 15 reference covering specified practices or activities. The 1956 Act withdrew the proviso to Section 15(1) of the 1948 Act, which had limited the power of the Board of Trade in making such references to practices already examined by the Commission.[4]

5. The Board of Trade may still make a Section 12 reference to the Monopolies Commission where the appropriate conditions apply.

B. THE COMMISSION'S INTERPRETATION OF THE ACT

The Public Interest

Economists and philosophers may criticize the Commission for its interpretations of the public interest. It is scarcely possible, however, to suggest that any of the Commission's interpretations are in direct conflict

[1] Although in the latest statement made by the Registrar, he contends that certain open-price filing systems may be registrable under the 1956 Act.

[2] Section 8 (8) (a) of the 1956 Act.

[3] If, however, the agreement contains registrable restictions relating in part, e.g. to the export of goods from the UK, but also in part to home trade, the entire agreement will fall within the jurisdiction of the Restrictive Practices Court. An example occurred in The Water-Tube Boilermakers' case—I.W.C.R. 1118.

[4] Although, to date, no Section 15 reference has been made since the passage of the 1956 Act.

with the directions imposed by the 1948 Act. The criteria established by the Act regarding the public interest are vague; they were designed to allow the Commission to formulate its own philosophy.

At first it was not the intention of the Labour Government to draft any public interest 'guiding lights' into the Act. At the instigation of the Opposition, however, and under pressure in particular from David Maxwell-Fyfe, Section 14 was drafted into the Act, providing the following guidance for the Monopolies Commission:[1]

> All matters which appear in the particular circumstances to be relevant shall be taken into account and, amongst other things, regard shall be had to the need, consistently with the general economic position of the United Kingdom, to achieve:
>
> (a) the production, treatment and distribution by the most efficient and economical means of goods of such types and qualities, in such volume and at such prices as will best meet the requirements of home and overseas markets;
>
> (b) the organization of industry and trade in such a way that their efficiency is progressively increased and new enterprise is encouraged;
>
> (c) the fullest use and best distribution of men, materials and industrial capacity in the United Kingdom; and
>
> (d) the development of technical improvements and the expansion of existing markets and the opening up of new markets.

These statements are pregnant with problems of definition; they were scarcely expected to be of practical use to the Monopolies Commission. This is no criticism of the Act, which was drafted against a background of uncertainty concerning the effects of monopoly and restrictive practices. In such circumstances it would have been unrealistic to define narrowly the limits within which the new body should direct its approach. The only specific guidance from Section 14 is the emphasis upon a nationalistic approach.

Oligopoly

Some confusion has emanated from Reports of the Commission relating to industries comprised of a few companies. The Commission has not clearly demonstrated whether it considers itself able to examine and report in detail upon the activities of firms within a referred industry other than the dominant firm itself. The wording of Sections 2 and 3 of the Act appears to be consistent with the broader interpretation.[2] The Monopolies Commission also interpreted the reference on the supply of matches as enabling it to formulate recommendations covering the

[1] Section 14 of the 1948 Act, op. cit.
[2] Supra.

entire industry.[1] It appears also that the intention of Government in drafting the 1948 Act was closer to the broader than the narrower interpretation of the Act.[2]

On the other hand, some commentators rely upon the Report on the Supply of Cigarettes and Tobacco to support the narrower viewpoint that the Commission investigates only dominant firms. The Commission made a point in its report of commenting upon the activities of The Imperial Tobacco Company[3] alone. The Commission omitted a detailed account of the operations of Gallaher and other smaller cigarette and tobacco producers.[4] If this is indicative of a narrow interpretation, Section 6 (i) (a) of the 1948 Act provides some legal support. It provides that a reference may be drafted: 'to limit the investigation and report to the facts, that is to say, to the question whether conditions to which this Act applies in fact prevail, and if so in what manner *and to what extent*, and to the things which are done *by the parties concerned* as a result of, or for the purpose of preserving, those conditions'; should the narrower interpretation be correct, outside companies may nevertheless be caught by the Act. Sections 3–5 of the Act cover arrangements and activities of firms which do not amount to a registrable agreement when such firms 'so conduct their respective affairs as in any way to prevent or restrict competition in connection with the supply (processing or exporting) of goods of the description in question'. This was certainly considered by the Labour Government to cover oligopolistic situations.[5]

> Subsection (2) of Clause 3 goes much further than that and covers cases where there may be no arrangement, formal or informal, between supplying firms. This authorizes the Commission to go into conditions usually referred to as 'price leadership' where a single firm, without being in a monopolist position, and without there being any formal cartel or price-fixing association, is in a position to influence price and other conditions of supply; in such cases the price set by the leader is invariably followed, even though there may be no formal arrangement to do so.

The Monopolies Commission displayed its awareness of this clause,

[1] 1953, H.C.P. 161, p. 91. 'We recommend that the Government should assume for the future a definite and continuing responsibility for the supervision of the costs and prices of manufacturers, importers and distributors of matches.'

[2] See House of Commons Debates, April 22, 1948, H. Wilson, as President of the Board of Trade.

[3] Report on the Supply of Cigarettes and Tobacco, etc. H.C.P. 218, p. 212. 'The retention by Imperial of its shareholding in Gallaher and Imperial's practice of allowing a bonus to distributors conditional upon. . . .'

[4] It is interesting that action taken by the Board of Trade regarding bonus payments was made operative throughout the industry. This was not recommended by the Commission. Infra.

[5] H. of C. Debates, April 22, 1948, col. 2033—H. Wilson.

and announced its willingness to make use of it where necessary. It was called upon to do so only once, when inquiring into the activities of the Tyre Manufacturers' Conference.[1]

One member of the Monopolies Commission emphasized the need to investigate the entire industry when dealing with oligopolistic conditions. He was adamant in his belief that such an inquiry was not outside the scope of the 1948 legislation. He admitted that in certain cases information relating to smaller competitors of dominant firms had not been included in the reports. This was not indicative of lack of investigation of such companies. The material had been omitted on the grounds that it was of no importance to the inquiry.

Both the Chairman and the Secretary of the Monopolies Commission stated that the Commission had full powers to investigate oligopolies. They admitted that the Commission, in its reports, might have given a contrary impression. The Monopolies Commission was always more concerned to publish information relating to a dominant firm than it was in the case of a small competitor.

Agreements Registrable under the 1956 *Act*

Since 1956 the Monopolies Commission has been prevented from commenting upon agreements registrable with the Registrar of Restrictive Trading Agreements; it may refer to such agreements for the purpose of the survey required by Section 7 (i) of the 1948 Act. The Commission is not precluded from assessing the effects on the public interest of the participation of a dominant firm in a registrable agreement.

The Monopolies Commission encountered such a registrable agreement in the course of its inquiry into chemical fertilizers. Imperial Chemical Industries was party to certain agreements operated by the British Sulphate of Ammonia Federation. The Monopolies Commission pointed out that 'we are precluded by Section 29 (i) of the Restrictive Trade Practices Act, 1956, from reporting whether any such agreements to which the monopoly suppliers are party "operate or may be expected to operate as such against the public interest"'.[2] There can be little doubt that the Commission has deliberately given preference to the Court in this field.

[1] The Report on the Supply and Export of Pneumatic Tyres, 1955, H.C.P. 133. See also The Report on the Supply of Certain Rubber Footwear, 1956, H.C.P. 328, p. 73. 'In our opinion, therefore, the RFMA's uniform prices for basic standard lines are the result of agreement among members. But even if this were not so, we are satisfied that their price consultations are restrictive of competition.'

[2] Report on the Supply of Chemical Fertilizers, p. 199. The remarks related to the Sellers' Agreements between BSAF and its members, the Agency Agreement between the BSAF and ICI, and to the purchase and sale agreements of BBS with its members.

Ability to Investigate Foreign-Owned Subsidiaries

A number of references have related to companies which were subsidiaries of overseas organizations. In such cases the Commission has been confronted with problems concerning its powers to examine documents and to extract financial information. This difficulty was most apparent in the chemical fertilizer case. Potash Limited was a subsidiary of suppliers from West Germany and France. It informed the Commission that it had no knowledge of its production costs. The Commission admitted that it had 'no means of determining whether the price at which it sells potash is reasonable in relation to the costs of all or any of the producers'.[1] Lack of information prevented the Monopolies Commission from deriving a satisfactory conclusion regarding the operations of this company. It was not possible for the Commission to demand information from the foreign parent companies involved.

The immunity of foreign companies from an inquiry of the Monopolies Commission has concerned a number of British companies. They have pointed out the ease with which documents may be withheld from a British subsidiary of a foreign owned company. British companies would then be bound to disclose information which their foreign competitors had decided to withhold from the Commission.

Short of an international agreement there is little that can be done at present to remedy this bias in the working of the 1948 legislation. It is important that the Monopolies Commission should take great care when sifting information under such conditions.

Export Investigations

Thc Monopolies Commission has taken little interest in the export activities of trade associations and companies in the absence of a specific export reference. The Commission decided that exports were outside the scope of a domestic inquiry. Even where export activities assumed an important position in the reference trade, no serious attempt was made to examine its influence upon domestic operations. Perhaps the outstanding example occurred in the inquiry into the process of calico printing, where omission of export activities encouraged the production of a largely irrelevant and somewhat doctrinaire report. A number of companies and trade associations expressed concern at this attitude. They considered that export performance was of substantial importance for understanding domestic operations.

The Secretary of the Commission, Mr Gilbert, CBE, emphasized the statutory limitations within which the Commission conducted its inquiries. The Commission might demand evidence on matters directly referred to it by the Board of Trade. This did not include export performance in the case of a domestic reference. In certain instances trade

[1] ibid., p. 223.

associations and companies had submitted evidence relating to export performance. Such evidence would always be examined, but could not be tested for its reliability. Foreign governments had complained bitterly about price rings in the electrical machinery industries. The same governments had refused to submit evidence to the Monopolies Commission.

The Chairman of the Commission, Mr Levy, QC, substantiated this point. In the absence of an export reference he considered that the Commission would be *ultra vires* if it attempted to demand information on export activities. The Chairman suggested that the Government was not always keen to institute an inquiry into export activities. Political complications were common in the export field.

The unwillingness of the Monopolies Commission to examine export activities may create considerable hardship for companies under examination. To take one example, Ilford consider Eire as home territory. They produce their financial data in this light. The Monopolies Commission will no doubt insist upon a division between the United Kingdom and the Eire markets, creating statistical problems for the company.

The narrow interpretation of the Commission's powers in the export field is incorrect. It results from a mis-reading of the Act, and undoubtedly results in ill-balanced reports. Remedial action in this instance lies within the power of the Monopolies Commission. New legislation is not required.

The Monopolies Commission and a Restricted Reference

The only restricted reference examined by the Monopolies Commission occurred in the Inquiry into the Supply of Wallpaper.[1] This limited the public interest analysis of the Monopolies Commission to selected issues. The reasons for making a restricted reference in this industry are not clear. The Board of Trade had been in close contact with the industry between 1945 and 1951, and certainly had knowledge of the pricing system of the dominant firm in the industry. It has been argued that a full reference would have wasted the time of the Monopolies Commission. It is apparent that the novelty of a restricted reference created certain difficulties for the Commission. The final report was insubstantial, providing more fuel for the politician than information for those interested in the economic performance of a dominant firm.

C. THE AUTHORITY OF THE MONOPOLIES COMMISSION

The Monopolies Commission is an advisory body. Its recommendations and conclusions have no judicial effect. This lack of power produced a

[1] Report on the Supply of Wallpaper, 1964. H.C.P. 59.

great deal of criticism from economists. The following passage contains the kernel of the criticism:

> If Parliament really takes advantage of this provision, and debates these reports, as seems to be intended, then the prestige of the tribunal will soon suffer irreparable damage. For the parties involved in these cases will seldom accept either the tribunal's findings on the facts, or its opinion of the public interest. In the USA the findings of original courts have almost always been challenged by appeal; why should we expect the findings of a tribunal, sitting probably in secret, to be more readily accepted? We have had a foretaste of what will happen in the reception accorded to the report of the Committee on the Distribution of Building Materials and Components. The findings of the Committee both as to the facts and as to the public interest were challenged by the interested parties as soon as the report was published, and no action has been taken on the report.[1]

Where the Monopolies Commission decides that the relevant conditions within a reference field operate or may be expected to operate against the public interest, it must then consider the remedial action required. At its discretion the Commission may recommend appropriate action in its report. Dissenting members are able to signify their dissent and the reasons for such dissent in minority addenda to the report.

The Monopolies Commission reports to the Board of Trade. Once signed, the report is despatched to Whitehall and the Commission's interest in the inquiry is terminated.

Upon receipt of a Monopolies Commission Report, the Board of Trade may, 'and unless the reference was so framed as to limit the investigation and report to the facts, shall',[2] lay the report before each House of Parliament. This measure is designed to attract publicity to the reports and to provide for discussion and dissemination of the conclusions and information provided.

In laying the report before Parliament, however, the Board of Trade must omit sections where publication would not be in the public interest. In addition, where published information would 'damage the legitimate business interest of any person',[3] and where the Board also feel that 'the portions of the report embodying that information could be omitted from the report without substantially affecting the sense, clarity or cogency of the report, or the value thereof as an aid to the proper under-

[1] W. A. Lewis, *The British Monopolies Act*, Manchester School, 1949, p. 210.

[2] Section 9 of the 1948 Act. The Board of Trade is not obliged to publish reports made by the Commission under Section 15 of the Act.

[3] Section 9 (b) of the 1948 Act.

standing of the subject matter of the reference',[1] the Board of Trade is obliged to omit such information.[2]

The Powers of the Competent Authority

The Act provides for action by statutory order at the discretion of the competent[3] authority in cases where the Commission finds that the appropriate conditions, or things done to preserve the conditions, operate or may be expected to operate against the public interest.[4]

Conditions necessary for a statutory order may be fulfilled even where the Commission makes no contrary conclusions. It is necessary in such a case to pass a resolution through the House of Commons declaring that 'those conditions, or any things which, according to the report, as laid before Parliament, are done by the parties concerned as a result of, or for the purpose of preserving, those conditions, operate or may be expected to operate as aforesaid'.[5]

Once either of these conditions has been fulfilled it is open to the competent authority to make a statutory order declaring unlawful specified arrangements to which exception has been taken. The order itself states the time allowed for termination of the activity and the extent to which termination should occur. The order may declare the activity unlawful for all persons or for such persons as may be specified.[6] Orders carry no authority over any person in relation to his conduct outside the United Kingdom unless such a person is a British subject, a body corporate incorporated under the law of the United Kingdom, or a person who carries on business in the United Kingdom, either alone or in partnership.[7]

The Act stipulates that no order made under the Act may conflict with powers to prevent an infringement of a United Kingdom patent, or to restrict the conditions attached to a licence to do anything, the doing of which, save for the licence, would amount to an infringement of a United Kingdom patent.[8]

[1] Section 9 (b) of the 1948 Act.

[2] Proviso (b) to Section 9 of the 1948 Act limits this to information as to a secret process of manufacture, or as to the presence, etc., of any mineral or other deposits or as to any other similar matter.

[3] The Act defines the 'competent authority' in Section 20 (1); it is the so-called 'production department' of the industry in question and will be one of the existing ministries.

[4] Section 10 (1) of the 1948 Act. It is notable that reports upon any references under Section 15 of the Act upon specified practices do not satisfy the conditions of the Act. General legislation is necessary for any action under this Section.

[5] Section 10 (1) (e) (ii) of the 1948 Act.

[6] Section 10 (2) of the Act. In fact only two Orders have been made under the 1948 Act. See infra.

[7] Section 10 (4) of the 1948 Act.

[8] Section 10 (5) of the 1948 Act.

The power to make an Order is exercisable by statutory instrument, and no order becomes effective until a draft has been laid before each House of Parliament, and has been approved by a resolution of each House. Any such order, once made, may be revoked or varied by a subsequent order by the competent authority.[1]

It was not the aim of the 1948 Act to establish a new criminal offence. The Act stipulated that no criminal proceedings may lie against any person on the grounds that he has 'committed, or aided, abetted, counselled, or procured the commission of, or conspired or attempted to commit, or incited others to commit, any contravention of the order'.[2]

On the other hand in the event of any contravention, or attempted contravention of an Order, compliance with such Order 'shall be enforceable by civil proceedings by the Crown for an injunction or for any other appropriate relief'.[3] This clause again met with criticism:

> Here most of the case will probably be argued again. First, was the order made within the terms of the Act? Secondly, does the order prohibit the acts the defendant is alleged to be committing or has he found a loophole in the order, e.g. started a new practice not precisely covered by the terms of the order, or varied the old practice slightly? And thirdly, is he in fact doing what he is alleged to be doing? If the framers of the Act chose this sort of machinery because they hoped to avoid litigation they are doomed to disappointment. There will be as much litigation to challenge orders made by a competent authority as there would have been over the clauses of an Act of Parliament.[4]

The Act provided that any person might bring civil proceedings in respect of such an infringement. In this respect Section 4 of the Trade Disputes Act, 1906, which prohibits actions in tort against trade unions does not apply.

The Government is not obliged, however, to take such measures as it may wish through the process of a statutory instrument. It may extract an undertaking from those concerned relating to the activities under review. This has been the favourite device of the Government of the day in acting upon reports of the Monopolies Commission. Voluntary undertakings do not involve any legal commitment. The Board of Trade may if it so wishes request a Section 12 'follow-up' reference from the Monopolies Commission if it has reason to believe that the undertakings are not being honoured. Little use has been made of this facility. The Government was criticized for not using Section 12 in 1953:

[1] Section 10 (6) and (7) of the 1948 Act.
[2] Section 11 (1) of the 1948 Act.
[3] Section 11 (2) of the 1948 Act.
[4] W. A. Lewis, op. cit., p. 211.

> [they] consider that the effectiveness of the Commission will be prejudiced if it becomes apparent that adherence to voluntary agreements is not subsequently examined. They realize that investigations of the kind provided for in the Act would add to the matters already long awaiting the Commission's attention. They recommend that the Board of Trade should establish an effective procedure to ensure that those industries which have become parties to voluntary agreements based on the Commission's recommendations are complying with the terms of those agreements.[1]

It is impossible to make a Section 12 reference once a Statutory Order has been made by the Government. Appropriate legal remedies are then available to deal with any breach of the conditions of an Order.

CONCLUSIONS

The 1948 legislation placed the responsibility for initiating inquiries solely with the Board of Trade. This decision might well be altered. The Board of Trade must of course preserve its right to make references. This is an important function of Government. The Monopolies Commission itself, however, is closely concerned with the affairs of industry and commerce. The Monopolies Commission might well be allowed to initiate inquiries. This would raise the status of the Monopolies Commission in the eyes of industry. It would furnish the Commission with flexible powers of selection not dissimilar to those of the American Federal Trade Commission.

The 1948 legislation may be criticized for its exclusion of the service sector from the scope of the Monopolies Commission. There is no reason for this exclusion. The service trades are as prone to market dominance as production and processing. Fortunately this criticism is short-lived. The Bill recently introduced into the House of Commons by the Labour Government is designed to remedy this fault.

A later chapter deals at some length with the authority of the Monopolies Commission. It would be inopportune at this stage to anticipate subsequent analysis. Important alterations are requircd in this critical area of the 1948 legislation.

It is far from easy to legislate well in relation to the scope of a body designed to investigate conditions of market dominance. The 1948 legislation bears its fair share of faults. However, it would be shabby to condemn a complex and lengthy piece of legislation on the ground of a few faults. Much of the Act is excellent, and it is clear and unambiguous in the main. The very few problems that have arisen in respect to the scope of the 1948 legislation is itself a tribute to those responsible for it.

[1] The Select Committee on Estimates, 1953, op. cit., p. (ix).

Chapter Five

THE INVESTIGATING PROCEDURE OF THE MONOPOLIES COMMISSION

A. THE LEGISLATIVE FRAMEWORK

The 1948 Act conferred upon the Commission considerable discretion in the determination of its procedure of inquiry and report.[1] The Commission could determine whether, and to what extent, interested persons should be present or heard at its meetings, whether such persons, if present, should cross-examine witnesses, and whether its sessions should be held in private or in public.

The Monopolies Commission must consider all evidence, written or oral, submitted to it by substantially interested parties or by their representatives. Such parties must be heard orally by the Commission or by members of the Commission 'unless in all the circumstances they consider that it is not reasonably necessary or is not reasonably practicable so to do'.[2] The Commission alone must decide the meaning of such phrases as 'substantially interested', 'reasonably necessary' and 'reasonably practicable'.[3] The Commission may obtain evidence on oath if it so wishes, may specify the time and place at which evidence shall be submitted, and may demand access to all necessary documents, estimates, returns and other information; it may specify the form in which such material shall be presented.

Sanctions may be imposed against those who fail to fulfil these obligations. Penalties are prescribed for those who contravene the Act.[4] The maximum penalty for any single offence under the Act is imprisonment for three months and a fine of one hundred pounds.[5] Any sub-

[1] Section 8 (i) of the Act. [2] ibid., p. 8.

[3] During the debate over the Bill in the House of Commons the Government was pressed to give all interested persons an express right to be present at hearings and to empower them to cross-examine witnesses. Such pressure was resisted on the ground that proceedings should be as informal as possible and that 'the Commission will be playing the part of a Royal Commission rather than that of a Chancery Judge', J. Belcher, H. of C. Debates, June 29, 1948, col. 2127.

[4] Section 8 (c), p. 8. [5] Section 18 (i).

sequent contravention would constitute a further offence and would be subject to the appropriate penalties.

The requests made by the Commission upon the time and resources of those subjected to investigation may well involve heavy expense. Where appropriate, therefore, the Commission may pay expenses. Expenses may not be paid to parties providing estimates, returns, or other information, unless the conditions to which the Act applies do not prevail in relation to the subject matter of the reference.

In many inquiries counsel for the investigated parties will gain access to highly-confidential material. Legal representatives may not be pressed by the Monopolies Commission into a disclosure of privileged information received by them in their official capacity.

The Act empowers the Board of Trade to issue general directions to the Commission regarding its procedure and the exercise of its powers.[1] The Board must lay before each House of Parliament a copy of any such direction.[2]

Procedure for an Industry Reference

The Board of Trade is not concerned with an inquiry once the reference has been received by the Monopolies Commission until the return of a signed copy of the Report to Whitehall. The Board may intervene to vary a reference[3] but otherwise leaves the Commission to pursue its inquiry free from interference and supervision.

Fourteen years of inquiry under the 1948 Act have resulted, inevitably perhaps, in an adjustment of the procedure of the Monopolies Commission. A number of companies and associations testify to the flexibility of the Commission in responding to constructive criticism. Nevertheless a standard form of procedure has developed over the years.

Upon receipt of a reference the Monopolies Commission immediately advertises its exact nature as widely as possible.[4] All interested parties are encouraged to communicate so that the final report may be based upon the fullest possible information. Preliminary rounds of informal discussions are held with representatives of bodies involved in the inquiry. The Commission begins to accumulate and to analyse relevant published information concerning the referred industry. Such preparatory investigations are effected by small panels of Commissioners who

[1] Section 8 (c) (6).

[2] In 1949 the Commission was invited by the Board of Trade to give some priority to investigations of referred industries in which the practice of resale price maintenance was apparent.

[3] The Board has intervened in this way on a few occasions under S. 6 (4).

[4] Sir Archibald Carter, 'Minutes of Evidence of Select Committee on Estimates, 1953', p. 3. (122)—'We advertise them and say we would be glad to hear from anyone who wants to address us.' The Commission would normally proceed with all references simultaneously during the early stages.

supervise staff teams allocated to the inquiry. The preparatory stage is important in directing the inquiry towards the critical issues, and in the formulation of subsequent questionnaires.

The foundations are thus laid; the task of accumulating factual information now commences in earnest. Questionnaires containing comprehensive sets of questions are issued, not only to suppliers and processors, but also to users and consumers of the referred goods. The Commission is anxious to obtain the maximum possible co-operation from bodies under investigation. At the same time the Commission briefs its staff to seek out relevant information. The staff tend to concentrate upon the Minutes of Board meetings, often seeking access to documents covering events in the distant past. Most companies criticize this aspect of the inquiry. They fear that Minutes may provide only a brief synopsis of the decisions made, and that sound reasons for the decisions may be omitted. In addition this part of the inquiry is costly and time-consuming.

Members of the Monopolies Commission and their staff may request a visit to the plant and machinery of the companies concerned in the inquiry. Such visits are intended to provide atmosphere, and to familiarize the Monopolies Commission with products and production techniques. They are designed to provide background information only: 'They are really only go, look and see, by way of background, to get some sort of idea of what the processes of manufacture are, to have some idea of what we are talking about and what we have got to consider.'[1]

It is quite clear that these visits are not designed to obtain economic and technical information relating to plant layout and operational efficiency. The Select Committee on Estimates, 1953,[2] argued that the existence or absence of restrictive trade practices could not be discovered merely by visiting factories. Members of the Monopolies Commission complain that the visits are boring and time-consuming. Visits are normally pressed into a single day, on some occasions indeed into a few hours.

The Commission's staff always produce a detailed historical account of the developments within the referred industry. The Act expressly encourages such effort.[3] The Commission appears to attach considerable importance to historical data using such information as a key to understanding current activities. The staff often spend twelve months in accumulating historical data relating to an inquiry.

Once the Monopolies Commission has launched the factual investigation it turns to its accounting staff for an investigation of financial data relating to the referred goods. The accountants are seconded from the Board of Trade. On rare occasions—calico printing is an example—

[1] Sir Archibald Carter, Select Committee on Estimates, op. cit., Section 131.
[2] ibid. [3] Section 7 (i).

outside firms of accountants have been used. In general this has been avoided. It is often difficult to find suitable firms of accountants that are not already employed by one or other of the bodies under examination.

Statistics are collected relating to the total supply of the referred goods in the referred market, and the proportion attributable to each company. Financial relations between the more important companies are subjected to close scrutiny. Data relating to prices, costs, profit, and capital employed in the relevant market are extracted and analysed.

Inevitably the financial investigation tends to be time-consuming. In part this is the fault of the companies concerned, who frequently dawdle in producing the required information. In part it is the fault of the Monopolies Commission's accounting team which is occasionally overworked. Primarily, however, the investigation is delayed by the difficulty in organizing and analysing information produced for purposes other than a Monopolies Commission inquiry.

The Monopolies Commission has rarely made use of its statutory powers to obtain information. Occasionally it has issued oaths, subpoenaed witnesses, and demanded documents. From time to time it has issued a deadline for presentation of evidence. Companies exposed to such deadlines accept that they have been generous. The Monopolies Commission has always preferred to execute its inquiry with the cooperation of those involved rather than by resorting to the compulsory powers conferred upon it.

The factual information obtained by the Commission's staff is assembled and analysed. Where necessary supplementary inquiries are effected to resolve ambiguities. The stage is then set for the Clarification Hearing.

The Clarification Hearing is the climax of the factual part of the Commission's inquiry. The bodies involved in the inquiry are invited individually to a formal meeting with members of the Commission. Most companies are not formally represented by counsel at this meeting; a few request their prospective counsel to attend the meeting to obtain atmosphere. The Clarification Hearing is limited to discussion of matters of fact. In practice discussion tends to concentrate upon, indeed to foreshadow, the critical issues relating to the public interest aspect of the inquiry. Nevertheless, the main function of the Hearing is to eliminate factual errors and to provide a sound basis for launching the public interest investigation.

The public interest inquiry commences with the despatch of a 'public interest' letter by the Commission to each company. This letter divides into two parts. Section One contains the Commission's summary of the facts, whilst Section Two carefully attempts to define the important public interest issues. No opinion is expressed upon these issues. The companies are requested to comment upon the issues listed, where possible providing substantiating evidence for their views. In certain instances supplementary questionnaires are sent out following the companies' replies. Once the Commission has digested the information, each company is invited to attend a Public Interest Hearing.

The Public Interest Hearing is formal; companies are usually, but not invariably, represented by counsel. Discussion centres, at this stage, upon the critical public interest issues. The companies often lead off, as they might in a judicial hearing, with a prepared 'statement of case' delivered by counsel. The 'defence', however, proceeds in a Kafkaesque atmosphere since the Commission issues no indictment and provides few indications of its attitude towards the selected issues. Many organizations have severely criticized this aspect of the inquiry.

Subsequent upon the Public Interest Hearing the Commission may contact the companies involved once again. Firms may put in information up to the moment that the Report is signed. In fact, however, the main emphasis of the inquiry is switched to the formulation of recommendations and conclusions. This stage of the inquiry imposes a heavy strain on the Commissioners. At this point the investigation nearest to completion takes preference; other inquiries are postponed or slowed down. The Commission may listen to requests that confidential information should be omitted from its Report. It will exclude all irrelevant material, and may advise the Board of Trade concerning the possibility of further excisions on public interest grounds. The Report is then signed and delivered to the President of the Board of Trade. Any further contact between the Board and the Commission occur solely at the former's request. The task of the Commission is otherwise completed.

The Impact of the 1953 *Act*

The 1953 Act altered the procedure of the Monopolies Commission. It increased the maximum number of Commissioners from ten to twenty-five, empowering the Commission, at the discretion of its Chairman, to operate in groups of not less than five Commissioners. The groups would be selected by the Chairman; he could select any Commissioner to act as chairman of a group. Any Commissioner, at the invitation of the Chairman, could attend meetings and take part in proceedings of other groups. He would not vote on any matter considered by that group.

The expansion in the size of the Commission did not result immediately in a *pro rata* expansion in the number of inquiries. The eleven newly appointed members outnumbered those with experience by more than two to one. A break in continuity was feared. The Commission was divided into two groups, one of eight, the other of nine Commissioners; each was presided over by the Chairman. Three experienced members were allocated to one team, two to the other. Consistency of procedure and approach between the groups was ensured by the common presence of the Chairman. Each group comprised the variety of individual experiences considered so necessary by the Government in drafting the 1948 Act. The composition of the groups was occasionally altered, where the Chairman considered such action desirable. Team changes were made for the pneumatic tyre reference,[1] and the Collective Discrimination report, which was dealt with by a mixed group of ten Commissioners.

The new legislation certainly accelerated the pace of investigation. Most notably the Monopolies Commission could complete a larger number of inquiries within a given time period.

The Impact of Legislation in 1956

The Restrictive Trade Practices Act, 1956, reduced the scope of the Monopolies Commission. It reconstituted the Commission on the 1948 pattern, providing for a maximum of ten Commissioners. This involved the Monopolies Commission in a return to the single group investigation. The pace of inquiry was inevitably lowered. This action was part of a general downgrading of the Monopolies Commission by the Conservative Government. The 1956 Act has been criticized severely in this respect, and current legislation provides for a return to the 1953 pattern of inquiry. The Conservative Party accepted the need for such legislation. Two Conservative committees of inquiry[2] recently reported to this effect.

Procedure for a Section 15 *Reference*

The Commission has only completed one Section 15 reference—the Collective Discrimination Report of June 1955.[3] The reference was received on December 17, 1952. As a result of the 1953 Act a Group was constituted for the inquiry on May 24, 1954. The report itself was signed by this group of ten Commissioners, drawn from both the groups formally constituted for industry inquiries.

The Monopolies Commission is not provided with the same statutory powers to obtain information for a Section 15 inquiry, as it has in the case of an industry inquiry. The Commission did not consider itself handicapped. Representatives of trade and industry were helpful and co-operative.

Upon receipt of the reference, the Commission issued a press notice

[1] Mr Davidson, as a director of the Bristol Aircraft Company, dropped out from this inquiry.

[2] The Bow Group, February 1963, op. cit., p. 73. C.P.C.—Monopoly and the Public Interest, March 1963, op. cit., p. 27.

[3] Cmnd. 9504.

inviting persons operating or affected by the specified practices to send factual information and a statement of their views. The announcements received considerable notice both in the national and the trade press.

In addition, the Commission undertook extensive inquiries among associations of traders and similar bodies. Detailed questionnaires were despatched to about 200 trade associations in the spring and early summer of 1953. Supplementary questionnaires were issued as the inquiry developed, sometimes at the request of trade associations. In total, the Commission contacted almost 300 trade associations or groups of traders in a wide range of industries and trades. Of these, about 160 submitted statements concerning specified practices to which they themselves were parties. The very large majority of these related to the supply of goods, few to processing, although the Commission found no need to distinguish between the two categories.

During the later stages of the investigation the Commission sought out firms which had not provided evidence, and which were not parties to Collective Discrimination agreements. In addition representative national bodies in trade and industry were invited to submit general evidence. The Federation of British Industries, the Parliamentary Committee of the Co-operative Union, and the Trades Union Congress submitted such evidence.

Much of the evidence received by the Commission was in writing. Hearings were arranged, both at the insistence of certain associations and when evidence received by the Commission appeared of special importance.

In addition, as envisaged by the 1948 Act, the Monopolies Commission was able to utilize information and experience gained in its previous industry studies. Evidence from these inquiries, of course, had been obtained with the full sanctions of the 1948 Act.

The Monopolies Commission was fully satisfied with the powers at its disposal and the procedure adopted in this inquiry. Nevertheless, it would appear desirable to provide the Monopolies Commission with statutory powers similar to those available for industry references. There is no point in limiting the probing ability of the Commission by providing insufficient authority.

Procedure for a Section 12 Reference

A Section 12(i) reference was made in February 1957 covering the imported timber industry.[1]

The Commission requested, and received, copies of correspondence between the Board of Trade and the Timber Trade Federation

[1] Imported Timber: Report on whether and to what extent the Recommendation of the Commission has been complied with. 1958, H.C.P. 274.

consequent upon the Report. In the light of this information questions were addressed to the TTF and replies received.

The Commission further advertised its readiness to receive evidence from dealers and users of imported timber; a number of traders and associations were approached directly. Written evidence was received from users, merchants, and a few importers or agents. Certain witnesses were heard orally. Commission staff examined the minutes and other records of the TTF, its members and its associates.

In February 1958 a statement of the factual evidence received was sent to the TTF. Members, supported by Counsel, attended a Hearing. The Hearing was designed to establish the accuracy of the factual evidence; those concerned could submit interpretations of the facts. Following this Hearing the Commission formulated its conclusions and drafted the Report. The inquiry itself was far less exacting and time-consuming than industry inquiries; the task of the Commission was greatly reduced.

B. THE PROCEDURE OF INVESTIGATION—A CRITICAL ASSESSMENT

Time Period of the Inquiry

The Monopolies Commission has been severely ciriticized both for the time taken on individual inquiries, and for the small number of references completed within a given time-period. Statistics do indeed indicate a slow programme of inquiry:

TABLE 2

*The Time Period of Investigation**

A	*All inquiries.* Average time period	2 yrs. 4 mths.
	Maximum time-period	4 yrs. 1 mth.
	Minimum time-period	1 yr. 0 mths.
B	Dominant Firm Inquiries. Average	3 yrs. 5 mths.
C	Trade Association Inquiries. Average	2 yrs. 1 mth.

* This table excludes the reports published after August 1964.

Recent inquiries have been rather more lengthy than the averages would suggest. Dominant firm inquiries produce complexities that were rarely encountered when the Monopolies Commission examined restrictive trading agreements. The inquiry into petrol distribution was a particularly vast exercise for a small body with limited personnel and other important commitments.

A number of those closely connected with the intimate work of the Monopolies Commission[1] emphasize the delays created by companies

[1] The Chairman, One Commissioner, and the Secretary of the Monopolies Commission.

which do not respond speedily to questionnaires; they complain of the submission of bulky, poorly organized information which must be overhauled subsequently by the Commission. They point out that companies demand lengthy preparation periods for both the Clarification Hearing and the Public Interest Hearing. These are delays for which the Monopolies Commission cannot be held responsible.

At the same time the Commission must undertake a thorough, comprehensive inquiry and must effect a historical survey to satisfy the requirements of the 1948 Act. All information received must be examined, however late it arrives. The length of the inquiry is the necessary price for care.

Numerous criticisms have been levelled at the Monopolies Commission and its staff in relation to the procedure of inquiry. The Select Committee on Estimates in 1953 hinted that the historical survey might well be abbreviated:[1] 'Your committee . . . consider that it should be possible, as experience is gained, to eliminate certain lines of inquiry or at least to decide at an early stage in an investigation to bring any unprofitable lines of inquiry to an end.'

Despite this warning recent reports have been padded with extensive historical surveys, sometimes dealing at great length with events that occurred fifty or more years prior to the inquiry. A historical account may be extremely useful. One suspects upon occasion however that the Monopolies Commission allows itself to be mesmerized by a wad of interesting but nevertheless completely irrelevant information. This tendency has met with recent criticism:

> One of the most important reasons for the inordinant time spent on Monopoly [*sic*] Commission inquiries has been its tendency to investigate matters of doubtful importance. Its reports contain large sections on general industrial background and on company histories . . . it is of little immediate value and we consider that stricter tests of relevance should be applied.[2]

Many firms and trade associations have confirmed this criticism. They complain bitterly of the delay and the problems created by such exercises, and place the prime responsibility upon the Commission's staff.

There was a general feeling that the staff of the Monopolies Commission had little discipline in the technique of inquiry. They refused to make use of modern equipment to accelerate the inquiry, and they tended to pursue irrelevant issues quite excessively. It was noted earlier that the blame for this must rest partly with the Commissioners for failure to provide adequate direction to their staff.

[1] op. cit., p. IX.

[2] Bow Group, February 1963, op. cit., p. 74.

The majority of organizations considered that the questions asked both by the Monopolies Commission and by its staff were unduly imprecise. In certain cases imprecision was clearly the result of poor preparatory work. Whether such imprecision resulted from laziness or lack of competence is not clear.

It is easy to criticize the Monopolies Commission from an *ex post* vantage point. During an inquiry the Commission and its staff are inevitably working to a certain extent in the dark. Tactical errors are bound to occur under such conditions. An intelligent staff well-trained in industrial detective techniques might succeed nevertheless in abbreviating irrelevant lines of inquiry. Much time and wasteful effort might then be saved.

The conflict between time and thoroughness occurs in all types of investigation. Firms themselves appreciate this point. The majority would always select a lengthy but authoritative Report. They criticize, however, unnecessary and wasteful delay. The time period of inquiry may be of crucial importance when important investment decisions are due to be taken. This point was made by the Bow Group: 'Delay does not only involve the direct cost of the prolonged existence of an old and probably unsatisfactory order of things, but there are also the undesirable consequences of mistiming and lost opportunities.'[1]

A company might fear, for instance, a recommendation that a delivered pricing system should be replaced by an ex works pricing system. A Government acceptance of this might well involve issues affecting plant size and plant location. Two companies complained that investment plans had been delayed awaiting a Monopolies Commission Report. The task of the Monopolies Commission is to encourage and not to retard economic development.

The Cost of Monopolies Commission Inquiries

The annual cost to the Treasury of Monopolies Commission inquiries is indicated in the Annual Reports of the Board of Trade. By international standards the cost of British operations has been, and still is, extremely low. The cost stated in Table 3 exclude the cost of accommodation, heat, light, telephones, stationery, etc. which are included in general Board of Trade expenditure.

These costs, however, in no way indicate the cost to those under examination. The monetary costs assessed by such organizations themselves give precious little indication of the opportunity cost. Many companies are not familiar with the concept of opportunity cost; but all of them emphasize the important time of top-level executives taken up by Commission inquiries. Monopolies Commission work cannot in many cases

[1] op. cit., p. 71.

be delegated by senior executives. They alone, too often, are familiar with the information required by the Commission.[1]

TABLE 3

Financial Year Expenditure

	£
1949–50	32,741
1951–2	51,034
1953–4	76,354
(1953 Act increased number of Commission and staff)	
1955–6	106,363
(1956 Act reduced number of Commission and staff)	
1957–8	59,624
1959–60	56,474
1961–2	64,615

The Imperial Tobacco Company estimated that 35,000 man-hours were spent by the Company on Commission work, the majority by top executives. The opportunity cost of this time was very great indeed. Another large organization estimated that 'something in the region of 10,000 man-hours were spent by senior executives on work in connection with this inquiry'.

This point was substantiated by the Bow Group: 'The strain they impose on the companies being investigated and the amount of time of senior executives they consume most seriously diminish the efficiency of the industries which it is the Commission's main purpose to encourage.'[2]

A number of organizations provided details of monetary expenditure upon Monopolies Commission inquiries:

TABLE 4

Organization	*Nature of Expenditure*	*Amount of Expenditure* £
1	Solicitors' and Counsel fees	1,000+
2	Accountants' fees	2,100
3	Direct Financial Outlay	25,000
	Direct Cost	70,000
4	Total Financial Outlay	320,000
5	Legal and Financial fees	12,000
6	Total Cost	100,000

The Select Committee estimated in 1953 that the cost of an inquiry to the companies and trade associations concerned had ranged between

[1] e.g. The Metal Windows Association. 'The greatest cost, however, which exceeds the out of pocket expenses, is in the time spent and the work that has to be done by senior people in member firms and in the Association, as it distracts their attention from the constructive side of their business.'

[2] op. cit., p. 48.

£15,000 and £20,000. Since that date it would appear that the costs have risen considerably. The monetary estimates are almost certainly a poor reflection of the opportunity cost involved in such an inquiry. One representative commented that nothing would please his company more than to hear that the dominant supplier in an industry in which they were a minor competitor had been referred to the Monopolies Commission. The subsequent inquiry would distract the attention of the dominant supplier, and enable them to consolidate their position within the reference industry.

The Opportunity to Rebut Complaints

Many companies and trade associations strongly criticized the Monopolies Commission for refusing them an opportunity to rebut trade complaints. The Select Committee was a little dissatisfied with the Commission in this respect, suggesting that the Monopolies Commission should allow those under investigation the right to counter specific charges from known bodies.

Selected complaints are shown to companies in the public interest letter. They appear to be formulated in a vague and impersonal manner; only rarely are the names of complainants appended. In the early years especially trade associations were critical of the system:

> It was our view that the system of the Monopolies Commission could not result in a completely fair report for the reason that the names of the complainants and the exact nature of their complaints are not disclosed to the trade under investigation. Obviously, in many cases a complete answer to the criticism can be given when the source of the complaint is known and the precise matter concerned. We found that the Report, when published, referred to a number of complaints which were never mentioned to us and some of which were manifestly absurd.

The Federation of Calico Printers suspected that complaints referred to by the Commission had stemmed from a small minority of discontented customers. In the absence of detailed information concerning the complainants the Federation had been unable to substantiate this belief.

On many occasions organizations have requested the right to cross-examine complainants, as they would under a judicial system. On no known occasion has this request been granted. It is not surprising, therefore, that companies doubt the impartiality of the Commission's procedure.

In recent inquiries, however, the Commission shows signs of having remedied many weaknesses of this type. Companies subjected to more recent inquiries have emphasized their satisfaction with the Commission's handling of complaints. The Commission has provided the names of many complainants and encouraged the companies to comment in detail. The companies believed that the Commission had not been influenced adversely by criticisms received.

The Commission's Secretary commented that it was existing policy to disclose identity where complainants were co-operative, or where the Commission considered disclosure justified in order to maintain impartiality.[1] He admitted that many witnesses feared reprisals.[2] He stressed that valuable information would certainly be withheld in some cases if cross-examinations were allowed. It is difficult to disagree with this contention. The recent instance of trade retaliation against a critical witness in the Restrictive Practices Court underlines the dangers involved.[3]

No libel suit could possibly result from complaints printed in the Monopolies Commission's reports. All such reports are protected by Parliamentary privilege. If cross-examination was allowed, however, it is far from certain that unqualified privilege would be available for complainants. Qualified privilege would certainly be available, but would not protect complainants if their criticism was malicious and unfounded. Delicately-balanced libel suits might therefore emerge from proceedings under the Act.

It would seem desirable that full details of the nature and sources of criticism should be made available to investigated organizations.[4] It would be less sensible to allow automatically for cross-examination of complainants unless such complainants are fully co-operative or unless the complaints prove to be of substantial importance.

Indication of the 'Critical Issues'

The Monopolies Commission has been criticized for failing to make known the critical issues of an inquiry or even the charges levelled against an investigated organization. Companies and associations complain that they are not provided with any guidance from the Commission; they are therefore pressed into producing vast quantities of useless

[1] This should be contrasted with the comment of Sir A. Carter before the Select Committee, op. cit., p. 10. 'I think it would be very dangerous indeed to promise to show the industry every criticism that was sent to us. I think the only result would be we would cease to get any criticism at all.'

[2] Bow Group, February 1963, op. cit., p. 46. 'It may be necessary to protect witnesses with anonymity in order to get them to come forward, but we doubt it.'

[3] In re Newspaper Proprietors' Agreement. The case ended successfully for the trade witness. The respondents' action against him was held by the Court of Appeal to constitute action in contempt of court.

[4] Bow Group, February 1963, op. cit., p. 74. 'Consideration should also be given to identifying all those who make specific complaints against a company where these are likely to influence the Commission's view seriously.'

evidence relating to activities outside the Monopolies Commission's interest. Companies contrast this uncertainty with the much greater specificity regarding allegations that results from an adversary procedure. They point out that the questionnaires at all stages of the inquiry are phrased ambiguously and provide little indication of Commission attitude.[1] Throughout the inquiry those under examination are unable to judge which arguments to press most strongly. Those with experience of judicial proceedings are deeply perturbed at the comparative uncertainty of an investigation by tribunal. A number of Commissioners have emphasized that it is not the function of the Commission to make charges. The purpose of the inquiry is to analyse the effects of relevant industrial activities in the light of the public interest. In the course of a lengthy and comprehensive inquiry it is impossible to be completely unaware of the critical issues. Arguments to the contrary are a little ingenuous. In particular, the Public Interest letter provides a useful indication of the issues involved. The Commission may not divulge its findings to organizations prior to publication of the Report. Any such divulgence might be construed as a breach of Parliamentary privilege.

It was to be expected that the Commission would not provide a narrow direction to its early inquiries since a fundamental reason for the 1948 Act had been a lack of philosophy towards monopoly and restrictive practices. In more recent inquiries however the Commission's approach has lacked clarity partly because of the nature of dominant firm references. The existence of specified restrictive agreements had at least provided an obvious starting point for an investigation. No such focal points exist in dominant firm inquiries.

Despite its arguments to the contrary it is quite clear that the Monopolies Commission does make charges against referred companies. By the nature of its function it is bound to do so. On the other hand, its present procedure does not enable the Commission to specify the more important aspects of its inquiry before the Public Interest letter is despatched.[2] One reason for such a delay in indicating the critical issues has been the lack of close contact between the Monopolies Commission and the referred company before the Public Interest Hearing.

It would be wise to abandon the formal Clarification Hearing which

[1] One organization commented: 'The Commission will not suggest to an industry that its profits are too high; it will merely put forward for consideration the question "whether the profits are unreasonably high", but no indication is given as to what reasonable profits are.'

[2] See, however, Report on the Supply of Electrical Equipment for Mechanically Propelled Land Vehicles, 1963, H.C.P. 21, p. VIII. 'And we notified them of the respects in which it might be contended, so far as each of them was concerned, the conditions, or the things done as a result of or for the purpose of preserving the conditions, operated or might be expected to operate against the public interest.'

has been severely criticized by companies investigated, especially in recent years. It should be replaced by a series of informal meetings between the Monopolies Commission and the relevant company designed to stimulate discussion on the details of accumulated factual information.[1] These discussions would be of great help to the Commission in drafting a pertinent, relatively unambiguous Public Interest letter.[2] The decreased formality of procedure resulting from this recommendation would capitalize upon one major advantage of the tribunal system of inquiry. The close relationship that would develop between the Commission and the company would be extremely valuable at the Public Interest Hearing. One suspects that in the past lack of this kind of contact has contributed towards the doctrinaire elements in Reports of the Monopolies Commission. The Commission must retain the mantle of pragmatism if it is to secure any co-operation from those subjected to an investigation.

Judge, Jury and Prosecutor

The Commission has been criticized from its beginning by those who believe that the functions of judge, jury and prosecutor are uneasy bedfellows.[3] The belief that an effective prosecutor becomes personally involved in his case clearly conflicts with a desire to maintain complete impartiality in adjudication. Criticism of the Monopolies Commission in this respect is only one facet of the general mistrust of administrative tribunals, particularly by those experienced in the judicial system of review and judgment. The argument against tribunals was thoroughly expounded by Lord Symonds in the House of Lords when opposing the resolution to appoint the Lynskey Tribunal:

> Your Lordships will at once see two glaring defects in such a system, the first not so important but not negligible; that the Tribunal could cross-examine only with the material which had been already put before them in due sequence. That is very different from the procedure with counsel, who can rely, if they are well instructed, upon the surprise effect of information not yet revealed to the witness. But far more important was the difficulty, as anybody who has had experience will recognize, of cross-examining and appearing to be

[1] Although this alteration was not recommended by the Bow Group, February 1963, op. cit., it would go far towards satisfying their suggestion: p. 74. 'We suggest that the companies being investigated should be given more opportunity of making their positions clear. In particular they should be allowed to comment on the whole of the factual part of the report; and the Commission's preliminary findings (following the public interest hearing) should be discussed with them fully.'

[2] The Franks Committee. Cmnd. 218 (1957), p. 17. 'Citizens should know in good time the case which they will have to meet.'

[3] W. A. Lewis, Manchester School, 1949.

> impartial. Truth lies often at the bottom of a well, and in the case of a reluctant witness the questioner must be severe to the point of harshness. In the case of an evasive witness, from time to time . . . guile must be met with guile and, the evasive witness led to the admission of a truth which he would fain conceal. Can he be harshly severe or compact of guile and, at the same time, appear an even-handed figure of justice?

Several organizations expressed dissatisfaction at the combination of functions united in the Monopolies Commission. They felt that the whole system encouraged partiality by the Commission against those under investigation. One trade association was especially critical of the Monopolies Commission:

> By its constitution the Commission acts virtually as prosecutor, jury, and judge. Its staff tend to become witch-hunters. The impression gained . . . during the inquiry was that there was a tendency by the staff to endeavour to collate all the facts which were adverse to the industry in order to support an adverse verdict. . . . The impression obtained at the hearing before the Commission is not of an impartial tribunal attempting to obtain the true facts; the impression is of an inquisitor attempting, if possible, to convict the accused out of their own mouths. In such circumstances it is difficult to feel that there has been a fair trial.

It has been suggested[1] that a new procedure, involving a separation of functions, should supersede the existing system of investigation. The Monopolies Commission itself would retain its present function of adjudication. A newly-appointed Registrar would be responsible for presentation of evidence. Such a separation, it is urged, would enable issues to be clarified at an earlier stage, and would thereby eliminate tiresome and expensive delay and uncertainty. The Registrar would be responsible for the 'clarification' stages of the inquiry, allowing the Commission to concentrate upon the 'public interest' issues in a manner analogous to the Restrictive Practices Court.

These recommendations are based upon a misconception of the Monopolies Commission's task. The Commission is usually required to assess the effect of conditions upon the public interest; it may also put forward recommendations for Government action. This process clearly involves the exercise of a 'judicial' function. In addition, however, it must collate factual information relating to the conditions of the 1948 Act. In so doing it may make use of certain statutory powers. This task does not place the Commission in the position of prosecuting counsel. The latter is completely bound up with prosecution. He is personally

[1] C.P.C., March 1963, op. cit., p. 20.

committed to so manipulate the evidence as to secure a 'conviction'. The Commission, on the other hand, correctly points out that its task may be effected with complete satisfaction by completely vindicating a company. There is no presumption written into the Act. This distinction is of immense importance. The Registrar of the Restrictive Practices Court is known to dislike 'losing' a case. The Commission, in one instance at least,[1] has shown sincere satisfaction when vindicating an industry. Companies which see the Commission as an unrelenting prosecution counsel are completely misinterpreting its task.

It would be extremely foolish to separate the Monopolies Commission's functions. Such action would eliminate the advantages of tribunal inquiry. An administrative approach provides opportunities for informality, flexibility, and close contact between the tribunal and the company that would not be possible should the functions be separated.[2] The inquiry is economic rather than judicial and the philosophy of the legislation is one of pragmatism and flexibility. Under no circumstances should these aims be placed in jeopardy. The recommendations of the Poole Committee run contrary to the intention of the 1948 legislation.

Judicial v. Administrative Procedure

The present British approach[3] towards monopoly control involves two divergent systems. Dominant firms, export agreements and concerted practices are subjected to an administrative procedure; domestic restrictive trading agreements relating to goods are covered by judicial review. Many critics of the Monopolies Commission contend that a system of judicial examination should supersede administrative investigation in sectors at present delegated to the Commission. It is essential to review briefly the procedure of the Restrictive Practices Court before assessing the relative merits of the two approaches.

The Registrar of Restrictive Trading Agreements selects the order of references for the Court. The Board of Trade may make directions regarding the order of priority with which registered agreements should be dealt. During 1957 and 1958 directions of this kind covered sixty-three commodities. In October 1958 previous directions were rescinded, leaving the Registrar with unfettered freedom of selection.

A notice of Reference is filed on interested organizations by the Court at the application of the Registrar. This is usually followed by arrange-

[1] Report on the Supply of Insulin, 1952, H.C.P. 296, op. cit.

[2] Mr J. Belcher emphasized this in H. of C. Debates, 29.648, col. 2127. He argued that a more formal procedure 'would rule out these informal discussions through which alone we feel it is possible to find out the real motives and attitudes in business arrangements, and it would turn the whole atmosphere into one of litigation instead of co-operation in finding out the trouble'.

[3] Since 1956.

ments for an Order allowing the respondent companies to be represented in Court by a representative respondent, normally the trade association or Federation representing the industry.

The first pleading in the review—the Statement of Case—is then filed by the representative respondent, specifying restrictive practices admitted by the companies. The respondents plead first because the onus of proof is weighted against them by the 1956 Act. The Statement of Case must be accompanied by a full list of documents relevant to the proceedings which are or have been in the possession or power of the respondent. The respondent must indicate for which documents he claims privilege and the grounds for such claim. The Registrar may require production of unprivileged documents. He may also provide for accountancy investigations and for interrogations.[1]

At this stage preliminary meetings are usually arranged between the Registrar and the respondents.[2] These are designed to discuss the pattern of the accountancy investigation and to arrange for an examination of voluminous documents; they assist the Registrar in placing relevant material before the Court in an appropriate form. Parties to restrictive agreements are usually fully co-operative in allowing the Registrar's staff, together with co-opted experts, to inspect factories and works premises.

The Registrar issues an open invitation for persons with relevant information to place it before his staff. Evidence is also supplied by economists, accountants and on occasion by scientists and engineers relating to the effect of specified practices. The Registrar has been fortunate in obtaining the services of distinguished members of their respective professions for this purpose.

Subsequent upon a detailed investigation, the Registrar files an Answer to the respondent's Statement, admitting or denying facts and contentions; the statement specifies all restrictive practices not admitted by the respondent together with the detriments alleged to result. This may be the first indication provided to the respondent of the Registrar's case. The respondent may, if he so wishes, file a Reply relating to any other matters not referred to by the Registrar.

Once the Court hearing commences procedure is very similar to that of any civil court. The Restrictive Practices Court has ruled that no advantage will be allowed from surprise. A premium is thereby placed upon exchanging as much evidence as possible between the parties before the hearing commences. The Court has also ruled that the

[1] Requests for information to be answered on oath.

[2] Registrar of Restrictive Trading Agreements Report for the period August 7 to December 31, 1959. Cmnd. 1273, p. 13. 'I believe co-operation leads to an earlier ascertainment of the issues with a consequent saving in time and money to both sides. . . .'

evidence of trade witnesses need not be duplicated. This is designed to save time and to prevent an endless procession of semi-literate witnesses from parading through the Court. The Court is a civil court and facts need be established only on balance of probabilities, not beyond all reasonable doubt. This contrasts sharply with the judicial system of the United States of America.

The Court is presided over by a Judge,[1] who is assisted by a body of lay members drawn from a varied background of specialisms. No economist is represented on the body of lay members—a situation in sharp contrast to the Monopolies Commission. The judge may be overruled on points of fact but is dominant on all matters of law. The Restrictive Practices Court has the status of High Court. Appeal on matters of law may be made to the Court of Appeal and, with appropriate consent, to the House of Lords.

The majority of dominant companies preferred an administrative inquiry into their practices and activities. Trade associations on the other hand were more evenly balanced, marginally preferring a judicial procedure.[2] To a large extent this divergence of view is indicative of the different problems involved.

Many organizations welcomed the greater flexibility and informality of an administrative procedure. They felt that in court techniques of presentation and cross-examination might prove of greater importance than a straightforward analysis of the facts.

One company pointed out that the Restrictive Practices Court did not operate in all respects as originally intended. In particular, it was often difficult for the Respondents to obtain from the Registrar at a sufficiently early stage in the proceedings full details of his Case; indeed the Registrar's Case was sometimes not fully disclosed until the Hearing before the Court was well under way.

Another criticism directed at the judicial system is the need to 'defend' and to 'attack' specified practices. It is not unknown for respondents to alter their pleading during the Court proceedings,[3] rendering complex briefs provided by expert witnesses completely valueless. An administrative inquiry may cope more flexibly with this

[1] The Act provided for five judges and not more than ten other members. The Court for any case must comprise at least a presiding judge and two other members; it may thus sit in two or more divisions concurrently.

[2] e.g. 'The Commission is given the widest roaming authority to visit, inspect and demand information anywhere. Under the Restrictive Practices Court procedure, on the other hand, issues are determined by pleading, and inspection is confined to the parties of the agreement under investigation and not to the whole trade of the country in the goods in question. . . .'

[3] This certainly occurred in the Glass Bottle Case and the Black Nut and Bolt Case, angering the expert economists representing the Registrar, Professor J. H. B. Tew and Mr Worswick respectively.

form of activity than a Court bound by legal conventions and procedural precedents.

Under the existing Court procedure trade associations may encourage the Registrar to prepare detailed briefs, subsequently announcing the termination of the agreements under review.[1] This practice carries no legal penalty and has occurred on several occasions. The provision for reviewing abandoned agreements may weaken this tendency to waste time but it cannot be highly effective when so many existing practices remain for examination.

The Restrictive Practices Court procedure places considerable responsibility upon the presiding Judge[2] who tends to dominate his lay panel. This contrasts with the more even balance between members of the Commission. The lack of economic intelligence in the Court has resulted in occasional errors of analysis in Court decisions. The decision in the Cement Case in particular reads strangely to an economist.[3]

The Court system of investigation for dominant firms and trade associations has long existed in the United States of America. One of its most serious weaknesses is the costly and time-consuming system of appeals, and the legal dodges derived to evade the impact of legislation. The Federal Trade Commission's 'consent decrees' are probably far more extensively successful than Court judgments, especially at times when a weak or a conservative Attorney-General is in office.

It is true that a powerful case may be made for the judicial review of restrictive agreements. Agreements provide immediate focal points for the review; enough is known about restrictive practices to establish a burden of proof together with reasonably precise criteria upon which the Judgment may rest. The comparative speed of the judicial review under such conditions may be preferred to the increase in comprehension which may result from an administrative review.

In the case of the dominant firm these arguments do not obtain. It would be most difficult at present to fashion any general presumption. The practices and activities of dominant firms are not clear-cut, as they are where agreements are concerned. A decision to place dominant firms under judicial review would be misguided at this stage. To allow the intimate details of company finances and activities to be the subject-matter of public debate might have disastrous commercial repercussions for the company concerned and indeed for the British export

[1] This occurred in the radio valve investigation, resulting in a blank period for the Court during which the Registrar prepared another brief.

[2] Justice Devlin (now President of the Press Council) in particular was dominant in his Judgments.

[3] This decision provided some dubious economic analysis in relation to uncertainty and the supply price of capital under conditions of competition and monopoly.

market. An examination of the dominant firm may be carried out with any degree of success only by a team of experts covering such areas as economics, accountancy, law, statistics, and industrial sociology. It is not surprising, therefore, that representatives of almost all the large companies, with which the issue was discussed, indicated a preference for an administrative inquiry.

The Public Interest and Economic Efficiency

The concept of economic efficiency is most complex and controversial. Criteria such as rate of return on capital, output per manhour, average cost of production and the like compete with each other for economists' favours. Each criterion, in its own way, is riddled with ambiguity. Clearly, however, any study concerned with the public interest must take notice of the problems involved in assessing economic efficiency.

The Monopolies Commission has taken efficiency into account when examining the effect of practices and activities upon the public interest. It has compared the unit production costs of members of trade associations, railing against any lack of uniformity in costing techniques. It has examined the relative plant costs of multi-plant companies, usually criticizing a wide spread of costs. It always compiles detailed statistics relating to rate of return on capital and/or on sales, and attempts a rudimentary analysis of such information. It examines forces likely to encourage or to impede invention and innovation. All these efforts are aimed at assessing the 'economic efficiency' of the organization under review.

Many representatives of investigated companies are not satisfied, however, that the Commission is really interested in efficiency:

> It was always realized that it would be exceedingly difficult to place before the Monopolies Commission a case prepared in such a way that the Commission would understand all the technical implications and problems. Although great pains were taken with this it was the opinion of the industry . . . that much of the technical aspects of the case had not registered with the Commission. . . .

One company complained that the Commission's Report had fallen palpably short of understanding the technical and economic problems facing the industry. It felt that the Commission's concept of efficiency did not extend far beyond rudimentary cost accounting techniques and the like. The organization was not alone in commenting adversely on the offhand manner in which Commissioners visited factories and works premises, and their lack of interest in plant layout, labour facilities, management communications, etc. The Select Committee examined this aspect of the Commission's work in 1953. It raised the possibility of making use of professional advisers on industrial matters:

> They were told that it had not been considered, as the need for such advice had not so far been felt. The Commission see no reason why they should not take professional advice of this kind, but they pointed out that the Act gives no power for the Commission or their servants to enter and inspect premises. Your Committee appreciate that the Commission are not expected to be technical specialists in all the matters referred to them. Moreover, they do not think that the existence or absence of restrictive trade practices can be discovered merely by visiting factories. They recommend that the Commission should consider whether there might not be advantages in the employment, in some instances for certain types of inquiry, of professional industrial advisers, subject to the safeguarding of confidential information.[1]

Sir Archibald Carter had firmly rejected the notion that the Commission was in any sense 'a technical' committee of inquiry. He commented that even those Commissioners most conversant with industrial techniques 'are rather cautious about what they think of the efficiency of the factory, except, possibly, in very extreme cases. . . .'[2]

More recently one Commissioner stressed that the employment of management consultants would alter the nature of the Commission's work. At present the Commission was more concerned with market dominance and the existence of certain practices and activities than with efficiency itself. He argued that companies desiring a consultancy investigation were quite free to organize one. The Commission would always examine carefully reports submitted to it in this field. He stressed the limitations imposed by the Act regarding the Commission's powers to enter and examine premises.

The problems of obtaining companies' co-operation in the Commission's consultancy exercise, or of legislating afresh, are not the only difficulties attaching to such a development. A major difficulty would be the appointment of suitable staff for the consultancy team. It would scarcely be possible to obtain a high-powered team of experts technically qualified in the industry under examination without sacrificing impartiality. The alternative would be a team drawn from widely varied professions and experienced in various kinds of industrial activities. The occasional employment of outside consultants might suffice; such an operation would impair the confidence between Monopolies Commission and staff resulting from a long period of close co-operation.

The remaining solution would be the replacement of the majority of

[1] op. cit., p. VIII.
[2] ibid., p. 4.

present staff by full-time staff drawn from consultancy teams and suitable professions.[1] Such an operation would involve placing greater authority[2] in the hands of staff, paying much higher salaries, and providing long-term contracts. Promotion from staff to the Commission itself might then be considered in suitable instances. Such an improvement in the calibre of Monopolies Commission staff is highly desirable whether 'efficiency audits' become a regular feature of Commission inquiries or not.

Management consultancy investigations are conducted, usually, by invitation of the Board of Directors. Companies invite such investigations to help in lowering production costs, improving management communications and labour relations, and in the last analysis as a means of raising profits or increasing the security of existing profit levels. The consultants are responsible to senior management and derive delegated authority from senior management whilst conducting their inquiries.

The Monopolies Commission's staff would be forced to conduct their inquiries with a different purpose and in a vastly less co-operative atmosphere. Access to information might be less readily granted, and the tenor of the entire exercise might easily be lowered. This would undoubtedly weaken public acceptance of the investigation even if it did not mar its practical effectiveness.[3]

Companies hold widely differing views on the desirability of the Monopolies Commission undertaking efficiency audits of this kind. One large company felt that if the Commission wished to make a valid judgment on the level of efficiency in manufacture and marketing of the reference goods a full-scale consultants' exercise would have been necessary.

On the other hand a number of companies were equally firmly opposed to efficiency audits. A representative of one large company commented that it was not too difficult to determine if the industry under examination was inefficient. However there were many different criteria of efficiency and even the most eminent of outside consultants might fail to make a correct appraisement of an industry's performance. It was thought, therefore, that firms would not welcome the imposition of industrial consultants upon them by an outside body such as the Commission. Nor was it considered that this was the right way for the Commission to go about its business, which was primarily to establish the

[1] e.g. Statisticians, economists, econometricians, accountants, lawyers, line management recruits and the like.

[2] And, therefore, commensurate responsibility.

[3] L. C. Hawkins, *Oxford Economic Papers*, 1950, p. 49. 'I cannot at present see how external efficiency audits of management, undertaken without responsibility to or for the management, are likely to further the task of management and so benefit the public by an improved relationship of price to service. The opposite seems more probable.'

facts about monopoly under the terms of the Act and to judge whether monopoly power had been used in a fashion contrary to the public interest.

A few companies would be prepared to accept an efficiency audit where the reference involves single-product companies. They are reluctant to commend such an audit for one section of a multi-product company. This is a real problem for the Monopolies Commission. It is sufficiently difficult to organize an effective accountancy inquiry into the referred products of a multi-product company. Efforts of this kind have been criticized severely in recent years. The problems would be far more intractable in the case of a fully-fledged efficiency audit.

Nevertheless, many companies would like to see the Monopolies Commission more closely concerned with the more superficial symptoms of economic efficiency. They feel that the Monopolies Commission often does not understand the nature of their markets. The Wall Paper Manufacturers were particularly upset on this issue. They argued that the Commission displayed no interest in the technical aspects of the trade. Pattern ranges were provided for inspection but were not examined. The Commissioners did not visit any of the mills. As a result the Commissioners persistently failed to perceive that wallpaper production was a fashion industry subject to emphasis upon new patterns and designs.

The Chairman and the Secretary of the Monopolies Commission rejected the idea of making use of consultancy inquiries. They emphasized that the Monopolies Commission was not concerned as such with business or economic efficiency. Developments of this kind would be opposed keenly by the Federation of British Industries as involving undue interference by Government in the affairs of trade and commerce. At the same time efficiency audits would inevitably delay the process of a Monopolies Commission inquiry. This would expose the Commission to further public criticism.

CONCLUSIONS

It is important that the Monopolies Commission should establish a team of highly skilled, diversely qualified staff, capable of examining closely relationships between market dominance and efficiency in manufacture and distribution. Past experience indicates the need for a tough, well-organized, professional approach to a reference, if the Monopolies Commission is ever to raise more than a quiet smile in business circles. Legislation is required enabling the Monopolies Commission to enter factory and office premises and to seize documents. Irrespective of the ability of the Monopolies Commission to effect a full efficiency audit—and this depends on the nature of the reference—it is most important that a closer analysis of economic efficiency should be undertaken.[1] It is impossible to assess the impact of the affairs of a dominant firm upon the public interest in the absence of such analysis. Failure to recognize this point has marred the procedure of investigation of the Monopolies Commission.

[1] Bow Group, February 1963, op. cit., p. 74. 'It is important to control unfairness, but we should be far more concerned about sloth.'

PART III

TRADE ASSOCIATION INQUIRIES

Power, like a desolating pestilence,
Pollutes whate'er it touches; and obedience,
Bane of all genius, virtue, freedom, truth,
Makes slaves of men, and of the human frame
A mechanized automaton.

Shelley, *Queen Mab*, III, p. 222

Chapter Six

THE MONOPOLIES COMMISSION AND PRICE AGREEMENTS

INTRODUCTION

Competition, in the context of the modern business environment, takes many forms and occasionally stems from somewhat surprising sources. From the viewpoint of the firm competition is often a synonym for insecurity. Where competition, and therefore insecurity, is keen it is little surprising that those affected by it should formulate practices designed to contain, to control, indeed to eliminate it insofar as this is possible.

Price fixing schemes take pride of place among attempts at reducing the direct impact of the competitive process. Effective price fixing schemes eliminate an important facet of the competitive process. It is not surprising, therefore, that most trade associations consider the establishment and/or the maintenance of price fixing arrangements as an important objective. For many industries arrangements relating to research, innovation, and advertising may be of equal importance;[1] this is rarely recognized, however, by trade associations. A study of price arrangements thus provides a logical basis for any analysis of public policy towards restrictive trading agreements.

Any attempt to assess the impact of price arrangements on the public interest, in the absence of a detailed examination of relationships between costs, profits, sales, and capital employed is like 'Hamlet' without the Prince of Denmark. No matter how desirable a price fixing system may be it must be treated with suspicion if it results in extremely high levels of profit or in high-cost production, by whatever criteria these should most suitably be assessed. Nevertheless, convenience recommends an examination of price fixing agreements in advance of a fundamental analysis relating to the impact of such agreements.

Price fixing schemes may take three basic forms; since the economic

[1] See e.g. H. Edwards, *Competition and Monopoly in the British Soap Industry*, Oxford, 1962.

consequences of each form may differ considerably it is important to distinguish between each form at this stage.

Minimum Price Agreements

Many companies are afraid lest unfettered price competition within their respective industries should result in cut-throat competition. The risk of cut-throat competition is high in highly-capitalized industries subjected to substantial fluctuations in the level of economic activity. Companies producing under these conditions are under keen commercial pressures to provide a 'floor' to price competition through the medium of a minimum price agreement. Price agreements of this genre are not designed to fetter the freedom of companies concerned to establish prices at levels above the agreed minima.

In certain cases, of course, the agreed minima are rarely if ever exceeded in practice by participating companies. Where this occurs over a lengthy time-period the price agreements are *de facto* common rather than minima.

Common Price Agreements

Common price agreements are more tightly drawn than minimum price agreements. They specify in detail the precise prices that must be charged for precisely specified commodities. Participating companies are required to surrender their individual sovereignty in relation to price determination. They must subject this process to group decision. Common price systems were common in reference industries before the Monopolies Commission prior to the Restrictive Trade Practices Act, 1956. Common price agreements usually require detailed supplementary agreements relating to discounts, bonuses, qualities, after sales service and the like, to prevent widespread avoidance of agreed prices in difficult trading conditions.

Maximum Price Agreements

Agreements specifying maximum prices, in the absence of a common price system, are rarely negotiated in British industry. No such agreement has been encountered by the Monopolies Commission. In the absence of the public regulation of prices, maximum price agreements are unlikely to be encountered in practice.[1]

PRICE FIXING AGREEMENTS AND THE PUBLIC INTEREST

A great deal of public discussion has centred upon the relationship between price fixing agreements and the public interest. The Monopolies

[1] It is likely in most cases of public regulation that prices will be *de facto* common.

Commission devoted considerable space in its reports to an analysis of the economic and social impact of individual price fixing systems. Some economists would attempt to distinguish the static from the dynamic effects of such practices. Static analysis has been far more susceptible to treatment by classical welfare techniques than analysis under dynamic conditions. For the most part distinctions of this kind are unrealistic; they may be very misleading under dynamic conditions. The eight main categories into which subsequent analysis has been compressed are listed below. Each category comprises a mixture of static and dynamic economic analysis.

1. Stability
2. Quality
3. Unemployment
4. Concentration
5. Countervailing Power
6. Exports
7. Research, Development and Innovation
8. Wasteful Investment Expenditure and Product Standardization

PRICE AGREEMENTS AND STABILITY

Price fixing agreements are often defended as encouraging stability. The term stability is not unambiguous: care must be exercised to define the term precisely so that its separate interpretations may be isolated. Most trade associations are only concerned with the stability of their own industries; this definition must be clearly distinguished from stability of the economy. There are three forms of stability which may be distinguished usefully at the level of the trade association: price stability, quantity stability and income stability. Each is a temporal concept.

Certain associations argue that the demand schedule facing their respective industries shifts bodily from time to time in greater, or lesser, degree and in a more, or less, foreseeable manner. Under such conditions, it is argued, price fixing schemes stabilize prices. The argument is rarely expanded in regard to the output repercussions of such schemes. Attempts to stabilize price in this manner in the absence of induced changes in the fluctuations of the demand schedule are likely to produce greater fluctuations in output than would otherwise occur.[1] In the absence of detailed knowledge about the relevant elasticities of supply and demand, it is impossible to stipulate the likely effect upon income levels of such activity. It may be useful at this stage to examine

[1] E. A. G. Robinson, *Monopoly*, p. 151. 'Though a monopolist sometimes possesses the power to convert demand in the present into demand in the future (output stabilization), it must be remembered that by so doing he will often reduce the price that he receives. He will only transfer demand from the present to the future if the prospective and discounted saving of cost exceeds the prospective and discounted loss of receipts.'

the impact of price agreements upon price stability from the viewpoint of the industry concerned.

Price stability arguments must be analysed within two distinct situations—a secular downward shift in the demand schedule and fluctuations in the level of the demand schedule facing the industry.[1]

Price Stability and Secular Decline in Demand

Trade associations may produce price fixing agreements—minimum or common—when their respective industries are faced with secular decline; the pressure for such action usually mounts as excess capacity develops. It is not easy to decide whether secular decline is inevitable, nor is it easy to decide upon the eventual extent of such a decline in demand:

> It is, of course, by no means easy to decide, when depression overtakes a particular industry, whether it is likely to be temporary or prolonged, whether the circumstances are such as to lead to contraction followed by stability at a reduced level, or to a virtual disappearance of the industry.[2]

Where an essential feature of the situation is the inevitable reduction in the level of activity of an industry the problem facing the companies concerned resolves itself into that of deciding how best a reduction in productive capacity should be effected, and how rapid the process should be.

One school of thought strongly favours the use of unfettered market forces as a tool in reducing capacity. A period of keen price competition —and the consequent losses made by substantial sections of the industry—are felt to operate swiftly and effectively in reducing capacity. Prices reflecting merely short-run average variable costs during the period should not be condemned. Bygones are bygones and much of the plant and capacity in the industry must be valueless, at least in its present occupation. Price-levels would merely reflect this phenomenon. Economists of this 'genre' condemn the fear of bankruptcy and industrial dislocation as a fear of economic progress with its implied changes.

The thesis might be justifiable where market forces effect the required contraction at the desired pace and eliminate the least desirable capacity without imposing adverse effects upon the economic efficiency of remaining capacity. These requirements are not always fulfilled in practice, as any close study of the inter-war period underlines. There are

[1] The distinction is often far from clear *ex ante*. Many firms believe they face temporary depression when in fact their markets are subject to secular decline. The opposite situation occasionally occurs.

[2] G. C. Allen, 'An Aspect of Industrial Organization', *Economic Journal*, 1945, p. 185.

many instances of persistent and stubborn resistance, on the part both of labour and of capital, to acknowledge that bygones are indeed bygones. The price mechanism may prove a lengthy and arbitrary technique for inducing a fall in capacity under such conditions. Resistance to decline is likely to be particularly stubborn when the opportunity cost of employed factors is low and when transport costs are high. It is likely to be further intensified if many producers in the industry are unduly optimistic about the degree of contraction necessitated by demand changes, or about their respective individual abilities to survive a contraction process.[1]

In the meantime the low profitability of the industry may have serious detrimental effects upon the technical and economic efficiency of member firms. Low-cost companies may be unable to maintain the efficiency of their plant and equipment, let alone to introduce cost-reducing innovations. Even where they are able to do so they may lack the necessary incentives under conditions of extensive hardship and low profits. Consequently, unit production costs may move in favour of overseas competitors; this will exacerbate the required decline of domestic capacity.

It is dangerous to assume that cut-throat competition eliminates the least efficient productive capacity. Factors such as the degree of liquidity, the size and degree of diversification of the companies concerned, may be more important than low unit production costs in the fight for economic survival. Where the process of contraction is lengthy and unrewarding the most dynamic companies may be the first to quit. Those that remain may be the least progressive and most apathetic units. The survivors of a process of secular decline stand in testament of their fitness to survive; this is no obvious indication of their ability to serve best the future requirements of the industry. Finally, it should not be assumed too readily that the elimination of companies necessarily involves the sterilization of their productive capacity. Where such capacity carries a low opportunity cost it may be extremely difficult to eliminate completely.

These problems of contraction through price competition cast shadows over the sanguine expectations of those inclined to the *laissez-faire* solution. They should not, however, encourage a blind acceptance of the alternatives proposed by members of trade associations.

Minimum or common price systems cannot prevent an eventual reduction in the productive capacity of an industry faced with secular

[1] J. M. Clark, *Competition as a Dynamic Process*, 1961, p. 69. 'Under excess capacity [in the nineteenth century] unrestricted competition tended to drive prices towards short-run marginal cost as a limit, this being less than average operating expenses. Resulting losses did not eliminate excess capacity with any readiness.'

decline unless in some way the decline itself is not independent of the price system adopted in the industry. Schemes may be designed to reduce the decline in prices and industrial profits; such action, save in exceptional circumstances, must involve an aggravated decline in the quantity demanded. Under such conditions a price system is unlikely to operate effectively in the absence of market sharing agreements[1] and a planned reduction of plant and equipment. The price agreement does not eliminate the problem of disequilibrium; it merely masks its symptoms. Any delay in reacting to the crisis may intensify the difficulties of the industry. Price systems fortified by market sharing may stimulate or reduce the speed of contraction depending upon the reaction of member firms. On the one hand the possibility of selling one's allocated market share may encourage firms to leave the industry more quickly than they otherwise would. On the other hand higher group profits may reduce the pressure to leave the industry, especially if high-cost firms are protected from their more efficient fellow-members by savage penalties placed upon production in excess of quota. Redundancy schemes fortifying the price systems may succeed in sterilizing plant disposed of by outgoing firms. On the other hand such schemes usually involve compensation from those remaining; this involves interest payments not merely on redundant but upon scrapped capacity, aggravating the serious financial difficulties of those left behind.

It is not clear, therefore, that price fixing agreements are desirable responses to secular decline. The Monopolies Commission certainly has not viewed the defence with favour. A case in point occurred in the calico printing inquiry.[2]

Calico printing had been involved in the heavy contraction of the Lancashire cotton industry during the inter-war period, and had witnessed the collapse of the price system operated by its Federation. Following the Second World War the Federation established a new system of minimum prices, fortified by detailed market sharing and redundancy agreements. The Federation defended this scheme as being necessary to prevent cut-throat competition in calico printing. The Federation argued that a further contraction of the cotton industry was likely to occur in the post-war period and that the price system provided 'a breakwater against the storms which have beset the Industry over the past sixty years and to discourage the fall in prices to a level which could only result in losses'.[3]

[1] T. Wilson (J. Miller, Ed.), *Competition, Cartels and Their Regulations*, North-Holland P.C., 1962, p. 144. 'The fixing of prices and the allocation of quotas will scarcely put the industry in a position where it will be attractive to dynamic managers: on the contrary it will then be so organized as to make a vigorous new manager more or less impotent.'

[2] Report on the Process of Calico Printing, 1954, H.C.P. 140.

[3] ibid., p. 61.

The Federation contended that unit production costs increased rapidly with any reduction in the level of production, and that this provided a strong incentive for price cutting on the part of individual printing firms. Extensive losses would result in the absence of minimum prices and this would put pressure upon quality standards and expenditure upon research and development in the industry.

The Monopolies Commission made a detailed study of existing and future demand conditions in the industry in the light of existing and potential capacity. This study did not indicate that the domestic market for calico printing was undergoing long-term decline, or that the industry itself was burdened with serious excess capacity. The Commission considered that the price system was more a product of inter-war depression philosophy, than of any detailed assessment of postwar conditions. It concluded that the Federation had misinterpreted short-term fluctuations in the demand schedule as being symptoms of secular decline.[1]

The Monopolies Commission in any event would not accept necessarily a price fixing system which effectively reduced the pace of contraction. In a fully-employed economy the retention of factors of production in occupations which should be eliminated on market grounds would be considered detrimental to the public interest unless the social cost of transferring such factors to other occupations is considerably in excess of the private cost. In the case of calico printing, had the case of secular decline been substantiated, the Federation could scarcely have pleaded that unemployment would be increased in Lancashire. Its Redundancy Scheme and its high prices served to speed up the process of contraction. Arguments in favour of price systems under conditions of secular decline are double-edge.

Price Stability and Demand Fluctuations

Minimum or common price agreements are defended frequently on the ground that they preserve price stability under fluctuating demand conditions. Most commonly they are defended in the case of products the demand for which is point inelastic with respect to price but highly elastic with respect to income. Whenever incomes fall, therefore, the demand schedule moves sharply to the left whilst a reduction in price does little to increase quantity demanded. If, in addition, supply is relatively price inelastic, or indeed subject to the 'cobweb' phenomenon, production, in the absence of a stabilization scheme, may not contract until severe losses have been inflicted for a lengthy period upon all

[1] ibid., p. 65. 'The demands in the home market will no doubt fluctuate from year to year according to the movements of fashion, but we see no reason to expect any long-term decline here.'

producers. Primary products of various kinds are most likely to suffer from these conditions. Government-sponsored marketing systems normally secure such producers from public supervision and control, other than by means of subsidy determination and/or import protection policy. This study is concerned with less pernicious market conditions.

Where fluctuations in the demand schedule are large it is inevitable, on an average of high and low levels of the schedule, that highly competitive industries will maintain considerable surplus capacity.

Nevertheless some companies within the industry, the more successful, may operate at a high degree of capacity at all times. Should this be the case less successful firms, operating considerably below capacity during trough periods, may regard sales expansion as being profitable so long as price does not fall beneath short-run average variable cost. Competitive action of this kind may press the more successful firms to follow suit. In highly-capitalized industries the result may be heavy short-run losses even in normal times,[1] the size of losses depending upon subjective interpretations by firms of the price elasticity at relevant points on the demand schedule, and the structure of marginal and average cost curves.[2]

When trough periods are extensive and price reductions severe certain firms may be driven out of the industry, thereby reducing total productive capacity. Once boom conditions return consumers would be faced with shortages at prevailing prices, price levels might soar, and new investment might not be forthcoming for an industry so recently the subject of difficult trading conditions. In this manner temporary price reductions during depression would be more than counterbalanced by high prices in times of boom. Price stability guaranteed by a price-fixing agreement is urged as a desirable alternative to competitive chaos.

This analysis may be criticized. If the association is successful in maintaining stable prices, and if the demand schedule is completely independent of the scheme, the members will have a larger output in good times and a smaller output in bad times than would result from competing firms operating on rising short-run supply (marginal cost) curves. The aggravation of employment fluctuations may operate in a manner contrary to the public interest.

In addition, firms eliminated during the depression must be ex-

[1] G. Richardson, *Information and Investment*, Oxford, 1960, p. 130. 'Under conditions of low elasticity of demand and high fixed costs, downward flexibility of prices might result in severe losses and widespread bankruptcy, both without economic justification.'

[2] ibid., p. 131. 'If demand is, in fact, inelastic the principal effect of a fall in prices may be merely a pointless (or indeed harmful) redistribution of income from firms to their customers.'

tremely short-sighted, illiquid, or inefficient.[1] Since the industry, by definition, is operating in roughly equilibrium conditions profitability incentives (discounting the cash flow at the appropriate interest rate) must be sufficient to maintain efficient and prudent firms in operation. In any event, the assets of bankrupted companies would not disappear necessarily from the industry, especially if they carry a low opportunity cost.[2]

Finally, if the demand fluctuations emanate from genuine switches in the pattern of consumers' preferences it may be desirable to reflect such switches in changing relative prices within the economy. It is far from simple, *ex ante*, to judge whether a movement in the demand schedule is temporary or permanent.

Industries characterized by highly differentiated products may be subject to another form of price instability in the absence of a price fixing agreement. Quality differences may be recognized between competing products but the appropriate price differentials may be in dispute. One company may consider that its product requires a slightly lower price than that of its rivals, contrary to the latter companies' interpretation of the situation. Under such conditions a downward price struggle may develop, culminating in prices that do not fully reflect unit production costs. This form of price instability occurs so rarely under conditions of oligopoly[3] as to justify its omission from more detailed analysis.

The Monopolies Commission encountered the 'demand fluctuations' defence for a price fixing scheme in the electrical and allied machinery and plant industry.[4] Signatory groups of the British Electrical and Allied Manufacturers' Association operated minimum price agreements covering both the domestic and the export market. Basically the price arrangements could be viewed as common price agreements.

The Groups contended that their price systems had originated as a defence measure under depressed market conditions, when price competition had resulted in widespread losses. The arrangements provided an indispensable safeguard against the return of such conditions.

The manufacturers were tied to extremely costly capital equipment, with an exceptionally high ratio of overheads to direct labour costs. Heavy fixed costs were committed to research and development programmes. In addition much of their output was 'one-off' production, subject to individual specifications, and often it was impossible to offset

[1] Especially if stocks are feasible as a technique for smoothing out the impact of fluctuations.

[2] More especially if prices truly soar in boom periods.

[3] The most likely industrial organization in which this form of dispute might be muted, but the least likely, many economists would argue, for an actual outbreak of price-cutting to take place.

[4] Report on the Supply and Export of Electrical and Allied Machinery and Plant, 1957. H.C.P. 42.

demand fluctuations by producing for stock. Yet at the same time heavy costs resulted from excess capacity during periods of depression. Under these conditions, and stimulated by the high value of individual orders, firms were tempted to pare tenders down to short-run average variable costs of production. An outbreak of this nature was aggravated by the fewness of sellers.

The Monopolies Commission's costing investigation substantiated the Group's contention that 'the ratio of fixed overhead costs to total costs is rather higher than in many industries, though not outstandingly so'.[1] On the other hand the Commission was not impressed by arguments that price arrangements maintained high levels of activity in periods of depression. Flexible rather than rigid pricing would help to obtain such an objective. In any event the Commission was convinced that the common prices would be unlikely to survive under chronic depression of the kind feared by the manufacturers.[2]

The Commission was unimpressed by fears that capacity would be eliminated in depression in the absence of the price system, and that boom conditions would result in high prices. It pointed out that discarded capacity might readily be reinstated if demand conditions should warrant it. On the other hand, the Commission considered that the concept of panic price cutting was itself not unambiguous. Cut-throat pricing in the eyes of one producer might be shrewd business in the eyes of another. The Commission recommended that each manufacturer should be free to decide his own tendering price, taking into consideration available capacity and his fixed production costs.

The Monopolies Commission's approach, admirably illustrated in this inquiry, strongly favoured the *laissez-faire* solution to fluctuating demand schedules. In many instances its arguments have been strong. In the BEAMA inquiry the Commission may have placed too little emphasis upon the changing nature of demand for heavy electrical equipment. The Central Electricity Authority (now the Central Electricity Generating Board) purchased almost the entire production of such equipment. Individual orders tend to be extremely costly and intermittent. Under these conditions firms desperate to maintain plant in operation may be tempted to cut prices to marginal cost. The Monopolies Commission failed to detail the importance of such market conditions in its Report. It may well be that this omission results from failure to conduct an extensive and detailed consultancy investigation related to the industry.

[1] Report on the Supply and Export of Electrical and Allied Machinery and Plant, 1957, H.C.P. 42, p. 248.

[2] ibid., p. 249. 'The manufacturers appear to us to overestimate the likelihood of a protracted weak market, to take a mistaken view of some of its effects if it should occur, to be unduly optimistic about the effectiveness of their own arrangements for maintaining the level of prices in such conditions, and to underestimate the buyer's interest in the quality of his purchase.'

Price Stability and 'Shopping Around'

The 'shopping around' defence for price fixing surprisingly seduced the Restrictive Practices Court in its judgment in the Black Nut and Bolt case.[1] In addition, certain more plausible aspects of the theory influenced the Monopolies Commission in the linoleum inquiry.[2]

Where the average level of trade association prices is considered reasonable, and where suppliers are numerous, it is argued that price stability carries great advantages to consumers,[3] especially to those carrying stocks of the commodity in question. Since every purchaser is then certain of the price of the product 'there is no need to make inquiries or obtain price lists before ordering goods from a particular manufacturer. . . .'[4] In the absence of a price agreement the trade would suffer the expense and inconvenience of having to 'go shopping', administrative costs would rise, and this would be mirrored by higher prices to the public. The argument was accepted by Justice Diplock:

> He knows the price that he can quote, he knows the price he must pay from whatever manufacturer he buys: date of delivery is the only matter of negotiation. . . . The margin of 7½ per cent . . . would, we are satisfied . . . be scarcely adequate to cover the additional costs involved in 'going shopping'.[5]

The judgment in the Black Nut and Bolt case was destroyed subsequently by the expert economic witness for the Registrar.[6] He first challenged the implied judgment of the Court that price stability could only be maintained by agreement. He argued on the contrary that price leadership, highly likely in the absence of agreement, might well produce considerable stability of prices. A price leadership system might encourage lower-cost suppliers 'to have a go',[7] quoting the leading firm's prices less a stated percentage discount. Customers, unimpressed by quality differences, would begin to switch their demand to the price-cutter's products, placing pressure upon remaining suppliers to reduce their prices. 'This is the very process of competition which the agreement inhibits and which, in my view, in this particular case would be likely to bring about a restoration of uniformity of price following a

[1] Delivered on July 15, 1960. [2] Report on the Supply of Linoleum.

[3] P. L. Cook. 'Orderly Marketing or Competition'. *Economic Journal*, September 1961, p. 505. 'Trading becomes extremely tedious, time consuming and wasteful when the number of variables to be settled is large. The large buyer will spend time on comparing all details, but the small buyer who is trading in many other products is unlikely to do this; it is not worth his while to waste time shopping around.'

[4] Judgment in *re* Black Nut and Bolt Association—Incorporated Council of Law Reporting. [5] ibid.

[6] Mr G. D. N. Worswick. 'On the benefits of being denied the opportunity to go shopping.' *Bulletin* of Oxford University Institute of Statistics, August 1961.

[7] ibid., p. 277.

departure from a previous uniformity, initiated by one, or more, firms.'[1]

Mr Worswick contended that keen buyers might well purchase direct from the manufacturers if stockholders attempted to cover additional expenses by raising prices. If, on the other hand, purchasers were not keen, stockholders would be placed under no compulsion to shop around.[2] 'Once again, the inability of stockholders to move out of line from manufacturers is a point which the judgment itself has made in a different context.'[3]

The Monopolies Commission examined the impact of price stability upon the incentive to hold stocks in the linoleum industry.[4] The Linoleum Manufacturers' Association defended its common price system on price stability grounds. It pointed out that raw material prices fluctuated considerably; its price system was designed to cushion the effects of this movement since members 'take a view of future costs when fixing their prices, so that the prices remain unaltered for some time'.[5]

The Monopolies Commission was impressed by the argument that common prices under such conditions created confidence in stockholding. 'We believe that is a convenience to users, as well as in the interests of the manufacturers and of smaller traders who do not normally obtain linoleum direct from manufacturers, that the trade should be encouraged to hold adequate stocks, and we conclude that the stability which gives such encouragement is an advantage of this common price system.'[6] In the sense that price stability did not merely prevent price fluctuations of all linoleum through time, but also prevented price fluctuations between various brands of linoleum, the argument is an interesting aspect of the shopping around theory.

One aspect of shopping around which was not discussed by either the Court or the Commission relates more directly to the housewife. The possibility of price variations in commodities may perturb consumers, particularly when they find they have not made the cheapest possible purchase. The argument rests upon the existence of resale price maintenance, since retailers would be free otherwise to vary their prices even though they purchase at common prices. In any event it does not appear to be an argument carrying any weight.[7] It would be surprising if the Commission was to consider such a thesis in a serious vein.

[1] *Bulletin* of Oxford University Institute of Statistics, August 1961, p. 277.

[2] D. E. Varley (in discussion). 'It is not a little surprising that the Restrictive Practices Court should concern itself with the well-being of the stomach-lining of the buying executive.'

[3] G. D. N. Worswick, op. cit., p. 279. [4] op. cit. [5] ibid., p. 54. [6] ibid., p. 55.

[7] G. D. N. Worswick, op. cit., p. 278. 'I have been told that people accustomed to a fixed price world do suffer neuroses if suddenly transported into a variable price world, e.g. United States (in some goods) or an oriental bazaar, but that for those of strong constitution the effects quickly wear off.'

Price Stability—The Investment Confidence Theory

Price fixing systems successful in promoting 'orderly marketing' are defended on the ground that they reduce day-to-day uncertainty, thereby encouraging management to concentrate upon long-term strategy.[1] Where prices are reasonable and the costing system efficient and uniform the thesis is put forward with vigour. It is argued that the chief determinant of profitability becomes long-term policy decisions and not the ability to take advantage of short-term price fluctuations under conditions of a moving demand schedule. The costs of short-term adjustment are eliminated, and prices will be lower on this account than in an unregulated market. Orderly marketing schemes are difficult to establish, and should, therefore, be tolerated in periods of relative trading stability.[2]

This argument is open to criticism. Monopolies Commission investigations do not indicate that price systems canalize corporative activity into long-term strategy. In many instances a great deal of energy is dissipated upon internal bickering and bargaining; in other instances the delights of the quiet life appear equally seductive in the long as in the short-run.

The problem of whether price stability implies 'income stability' in the face of movements in the demand schedule or in the relevant cost schedules is usually side-stepped by exponents of the theory. Where trade association prices are considerably out of line with the market indirect forms of price competition may raise costs of production and eliminate stability. In the last analysis extremely depressed conditions may result in complete and overt termination of stability and 'orderly marketing' policies.

It is by no means certain, in any event, that cost reductions resulting from a price fixing agreement will be reflected in lower prices. Even where public supervision is close and continuous, sufficient ambiguity exists concerning the relationship between profit, cost, and capital employed, to allow grave doubts about the efficacy of public supervision and control.

A more sophisticated thesis concerns the impact of price stability upon the incentive and the potential to invest. Firstly it is argued that the ability to concentrate upon the longer-run must result in improved investment decisions. The weakness of this contention has been exposed. Secondly it is argued that uncertainty is reduced, and that capital for investment will be forthcoming on a lower supply schedule than under

[1] P. L. Cook, op. cit., p. 510. 'Examination of the selling decisions which have to be made show that many involve very considerable risk. In unstable, highly competitive, bitter and confused conditions it is the risky selling decisions which may become the most important aspect of "efficiency", that is, the chief determinant of profits.'

[2] ibid., p. 511. 'Further, it is not easy when mutual confidence in orderly marketing has been lost to make the necessary agreements and to re-establish the necessary mutual confidence....'

price competition. The lower rate of return thereby necessitated might be translated into lower prices.

The investment thesis is suspect in many ways. Internal dispute between association members may be detrimental to investors' confidence. Price agreements, insofar as they shield high cost producers, may be detrimental to investment in innovation. Where capital supplies are 'cheaply' obtained due to high profits ploughed back by the trade association members present consumers may be subsidizing future consumers. This is by no means automatically desirable. In any event available evidence does not substantiate the thesis that enterprising companies are unable to undertake attractive investment programmes due to lack of capital. Should this be the case[1] the remedy is not restrictive price agreements but a reform of the institutions in the capital market.[2]

Price Fixing and Macro-economic Stability

Price fixing associations occasionally contend that their actions stimulate price stability throughout the economy or throughout a selected section of the economy. The Monopolies Commission itself is ill-equipped to examine such arguments, particularly where they relate to the entire economy. It has neither the powers nor the time to obtain relevant data. In addition, theories relating to stability of the general price level are highly complex. The distinctive role of micro-economic price fixing upon the price level is far from clear, even should all possible information be accumulated.[3] It would be necessary to obtain details concerning relative elasticities of supply and demand, relative marginal propensities to consume and to save, and relative investment incentive between sectors, between firms and between individuals. Information of this kind does not exist, and could never exist with accuracy in a dynamic economy.[4]

[1] e.g. In the supply of capital to small private limited companies.

[2] As for instance was recommended by The Radcliffe Committee Report. See also F. Machlup, op. cit., p. 396. 'There can be little doubt that, instead of erecting barriers to competition in order to increase the pioneer's or insider's gain, it is simpler and safer to increase it by letting him keep more of it—that is, by taking less through taxes.'

[3] J. M. Clark, 1961, op. cit., p. 82. 'But competition has some features that are incompatible with thorough-going stabilization: primarily the fact that programmes of investment and output are planned and carried out by different firms independently, without co-ordination, always contingent on adequate demand and subject to revision if the demand that materializes is not enough to validate them.'

[4] A case that price fixing lessened income and output fluctuations through time might be established if the association proved that its activities raised planned saving for the economy without increasing planned investment during an inflationary period, whilst reducing planned saving without lowering planned investment during deflationary conditions. Even then, the stable general price level may be 'bought' by great sectional fluctuations.

On the other hand, the Commission is much better equipped to examine 'vertical' relationships between an investigated industry and its major suppliers and consumers. It is able to obtain a great deal of background information concerning closely related industrial sectors during an industrial inquiry. From this kind of evidence it may be well placed to judge the effect of a price fixing scheme upon the operations of closely related sectors. Such an instance occurred in the calico printing inquiry.[1] The Federation of Calico Printers contended that its minimum price agreements provided some degree of stability in an industry whose recent history had been wrought with instability. The Monopolies Commission refused to examine the calico printing industry in isolation from the remainder of the cotton industry. It pointed out that prices maintained at levels higher than would have obtained under competitive conditions made it more difficult for merchants to sell cotton goods both at home and abroad. Thus the benefits accruing to calico printing were solely at the expense of the stability of other sectors of the cotton industry.[2]

In the case of vertical relationships the Monopolies Commission may have a role to play. Concerning the relationship between price fixing and the general price and output level it would be highly dangerous for the Commission to speak out at all. It has wisely refrained from so doing.

PRICE AGREEMENTS AND QUALITY

Arguments based upon a relationship between price fixing arrangements and quality follow two distinct lines: (a) that price fixing serves to maintain existing quality standards; (b) that price fixing agreements encourage quality improvement.

Price Fixing Agreements and Quality Maintenance

Certain trade associations defend price fixing agreements on the ground that they prevent cut-throat price competition from emerging in times of secular decline or in the face of a fluctuating demand schedule. Cut-throat competition would place companies under intense pressure to debase quality standards to the general detriment—indeed on occasion to the physical endangerment—of the consumer.[3]

[1] op. cit.

[2] ibid., p. 71. 'We cannot see how in the long run they can have results which their sponsors hope for, or how, even if for a time they had some of these results, this could be achieved except at the expense of other sections of the textile industry and of the wider public interest.'

[3] T. Wilson (J. Miller, Ed.), *Competition, Cartels and Their Regulation*, 1962, p. 147. 'Is it not therefore conceivable that firms might carry such competition too far in the circumstances in which they might also carry price-cutting too far? For some reason however this possibility is rarely mentioned.'

The Monopolies Commission was never impressed by such a thesis as argued by producers' goods manufacturers. It was content to rely upon technically-skilled buyers to insist upon the required level of quality in making purchases. The British Non-Ferrous Metals Federation[1] discovered, to its misfortune, the Monopolies Commission's approach in this respect. All non-ferrous metal manufacturers' associations operated minimum price systems, which they defended as being necessary to maintain high quality standards. Should unlimited price-cutting occur, it was argued, 'there would be a tendency for the conditions to favour firms which were prepared to sacrifice quality to reduce costs with a view to increasing their sales in certain fields'.[2] Producers would be pressed to reduce conversion costs, since they could not influence raw material prices.

Many customers stressed to the Commission the paramount importance placed upon high quality supplies. Consumers inspected their purchases on a sample basis to ensure that they were satisfactory.[3] This action provided satisfactory safeguards for quality maintenance. Those who pared quality would quickly lose custom.

The Commission was far more concerned about quality debasement in the case of consumer products, especially where quality was difficult to assess in the absence of technical knowledge of the product. The Commission encountered such a situation in its inquiry into the linoleum industry.

The Linoleum Manufacturers' Association contended that price competition in times of depression must lead to quality debasement. Quality of linoleum products, it was argued, was extremely difficult to assess. Wearability,[4] in particular, could be assessed only after a number of years in use. The Monopolies Commission was impressed by the argument. It agreed that price competition might result in such debasement of linoleum qualities, and that the consumer could be deceived in this respect. This conclusion influenced the Monopolies Commission into recommending a limited and closely-supervised price system for the linoleum industry. The particular conditions that prevailed in the linoleum industry might be encountered rarely in Monopolies Commission inquiries. The decision did not foreshadow a slack interpretation of arguments relating price systems to the maintenance of quality.

[1] Report on the Supply and Export of Certain Semi-Manufactures of Copper and Copper-Based Alloys, 1955. H.C.P. 56.

[2] ibid., p. 85.

[3] Standard specifications had in fact been published for many of the Federation's products. These specifications covered quality as well as dimensions.

[4] As opposed to appearance.

Price Fixing Agreements and Quality Improvement

Price fixing agreements may canalize competition into the quality dimension, raising the general level of quality to the consuming public. Trade associations frequently put forward this thesis in support of their price systems. The Monopolies Commission always viewed this contention with suspicion.

When consumers are presented with a choice between low quality cheaply priced goods and better quality but more expensive goods they will select the most desirable combination. A price fixing agreement, if it is effective, eliminates such choice; it may compel consumers to purchase less satisfactory price-qualtiy combinations of the relevant commodity.

The Federation of Calico Printers[1] contended that its minimum price agreements stimulated competition both in quality and in service. This form of competitive strategy was far more effective in its own industry than straightforward price competition. The Cotton and Rayon Merchants' Association flatly contradicted this supposition. The Monopolies Commission dismissed the Federation's argument, pointing out that the system prevented the supply of a lower priced, lower quality treatment 'even though in the view of the merchant this is what his market requires'.[2] The Commission felt that the system imposed an undesirable restriction on consumer choice. Federation members accounted for 98 per cent of total calico printing in the United Kingdom.

On the other hand the Commission viewed a similar argument more favourably during its inquiry into the linoleum industry. In this case, however, the Association provided a full range of qualities, from the most expensive inlaid to the cheapest printed linoleum. In addition there was strong competition from independent producers producing to the specifications of the British Standards Institute. The linoleum produced by the Independents retailed at prices 5–10 per cent below those of the Linoleum Manufacturers' Association. The Monopolies Commission concluded that an adequate price/quality selection was provided in the industry, and that consumer choice was not unduly restricted.

In general the Commission has not been impressed by quality improvement arguments, pointing out that high quality products will be marketed in the absence of price agreements if the production of such commodities is desirable. The Monopolies Commission is not usually prepared to restrict consumers from purchasing poorer quality commodities at lower prices. In this respect the Commission may be criticized for failing to relate arguments concerning research expenditures with those concerning quality improvement.

[1] op. cit.
[2] op. cit., 1954, p. 71.

PRICE AGREEMENTS AND UNEMPLOYMENT

The White Paper on Employment Policy,[1] published in May 1944, pledged a high and stable level of employment as a prime aim and responsibility of Government in the postwar period. The promise did not guarantee that each worker would be provided with one particular occupation for the whole of his working life. The Paper was concerned with aggregates, emphasizing the necessity for a high mobility of labour in a dynamically expanding economy.[2]

A few associations, nevertheless, defended price fixing agreements on the ground that they contributed to the maintenance of employment within the reference industry. Typically, this argument is not related to the short run. Action successful in maintaining prices above market levels, assuming independence of the demand schedule and absence of stock piling, must reduce the quantity demanded as compared with a freely competitive system. Employment is closely correlated to output in most industries, especially in the short run. Associations rarely argue that their price fixing systems provide lower short-run prices than would occur under price competition.[3]

Associations emphasized the longer-term effects of price systems upon employment. Some argued that cut-throat competition under depressed market conditions would lead to a reduction in the number of firms in the industry and to a reduction in total output. This would reduce employment opportunities in the industry. This thesis must be examined separately in cases of secular decline and of fluctuations in the level of activity. A further contention relating to the impact of investment in innovation upon future labour requirements must also be examined.

Unemployment and Secular Decline

Measures designed to prevent or slow-down the outflow of resources from an industry faced with secular decline may be criticized. It may be argued that such resources are more highly valued in alternative employments, and that they should be encouraged to move. The argument regarding price fixing agreements then resolves itself into a discussion of the relative speed and efficiency with which factors are shifted by price fixing or price competition. There is a powerful prima facie case for arguing that price fixing will accentuate the outward movement of labour[4] whilst retarding the outward movement of capital.[5]

In regard to capital, however, the argument is more complex than

[1] Cmnd. 6527.

[2] More especially in an economy susceptible to international trade fluctuations.

[3] They were usually much more concerned with demonstrating the evils of cut-throat competition in the absence of price fixing agreements.

[4] By reducing quantity demanded of the product in question.

[5] By raising existing and expected profit levels in the industry.

this. Under keen price competition, capital may be retained by companies even where price fails to meet short-run average variable costs of production. Optimism regarding future prospects may see to that. Low opportunity costs will provide a further incentive to retain capital in its existing occupation.[1] Much plant and equipment is affected in this manner. In such circumstances the owners may be unwilling to realize large reductions in the value of their capital; they may not wish to face an unpleasant reality.

It may not always be desirable to obtain a swift release of labour resources from an industry that is declining. The opportunity cost of specialized labour may be extremely low, even in a fully-employed economy. Retraining schemes may be unavailable or unacceptable to the relevant trade unions. Immobility of labour between regions may result in serious regional employment problems.[2] Where such conditions prevail the social cost of retaining labour in existing occupations may be lower than the private cost of so doing. A price fixing scheme might then be criticized for accelerating the release of labour from a declining industry.

So much for problems relating to the speed of decline. There is an additional problem in deciding *ex ante* that the decline is secular and not merely seasonal or cyclical. A misjudgment at this stage could have serious welfare repercussions at a later stage both in the case of unduly optimistic and in the case of unduly pessimistic expectations.

The analysis is further complicated by the need to judge the impact of price fixing upon the quality of released resources. This involves deciding whether the least or most effective resources should be released; the likely consequences of price fixing agreements and free competition should then be examined from this viewpoint. The problem of price fixing agreements and unemployment under secular decline is complex. It is perhaps fortunate, therefore, that the Monopolies Commission was not called upon to analyse such a situation.

Unemployment and Demand Fluctuations

It is more common to encounter the argument relating to price fixing and unemployment in industries characterized by cyclical or seasonal demand fluctuations. Trade associations fear that such conditions may lead to price wars and to unnecessary elimination of productive capacity. Where this occurred during a trough, the eliminated capacity might not return in the peak. The level of employment in the industry—both labour and capital—might be lowered permanently.

Insofar as this contention relates to the short-run it is suspect. The

[1] In certain instances—railway tunnels—opportunity cost may be zero.

[2] The problem is more intractable when the level of employment is considered to be high throughout the economy.

prevention of downward price movements in depression must usually lower the employment of labour and intensify excess capacity in productive equipment. It is possible, nevertheless, that under-employed labour and capital may be retained by companies secured from the worst dangers of cut-throat competition. Once again an interesting contrast is exposed between potential and incentive.

Excessive hoarding of labour under general conditions of full employment runs counter to the designs of public policy. The 'payroll tax' which may be imposed upon companies was designed to penalize such anti-social behaviour. As ever, however, politicians are susceptible to the pressures of vested interests. Measures designed to support declining industries are usually inspired by political fears of one kind or another relating to the labour force that would be dismissed. It is quite natural, therefore, that price system defences relating to employment were argued strongly before the Monopolies Commission.

The defence was argued by the Federation of Calico Printers. The Federation argued that unemployment in Lancashire might re-emerge on a similar scale to that of the inter-war period. Although calico printing itself accounted for only 12,000 employees, the employment was localized in parts of Lancashire.

The Monopolies Commission was sceptical about these fears. Inter-war conditions were no longer apparent in the British cotton industry and could not reasonably be forecast for the future. Indeed, under-employment of capital equipment in postwar years had resulted, not from depressed demand conditions, but from labour shortages.

Even, however, should depressed conditions emerge in the industry the Commission could not accept the Federation's price system as a palliative to unemployment. The price scheme could only succeed, under such conditions, in extending unemployment of labour in the industry. The Monopolies Commission was particularly concerned about the impact of the Federation's scheme upon employment throughout the cotton industry. It pointed out that price rigidity 'must result in a loss of orders for cloth to overseas competitors, and so in a smaller volume of business being done than could have been secured if printing prices were lower'.[1] A reduction in the volume of business would find its expression not only in calico printing, but also in spinning, weaving and other sections of the cotton industry.

The Monopolies Commission, typically, was unimpressed by the unemployment defence for price fixing agreements. The Monopolies Commission usually paid insufficient attention to the quality[2] as well as the volume of employment of capital and of labour under such condi-

[1] op. cit., 1954, p. 71.

[2] e.g. whether periodic fluctuations encouraged more enterprising factors to leave the industry.

tions. In general, nevertheless, the Commission's approach to the unemployment problem tallied with the existing emphasis on the need for flexibility and resource mobility.

Price Fixing, Long-term Investment, and Unemployment

Trade associations occasionally argued that price fixing agreements in conditions of demand fluctuations improved income stability and induced a higher level of gross investment on the part of the industry. The higher level of investment, it was suggested, would raise long-term employment within the industry. Once again, however, the contention may be criticized on various grounds. A higher rate of gross investment may imply a greater volume of capital commitment in the industry, a more rapid depreciation of capital equipment, or merely a complete squandering of capital. Should the capital employed in the industry expand as a result of price arrangements this may involve an undesirable canalization of scarce resources from a competitive to a monopolistic sector of the economy. Similarly in the case of labour, any increase in labour requirements may result in welfare distortions. It is by no means certain, in any event, that capital investment will increase labour utilization. Where such investment concentrates upon labour-saving equipment, and where the relevant elasticities provide little scope for further market penetration, the employment of labour may be heavily reduced in the long-run. The relationships between price fixing, capital investment, and the employment of labour and capital are not simple, even at the level of one industry.

The argument was adopted nevertheless both by the Federation of Calico Printers and by the Hard Fibre Cordage Federation.[1] Both federations contended that investment would be stimulated by price fixing and that this would stimulate the employment of labour in the long-run. The Monopolies Commission adamantly rejected both contentions. It suggested that the price systems would tend to create a false sense of security and that this would delay the required adjustments and redeployment of resources.

It is true, of course, that an increase in the level of investment initiated by one association will generate income. The multiplier effects of the initial rise in material investment will cause a secondary increase in the National Income; the pace and extent of this secondary increase will depend upon the relevant time-lags, and the relevant marginal propensity to consume.[2] It is also feasible that income expansion as described above may inaugerate a climate favourable to further investment

[1] Report on the Supply of Hard Fibre Cordage, 1956. H.C.P. 294.

[2] $K=\frac{I}{I-C}$ where C is the marginal propensity to consume.

expenditure in other industries—the accelerator effect.[1] The Commission has not considered such speculation to be part of its function. In this respect it has been sensible.

PRICE AGREEMENTS AND INDUSTRIAL CONCENTRATION

A number of associations subjected to Monopolies Commission inquiry defended price agreements on the ground that they prevented concentration of production within their respective industries. They argued that the elimination of their agreements would be followed by price cutting which would drive many producers out of the industry. The remaining firms would subsequently raise their prices and exploit an entrenched monopolistic position, to the general detriment of the consuming public. The Monopolies Commission viewed such contentions with more than a modicum of suspicion.

Price competition of the kind required to effect substantial industrial concentration is unlikely to occur in the absence of a wide spread of unit cost within the relevant industry. A wide unit cost spread implies that prices fixed by the trade association must provide high profits for low-cost producers so that high-cost companies may remain within the industry. Featherbedding of this variety is scarcely an attractive alternative to industrial concentration.

A price fixing agreement which deters the relative expansion of low-cost companies may sacrifice scale economies, and may lower the desire to innovate, and to fulfil the risk-taking function of business enterprise. These are serious weaknesses in the arguments that are typically used.

It is feasible, nevertheless, that a price war might be initiated by large, liquid, multi-product companies in a determined attempt to dominate the market. Survival of the fattest could supersede survival of the fittest under these circumstances. Members of the electric wires and cables industry suspected such motives behind the price war commenced in 1960 by British Insulated Callender's Cables and Associated Electrical Industries. A concentration process is taking place at present in calico printing.

The present system of public supervision is weak in respect to activities of this kind. The situation may not be referred to the Monopolies Commission until dominant firm status has been achieved. Small companies may have been eliminated or taken over prior to the commencement of an inquiry. Certain economists[2] have made light of the danger of

[1] The pace and extent of this further round of income expansion will depend upon the initial relationship between the optimum and the actual stock of capital, the capital-output ratio, and the relevant time-lags involved.

[2] e.g. J. Downie, *The Competitive Process*.

industrial concentration. It is argued that concentration will lower automatically unit production costs to the lowest level ruling prior to the concentration process. Evidence from Monopolies Commission reports does not substantiate this belief. The Imperial Tobacco Company was criticized by the Monopolies Commission for retaining high-cost plant and an excessive number of cigarette brands.

On the other hand a process of concentration and consolidation may produce favourable results. Scale economies may be reaped by low-cost companies, which would be unavailable within a price agreement. Concentration may result in lower prices through this process. The stimulus towards price reductions will be dependent upon the availability of competitive substitutes, upon potential competition, and upon the profit-seeking policies of companies that remain in business. The Monopolies Commission examined the concentration contention with care. An interesting example occurred in the copper semis inquiry.

The Federation argued that member companies, in the absence of price arrangements, would specialize individually in particular groups of commodities. A considerable degree of monopolistic power might result. The Federation admitted that the price agreements encouraged the existence of suboptimal sized firms, but contended that the scale advantages thereby sacrificed were outweighed by the greater effectiveness of competition currently existing.

The Monopolies Commission noted that large-scale expensive plant was used in the industry, especially for hot-working. Continuous operation of such plant was essential on profitability grounds. The nature of the production function, therefore, encouraged concentration. Potential competition, particularly from industrial consumers, provided adequate safeguards against abuse of a dominant market position. The Monopolies Commission was undoubtedly influenced by the evidence of wide cost differences in the industry. It was convinced not only that the price arrangements encouraged undue diversification of production, but that it provided effective shelter for high cost firms.[1]

The Commission placed greater emphasis upon the evils of high cost production than upon the risk of a dominant company taking advantage of its market position. The Monopolies Commission was prepared to rely upon the constraints imposed by the competitive process as a safeguard against the latter phenomenon. It remains to be seen whether this confidence was ill-placed.

[1] At the time of investigation there were about 140 concerns in the industry of which seventy accounted for 75 per cent of output. The scope for concentration was, therefore, very great.

PRICE AGREEMENTS AND COUNTERVAILING POWER

A number of economists[1] see no problems for public policy in relation to market dominance. They look to automatic safeguards provided within the capitalist system to prevent activities that run counter to the public interest. They suggest that the existence of monopolistic powers in selling will encourage the establishment of monopsonist powers on the other side of the relevant markets; these powers would be used to curb the sellers' attempts at exploitation.[2]

This theory has been severely criticized both on grounds of logic and on grounds of fact in recent years.[3] One might expect, nevertheless, that trade associations faced by powerful purchasers would rely upon the countervailing power argument as a justification for their restrictive practices. There were two forms in which the defence occurred: (a) that price agreements prevent exploitation by powerful buyers and (b) that powerful purchasers safeguard the public interest.

Countervailing Power and Fear of Depressed Prices

A number of trade associations pleaded that powerful buyers, in the absence of price arrangements, would take advantage of their members and impose drastic price reductions upon the trade; this would culminate in deterioration of quality, research and development, and new investment. The price systems eliminated the danger of such developments. The contention was put forward by the British Electrical and Allied Manufacturers' Association, with regard to price fixing in the supply of turbines and transformers for the British market.

The Central Electricity Authority had purchased 78·5 per cent of the turbines and allied equipment supplied by the associated companies in 1952 to the domestic market. Together with the Area Boards, the Authority had accounted for 66 per cent of the transformers supplied by these companies for the domestic market in 1952. The Groups pleaded that their selling position, in the absence of a price system, would be exploited 'by these great monopolies'.[4] The Central Electricity Authority would pressurize individual producers into price reductions. The negotiated prices would subsequently become standard throughout the industry; production would become uneconomic.

The argument did not convince the Monopolies Commission. The

[1] e.g. J. K. Galbraith, *American Capitalism*, The Concept of Countervailing Power, London, Hamish Hamilton, 1957.

[2] J. K. Galbraith, 1957, ibid., p. 119. 'In the typical modern market of few sellers, the active restraint is provided not by competitors but from the other side of the market by strong buyers.'

[3] For a devastating critique of the concept see G. Stigler, *Proceedings of the American Economic Association*, 1954.

[4] op. cit., 1957, p. 238.

common price system had been operated long before the establishment of the Authority; the latter had attempted, consequently, to stimulate price competition or obtain a justification for prices charged on the basis of disclosed costs. Member firms had strongly resisted all attempts to obtain cost disclosures. The CEA had therefore concentrated upon fostering competition in the industry. One manufacturer, Parsons, had left the Association and the CEA had promised to place a specified volume of orders with the company in consideration for its lower prices. In the case of transformers the CEA had made use of independent competitors to lower the price level. It had persuaded certain independants to manufacture large transformers; this competition placed a constraint upon Group prices. The CEA would have been prepared to invite tenders from all manufacturers if the market had been competitive; it would have placed its order with the lowest tender 'provided it was satisfied that they had the capacity available to give the required delivery'.[1] The CEA had no desire to encourage uneconomic prices and would carefully examine exceptionally low tenders from this viewpoint.

The Monopolies Commission concluded that the unification of the electricity supply industry had not greatly affected the balance of bargaining power between buyer and seller. Abolition of the price arrangements would not tip the balance decisively against the manufacturers. The Monopolies Commission rejected the Association's contention. Its conclusion was scarcely surprising. The nationalized industries have been criticized, in general, not for attempting to exploit dominant buying powers, but for being insufficiently cost-conscious and for failing to shop around for supplies. The large public companies concerned in the inquiry were capable individually of negotiating on equal terms with the Central Electricity Authority.

The problem of dominant buying power may assume greater significance where it lies in private hands. The Monopolies Commission was faced with this contention in the hard fibre cordage inquiry. The Federation pleaded that its members faced highly organized buyers, in addition to powerful raw material suppliers. Member companies would face serious hardship if restricted from countering such power collectively.

The Monopolies Commission was not impressed. It considered economic pressure from purchasers to be unlikely. Hard fibre cordage formed an insignificant outlay for most users and there was no evidence that they were cost-conscious. The only really dominant purchaser was the National Association of Rope and Twine Merchants, whose members handled rather less than 10 per cent of hard fibre cordage sold by the Federation in Britain. There was no evidence that this Association had been able or interested in exerting abnormal pressure upon price-levels in the industry.

[1] op. cit., 1957, p. 225.

It is rarely in the self-interest of monopsonistic purchasers to press uneconomic prices upon suppliers, especially if they intend to remain in the industry for a considerable time-period. In the long-run their attempts will result in quality deterioration of supplies or a reduction in the size of the supplying industry and a reversal of the market bargaining position. The technique may be tempting for 'fly-by-night' purchasers intent upon short-term profit. Such companies are unlikely to possess monopsonist power. Alternatively, evidence may be produced that buyers assume an unduly optimistic view of suppliers' unit production costs. It is right that the Monopolies Commission treated such suggestions with suspicion.

Countervailing Power as a Public Safeguard

The argument that powerful purchasers prevent monopolistic price fixing associations from exploiting their position was examined frequently by the Monopolies Commission. Where the trade association is faced by dominant industrial buyers the argument has its points. Industrial buyers are likely to have the detailed cost information required to estimate (a) whether prices are reasonable in relation to unit production costs and (b) whether the costs themselves indicate low or high efficiency levels in the supplying industry. Industrial purchasers are likely to hold the threat of backward integration should they be dissatisfied consistently with the supplies they receive. In boom conditions, however, purchasers may not be cost-conscious; they may feel able to pass on cost additions to the final consumer.[1] An interesting example of purchasing dominance relating to producer goods occurred in the electric wires and cables industry.[2] The Cable Makers' Association operated an effective price fixing agreement for supertension and mains cable. The Association was faced with a preponderant buyer, the British Electricity Authority, which accounted for 73 per cent of mains cables purchases in Britain and 87 per cent of supertension cable. The Monopolies Commission recognized that the Authority was powerful enough to insist upon reasonable prices from the Association.[3] The Authority had recently arranged an independent cost investigation of the six types of cable produced by the Association, and the Commission praised this innovation. It decided not to condemn the price arrangements as long as the CMA was prepared to submit costs for regular investigation by the BEA. The purchasers of mains cable other than the BEA, however, would

[1] Indeed, if they operate on a cost plus per cent mark-up, they may increase their profits per unit. (Not necessarily total profits however.)

[2] Report on the Supply of Insulated Electric Wires and Cables, 1952. H.C.P. 209.

[3] ibid., p. 79. 'It does not seem to us, however, that this situation in which a near monopoly buyer faces a near monopoly seller should, or could, be transformed into one of ordinary competition.'

not be protected by such action. The Monopolies Commission, therefore, recommended that Association prices to these purchasers should bear a direct relationship to prices for BEA supplies, and that the relationship should be made known to all buyers.[1]

A similar plea, by the Non-Ferrous Metals Federation,[2] was dismissed by the Commission. The Commission discovered that backward integration by powerfully organized purchasers was discouraged by price discrimination; certain non-standard specifications were supplied at prices below the average cost of production. The Commission concluded that this policy discriminated in favour of the large customer, and provided no safeguard against unreasonable prices in general. The preponderant buyers in this industry were not nationalized corporations.

Even where the buyer is dominant, vigilant, and State-owned the Commission has examined circumspectly for undesirable side effects.

An instance is found in the inquiry into land telephone cable price arrangements operated through the Cable Makers' Association. The General Post Office placed a bulk order for land telephone cable with the Telephone Cable Makers' Association.[3] This order was subsequently allocated among Association members. The negotiated agreements between the GPO and the Association covered a five year period. Prices were fixed on the basis of cost investigations conducted by the GPO. Cost reductions achieved during the currency of an agreement would not be passed on in reduced prices until the next agreement. The GPO was fully satisfied with this system.

The Monopolies Commission was less happy. The system had resulted in 'something very like a "closed shop" in land telephone cable, and the obvious danger to be guarded against is that of excessive rigidity and lack of enterprise on the part of the organized industry and of the permanent exclusion of "new blood" '.[4] The Commission accepted that recent modifications had lessened this rigidity, allowing the GPO freedom to purchase cable embodying new techniques from concerns outside the TCMA. In addition orders could be placed with independent producers where this would aid British exports. The Commission concluded that the GPO should not limit its future purchases exclusively to TCMA supplies, and that its bulk orders to the Association should be publicly announced so that independent firms would be aware of commercial opportunities. The Commission stressed its concern that the GPO should take full precautions to maintain efficient independent competition in the telephone cable making industry.

[1] This latter recommendation was later rejected by the Board of Trade (infra).

[2] Report on the Supply of Cast Iron Rainwater Goods, 1951. H.C.P. 136.

[3] The GPO accounted for 90 per cent of sales of telephone cable in the British market.

[4] op. cit., p. 84.

The Monopolies Commission reacted favourably to the countervailing power defence of price fixing arrangements where nationalized industries accounted for a substantial majority of trade association supplies. It was concerned throughout lest the close relationship between Association and buyer should encourage undue rigidity within the producing industry, and in particular lest independent competition should be eliminated or potential competition be rendered ineffective. The Monopolies Commission would ascertain whether the buyer in question was able and willing to insist upon cost investigations and to maintain a reasonable relationship between prices and unit production costs. In this respect it displayed greater suspicion where private enterprise buyers were concerned than it did with State-owned buyers. Many economists would criticize this dichotomy. The lack of cost-consciousness in the nationalized industries has been criticized throughout the postwar period. Inadequate cost inquiries might allow trade associations to maintain unduly high prices and excessively high cost production. A more healthy suspicion of the nationalized industries' role of public watch-dog was required especially where the nationalized industry itself was under no pressure to lower costs in order to fulfil its statutory obligations.

PRICE AGREEMENTS AND EXPORTS

Trade associations defended price fixing agreements on the grounds that they improved the United Kingdom balance of payments and/or increased the volume of exports. Separate arguments were put forward in relation to price fixing for domestic supplies and price fixing for export production.

Domestic Price Agreements and Exports

Certain trade associations, subject to periodic fluctuations in domestic demand, contended that price wars would eliminate efficient productive capacity, would endanger research and development within the industry, and would eventually lead to quality deterioration. These developments might damage export trade. If high quality production was maintained for the export market alone, unit production costs would be higher for such supplies unless available internal economies of scale were limited. On the other hand, if low quality/cheaper priced exports proved attractive to overseas buyers the UK balance of payments might suffer. Where the import content of exports was high, and conversion costs were relatively low, cheaper exports might lower net foreign exchange earned, even though the profit of individual suppliers remained at a satisfactory level.

Some would contend that a sound domestic market, reinforced by price arrangements, might provide a useful basis upon which to launch an export drive. Companies would be able and willing to indulge in export sales promotion. They might be prepared to lower export prices in the face of keen competition. Action of the latter variety might contravene the General Agreement on Trade and Tariffs. Dumping on the part of overseas producers in the British market is resented by British suppliers. Nevertheless the nationalism involved in the suggestion would not be disqualified before the Monopolies Commission. The 1948 legislation was overtly nationalistic.

On the other hand a high domestic price level, by reducing the volume of sales on the domestic market, might prevent companies from the exploitation of internal scale-economies; export prices might be unduly high as a result, perhaps leading to unduly low export earnings. Furthermore, a soft domestic market may provide little stimulus towards active entry into keenly competitive export markets. Lack of interest in developing export markets has been a recurrent criticism of domestically-protected British companies. The Monopolies Commission has not concerned itself seriously with analysing export trade in the absence of a specific export reference. The linoleum inquiry is a case in point.

The Linoleum Manufacturers' Association defended its domestic price system as being beneficial to the British balance of payments. The Association argued[1] that price competition would result in quality debasement, and that this would render imported raw materials a more important part of total export price than occurred under the price system. Lower net earning of foreign exchange would result. The Monopolies Commission was favourably impressed by the argument. In the absence of a specific export reference, however, it refused to examine in detail the effect of the domestic price scheme upon linoleum exports.[2] In this respect the Monopolies Commission misinterpreted its terms of reference. Export revenue is of great importance to the British public interest. In addition, insofar as an increase or reduction of export sales might affect unit production costs in the domestic market, and/or investment decisions, the domestic impact may be of very great importance. A detailed examination of export performance should have been conducted in inquiries relating to the domestic market. The Monopolies Commission must be seriously criticized for failing to do so.

[1] This argument is dependent upon certain assumptions regarding demand elasticity.

[2] LMA. 'The Monopolies Commission investigation was confined to the home trade only, and it is to be hoped that, because of the restricted nature of the terms of reference, for which the Commission was in no way responsible, it will not have been led to conclusions which it would not otherwise have reached, and which in the last analysis would be damaging to the country's export earnings.'

British Export Price Agreements

Armed with an export reference, the Monopolies Commission was fully prepared to examine price fixing agreements between British firms relating to export trade. The Groups concerned in the BEAMA inquiry operated common minimum price systems for export sales. They argued that the price agreement was the fundamental part of a system involving the exchange and pooling of export market information in the electrical and allied plant industry. In addition the minimum price arrangements maintained export prices at the highest levels possible, having regard to overseas competition; on occasion they maintained higher export earnings than would have obtained under price competition.[1]

The Monopolies Commission was concerned lest a dislike on the part of overseas purchasers of collective pricing systems should lose orders for British manufacturers. An intensive investigation demonstrated that one such order, the Snowy Mountains contract, had been lost on these grounds, despite a highly competitive Group tender.[2] This risk was considered a disadvantage of the collective system. However, the Commission condemned the price agreements for exports on more general grounds. It stressed the advantages of allowing each manufacturer to operate independently in the light of his own costs of production and capacity of operation. The Commission recommended that the export price agreements should be terminated.

International Price Agreements

In its examination of export references, the Monopolies Commission discovered a number of international price agreements. British trade associations argued that international agreements were necessary to protect their export markets, and to secure their export earnings. They were at pains to demonstrate their freedom to extend overseas market shares through indirect forms of price competition.

The whole question of international price agreements was examined in the copper semis inquiry. British manufacturers were involved in two major international price agreements. The Lausanne Agreement required signatories to observe each other's domestic prices in their individual markets, whilst a further agreement obliged them to observe minimum prices in the majority of remaining markets.

The British Federation claimed a discouraging outlook for exports; copper prices had risen much more rapidly than general price levels and

[1] This could occur where keen price competition between British firms lowered export prices below that obtainable as a Group. The Groups indicated that, especially in the case of large plant, on-off production prevailed and lower prices were highly unlikely to increase quantity demanded.

[2] op. cit., 1957, p. 160. 'In this instance, at least, the collective judgment appears to have defeated its own purpose by failing to foresee, or give sufficient weight to, the purchaser's dislike of collective tendering.'

this had rendered copper semis vulnerable to competition from substitute materials.[1] At the same time there was a growing tendency for former importing countries to manufacture their own copper semi requirements. The Federation feared that surplus production might be sold in world markets at uneconomic prices. The common minimum price system acted as a barrier to such destructive competition.

The Monopolies Commission agreed that termination of the Agreements might result in lower export prices. This would damage the British balance of payments unless demand was price elastic. The Monopolies Commission was convinced that overseas demand for copper semis was price elastic. In particular lower export prices would enable British manufacturers to enter markets previously completely closed to them, and thereby to extend the range and variety of their products.[2] The Commission felt that the international agreements discouraged cost reductions and concentration of production in low cost units. The Monopolies Commission admitted the speculative nature of its conclusions;[3] it was dissatisfied, nevertheless, with certain aspects of the international agreements, insofar as they related to exports.

The Monopolies Commission did not always find it easy to obtain information relevant to export agreements. It had no powers to demand information from overseas signatories and was pressed occasionally into intelligent speculation. The fault, in this respect, lay not with the Monopolies Commission, but with economic nationalism in the Western World. Indeed, the British legislation of 1948 imposed a nationalist interpretation of the public interest upon the Monopolies Commission. This prevented any discussion by the Commission of the international welfare implications of international or national agreements affecting exports. Any criticism attaching to this limitation must be aimed not at the Monopolies Commission, but at the legislation of 1948 as subsequently modified.

PRICE AGREEMENTS, RESEARCH, DEVELOPMENT, AND INNOVATION

The majority of trade associations subjected to a Monopolies Commission inquiry urged the importance of price fixing schemes for co-operation in research and development, and thereby for the provision of investment opportunities. The Monopolies Commission always examined

[1] It will be remembered that raw material costs formed a heavy proportion of total cost of copper semis production.

[2] Presumably without sacrificing economies of specialization.

[3] It would be impossible to forecast the reaction of overseas Governments to successful independent competition by British producers in their markets.

research and development arguments together; there are sufficient distinctive features, however, to warrant individual treatment.

Research has been defined as 'attempts on the part of firms consciously to organize for the purpose of increasing the flow of inventions'.[1] Research may be concerned with technique, management, organization and marketing. It is inaccurate to associate research only with the first-mentioned aspect of business enterprise. Organization for research normally involves employment of specialists to study problems of fundamental and/or applied importance. In addition such organization may be extended to encompass voluntary suggestions and data supplied by outside researchers.

Co-operation in research matters between a number of legally independent firms may involve a sharing of independently-produced research knowledge; or it may be extended further to provide for participation in co-operative research programmes. Companies would then pool, in addition to relevant knowledge, experts, laboratories and research equipment. The two systems merit individual examination.

At first sight the advantages of sharing research knowledge seem clear and unambiguous. The more rapidly scientific knowledge spreads throughout the economy the greater the likelihood of important commercial innovations of benefit to the general public. In reality however the situation is more complex. A major incentive towards research under regulated capitalism are the quasi-rents offered to successful companies supported by the patent system. Automatic sharing of research knowledge may imply the sacrifice of such quasi-rents on the part of successful companies. At best it must involve a shortening of the period in which quasi-rents may be extracted. The incentive towards research may be weakened by research sharing arrangements.[2] This may react to the long-term detriment of the general public. Even where the most enterprising companies maintain an active interest in research, co-operation may provide less active participants with the opportunity to cease all research and to rely parasitically upon the research results of others.

Moreover, research sharing schemes may result in less-intensive research efforts, since the fear of market-loss through successful research by rival companies is weakened.[3] Time-lags in the provision of invention are often of critical importance in a dynamic economy, where one invention provides a launching-pad for further research programmes.

[1] Jewkes, D. Sawers, R. Stillerman. *The Sources of Invention*, London, Macmillan, 1961, p. 129.

[2] Most particularly this is likely where the research expenditure is likely to be heavy, the risk of complete failure relatively high, and market penetration from a successful invention relatively low.

[3] In many industries the main emphasis of the competitive process in recent years has moved from price stategy to the research laboratories.

This further underlines the complexity of the relationship between research sharing and the public interest.

An analysis of the economic consequences of active co-operation in research is obstructed by a shortage of empirical data. During the post-war period it has become a fetish on the part of certain economists to laud the advantages of large-scale organization of research,[1] contending that individual researchers and small-scale research organization no longer play an important role in the dynamic process.[2] They contend that scientific frontiers are now so advanced and, moreover, are advancing so rapidly that research must be conducted in expensive laboratories with large teams of experts drawn from varying academic disciplines. Broad generalizations of this kind are drawn from the thinnest possible empirical evidence.

One recent study[3] does not fully support the contention that research must be conducted upon the grand scale. Detailed examples are provided of important inventions in recent years that resulted from the research of individual inventors and from small-scale research laboratories.[4] Indeed it may be argued that many forms of research are better carried out by individuals or by small research teams freed from the intellectual discipline characteristic in large research laboratories under the supervision of a research director. It is often the fresh approach, possibly from a relatively untrained, relatively unconditioned mind, that provides the degree of originality essential for a fundamental discovery.[5] Another danger of large-scale research is that of introversion. A large-scale organization may develop resistance to outside ideas in a manner alien to a small laboratory. As a result valuable ideas may remain unexplored on the ground that no organization is receptive to their importance. Competitive research may be wasteful, it is true, but the wastefulness is essentially an *ex post* assessment. On occasion the existence of competitive teams may result in a faster solution to a problem; on

[1] J. K. Galbraith. *American Capitalism*, 1957, p. 91. 'There is no more pleasant fiction than that technical change is the product of the matchless ingenuity of the small man forced by competition to employ his wits to better his neighbour. Unhappily it is fiction. . . . Most of the cheap and simple inventions have, to put it bluntly, been made.'

[2] A. Hunter. *Lloyds Bank Review*, October 1956. 'The days when one individual's inventiveness and enterprise could transform an industry are in the past. In this context the big firm again shows to advantage. Perhaps we are labouring the obvious. These are well-known facts of economic life.'

[3] J. Jewkes, *et alia*, 1958, op. cit.

[4] To cite a few examples: A. Fleming—Penicillin; E. J. de Normanville—Automobile Transmissions; A. Steckel—Steel Rolling Process; K. Gillette—Razor Blades.

[5] J. Jewkes, *et alia*, 1958, op. cit., p. 116. 'If invention ever became the prerogative of full-time professional employees there are grounds for believing that it would be weakened in range, liveliness and fertility.'

occasion it may result in discoveries of unexpected but fundamental importance.

Even should it be assumed that co-operation in research is beneficial to the public interest, it is by no means certain that price fixing agreements are a necessary complement to such arrangements. In Britain contentions of this kind have only become commonplace since the end of the Second World War.

Trade associations suggested on a number of occasions that price agreements created an atmosphere of security which was conducive to co-operation between firms in the field of research. They considered that such co-operation must be an advantage of the price fixing agreement.

It is far from easy to see why price fixing agreements, in the absence of further restrictions, should encourage the more progressive companies to share the fruits of their individual research programmes with less progressive parties to the agreement. Indeed, since competition through price would be eliminated in a direct form, progressive companies might well wish to take full advantage of other facets of the competitive process to expand their share of the association's total market. Where the price agreement was fortified by secondary market-sharing agreements there would be less incentive to withhold research information. But in the latter case further rigidity would be imposed upon the structure of the market and upon the performance of individual members of the association.

A closely-regulated price agreement, supported by a market-sharing system, may prevent market expansion on the part of the more efficient companies within the trade association. If this results in a more atomistic industrial structure than would be justified on scale grounds, the implications may be serious for research at the company level. The companies that are party to the agreements may be too small to carry viable research units of an individual variety. In the absence of the agreement the more successful companies might have been able to produce independent research units.

In such cases, co-operation in research, supported by restrictive arrangements of one kind and another, may be undesirable. The loss of the competitive impetus, not only in the broad strategies of the companies concerned, but also in the field of research itself, may be an excessive price for the general public to pay for research programmes that could be secured under conditions of free competition.

Development may be defined as the application of known methods to new or existing problems. The ground for development has normally been prepared by prior research programmes and consequent inventions.[1] At the development stage commercial or market considerations

[1] J. Jewkes, 1958, *et alia*, op. cit., p. 18. 'Invention is the stage at which the scent is first picked up, development the stage at which the hunt is in full cry.'

are systematically analysed to prepare the ground for subsequent innovation.

Economists are on strong ground in contending that development costs have increased spectacularly during the twentieth century. Small companies may be unable to obtain the necessary finance to undertake commercially attractive development programmes on their own. Co-operative development may provide a satisfactory solution.

In many respects development expenditure is less subject to uncertainty than research expenditures. The alternative forms of action have been reduced by the specific fruits of research. Therefore the danger that co-operation will rigidify companies' operations is less important in development than in research. Co-operative development programmes may eliminate wasteful competitive expenditure. Whether or not price fixing agreements are necessary for such co-operation is another matter. Associations argue that the security of price-fixing stimulates companies into co-operative development and innovation of inventions.[1] On the other hand, if the companies are effectively sheltered from competition, there may be little incentive to proceed with development which may transform production techniques. Reluctance to develop inventions may persevere in the face of high prospective profits if members fear that the innovation might eventually expose them to competition from companies currently operating in other fields.[2]

Allegations that important inventions had been destroyed or immobilized by trade associations were common during the inter-war period. Evidence accumulated by the Monopolies Commission and the Restrictive Practices Court has not substantiated such allegations. Information is difficult to obtain and the destruction of a series of individually less important inventions may have very serious effects upon development in the longer term. If price agreements inhibit the expansion of progressive firms they may consider that the risks and expense involved in expensive development and innovative campaigns are unjustified.

The Monopolies Commission usually examined the impact of price fixing agreements upon research, development and innovation simultaneously. An interesting instance occurs in the insulin Report.[3] In 1949 members of the British Insulin Manufacturers agreed 'to the fullest possible extent and with the fullest exchange of technical information to collaborate in a field covering *inter alia* "all aspects of research, develop-

[1] ibid., p. 182. 'It is odd that stability, through the suppression of price competition, should be sought for as a means of speeding up innovation, which in itself is a form of instability.'

[2] The development of electrically powered motor cars would open up motor-car assembly to competition from large electrical engineering companies such as Associated Electrical Industries.

[3] Report on the Supply of Insulin.

ment and production . . ." '.[1] Members were prohibited from providing information or from granting licences under any patents resulting from collaboration to non-members of the BIM.

In fact the essential know-how of the BIM was not protected by patents; it was a closely-guarded secret. The BIM regarded their know-how as a principal factor in the high rate of yield obtained from available pancreas. At the time of the inquiry members were involved in a carefully worked out programme of research in which the scientific staff of members of the BIM co-operated with various academic workers. The Ministry of Health and the Director of Biological Standards of the National Institute for Medical Research commended British insulin as being of extremely high quality and praised the successful research endeavours of the British manufacturers.

The Monopolies Commission was satisfied by the extent and thoroughness of technical collaboration within the industry. It noted valuable improvements introduced by the BIM concerning the packing and presentation of insulin. It was pleased by the existing programme of research in the industry. The Commission had no fears that collaboration within the BIM might prove detrimental to individual companies' collaboration with overseas manufacturers. The Commission considered that American producers in particular were in no position to offer useful information to the British manufacturers.

It would appear, however, that the Commission was excessively eager to associate valuable developments in insulin production with price arrangements in the industry. A careful examination does not justify the Commission's view. Following the initial discovery of insulin by Banting, protamine insulin had been introduced by Dr Hagadorn of the Nordisk Insulin Laboratorium before 1936. Protamine zinc insulin had been discovered at the University of Toronto in 1937. Globulin insulin had been derived by the American subsidiary of Burroughs Wellcome, the nearest instance of a major British innovation, and NPH insulin had been derived by researchers at the Nordisk Laboratorium. The evidence indicates that outstanding innovations had not evolved from British companies either before or after the price association was formed.

The Electric Lamp Manufacturers' Association[2] operated a patent pool at the time of investigation. A complex system of cross-licensing of patents provided complete freedom of access for members to the research results of any signatory company. At the time of investigation six members of the Association operated research programmes. Two companies, British Thomson-Houston and the General Electric Company, did so on a very large scale. Research programmes covered materials, glass technology, lamp design, and certain special applications of light-

[1] Report on the Supply of Insulin, p. 23.

[2] Report on the Supply of Electric Lamps, 1951. H.C.P. 287.

ing. Under international agreements the larger companies obtained benefit from a great deal of overseas research.

The Association contended that common manufacturing prices were an essential and fundamental feature of the entire organization without which the component members of ELMA would not be prepared to co-operate. The voluntary waiving of exclusive rights to a patent—a direct result of pooling—implied that a new invention or development became available to the public at the earliest possible moment, through the widest possible distributive channels. The Association had decided to adopt an even more liberal attitude in the future. The proposed licensing arrangements guaranteed access for non-member companies to all ELMA patents on the condition that they maintained Association prices for the relevant products and paid reasonable royalties.

The Monopolies Commission agreed that the exchange of technical knowledge between companies was desirable. The Commission agreed that the price system was a prerequisite for the scheme's continued existence. In allowing the association to maintain its price system the Commission stressed that the Association should extend the exchange of technical knowledge to all manufacturers within the system of common prices.

Once again it would seem that the Commission was too easily seduced by the Association's argument. Evidence relating to innovation within the electric lamp industry does not substantiate the Commission's conclusions. The commercial development of the electric lamp commenced in 1878 with the simultaneous invention of the carbon filament lamp by Swan in the UK and Edison in the USA. Patent disputes between the two companies ended in 1883 with the formation of Ediswan.

Between 1906 and 1935 British companies were not responsible for any technical development of significance. They played little or no part in the innovation of sodium and high pressure mercury vapour lamps in the mid-1930s; they claimed responsibility for the development of the modern fluorescent lamp, but appear to have been preceded in the field by the American General Electric Company, who marketed the product in 1938, a year ahead of British Thomson-Houston. The Commission appears to have paid too much attention to research expenditure, too little to practical results and to overseas comparisons, in evolving its conclusions.

The Monopolies Commission was far more critical of the defence in the copper semis inquiry. The Federation argued that collaboration on price had directed competition into research and development; the Federation argued that industrial stability encouraged investment in new methods of production and in the development of new products. The Federation's Research Association had been constituted in 1920 and had provided important discoveries relating to ships' condensers following difficulties during World War One. The Development Association had developed light gauge copper tube for domestic water services as an alternative to lead piping. The Federation considered that the industry had an outstanding record in the development of technical improvements.

The Monopolies Commission was impressed by the Federation's research. It was not convinced that the research programmes rested on price agreements. Most of the research had been conducted by individual companies actuated very properly by their own commercial interests. The Monopolies Commission was convinced that adequate research on an individual and joint basis would continue to take place in the absence of price agreements.

The Monopolies Commission always paid attention to research, development and innovation in relation to price fixing agreements. The Commission was rarely willing to accept that an end to price arrangements would destroy co-operative research programmes. Where it did accept the thesis it probably overestimated the practical results of research expenditure and underestimated the resilience of teams of scientists in resisting attempts at eliminating their programmes. The Commission may be criticized for a lack of attention to research and innovation in non-technical spheres.

PRICE AGREEMENTS, WASTEFUL INVESTMENT, AND PRODUCT STANDARDIZATION

Trade associations sometimes argued that their price agreements fostered desirable standardization of production. Monopolistic competition has been criticized by some economists for the 'wastes' supposedly arising from product differentiation. In recent years this argument has been exposed as stemming from untenable welfare assumptions. Nevertheless, under keenly competitive conditions a great deal of product differentiation may occur and very limited attempts at standardization may economize in the use of resources.

The Metal Windows Association stressed the contributions made by its price system towards standardized production. The British Standards Institution agreed that the Association's contribution compared favourably with that of trade associations in most other industries. The Commission, however, considered that co-operation in standards would proceed—as it had done in the 1920s—in the absence of price agreement. In addition the MWA pointed out that differential rates of profit were applied in calculating prices to discourage or to encourage the sale of specified windows; the system had been devised to reap the cost reductions involved in long runs. The Monopolies Commission decided that the common price system was in no way significant in relation to standardization.

The Federation of Calico Printers defended its Engraving Rental Scheme as deterring converters from making extravagant and wasteful demands for engraving, and from reserving the right to the use of designs in markets in which they were not interested, thereby restricting their full exploitation. The Monopolies Commission did not dispute these results; it considered the system a sensible one for individual printers to adopt. It concluded, nevertheless, that the obligatory nature of the scheme was undesirable, and that the sanctions should be terminated.

The small machinery groups of the British Electrical and Allied Machinery Association provided a price concession scheme for 'special orders'; such orders were subsidized by profits earned on standard orders. The Monopolies Commission condemned the arrangement, arguing that the public interest would be better served if the purchasers of 'special' machines had to choose between paying the full economic price and doing without them. In this manner purchasers of standard equipment would benefit from reduced prices.

The Commission was swift to condemn common price schemes designed to foster product differentiation. It was reluctant to accept that common prices were a prerequisite for product standardization; it was suspicious of agreements which obliged members to penalize demands for product differentiation.[1]

A much less common, but highly relevant, argument related price agreements to co-operative planning of investment outlays and to the flow of market information required for the making of sound investment decisions. Arguments of this kind may be particularly valid where investment expenditure proceeds in large indivisible units, such as strip rolling mills in steel supply; paradoxically it is also relevant where the capital outlay required for new entry into an industry is comparatively low, as for instance in road haulage.

Where investment outlays are indivisible the cost of error may be very high; the result of excessive optimism may be over-investment with consequential excess capacity. Where entry is inexpensive the danger of excessive investment may also be high, most especially where market information is poor. In such cases a high rate of annual bankruptcy may be the price paid for free competition.

It may be argued, therefore, in selected instances, that measures of planning and co-operation should be adopted with regard to investment decision-taking, to reduce market uncertainties to tolerable limits. Trade associations emphasized that such schemes should be privately

[1] T. Wilson (J. Miller, ed.), 1962, op. cit., p. 155. 'Trade associations have performed a useful function in achieving greater standardization, but there is no presumption that in order to do so they must also fix prices. Standardization may undoubtedly make it easier to fix prices if, on other grounds, firms wish to do so.'

organized. An example of public regulation of investment outlays in this country occurred in the steel industry following de-nationalization during the 1950s.

Trade associations occasionally argued the importance of price agreements as vehicles for investment planning at the industry level. They argued that price agreements, reducing the level of production intensity in the light of existing capacity, might succeed in directing the pattern and volume of future investment more efficiently than would result under free competition. The argument implied that the price agreements raised the stability of income expectations, and stimulated pooling of information relevant to investment determination. A number of economists have supported this thesis in a limited form.[1]

On the other hand it would be unwise to evade the dangers involved in such an exercise. Investment planning within a trade association will undoubtedly tighten the effectiveness of a price fixing system. Indeed, investment allocation schemes may limit the expansion of efficient units more efficiently than a simple market sharing scheme. The recent co-operation between French industrial units in the French planning programmes has encouraged the development of market rigidities, and has provided a stimulus to market dominance in France.

It is far from simple to weigh the advantages of investment co-ordination against the advantages of the competitive process. The Monopolies Commission must be criticized for omitting to examine any of the relevant arguments.[2] The omission is serious, indicating a static approach towards problems of price agreements and the public interest.

[1] See G. Richardson, *Information and Investment*, 1960, p. 136.

[2] The problem was touched upon in the rubber footwear inquiry, op. cit., p. 78.

Chapter Seven

TRADE ASSOCIATIONS AND THE COMPETITIVE PROCESS

Competition between producers of homogeneous commodities in price is perhaps the aspect of the competitive process most commonly referred to in economic textbooks. Price competition of this kind is important, of course, and must be closely analysed in any study of the competitive process. On the other hand, there are many other important facets of the competitive process which are not readily recognized by many textbook writers, but which require the attention of any body inquiring into the economic implications of market dominance. This chapter provides a brief analysis of the forces comprising the competitive process, in the light of the inquiries of the Monopolies Commission into the affairs of trade associations.

INTER-PARTY COMPETITION

It is dangerous to assume that all members of a trade association will act jointly with the sole concern of maximizing group profits. Such an assumption ignores the diversity of interest, and the complex pattern of negotiations that are a feature of trade associations. In this respect, the trade association has been likened to an alliance between a group of nations:

> Such an association is similar to an alliance between a group of nations who may be prepared to sacrifice some degree of independence in face of a common peril without abandoning completely their separate interests. The instability of alliances is a familiar theme of political history as rivalries revive and countries try to assert their claims at the expense of their allies. Cartels are likely to experience strains of a similar nature.[1]

Individual companies may be unwilling to accept the conditions required for a maximization of group profit, especially where a considerable loss of independence would be required. Incompatibility of wishes

[1] T. Wilson (J. Miller, ed.), 1962, op. cit., p. 129.

occurs in its most acute form where the spread of unit production costs between members is wide and/or where individual companies conceive substantially different subjective demand schedules either for their own products or for the group in total. Differences of this kind may provoke major conflicts at price review sessions of the association.

Low-cost firms may be reluctant to forgo opportunities for relative expansion *vis-à-vis* high-cost associates. They are likely to press for price levels which would secure satisfactory profit levels for efficient companies but which would seriously distress less efficient parties to the agreement.

It is unlikely, in general, that low-cost producers would insist upon a level of prices capable of forcing many high-cost firms to leave the industry. High-cost parties persuaded to accept the agreement would not lightly contemplate commercial suicide. It is more realistic to assume that low-cost producers would compromise with their fellow-associates to win their co-operation.

At first sight it may appear foolish for efficient companies to fetter their commercial freedom in this way. The reason is found in the lack of close correlation between economic efficiency and economic strength. Large, high-cost, but financially liquid, multi-product firms may threaten lower-cost specialized producers with a subsidized price-war in the absence of price-fixing concessions. Under such threats a compromise solution would normally be obtainable. Indeed it is far from uncommon to encounter price-leadership on the part of high-cost producers, such as the Dunlop Rubber Company in pneumatic tyre production.

A Danish professor, and one-time member of the Danish Monopolies Commission, suggested that, in practice, large companies tended to favour lower prices than smaller companies irrespective of their relative unit production costs.[1] In part this reflected a more circumspect long-run policy on the part of large companies. In part it indicated the greater difficulty of large firms in providing secret discounts from list prices. For this reason large firms had every interest in keeping the cartel price sufficiently low to remove the temptation to offer individual discounts.

Trade associations may be compelled to fix relatively low prices for their commodities, to retain existing membership. High internal prices may encourage ambitious mavericks to expand profitably outside the association under the high association 'price-umbrella'.

Mutual fear and suspicion may be a common feature of trade association meetings. The suspicion may centre not merely upon the immediate motives of companies involved in the price discussions, but also upon their longer term interests. B. Fog illustrated[2] the problems that could

[1] Bjarke Fog, How are Cartel Prices Determined? *Journal of Industrial Economics*, November 1956.

[2] op. cit., p. 23.

arise through excessive inter-company suspicion when attempts were made to raise trade association prices. A trade association in 1955 had been suffering from a general reduction in the level of profits. Each firm within the association wished to raise price in response to the situation. At the meeting, however, each company evaded the issue for fear that its suggestion might be construed as indicating a weak position within the industry. Eventually, a medium sized member of the association broached the subject; two larger companies immediately rejected the proposition in order to demonstrate their strength.

The Monopolies Commission commonly examined the nature of inter-member competition in its assessment of trade association market dominance. An interesting example occurred in the copper semis inquiry. The trade associations established in the industry had organized minimum price schemes. They claimed that the more efficient companies played an important role in price determination. Each firm was free to suggest that it was able to produce any item at prices below the minimum established by the associations. In such instances an appropriate reduction would be made in the minimum prices of the associations involved. The Monopolies Commission was provided with nine instances within one association during 1953 and 1954 in which individual members had requested and had obtained a reduction in minimum prices or alternatively had opposed and prevented a proposed increase in minimum prices.

The Monopolies Commission was dissatisfied with this evidence. Production had rarely been terminated on grounds that individual companies had been unable to operate profitably. Excessively high trade association minimum prices had deprived the public of benefits which would obtain if low-cost producers had been free to lower prices in the light of cost advantages.

Two members of the Electric Lamp Manufacturers' Association—the General Electric Company, and Associated Electrical Industries—customarily took the initiative in proposing changes in lamp prices. The Association contended that prices had never protected high cost producers. The Monopolies Commission accepted this contention, noting evidence of a 'tug-of-war' between high and low cost producers. The prices eventually agreed represented a compromise between divergent interests. During 1952 there had been few instances of individual firms incurring trading losses on the sale of particular categories of lamp. In very weak market conditions this was not surprising since high cost association members would otherwise be eliminated from the industry.

Where there are few producers within an industry and where each producer is aware of potential retaliation against its price adjustments by rival companies prices may be relatively stable. Under such conditions a price fixing agreement may do little more than reflect a situation that would exist in its absence. Should one company be larger and more powerful than its rivals price leadership may develop, with or without collusion. Such was the situation in the rubber footwear industry.[1]

There were eight producers of rubber footwear in Britain at the time of investigation. In 1954 the Dunlop Rubber Company had supplied 45·4 per cent by value of total sales of rubber boots in the United Kingdom, and rather less than 33 per cent of canvas footwear. Consultations between the eight manufacturers occurred through the Rubber Footwear Manufacturers' Association. Uniform prices ruled in the industry.

The Association argued that price uniformity was a natural consequence of perfect competition, and that consultations merely produced competitive results more effectively and rapidly than any other system. In view of the fewness of competitors, and the accepted differentiation of products in the industry at the time, the theory was totally unacceptable. The Monopolies Commission dismissed the contention, emphasizing the existence of product heterogeneity and brand attachment. It concluded that a price agreement did exist and strengthened the natural tendency towards price uniformity in the industry.

The Commission agreed on a number of occasions that inter-member competition might check the abuse of a dominant market position. On no occasion did it feel that this safeguard alone justified the acceptance of a price fixing agreement. It was disturbed by evidence of the continued existence of high cost units and of price compromises accepted by low cost members. The prima facie disadvantages of price compromises, especially where unit costs were spread widely, always proved difficult to shift. Even where there was little prospect of keen price competition in the absence of agreement, the Commission anticipated the development of slightly closer individual relationships between unit costs of production and prices than occurred under price fixing systems.

COMPETITION FROM INDEPENDENT REFERENCE GOOD SUPPLIERS

Competition of this variety is the most commonly-conceived of all forms of competition. The majority of trade associations subjected to a Monopolies Commission inquiry encountered direct competition within their reference field. The effectiveness of independent competition of this kind depends in part upon their proportion of total sales, in part upon the ability and willingness of the association to obstruct independents from expanding and/or to reduce their existing market share; to some extent these factors depend on the comparative cost functions of the trade association members and of the independent producers. In the longer-run the effectiveness of independent competition may be

[1] Report on the Supply of Certain Rubber Footwear, 1956. H.C.P. 328.

dependent upon comparative performances in the field of innovation. Willingness among the independents to compete actively, and not merely to accept sheltered profits provided by a high association price system is clearly of importance in safeguarding the general public from high prices and inefficient production.

Members of the Electric Lamp Manufacturers' Association experienced considerable independent competition.[1] Independent producers normally manufactured general service filament lamps, motor lamps, and specialized products such as flashlamps and miniature medical lamps. They did not produce discharge lamps other than fluorescent lamps and neon tubes. No independent firm produced ranges of filament lamps comparable with those of the General Electric Company and of Associated Electrical Industries. Two independents, Thorn Ltd and its subsidiary Ekco-Ensign, had developed rapidly during the war and produced on a large scale with a high degree of mechanization. Thorn Ltd claimed that it was the largest individual producer of fluorescent lamps in the United Kingdom. At the time of investigation, however, the majority of its production was for export. The Monopolies Commission failed to discover a single attempt by the company to undercut retail prices fixed by the Association in the home market; the Company did claim that it had doubled the life of bulbs which still sold at the Association prices.

The Commission attached great importance to the continued existence of independent competition in deciding in favour of some form of price fixing in lamp production. It recommended that any reduction in the level of independent competition should be treated as a strong ground for introducing a fresh inquiry.[2]

Keen independent competition existed in the lighter sections of copper semi production. A number of small companies competed with trade association members in such fields as fine wire drawing and rerolling of sheet. The Wednesbury Tube Company had been at one time a large, efficient, independent producer of tubes. Its competition had substantially lowered tube prices.

A costing investigation conducted by the Monopolies Commission indicated that members of the Tube Association in 1953 had made losses on their entire tube production; they had reduced prices for Wednesbury's speciality, building service tubes. The latter company, completely specialized in tube production, had feared for its livelihood in the face of subsidized Association supplies. It had decided to enter into the Association's price agreement.

[1] At the time of investigation Independents were responsible for 27 per cent of UK sales of filament lamps and 38 per cent of discharge lamps.

[2] A fresh reference relating to electric lamps was placed before the Commission in late 1965.

The Commission pointed out that further reductions in Wednesbury's costs in the future could be reflected in prices thenceforth only with the consent of the Association, and competition from this source, formerly important, had been restricted. The Commission concluded that 'the prudent independent will be content to sell just below the Association prices and will not allow his trade to expand beyond the point at which members of the Association . . . will act together to undercut him'.[1] The Commission felt that the association prices in general were higher than they would have been if members were to compete actively in price.

The Monopolies Commission attached considerable importance to the existence of vigorous independent competition. Upon occasion, the willingness of the Commission to support price agreements rested upon the pressures exerted through such competition.

COMPETITION FROM NON-REFERENCE GOOD SUPPLIERS

The activities of some trade associations may be constrained by active competition from non-reference good suppliers. A high cross-elasticity of demand often exists between physically differentiated commodities, in the modern industrial economy. Product differentiation need not be a bar to pervasive competitive pressures.

Keen competition from standard wood windows faced members of the Standard Metal Windows Association. Wood and metal windows served approximately the same markets, although wood windows suffered from higher maintenance costs. During the inter-war years the ratio of wood to metal windows for house use had been three to two. Following the war, except for the period of steel economy measures, these proportions had been approximately reversed. In addition, especially where steel was scarce, aluminium windows threatened competition. In general, however, standard aluminium windows remained expensive. The Monopolies Commission was impressed by the existence of competition from wood window producers. The latter's existence confirmed its support for the price agreement in metal windows.

The British Ironfounders' Association supplied cast iron rainwater goods; members were confronted by keen competition from rainwater goods produced with competing materials. In 1949 non-cast iron rainwater goods accounted for 42 per cent of the total market.

Merchants accustomed to handling rainwater goods informed the Monopolies Commission that, whilst competition from other materials might become more or less permanent, there was still a general preference for cast iron. Cast iron sales were helped by the wording of some local authorities' by-laws requiring the use of cast iron or lead.

[1] op. cit., 1955, p. 93.

The Commission felt that the development of alternative materials for rainwater goods had been an outstanding postwar development. Relative price levels were of great importance in determining relative market shares. The Commission was convinced, under the circumstances, that profits on cast iron rainwater goods could scarcely reach excessive levels even if the Rainwater Agreements should remain.

The Monopolies Commission was concerned to estimate the effectiveness of competition. In this task it was not particularly concerned about the source of competition. Non-reference good competition was equally as relevant as competition within the reference field itself. The Monopolies Commission did not feel able to demand information from suppliers outside the reference field. This may have weakened the validity of certain conclusions drawn concerning non-reference goods.

COMPETITION FROM OVERSEAS SOURCES

Imports may provide effective competition for domestic price fixing associations. Nevertheless, competition from imports may not always find Government favour. Dominant trade associations in this country are frequently afforded tariff protection on balance of payments grounds. Imports may be excluded as being excessively competitive, in order to avoid the development of excess capacity in Britain. Trade regulations which limit the importation of cheap cotton textiles from Japan, Hong Kong and India were imposed at the insistence of British textile producers despite the existence of powerful trade associations in yarn spinning and calico printing.

British manufacturers of copper semis were protected by the Government from imported competition at the time of the Monopolies Commission inquiry. *Ad valorem* duties ranging from 15 per cent to 20 per cent had been imposed upon imported copper semis; this constituted a higher level of protection than before the war. In addition, the price of copper had risen more rapidly than the conversion costs involved in producing copper semis. Since import duties were levied on the total price for copper semis this provided further protection for British producers. Protection had been further extended during the postwar period by the virtual exclusion of copper semi imports from dollar countries.

British copper semi producers had been protected from imports by the Government. By contrast, the Linoleum Manufacturers' Association had limited import competition by private means. Despite the existence of an *ad valorem* duty of 20 per cent on imported linoleum, the Association had entered into restrictive arrangements with overseas suppliers. The Monopolies Commission refused to examine the nature of these overseas arrangements pleading that this was not within its terms of reference. It pointed out that the encouragement of linoleum imports might safeguard the general public from the ill-effects of the Association's common price scheme.

Competition from imported commodities played little part in regulating the activities of associations investigated by the Monopolies Commission. In part this was due to the existence of tariffs and of other impediments to trade; in part it was due, undoubtedly, to the competitive prices quoted by British trade associations. The Monopolies Commission was unwilling to press for a revision of tariff policy unless alternative measures designed to stimulate domestic competition were unavailable.

THE ROLE OF POTENTIAL COMPETITION

Trade associations are rarely in a position to disregard the possibility that high association prices, in relation to the unit production costs of low cost producers, may encourage the entry of new companies or the diversification of established companies into their industry. The prudent trade association will always take this risk into account when establishing its prices. A 'no-entry' price ceiling may serve as a reference in determining maximum obtainable prices. Prices exceeding the 'no-entry' ceiling may be allowed where high short-term profits are sought at the expense of inviting new competition. The presence or absence of barriers to new entry will influence the level of the 'no-entry ceiling'. In practice, of course, the 'no-entry ceiling' is highly subjective; errors are bound to occur, both on the part of associations desiring to forestall new competition, and on the part of potential entrants misjudging market possibilities. In the post-war period the most important source of potential competition facing capital goods producers has stemmed from the willingness of customers to expand backwards if such a policy should prove profitable.

The Monopolies Commission always emphasized the importance of potential competition. It carefully examined the nature of barriers to new entry and unfavourable conclusions resulted consistently where trade associations had erected barriers to new entry into their fields. Freedom of entry to a reference market was a corner-stone of the Commission's approach towards association dominance in reference fields.

In the covered conductor industry[1] a number of important consumers had seriously considered the possibility of integrating backwards. There was no protection from imported cables and high trade association prices might encourage keen competition from overseas. The Covered Conductor Association had imposed a condition with regard to its special price discount offers, that consumers should undertake to refrain

[1] Report on the Supply of Insulated Electric Wires and Cables, 1952. H.C.P. 209.

from covered conductors production. The Commission did not consider that covered conductor consumers were sufficiently well-organized to provide an adequate safeguard against undesirable price agreements in the industry.

In the lighter sections of the copper semis industry potential competition acted as a constraint on the prices imposed by the relevant trade associations. In wire drawing, consumers actively competed with the associated suppliers; they drew their own wire requirements. In most sections of copper semi production there were substantial obstacles to new entry. In particular, scale requirements obliged new entrants to commence production on a scale in excess of that justified by their own requirements. It was necessary to dispose of surplus production in difficult marketing conditions. The Monopolies Commission concluded that the effects of potential competition were 'limited in range and rather haphazard in their incidence. They result in discrimination in favour of the large customer and against the small one and they provide no safeguard against unreasonably high prices in general.'[1]

The Monopolies Commission repeatedly emphasized the need to maintain free entry, where this was economically possible. Wherever possible its conclusions were designed to lower entry barriers and, in particular, to increase the possibility of diversified entry from companies established in other industries. The Commission was concerned whenever the opportunity for new entry was limited.

COMPETITION FROM THE STATE

The British Government has not initiated and financed State competition in industries dominated by trade associations. The Labour Party has indicated interest in this kind of State participation, but has not publicly committed itself to such a policy.

State-sponsored competition, financed at market interest rates, and precluded from privileged access to information, might quickly dispose of high cost/high profit production on the part of powerful trade associations. The Monopolies Commission rarely paid serious attention to this remedy.

One member of the Monopolies Commission,[2] in an addendum to the electric lamp Report, asked for Government participation in the industry:

> It seems unrealistic to expect the Controlled Companies to compete freely and effectively with the members of ELMA while they continue to be owned by them. I therefore recommend that the Government should acquire the share capital of these companies at a fair valuation.

[1] op. cit., 1955, p. 94. [2] Mrs Joan Robinson.

> . . . By this means, these companies would be freed to take advantage of the situation created by the abolition of ELMA's exclusive dealing arrangements, a modicum of competition would be permanently secured, and the effect of our other recommendations generally strengthened.[1]

On no occasion was State participation supported by the majority report of the Commission. It may well be that the Commission failed to pay adequate attention to a useful, if publicly controversial, remedy for the more serious abuses of trade association power.

PUBLICITY AND THE COMPETITIVE PROCESS

Inter-war reports on industrial organization and commercial policy stressed the importance of publicity as a constraint upon the activities of powerful trade associations. Indeed certain reports concluded that publicity itself provided satisfactory safeguards for the general public. In the post-1945 period publicity has been considered a less satisfactory safeguard. In part this reflects the increased scope for abusing market power under boom conditions than in periods of depression. In part it reflects the change in the climate of informed opinion, which resulted in monopoly and restrictive practices legislation in 1948 and 1956. The reports of the Monopolies Commission and the case reports of the Restrictive Practices Court certainly provide a modicum of publicity. Active sanctions are feared far more by trade associations. Publicity may help to eliminate the more objectionable practices. It is far less successful in constraining activities which are less unambiguously undesirable; these practices may bear, nevertheless, seriously detrimental consequences for the general public.

THE MANAGERIAL REVOLUTION AND THE COMPETITIVE PROCESS

The Monopolies Commission never made a direct assessment of the impact of the managerial revolution upon the activities of trade associations. It treated member firms as though the interests of management and shareholders were identical. In certain cases this approach is justifiable. Members of trade associations are more likely to be organized upon family lines than are large companies dominant in their own right in specified fields of activity. Family concerns are less likely to be subjected to the divorce between ownership and control which commonly occurs in the giant public limited company. On the other hand, many a trade association can count among its members at least one giant company, the management of which appears to be acting in considerable in-

[1] op. cit., 1951, p. 101.

dependence from constraints of the equity shareholders. The Monopolies Commission frequently encountered such instances.[1]

The Monopolies Commission was never really concerned with assessing the objectives of trade association members. Clearly, of course, the results of trade association action must count more than the objectives which inspired such action. Nevertheless, objectives are not irrelevant. The Commission may be faulted in its neglect in this field.

THE CO-OPERATIVE MOVEMENT AND COMPETITION

In principle it is the policy of the co-operative movement to counteract monopolistic activities in the fields of production and distribution. In practice the extent of such action is limited. A relatively few examples or conscious intervention may be cited. Fifty years ago the Co-operative Wholesale Society took action against the Lever Soap Combine, with a limited degree of success. A few years ago, as a result of a boycott by a wholesale distributors' organization dealing in radio sets, the Co-operative Wholesale Society entered into production with Defiant Radio. Very recently, the Co-operative Movement attempted to engage in the motor car trade at Scunthorpe. Perhaps the most significant attempt by the Movement to counteract a price fixing association occurred in the lamp industry.[2]

The Electric Lamp Manufacturers' Association was formed in 1919, and members accounted for the majority of lamp sales in Britain. In 1925 the organization became international with the signing of the Phoebus Agreement. As a direct reaction to this development British Luma was established in 1937 as a result of an agreement between the Scottish Wholesale Society and the Swedish Ko-operative Forbundet. The company did not commence production until late 1939. The intervention of war deprived British Luma of much of the aid it would otherwise have received from the Swedish Co-operative Movement.

An agreement between the Phoebus Organization and the Swedish Movement, following lengthy patent litigation, tied British Luma firmly to the Phoebus rules. This agreement was formally terminated by British Luma in June 1951. The difficulties faced by British Luma reflect the problems of breaching a tightly monopolistic market. 'In view of its small output, and of the restrictions imposed on its prices and output, it is clear that the existence of British Luma could have exercised little competitive restraint on the electric lamp monopoly before 1951.'[3] The

[1] e.g. Associated Electrical Industries, Imperial Chemical Industries, the Dunlop Rubber Company, and the General Electric Company.

[2] Details are provided by F. Knox, *The Co-operative Movement and Monopoly in Britain*, p. 12.

[3] ibid., p. 14.

company's output increased quite rapidly between 1953–5, and by the latter date the prices of most of its products were below the prices of ELMA members, and below those of the two main independent manufacturers, Thorn and Philips.

At the time of inquiry by the Monopolies Commission, the Co-operative Movement was competing against trade associations in lamps, linoleum, hard fibre cordage, and tea. In no instance did the Commission consider that this competition was effective.

CONCLUSION

The competitive process is a complex concept. The Monopolies Commission approached the subject with considerable understanding and flexibility in the case of trade associations. There are important instances where its interpretation was narrow, but these were few in number. The Commission's approach must be commended in this respect as being more fruitful than that of the United States Supreme Court.

Chapter Eight

TRADE ASSOCIATION AGREEMENTS AND BARRIERS TO INTER-MEMBER COMPETITION

The forces of competition may limit the ability of trade associations to reap the desired fruits of price fixing arrangements. Trade associations are rarely unaware of this. Many associations establish a network of secondary agreements, designed to support and to extend common or minimum price agreements. Secondary agreements of this variety may be designed to prevent inter-member competition from damaging the price arrangements; they may be designed, alternatively, to limit extra-association competition. This chapter provides a short study of agreements, examined by the Monopolies Commission, which might limit inter-member competition.

MARKET SHARING AGREEMENTS AND THE PUBLIC INTEREST

Probably the most widespread and most effective secondary agreements of this kind, market sharing agreements were examined by the Monopolies Commission on numerous occasions. Occasionally, market sharing was a prime aim of the trade association; usually, however, it was a device designed to prevent inter-member competition from destroying the price fixing arrangements of a trade association.

Trade associations frequently argued that price agreements did not forestall competition, but canalized it into desirable fields such as quality improvement, after-sales service, and product innovation. Within these fields competition between members was as keen, and market uncertainty as great, as had existed before the establishment of the price system. Many economists, on the contrary, would argue that market sharing agreements prevent or modify the relative market expansion and decline of member firms, thereby frustrating the purpose of competition by secret price reduction, quality improvement and sales promotion expenditure. Quotas, therefore, are invaluable to associations operating under depressed or under fluctuating demand conditions, where the individual incentive to pare association prices may be great. A few trade associations defended their market sharing agreements as being breakwaters essential to the operation of price systems.[1] There are a number of forms in which market sharing agreements are found. It is important to distinguish between them.

The Fixed Quota

The fixed quota provides for a rigid allocation of sales between member firms, based usually upon such measures as weight, value, volume, or yardage. In practice, fixed quotas are more frequently allocated on the basis of past performance than on an assessment of relative production potential. The fixed quota system, if operated effectively, prevents firms from expanding their sales both absolutely and relative to other members for the duration of the agreement. An effective fixed quota system will rigidify the structure of production within the relevant industry.

The Fixed Percentage Quota

Allocation of output between firms on a percentage basis is less rigid than allocation on a fixed value basis. Within a percentage quota system no penalty attaches to sales expansion as long as all member firms increase their sales at a corresponding rate. The system prevents or penalizes relative expansion by individual members. This may prevent the more efficient companies from eliminating high-cost fellow associates and it may prevent certain companies from reaping the economies of larger-scale production.

The Moving Percentage Quota

The moving percentage quota provides for general sales expansion by the association members but penalizes relative expansion by member companies. Relative expansion in any period, however, is rewarded in subsequent periods by an appropriate extension of the company's percentage quota. Deficit companies are penalized by a corresponding reduction in their percentage allocations.

The moving percentage quota system does not condemn completely relative expansion and contraction within a trade association. The degree of flexibility so afforded may be evaluated only by examination of the penalties exacted for excess sales, the rate by which percentages are modified, and the time-lag between quota adjustments. In practice the moving percentage tends to function slowly and is designed primarily to retain the co-operation of low cost units.

[1] e.g. The Federation of Calico Printers.

Domestic Market Sharing Agreements

The Monopolies Commission encountered relatively few instances of purely domestic market sharing agreements. The majority of associations examined had extended such agreements into the export field. A domestic agreement was examined in the hard fibre cordage industry.

The Cordage Manufacturers' Association had established a moving percentage quota system, relating to domestic sales, in January 1950. Trade shares had been calculated for each year on the basis of output weights reported in the first five of the six years prior to the allocation. Between 1950 and 1953, the trade shares of each participant in every pool had changed. No change had exceeded five per cent of the total trade of any pool and no consistent pattern of change was discernible. The allocation system was defended as providing a safeguard against conditions experienced during the 1930s. The system had been retained during periods of relative prosperity in view of the difficulty of re-establishing it in a depression. The Association contended that payments into the pool were small in relation to profits. On the other hand compensation was sufficiently high to discourage cut-throat competition at times when certain firms had suffered a severe loss of business.

The Monopolies Commission noted that compensation rates were below penalty rates. The Association's contention was therefore difficult to accept. Penalty payments amounted to about 50 per cent of profit margins on excess sales. This was sufficient to lower the incentive to expand, even taking into consideration subsequent quota adjustments. The Commission concluded that the market sharing system was contrary to the public interest and recommended its termination.

Comprehensive Market Sharing Agreements

The Monopolies Commission encountered a number of quota systems covering both domestic and export production. One interesting example was the percentage quota system operated by the Federation of Calico Printers.

The scheme had been introduced by the Federation in 1949, and had been accepted by a large majority of its members. It was designed both as an aid to eliminating surplus capacity within the industry and as a breakwater against instability. The scheme spanned a ten year period, and members were free to leave the scheme only if they ceased to operate as calico printers or ceased to be entitled to a percentage quantum.

The scheme provided for an annual adjustment of the percentage market share initially allotted to each firm by one-tenth of the difference between allocated share and the proportion of total turnover in fact achieved during that year.[1] New entrants were not eligible for this adjustment during their initial year of membership.

The scheme provided for the sale of quanta, in whole or in part, between members. The vendor was obliged to sell his printing machines to the purchaser of his quantum, or covenant with the Print Trade Production Council for their permanent disposal. Penalties and compensation were payable respectively for excess and deficit production. A member in excess during any month paid a sum equal to 20 per cent of the excess turnover into the fund. Those in deficit received a similar sum. Any member who failed to operate commercially for twelve consecutive months could draw no compensation until he resumed operation. Members failing to operate for two years were eliminated from the scheme.

During the initial four years of the scheme six members, including the Calico Printers' Association,[2] had regularly exceeded their market shares. Twelve members had regularly fallen short. The Combined quotas of the six in excess had risen in that time from 58·8 per cent to 62·2 per cent of the total. No member had lost the benefit of his quantum by failing to operate.

The Federation of Calico Printers viewed the PQ scheme as 'a mutual aid and insurance scheme' providing a 'contribution to the uncovered overheads of a member who, owing to the unpredictable hazards of the trade, has not been able to keep his works adequately occupied during a period where one or more such temporary influences affect his particular type of production'.[3]

The Federation considered the PQ scheme as an essential reinforcement to its minimum price arrangements. Without the scheme prices would be cut during those trading periods for which price stability was most important. The Federation argued that the PQ scheme discouraged short-term uneconomic market invasions, but left long-term economic forces fully operative.

The Monopolies Commission concluded that the Federation had exaggerated the need for specialization in the industry. It noted that a number of printers worked in several styles, and that nearly one half of the output of the industry came from one firm, the Calico Printers Association, which worked in every style. The calico printers later refuted this criticism,[4] pointing out that the Calico Printers' Association was an amalgamation producing many styles but preserving a high

[1] op. cit., 1954, p. 34. 'The figure of one-tenth of the difference between quantum and performance for the annual adjustment has been explained as a reward to enterprise which would not endow the *status quo*.'

[2] Allocated a quota of 42 per cent.

[3] op. cit., 1954, p. 61.

[4] C. R. Hargreaves, 'Some Comments on the Calico Printing Industry . . .' C.P.A. Publication.

degree of specialization in each. The remaining firms were much smaller and would sacrifice important scale economies if they diversified without an extension of their total production. Unless the Commission anticipated concentration within the industry, following termination of the quota system, the evidence would suggest that its conclusion was incorrect. The weakness of the Monopolies Commission's approach to economic efficiency was exposed once more to public view.

The Commission pointed out that compensation payment might cause individual printers to delay adjustments in the face of fashion changes, or in the face of generally declining markets. This would dampen flexibility and initiative within the calico printing industry.

The Commission also rejected the claim that the PQ scheme hastened the elimination of redundant capacity by providing the printer with an asset (the quantum) which was worth selling. The Commission pointed out that in fact the scheme might have the opposite effect. Continued receipts from the fund, sustained by the slow rate at which the quantum declined, would encourage a printer to remain in business.

The Commission accepted that in the short-run individual printers might strive for new orders without too much concern for penalty payments. However, in the long run this would not be so.[1] The Commission was influenced by longer term factors in deciding that the PQ system operated in a manner contrary to the public interest.

International Market Sharing Agreements

An international market sharing system was encountered by the Monopolies Commission in the electric lamp industry.

A detailed system had been operated under the 1925 Phoebus Agreement in the lamp industry. Each party or group had then been allotted a local participating percentage in each territory in which it sold lamps. Penalties had been extracted from those in excess of their quota, and compensation had been received by those in deficit. Penalties had increased with the scale of the excess. The British Association had been given a single quota and this had then been allocated among its own members. This exceedingly rigid system had disappeared with the outbreak of the Second World War, and had been replaced in 1948 by the Lamp Agreement. Only British manufacturers together with Philips of the Netherlands were involved. Separate quotas were arranged for each of six main territorial divisions.

The new Agreement based local participating percentages upon those used in the Phoebus Agreement. Penalty provisions, however, were considerably modified. Parties in excess up to 7½ per cent of quota paid into a pool 30 per cent of net profit per unit of excess; on any further

[1] In particular, investment decisions would be conditioned by the PQ scheme.

excess 52½ per cent of the net profit earned was payable. No compensation was obtainable for deficits in excess of 15 per cent of quota. In the first year of the operation of the new system penalty payments amounted to one third of that which would have been extracted under the Phoebus Agreement.

The British Association argued that the quota system mitigated the impact of sales fluctuations, and that it encouraged investment and other long-term commitments, whilst providing adequate incentive for individual manufacturers to increase their market shares.[1] The Association argued that the international quota arrangements had protected the British market from an influx of surplus goods of foreign manufacture at uneconomic prices. It had not resulted in higher lamp prices on the home market.

The Monopolies Commission regarded the quota system with distaste. The system was largely based upon members' shares in 1924 regardless of subsequent changes in relative efficiencies. This rigidity conflicted with the need for flexibility emphasized in Section 14 of the 1948 Act. The Commission could see no justification, under boom conditions,[2] for compensating firms who failed to meet their quota. The Commission was very suspicious of the argument that the penalties were insufficient to dissuade members from maintaining their quotas.[3]

The Commission noted that quotas embraced such different articles as motor lamps and projector lamps. Any increase in a member's share of the market for one type of product must be offset by a decrease in his share for another type unless penalties were to be incurred. In this respect the Commission made special reference to the lack of adjustment in quotas established predominantly on filament lamp sales, consequent upon the introduction of fluorescent lamps. The Commission had no hesitation in recommending that the quota system should be abolished.

The Monopolies Commission in fact recommended that market sharing agreements should be terminated in all instances save insulin production. The latter industry was allowed to maintain an allocation system for ox-pancreas, an essential raw material, at that time in short supply.[4]

In condemning domestic market sharing the Commission emphasized a long run approach. It felt that market sharing rigidified investment plans to an intolerable degree, propped up the inefficient and limited the

[1] ELMA also argued that quotas were essential to the valuable co-operation provided internally between members.

[2] T. Wilson (J. Miller, ed.), 1962, op. cit., p. 140. 'A quota system of this kind seems more surprising in a modern growing industry, such as that producing electric lamps, than in an older industry, such as calico printing.'

[3] op. cit., 1951, p. 96. 'If the lower scale of payment and compensation . . . does not force members to keep to their quotas then an elaborate and unnecessary piece of administrative machinery is being maintained.'

[4] The system died a natural death once supplies became fully adequate.

development of low-cost suppliers. The attitude of the Commission, in this respect, reflected the reversal of inter-war attitudes. The major political parties during the 1930s had committed themselves to market sharing systems. The Commission's approach conflicted also with post-war Government policy in relation to agriculture and Government encouragement of international commodity stabilization schemes. This inconsistency did not pass unnoticed in the industrial sector.

Some critics have attacked the Monopolies Commission—and the Restrictive Practices Court—for its hostility to 'orderly marketing schemes' in times of prosperity.[1] They argue that market sharing is troublesome to organize when times are difficult. The Commission took a more optimistic view of the future of industries under review. The Commission always stressed that long-term dynamic factors must outweigh short-term justifications for market sharing.

The situation regarding international agreements is less clear. Where the scheme was beneficial to British interests the Commission had a clear duty to find in its favour, irrespective of the international gains and losses.[2] In fact no inquiry provided convincing evidence that British producers had been favoured by such a system. It is true that a dominant firm, the British Match Corporation,[3] was involved in such an agreement. Fear of national disadvantage restrained the Commission from recording an adverse judgment regarding the allocation of international markets for matches.

QUALITY AGREEMENTS AND THE PUBLIC INTEREST

Common price schemes may be frustrated, in depressed times particularly, by a tendency for members to improve the quality of a product sold at a specified price. The result is concealed price competition without any alteration in price levels. It is not surprising, therefore, that many common price systems are fortified by ancillary agreements relating to quality.

The Cordage Manufacturers' Association specified the sizes and runnages of cordage that might be offered for sale, and the breaking strains to be quoted. The Commission, noting that these agreements buttressed a common price system, nevertheless accepted that standardization of sizes provided economies in manufacture, and that safety arguments justified the adoption of a conservative basis regarding breaking strain claims.

[1] e.g. P. L. Cook. 'Orderly Marketing or Competition'. *Economic Journal*, September 1961.

[2] See Section 14 of the 1948 Act.

[3] Report on the Supply and Export of Matches and the Supply of Match-Making Machinery, 1953. H.C.P. 161.

The Register adopted by members of the Linoleum Manufacturers' Association contained rules prescribing the thickness to which members could manufacture linoleum, and prohibiting the supply of certain kinds of linoleum with painted back. The Commission concluded that these rules were designed solely to support the common price system. In themselves, they were not undesirable.

The Monopolies Commission usually approved of appropriate quality regulations when consenting to the retention of price fixing agreements. It was not interested in condemning quality agreements when it had condemned price fixing within an association. The Commission adopted a realistic approach to quality agreements. Under conditions of unfettered price competition quality agreements would rarely be of use to members and would be readily abandoned.

DISCOUNT AND REBATE AGREEMENTS AND THE PUBLIC INTEREST

Unregulated discount payments may place a common price system in jeopardy. Many trade associations provide detailed regulations relating to discounts and rebates payable to buyers of specified categories. Such a system was operated by the Cordage Manufacturers' Association. The Association argued on grounds of pre-war experience that common discounts were inevitable with or without the price system. It contended that there were no ancillary dangers of the scheme, such as the raising of new entry barriers. The Commission could see no objection to uniform discounts in the absence of common prices if such discount rates were recommended and in no manner obligatory.

Similarly, the Rubber Footwear Manufacturers' Association had offered uniform terms for prompt payment. The Monopolies Commission did not object to the practice in the absence of price fixing. It was influenced by the existence of substantial bargaining power exercised by consumers. A more complex user discount scheme was operated by members of the Tyre Manufacturers' Conference with application to mileage and replacement tyre sales. Discounts were fixed for users whose aggregated expenditure on car and giant tyres exceeded £500 per annum. A main object of the scheme was the prevention of price-cutting through the grant of excessive discounts to large commercial users. An undesirable side-effect of the agreement was the securing of substantial concessions for large commercial users at the expense of tyre distributors. Nevertheless, the Monopolies Commission refused to condemn the system, arguing that the abolition of price discussions in the industry would itself lead to abandonment of the user discount scheme. In the pneumatic tyre industry the largest producer, the Dunlop Rubber Company, admitted that it had paid confidential allowances to certain distributors in violation of the rules of the Tyre Trade Register, until the rules had been relaxed in January 1954. Dunlop argued that the allowances had been designed to retain old and valued customers and, on occasion, had been made in response to similar allowances provided by rival firms. Secret discounts had never made any serious impact on the trade, and since 1954 they had not contravened any regulation. The Commission considered that Dunlop's allowances did not operate against the public interest.

The Commission was not concerned about common discount systems as such unless they contained built-in barriers to new entry or to effective competition. It considered that discount systems would lose significance upon abandonment of a price scheme; where the price system itself was acceptable common discounts were an essential corollary and should therefore be tolerated.

SALES PROMOTION AGREEMENTS AND THE PUBLIC INTEREST

Common price systems may channel competition into the field of sales promotion and, in particular, into advertising. The aim of advertising is to shift the demand schedule to the right or at least to raise the point inelasticity of the demand schedule. Product differentiation created by advertising may achieve this end. It is not surprising, therefore, that some trade associations regulate the volume and/or direction of members' advertising expenditures.

Perhaps the most interesting instance occurred in the tyre industry. Members of the Tyre Manufacturers' Conference had accepted a limitation on the use of advertising media, which spanned publicity at traders' premises, gifts and other financial inducements to traders. The Conference contended that these restrictions avoided wasteful forms of publicity, and protected the public from misleading quality recommendations. The Commission had no doubt that its primary purpose was to prevent inter-member competition through advertising.

No penalties were provided for non-adherence to the agreement, although the schedules had always been couched in mandatory terms. Since restrictions did not apply to large-scale advertising in the national press the scheme could have only a limited effect in preventing 'wasteful advertising'. The Commission did not condemn the scheme, indicating the broad field of advertising that remained unfettered. The Monopolies Commission implied its opposition to a more tightly-drawn scheme.

Members of the Tyre Manufacturers' Conference were also parties to the Exhibition Bond and Supplemental Agreement of the Society of Motor Manufacturers and Traders. This Agreement prevented them from exhibiting tyres in shows not covered by the Bond. In particular, this affected local and county agricultural shows. The Conference argued that this restriction prevented wasteful sales promotion. The Commission pointed out the detriment to local traders who were unable to exhibit their stock. It recommended that the Agreement should be abolished.

The Monopolies Commission undoubtedly exhibited ambiguity in its attitude towards agreements relating to advertising. Its dilemma was partly a reflection of the public controversy surrounding advertising.[1] In the light of theoretical confusion it was sensible perhaps for the Commission to take a pragmatic view in relation to advertising agreements. The relationships between advertising, inter-member competition, and barriers to entry, are complex, and worthy of further empirical research.

CONCLUSIONS

The Commission was usually opposed to market sharing agreements, even when provisions were included to promote flexibility. It was less concerned by agreements of other kinds designed primarily to support price agreements by restricting inter-member competition. Where a price agreement was eliminated, the Commission was convinced that the ancillary agreements would die a natural death.

[1] For further details see N. Kaldor, 'Economic Aspects of Advertising', *Revue of Economic Studies*, 1950–1, p. 7.

Chapter Nine

TRADE ASSOCIATION AGREEMENTS AND BARRIERS TO INDEPENDENT COMPETITION

Trade associations are usually aware of the limits imposed upon their activities by the existence of independent competition. Restrictive practices are often designed primarily to obstruct and to forestall competition from this source. This chapter examines under four main classifications the form in which such practices were encountered by the Monopolies Commission prior to the establishment of the Restrictive Practices Court.

PRODUCT DIFFERENTIATION, ASSOCIATION BRAND ATTACHMENT AND THE PUBLIC INTEREST

The existence of a strong brand attachment for the products of association members may provide a useful barrier to outside competition, particularly during the short run. J. Bain, in his pioneer work in the field of entry barriers, concluded that 'product differentiation advantages of established firms loom larger than any other source of barriers to entry, and especially large as a source of high and very high barriers'.[1]

Trade associations attempted to raise or to maintain product differentiation barriers to outside competition and new entry by manipulation of association advertising, association patents, and association access to distributive outlets.

Association Advertising

Advertising campaigns on the part of trade associations may rigidify consumer preferences, thereby raising entry costs to outside companies and jeopardizing small-scale independent production. Quasi-rents may be obtained for association members, perhaps to the detriment of the consumer. In addition, heavy advertising expenditure itself may involve

[1] J. Bain, *Industrial Organization*. London, Wiley, 1959, p. 250.

an undesirable mis-allocation of resources in a fully-employed economy. Distortion of preferences through advertising is likely to be more significant for consumer products than in the case of expensive and complex capital products. Mr Justice Burton summed up the position in an American anti-trust suit:

> Such tremendous advertising, however, is also a widely published warning that these companies possess and know how to use a powerful offensive and defensive weapon against new competition. . . . Prevention of all potential competition is the natural programme for maintaining a monopoly here, rather than any programme of actual exclusion.[1]

Economists are divided at present concerning the public interest implications of large-scale advertising. On the one hand consequent market penetration may provide an opportunity to reap scale economies; on the other hand any weakening in the impact of competition may provide for the exploitation of market dominance. Evidence of collusive raising of advertising expenditure by trade associations whenever competition sharpened would certainly have alarmed the Monopolies Commission. In its absence, the Commission was unwilling to condemn individual action. The Commission made little attempt to analyse the relationship between advertising expenditure and market dominance on the part of trade associations. The subject is complex, but complexity alone cannot excuse this omission by a body so keen to ensure freedom of entry under conditions of market dominance.

Patent Agreements

A United Kingdom patent provides the patentee with sole rights to make, use, exercise and vend an accepted invention for a period of sixteen years. After the first four years the continuance of the patent is dependent upon the payment of annual renewal fees; very few patents are in fact renewed. Upon expiration of the patent an invention becomes public property. Patent rights issued in the United Kingdom apply solely to domestic production,[2] although patents for the same invention may be taken out in other countries at the same time. Patentees may assign their rights to others, or may licence producers to use the invention exclusively or non-exclusively. Conditions relating to prices and quantity may be attached to the licence.

In essence patents provide a limited form of monopoly power protected by legislation. At the same time the aim of the patent system is the stimulation of invention and innovation. Patents may sharpen competi-

[1] American Tobacco Co v. USA 328 US 781/1946.

[2] Including domestic production for export.

tion through innovation. Provided that the patenting system is sensible, both regarding the period of protection and the type of invention patentable, the system would generally be considered a just and desirable reward for enterprise.

The danger of abuse from use of patents increases considerably, however, when groups of firms adopt common patent policies to the detriment of independent production. The danger may take various forms, one of which is a product differentiation barrier to competition through denying outsiders access to important techniques or designs used by members of the trade association.

A policy of indiscriminate patenting of multifarious inventions, some economically worthless, some of critical economic significance, may completely bewilder outside firms. Threats of litigation for infringement of patents may persuade independent competitors to apply for Association membership. Less well-established companies may be induced to leave the industry and new entry may be forestalled.

The Monopolies Commission rarely encountered serious allegations of patent abuse by trade associations. The most important case was the electric lamp inquiry. The major British lamp manufacturers had pursued a patent pooling system for many years, adopting a restrictive attitude towards firms outside the Association.[1] In 1920 a Sub-Committee appointed under the Profiteering Acts investigated the industry. It concluded that many Association patents were of doubtful legal validity, but had remained unchallenged through fear of incurring costly legal expenses. The Committee concluded that 'it is undesirable that patent rights should be made an instrument for enforcing a monopoly wider than that afforded under the patents themselves'.[2]

The Monopolies Commission examined the patent activities of the British Association under the Phoebus Agreement most carefully. It concluded that members had regarded aggregate ownership of a number of patents as a useful means of persuading independent manufacturers to enter price/quota agreements and of attacking those who refused to co-operate.[3] In 1937, Crompton Ltd had been forced into signing the Agreement by threats of patent litigation. Following legislation in 1948 and 1949, the Association had revised its patent policy. Members had decided to grant licences at reasonable royalties to all competent lamp manufacturers. These would be issued subject only to acceptance of

[1] One outside company, British Luma, had been treated favourably throughout the inter-war years. This company was a Co-operative Society venture.

[2] H.C. 287, p. 26.

[3] op. cit., 1951, p. 26. 'It is clear . . . that the Phoebus organization intended to pool the litigious resources of the parties with the aim not only of defending the parties' actual patent rights, but also of maintaining the parties' share of the trade generally and of damaging the trade of the independent manufacturers generally.'

Association prices. No limitations on exports or quantity would be imposed.

The Commission welcomed this revision of policy. It recommended careful supervision of the new system and of its effects upon independent competition. The Commission noted that the new policy did not extend to Philips, a company closely collaborating with the Association. The Commission recommended that any abuse of the patent system by this company should be dealt with under the Patents Act of 1949.

Independent producers in the industry complained that association members deliberately accumulated patents to confuse and harass outside firms and to raise barriers to new entry. The Commission carefully examined the patent files of the General Electric Company and British Thomson-Houston[1] but could find no evidence substantiating the fears of the independents. The proportion of patents renewed for the maximum period had not been abnormal, and although one half of the patents in force had not been used commercially, many of these were of recent origin.

In general, the Monopolies Commission was willing to condone patent pooling when operated in conjunction with agreements providing for full co-operation on technical and scientific issues. Advantages of more effective research programmes and/or a more rapid dispersion of scientific knowledge weighed heavily with the Commission. Nevertheless, the Commission always insisted that outside companies should have reasonable access to Association patents and should not be subjected to obstructive threats of patent litigation. The majority of associations examined had relaxed their patent policies in the light of postwar legislation.

Association Access to Favoured Distributive Channels

Exclusive dealing agreements were frequently encountered by the Monopolies Commission. They involved reciprocal obligations by suppliers and purchasers to trade only with members of each group. Exclusive dealing agreements required precision, both in detailing the form of discrimination and in specifying the favoured buyers and sellers. It was necessary to establish a detailed list, both of suppliers and buyers, since both groups undertook obligations in return for preferential treatment. The Monopolies Commission commented that it 'is in an association with exclusive dealing agreements that we find some of the most rigidly defined qualifications for admission to approved lists. . . .'[2] Where qualifications for membership were specified periodic reviews were made to ensure that those on the list conform to agreed requirements. Penalties were normally imposed for breach of regulations, rang-

[1] The two most important patentees within the Association.

[2] Collective Discrimination Report, 1955. Cmd. 9504, p. 36.

ing from minor fines to deletion from the list and expulsion from the scheme. Expulsion could be very serious where the price concessions offered to parties were large, or where no dealings were allowed with non-members. Normally accused members could state their case and even appeal. Appeals tended to be heard by another committee or group within the trade.

Associations defended exclusive dealing on the ground that their goods required skilled distribution and that they must select their own outlets. They pointed to stringent qualification requirements for acceptable distributors[1] and to the need to prevent individual suppliers from unfair pressure by large buying associations. Emphasis was placed upon the need for protection from excessive competition and the advantages of a stable market.

The Monopolies Commission felt that the main disadvantage of exclusive dealing agreements was excessive rigidity, amounting at worst to the elimination of effective competition from traders outside the privileged group. There was always an acute risk that such schemes would result in a 'closed circle of suppliers and buyers, each with an equal interest in preserving the *status quo*'.[2] The Commission had no doubt that exclusive dealing arrangements were among those most clearly operating against the public interest, even when they supported desirable common price systems.

The Commission made adverse recommendations in every case of exclusive dealing encountered. The system adopted by the Association of Dental Manufacturers and Traders provided a foretaste of the Commission's general attitude. The Association operated a very tightly organized system of exclusive dealing covering nine-tenths of UK trade in dental goods. Membership of the Association was open only to traders satisfying stringent requirements. It was notable that even a company of the size and economic power of Imperial Chemical Industries had deemed it wise to enter the Association in order to market its dental products.

The Commission objected to the system strongly on social grounds. It felt that the system entailed 'practices and powers involving an extreme interference with the freedom of the subject to carry on lawful business'.[3] The Commission felt that the penalty of expulsion for breach of regulations was outrageous; this penalty alone would condemn an otherwise unobjectionable system in the absence of more acceptable techniques of enforcement.

The Monopolies Commission condemned exclusive dealing in dental

[1] Qualifications might include technical skills, years of experience in the trade, physical facilities of the retailer, size of retail turnover, trading capital, etc.

[2] Cmd. 9504, op. cit., p. 41.

[3] Report in the Supply of Dental Goods, 1950. H.C.P. 18, p. 71.

goods on economic grounds as well as social. It pointed out that the market for dental products was already protected to a large extent by the existence of the National Health Service. In an expanding industry of this kind there were major economic dangers in imposing such a rigid pattern of development upon the industry.

In some industries exclusive dealing was not explicitly practised, but financial arrangements[1] were adopted with results analogous to those of exclusive dealing. Such a system was operated by the Electric Lamp Manufacturers' Association. Retailers were free to purchase lamps from independent producers if they so wished. However, those agreeing to sell only association lamps received an additional rebate of 5 per cent on lamp prices. The Commission estimated that this sum was approximately equal to the net profit margin made by retailers on lamp sales. This special rebate placed pressure upon retailers to deal exclusively with the association, and limited the effectiveness of independent producers who competed by offering higher margins to retailers rather than lower prices to the general public. The effect of the Association's scheme was transference of competition from the consumer stage to that of the distributor. On this ground the Commission recommended the termination of the system.[2]

The Monopolies Commission disliked exclusive dealing arrangements, primarily because of their adverse effects upon effective competition. The Commission's alarm was greatest whenever the system spanned the majority of producers and distributors, where preferential treatment of members was pronounced, and where the opportunity to join the system was low. The Commission feared, under such circumstances, that the stimulus to cost reduction and innovation and the restraint upon pricing policy imposed by the competitive process would be sacrificed unless the system was destroyed.

Aggregated Rebate Agreements

Aggregated rebates are discounts or rebates calculated by members of an association at rates varying with total value of purchases from all members. A characteristic feature is the rebate rate which increases with purchases in a specified time period. In most of the cases examined by the Commission the scale was so applied that buyers earned rebate on all purchases from the group at the rate applicable to their marginal purchases.[3]

[1] Excluding aggregated rebate systems examined infra.

[2] op. cit., 1951, p. 99. 'It seems to us that competition in the margins allowed to distributors is a poor alternative to competition in price to the public.'

[3] Thus, for instance, if an association allowed 2 per cent on purchases up to £3,000 but 3 per cent on all purchases if they amount to £3,000, then a purchaser buying £100 of goods, so raising total purchases from £2,900 to £3,000, would in effect receive a rebate of £32 on his final order of £100.

Less often the rebate rate rose in a series of discrete steps. Aggregated rebates were made available sometimes only to purchasers in selected categories, commonly to merchants and wholesalers, occasionally also to large retailers or user buyers.

The system was defended as a legitimate extension of the quantity rebates offered by individual companies. Economic arguments such as economies in packaging and transport were used for aggregated rebates in the same way as for quantity rebates.

Associations contended that aggregated rebates were the only operational form of rebate within a common price system. A simple quantity rebate would encourage buyers to place orders with one member only of the association. This would be detrimental to the small manufacturer, in many cases leading to his elimination. On the other hand the aggregated rebate introduced flexibility into common price systems, enabling buyers to spread their purchases without loss of rebate. Suppliers could refuse supplies without damaging their customer's rebate rate.

Aggregated rebates do not serve the same ends as ordinary quantity discounts. The latter normally reflect real cost economies in production and distribution. The former tend to prevent such economies from materializing by encouraging buyers to spread their purchases.

More important, however, in the viewpoint of the Monopolies Commission, was the effect of aggregated rebates in raising barriers against effective competition. Independent suppliers were unable to compete with association members when the rebate paid by the latter was conditional upon exclusive purchasing. The amount of rebate the customer would lose on a single order by placing it outside the group would be calculated at the highest rate he could have earned by placing it within the group.

The Commission considered that this detriment outweighed the advantages of increased flexibility within a common price system. The Commission concluded that such arrangements generally operated against the public interest. In exceptional instances an aggregated rebate scheme might prove acceptable as an essential part of a desirable common price system. No such case involving the Commission occurred between 1949 and 1956.

ASSOCIATION COST ADVANTAGES AND THE PUBLIC INTEREST

Cost advantages may result from more efficient utilization by trade association members of resources available to all producers. On the other hand they may be the result of association patent policy, association control of factor supplies, favoured association access to distributive outlets, or to investment funds.

Patent Agreements

The importance of patents from the viewpoint of product differentiation has already been assessed. In the modern technological age it is usually possible to find substitutes for patented techniques. In many instances, however, the substitutes are more expensive, or less effective, than patented techniques; cost disadvantages are thereby incurred by trade association competitors.

The patent system encourages invention by the offer of quasi-rents to those who are commercially successful. Patent pooling by association members not only speeds up the transmission of knowledge; in addition it may lead to co-operation in research. These advantages must be carefully measured against any obstruction of competition. The attitude of the Commission was strongly influenced by the nature of the licensing system for non-members adopted by the association. Evidence of consciously predatory action by the association in the field of patents would certainly have been viewed suspiciously.[1] On the other hand the Commission did not expect members to surrender all advantages of their co-operation.[2] The Commission adopted a flexible approach to patent agreements.

Association Control over Factors of Production and Component Resources

Associations may preserve a cost advantage over outside firms by controlling favoured factors of production.[3] The degree of advantage would be dependent upon the extent of the association's control, the effectiveness of such control, and the relative efficiency of the factor in question compared with the best available substitute. Where suitable substitutes are available overseas the advantage of the association is dependent upon the level of tariffs and other impediments to international trade.

Prior to 1914 British lamp manufacturers were dependent upon imported supplies of lamp components. After the war Association members made a determined effort to eliminate their dependence. They established component manufacturing plants on a large scale, and by 1939 had almost reached a position of self-sufficiency. During the inter-war years members of the Association pursued a restrictive policy, forcing independent producers to rely almost exclusively upon imported lamp components. During the Second World War imports ceased com-

[1] e.g. the activities of the Electric Lamp Manufacturers' Association in the 1930s.

[2] See Report on Supply of Electric Lamps, 1951, op. cit., and Report on the Supply of Insulated Electric Wires and Cables, 1952, op. cit.

[3] Land, labour or capital equipment. Marshall himself assumed that quasi-rents might be earned by companies under keen competition if they owned factors with scarce attributes.

pletely, and from 1942 the British Government imposed a rigid allocation system upon the industry.

During the post-war period imported lamp components were higher in price and more variable in quality than their British counterparts. The independents were obliged to rely upon Association supplies. Under the 1948 Lamp Agreement the Association willingly supplied them with bulbs, glass tubing, rod, caps, wire, and electrolodes. It refused to supply filaments or fluorescent powders. For all supplies independent producers were charged higher prices than Association members.[1]

The Monopolies Commission examined independent companies' complaints that the association refused to supply components and/or delivered components of the wrong specifications. It failed to find any deliberate Association policy to this effect. The Commission noted that the General Electric Company and British Thomson-Houston had jointly promoted Glass Bulbs Ltd, which utilized two Corning Ribbon machines. Supplies from this source adequately catered for the total demand of the British market. Both companies had undertaken, at the instance of the Ministry of Supply in 1947, to supply without discrimination bulbs produced by these plants.

The Commission discovered one Association attempt to dissuade outside firms from laying component producing capacity. Favourable terms had been offered to the Co-operative Wholesale Society by the Association for supplies of tubing for fluorescent lamps; the Association justified the attempt by reference to the ample capacity already in existence.

In general the Commission was satisfied with the supply of lamp components to the independents.[2] It recommended that the Association should undertake to supply all components without discrimination in price. In periods of shortage it felt that the Association should keep in close contact with the relevant Government department.

The question of limitations on use of premises, altogether with restrictions on the sale of second-hand plant, occurred in the calico printing inquiry. In 1949 the majority of Federation members decided to co-operate in a redundancy scheme operated through Print Trade Reorganization Ltd. One clause in the agreement prohibited the selling or leasing of calico printing premises during the eleven year Levy Period unless covenants were obtained preventing their use for calico printing for the remainder of the Period. The Print Trade Redundancy Board could sell or lease printing premises only under a covenant preventing

[1] Major exceptions to this rule were the Controlled Companies, and British Luma.

[2] op. cit., 1951, p. 93. 'We recognize that the members of the ELMA cannot be expected to share all the benefits of their own knowledge and skill with their competitors, and we think the line is reasonably drawn at present.'

their use in the industry for ninety-nine years.[1] In addition, signatories to the Percentage-Quota scheme accepted a ban on the sale of second-hand plant to outside firms.

The Monopolies Commission was concerned by the restrictive covenant. It pointed out that calico printing required access to large water supplies. Such supplies were available in a limited number of areas. The Commission concluded that 'the existence of restrictive covenants on so large a number of sites must seriously obstruct the entry of new concerns into the industry'.[2] In this way, in an industry which was not declining, the covenants operated against the public interest. In addition the Commission condemned the ban on second-hand plant to non-signatories of the PQ agreement.

These two examples illustrate the Commission's hostility towards restrictions on the supply of resources to independent suppliers. Only where technical co-operation within the Association was extensive and where the fruits of such co-operation were substantial would the Commission allow any limitation upon supplies to outside firms. In certain respects this attitude conflicted with the Commission's greater leniency towards patent restrictions. In general, however, technical progress is less directly related to restrictions upon supplies than upon patented inventions. It would appear that the Commission's caution was completely justified.[3]

Association Control of Favoured Systems of Distribution

Exclusive dealing and aggregated rebate agreements may involve independent producers in heavy countervailing expenditure, resulting in higher unit costs than their association competitors. The Commission was influenced by this danger in the hostility it displayed towards such arrangements.

Favoured Association Access to Investment Finance.

Protected association members may have better access to finance capital than independent producers, who may have to offer high interest rates or may be unable to obtain large amounts of capital despite an attractive present value of future prospective earnings. Lack of capital is often an important impediment to effective competition. The Radcliffe Committee[4] in 1959 reported upon the weakness in capital market provisions for companies attempting to expand from small to medium size.

[1] Such convenants had been placed upon twelve premises by the Federation, but the Calico Printers' Association had placed many more of its own accord.

[2] op. cit., 1954, p. 73.

[3] In both instances the Commission had been impressed by the low price elasticity of supply of relevant factors outside association control.

[4] Report on the Working of the Monetary System. Cmnd. 827.

Where trade association members obtain a high proportion of finance capital from ploughed-back profit, outside companies may be at a serious disadvantage. In addition association members may have the added advantage of sharing scale economies internal to the association, but external to each member firm.[1] The advantage may be met by large companies in other industries diversifying into the field. This possibility was neglected by Bain in his analysis of cost advantages accruing to associations and dominant firms. The Monopolies Commission declined all discussion of the problem of investment finance.

TRADE ASSOCIATION SCALE ECONOMIES AND THE PUBLIC INTEREST

Economies of large-scale accruing to trade associations may confer significant disadvantages upon competitors. Technical and managerial economies are unlikely to be substantial in industries characterized by an association of many companies. Such economies would be equally available to outsiders in the absence of oligopoly or perhaps the existence of a dominant firm.

Economies of scale internal to the association, though external to each member firm, may be available, however, in the marketing, financial and risk-taking sectors of many industries. Outside companies, deprived of the use of common facilities, would be obliged either to operate on a larger scale than association members, perhaps involving considerable short-run excess capacity, or to operate at a suboptimal scale. In either case cost disadvantages would result, and effective competition would be impeded. In extreme cases, new entrants might involve market saturation. Entry would then be prevented by a low present value of future income streams. Effective competition would then rest on existing competitors and on the willingness of large multi-product companies to take advantage of common overheads, and to commence production on a smaller scale without corresponding cost disadvantages. This type of potential competition is an underrated force conditioning the activities of trade associations.

Where scale economies were substantial, associations often defended ancillary restrictions on entry as desirable to prevent excessive entry involving excess capacity. The social cost of entry might prove to be greater than the private cost.[2] New entrants would not only operate at suboptimal capacity themselves, but would force established member

[1] OEEC, op. cit., p. 36. 'A cartel may be open to newcomers and so probably enable entering firms to operate under more favourable conditions than would have been possible under a decentralized set-up.'

[2] i.e. that there are substantial external diseconomies of new entry.

companies to do the same; higher unit costs would result with prices in excess of those in the absence of entry.

If this contention were true, the remedy should scarcely be left to the judgment and will of an interested trade association. But the rationale of the contention may be seriously questioned. Economies of large scale may be derived not from lower-cost techniques, but from market dominance; monopsonistic buying powers may be exercised to obtain discounts on raw materials, and to pay less for labour than would be paid in competitive conditions. Impotent suppliers may be forced to recoup low profits on trade association sales by obtaining high profits on sales to less powerful independent firms. Elimination of entry barriers may then be required to prevent exploitation and resource mis-allocation.

The Monopolies Commission encountered the problems imposed by scale economies in the lamp industry. The supply of glass bulbs from Ribbon plant laid by the General Electric Company and British Thomson-Houston threatened 'a monopoly arising inevitably from technical development'.[1]

The new plant was capable of producing, in full production, more bulbs than were demanded by the entire British market within the relevant price range. There would be no room for competing plant. The producing companies had promised the Government that they would supply bulbs on uniform terms to all United Kingdom purchasers, providing slightly favourable prices for themselves and the Controlled Companies. The Commission recommended, as an additional safeguard, that a price list should be published indicating gross prices and quantity discounts.

Plant for the production of copper semis was very expensive and, in hot-working especially, required high capacity operation for the best returns. In most sections of the industry large-scale production had been concentrated in relatively few concerns. This development had reduced unit production costs without any sacrifice in quality. The Commission felt that the risk of abuse of monopoly power was low because outside capacity was considerable. In addition, customers were frequently prepared to integrate backwards. Many wire users drew sufficient wire for their own purposes. In certain branches of the industry, it is true, there were scale obstacles to such competition. Customers in the motor trade who decided to produce their own copper semis would have had to produce more than their own requirements to compete on cost grounds. It would not be easy to sell surplus produce on the open market. Under such conditions 'the price would have to be extremely high before even a user with great financial resources would think it worth while to incur the heavy capital outlay involved and take

[1] op. cit., 1951, p. 93.

the risk of selling his surplus in a market new to him, for the sake of satisfying his own requirements more cheaply'.[1]

Fear of new entry in a market subjected to fluctuating or increasing demand conditions may result in the maintenance of permanent excess capacity by members of the trade association. Surplus capacity may be held to provide flexibility in the face of market expansion, demand peaking, and demand fluctuations. An association interested in maintaining or expanding its market share in a growth industry must lay plant capacity in advance of demand increases. Failure to do so may allow outside companies to take advantage of high association marginal costs;[2] incursions might be made into the association's market. Excess capacity may provide an effective barrier to new entry when scale economies are large.

The foregoing analysis poses a problem in monopoly control. It is extremely difficult to decide whether association excess capacity is due to prudent provision for future market growth, whether it is due to unforeseen changes in demand, or whether it is part of a predatory design to frighten off potential entrants. The Monopolies Commission itself does not appear to have been aware of the possible significance of excess capacity. It must be criticized for this omission.

DIRECT ASSOCIATION AGREEMENTS TO RESTRAIN COMPETITION AND THE PUBLIC INTEREST

Import Agreements

Competition from import substitutes may provide, in the absence of Government protection, effective competition for dominant domestic trade associations. One justification for free trade was the reduced risk of abuse from dominant domestic organizations.

Trade associations are not unaware of the constraint imposed by imports upon their activities. There are many examples of agreements designed to reduce the competitive effect of import substitutes. The copper semis inquiry provided a typical example. Immediately after the Second World War an International Conference of Non-Ferrous Metal Manufacturers was held.[3] The manufacturers present signed the Lausanne Agreement to provide protection for their individual domestic markets and to provide stability in international markets. Minimum prices were prescribed for sales to their domestic markets plus Canada, Western Germany, the United States of America, and Holland. This International Price List was altered on no less than six occasions

[1] op. cit., 1955, p. 94.

[2] Especially where the gestation period for new investment was lengthy.

[3] The Conference was attended by representatives from Britain, Belgium, France, Sweden, and Switzerland.

to reflect changes in world trading conditions. The agreement did not cover West German producers who provided a degree of effective price competition in world markets.

The British Federation contended that the Lausanne Agreement safeguarded the British market from subsidized European exports. It argued that tariff protection was insufficient[1] and that the British Government was unable to raise tariff levels because of its commitments to freer international trade; private action was more flexible than public in this sphere.

The Monopolies Commission agreed that overseas producers might profitably export copper semis at prices below their domestic levels. Exported goods could be sold at marginal cost, which in an industry of decreasing cost would be well below average production costs[2] upon which home market prices would be based in all probability. On the other hand, the Commission considered that existing import duties protected British producers from imports priced at marginal cost. At ruling prices for copper, the existing tariff amounted to some 80 per cent of conversion cost. Unless copper prices slumped heavily there would be no serious danger to British price levels.

Even if allegations of dumping proved correct, the Government could always introduce anti-dumping legislation. Article VI of GATT allowed the imposition of anti-dumping tariffs under qualified circumstances. The Commission was completely opposed to private action regarding import protection. It felt that an aggrieved association should convince the Government that its claims were justified.[3] This would provide an automatic opportunity for comment by outside companies and would ensure that the action taken would receive wide publicity. On these grounds, the Commission condemned the Federation's import arrangements and recommended their termination.

The Commission rejected, during its investigations, contentions that import restrictions saved an unnecessary outflow of foreign currencies, and that they prevented unemployment in domestic industry.[4] In each case it stressed the danger of relying upon private action even where a strong case for intervention could be formulated. This has been the pre-

[1] At the time of investigation *ad valorem* tariffs ranged from 15 to 20 per cent. Retained imports ran at negligible levels.

[2] One suspects that the Commission did not distinguish between the short and the long run in this analysis.

[3] op. cit., 1955, p. 101. 'Important and far-reaching issues of public policy are involved in these matters; no one industry can take adequate account of the repercussions of its action on other industries, which in the case of semi-manufactures used as materials by other industries may be particularly dangerous.'

[4] e.g. Report on the Supply of Hard Fibre Cordage, 1956. H.C.P. 294, op. cit., p. 72.

dominant theme of the Commission's attitude towards import arrangements.

One fundamental criticism may be made regarding this aspect of the Commission's work. In certain inquiries the Commission refused to comment upon import arrangements on the ground that they were inextricably intermingled with unreferred export arrangements. This attitude involved a serious misconception of the public interest. If export or import arrangements play any part in influencing the structure of domestic industry, or if they affect domestic scales of production, they must be of direct relevance to the public interest. As such they should have been examined by the Commission.

Selective Price Cutting Agreements

Selective price cutting may be directed at a specified section of the products of an association, or at specified geographical regions, or at specified sections of the consuming public. Techniques adopted might range from joint ownership of special fighting companies to the production of specified fighting brands and to allowing price reductions for existing products under specified conditions.[1]

Selective price cutting is usually adopted to prevent the emergence of, or to eliminate, effective competition within a section of the market. An aggressive market policy normally involves heavy costs, in the sense of foregone profits, not only for those attacked but also for the aggressors. If the price war can be confined to a narrow area, or if a fighting brand can be used, the cost of the war will be less, both in terms of immediate financial cost and, in the latter instance, in terms of goodwill. The system is a highly effective protective weapon if used with prudence. In this sense the Commission's hostility is not surprising; no such system received its blessing.

There are theoretical arguments favouring the technique. Selective price cutting loosens up rigidly-organized common price systems, perhaps encouraging price cutting by members over areas wider than those at first envisaged. In general, however, this advantage is over-shadowed by the risk that outside competitors may be weakened or rendered completely ineffective by organized competition on a selective basis on the part of powerful trade associations.

Selective price cutting was a feature of the common price system of the Metal Windows Association. Before July 1956 the Secretariat of the Association had obtained information relating to outside competition for any tender, including, if possible, the prices quoted.[2] One member

[1] This was the system used by the Metal Windows Association.

[2] In 1953–4 the Association accounted for about 90 per cent of all sales of standard metal windows made in the United Kingdom. Enquiries were made about outside competition from wood window manufacturers as well as metal.

had then been authorized to quote below list price if this was necessary to win the contract. The remainder quoted prices slightly above that of the nominated member. The Secretariat, in selecting the member, noted its consumer connections with a view to selecting the member who was in the best position to secure the order.

This procedure was amended in July 1956. Henceforth, upon suspicion of outside competition, members would meet to decide upon a common tender price. Anyone wishing to quote the usual list price was free to do so. If, following the common tender, any firm was invited to reconsider, it could do so with the authorization of the Secretariat.

The Commission compiled statistics of the Association's price cutting scheme. From a sample survey it estimated that overall a weighted average price reduction of 6 per cent had been made to combat outside competition. In more than 10 per cent of the cases examined price cuts exceeded 20 per cent. It appeared that members had been nominated for price cutting purposes roughly in proportion to their percentage shares in standard metal window sales.

Independent manufacturers expressed concern at the Association's price cutting techniques. One producer commented that the cutting had been increasingly keen during the 1950s and that his company profits had consequently been reduced. A small independent producer had been warned by a member of the Association to leave the large contracts to Association members. The firm had not tendered, thereafter, for contracts in excess of £200.

The Metal Windows Association described its system as a defensive measure which it disliked but felt obliged to adopt. It argued that the independents obtained Association price lists and deliberately quoted lower prices. The Association pointed out that outside competition had not been eliminated, but on the contrary had remained at a constant level. In any event, only 7½ per cent of members' turnover had been affected by price cutting in 1954–5.

The Commission, however, believed the system to be aimed directly at the elimination of outside competition.[1] It was further disturbed by the fact that the Association had to fix its normal prices at a level which would enable the members to recover the profit lost on sales of reduced prices; the cost would ultimately fall on the general body of consumers.

The Commission concluded that Association fears of competition could be allayed by a general reduction in the level of its price schedules. Therefore the selective price cutting agreement operated against the public interest and should be terminated. There was no doubt at all in the Commission's mind that such predatory techniques should be condemned.

[1] op. cit., 1956, p. 81. 'The practice involves using the collective resources of a majority of the manufacturers with a view to defeating the competition of a minority.'

Chapter Ten

THE TRADE ASSOCIATION AND PUBLIC POLICY

Until 1956 the Monopolies Commission was primarily concerned with inquiries into the activities of trade associations. The Board of Trade selected its references carefully to range over as wide a field of business practices as possible. Many observers consider that the 1956 Restrictive Trade Practices Act was a logical outcome of the work of the Commission.

The Commission's inquiries into trade associations were facilitated by the existence of restrictive agreements, which served as focal points for the investigations. Concentration upon restrictive agreements was justified by their importance to all the associations examined by the Monopolies Commission.

It has been argued that price fixing agreements are distinct from all other association arrangements as being the prime activity. This has been disputed by economists writing in the field of restrictive trade practices:

> Typically, firms appear to enter trade association agreements to protect themselves. They are not concerned to choose the most advantageous point on their collective demand curve (although this conceivably can happen) so much as to keep the competitive spirit within bounds.... If this is the correct interpretation the price-fix appears as a subsidiary element of restrictive systems.[1]

Companies certainly form trade associations for protection. However, price fixing agreements provide perhaps the most important form of short-term protection. The evidence subsequent upon the termination of trade association agreements substantiates this viewpoint. Open price filing systems are normally instituted in the place of price

[1] See A. Hunter, 'The Monopolies Commission and Price Fixing', *Economic Journal*, 1956, p. 587.

agreements. Secondary forms of agreement are allowed to disappear.[1]

The Monopolies Commission concentrated upon the longer-term effects of price fixing agreements. It paid far more attention to arguments relating to research, development, innovation, standardization of production and the spread of technical knowledge, than to those relating to cut-throat competition, and localized unemployment. In particular the Commission was concerned to ensure that low cost firms might expand at the expense of their less efficient competitors. The Commission was willing to risk concentration in order to achieve this aim.

The Commission was antipathetic to the point of dogmatism where agreements rigidified the market shares of trade association members. All quota agreements were condemned[2] and agreements relating to advertising, and discounts from list price were treated with suspicion.

The Monopolies Commission was determined to provide reasonable opportunities for the existence of independent competition in industries dominated by trade restrictions. Exclusive dealing agreements, agreements limiting the supply of important factors to non-members, and import agreements were critically examined and almost always condemned. Selective price cutting agreements and the use of fighting companies against established competitors were severely criticized. The Commission considered that the elimination of entry barriers would go far towards weakening the ability of trade associations to exploit the public. It tended to overlook the possibility that natural entry barriers in the form of scale economies and other market limitations might nullify the effects of its recommendations.

The Monopolies Commission recommendations were basically correct in relation to trade associations composed of many firms characterized by a wide spread of costs. The elimination of entry barriers and the weakening of barriers to inter-member competition might be expected, in these circumstances, to weaken the restrictive powers of the association, even where the price fixing agreement was replaced by open price filing.

In the field of oligopoly, the Commission's approach was much weaker.[3] The Commission recognized the greater difficulty of stimulat-

[1] T. Wilson (J. Miller, ed.), 1962, op. cit., p. 612. 'Not only may the "open" price agreements be looser and less binding than the price structure explicitly determined by a cartel, but the other possible restrictive activities may have disappeared or been greatly weakened. . . .'

[2] Save an agreement for the allocation of ox-pancreas supplies among members of the British Insulin Manufacturers.

[3] A. Hunter, op. cit., p. 589. 'Common prices can be maintained with relatively little support where there is sufficient agreement within the industry. This occurs, for instance, if there are few manufacturers, where a relatively small territorial area is affected, if the organization has a strongly organized central invoicing system or where it has retained a pricing procedure dating from inter-war years.'

ing competition under such conditions, but appeared to be at a loss concerning appropriate action. Open price filing, especially under inflationary conditions, may be highly effective when the number of firms is few, scale barriers to new entry high, and countervailing power weak or nonexistent.

PART IV

THE DOMINANT FIRM

I repeat . . . that all power is a trust—that we are accountable for its exercise—that, from the people, and for the people, all springs, and all must exist.

B. Disraeli, *Sybil*, bk. VI, ch. 1

Chapter Eleven

THE DOMINANT FIRM AND OLIGOPOLY

Any company would be considered dominant in terms of the 1948 legislation if it catered for one third or more of a specified market. This definition of market dominance is clearly arbitrary. Many companies in this country serve more than one third of selected markets but are subjected to keen competition. Certainly, the one third requirement falls considerably short of the literal definition of monopoly, which involves exclusive control over the specified market. It is not surprising that a less rigid definition was adopted in the 1948 legislation. Very few companies would have fallen within the scope of the Act if the literal definition of monopoly had been adopted. Market dominance is less commonly characterized in this country by the single firm monopoly, than by competition between relatively few companies, one of which may be larger and more influential than its competitors. This latter situation is known as oligopoly.

The Monopolies Commission has dealt with many cases involving oligopoly. It has dealt with few which concerned monopoly. It is appropriate, therefore, that this chapter should provide an analytical framework for a study of the dominant firm under conditions of oligopoly.

Competition between a few companies accentuates the problem of uncertainty, which always exists within a competitive system. Uncertainty is enhanced by the close inter-relationships that exist between competitors. Success on the part of one company invariably reflects difficulties for the remainder. They may be compelled to retaliate by resort to any of a range of counter-strategies. The aggressive company must anticipate the reactions that it will provoke.

Clearly, competition between the few involves issues that are irrelevant in industries composed of many small sellers. Economists have recognized that oligopoly requires a type of analysis fundamentally different from that developed to tackle free and monopolistic competition. The classical approach, which draws analogies from mechanics and biology, has had to be discarded, and replaced by more dynamic equipment. The nature of competition in conditions of oligopoly is similar in some ways to that of warfare between nations: 'The oligopoly-theorist's classical literature can neither be Newton and Darwin nor can it be Freud; he will have to turn to Clausewitz's Principles of War.'[1]

THE KINKED DEMAND CURVE AND PRICE STABILITY

Economists often contend that competition between a few companies results in long periods of price stability. The contention is based less upon empirical evidence than upon theories relating to nature of uncertainty in the making of price adjustments.

It is argued that companies are unwilling to raise prices for fear that their rivals will not follow suit. They thus anticipate that demand will be extremely price elastic in response to price increases. At the same time, companies are reluctant to lower prices in case their rivals follow suit, leaving them with no particular advantage; a generally lower price level would result. Companies consider demand to be highly price inelastic in response to price reductions.

This theory anticipates a kink in each company's demand schedule at the ruling price. The corresponding marginal revenue schedule is discontinuous at the kink. The extent of the discontinuity is determined by the extent of the kink in the demand schedule. As a result companies are reluctant to change their prices in the absence of substantial alterations in cost conditions or unless they consider that prevailing circumstances render the kink irrelevant.

The theory of price stability under oligopoly is by no means adhered to universally by economists. Many economists[2] consider that the theory rests upon a degree of knowledge between rival companies that does not exist in practice. Lack of knowledge by rivals of a price reduction may involve a lagged response by rivals; market penetration during the interval may benefit the aggressor, and compensate him for later reactions on the part of rivals. In any case there has been little systematic attempt to test the theory empirically.

The kinked demand curve theory does not pretend to provide a theory of price determination under conditions of oligopoly. It merely purports to explain why prices remain constant. Certain economists believe that the problem of uncertainty in pricing is overcome by resort to an acceptable formula. Prices are determined by adding an accepted margin to estimates of average costs or to average variable costs of production. A system of this kind might materialize without formal agreement and might be consolidated by the tacit acquiescence of competing

[1] K. W. Rothschild, 'Price Theory and Oligopoly', AEA, *Readings in Price Theory*, p. 450.

[2] e.g. W. J. Baumol, *Business Behaviour, Value and Growth*, London, Macmillan, 1959, Chapter 3.

companies. This theory is compatible with empirical evidence that oligopolistic companies tend to adjust prices in reaction to a change in production costs common to the entire industry. In itself the theory says little about the factors determining the acceptable mark-up or about the process through which a mark-up may be altered.

Whatever the process by which prices are determined it is clear that most companies pay careful attention to the 'no-entry ceiling'. Prices in excess of this ceiling endanger new entry, and companies may wish to avoid this even when current market conditions warrant large price increases.

Price competition under oligopoly often manifests itself indirectly, through quality changes, through changes in credit facilities and discounts offered to purchaser or through changes in the level of advertising and after sales service provided by competing companies. There are sound reasons why competition should be edged into such channels. Direct price manipulation is open to immediate response. Indirect changes may invite less rapid response. They have been likened to 'tools for tactical manoeuvres in the enemy's territory, testing his strength without provoking a major conflict'.[1]

Quality changes may be particularly serviceable to this end. There is an inevitable time-lag before rival companies are able to retaliate in kind; this delay may enable the aggressor to penetrate into rival territory and to consolidate his position. Alternatively, an aggressive competitor may resort to offering secret discounts from list price. For a time such action may be extremely successful. There is always a risk that price reductions of this type may escalate and eventually culminate in a downward revision of list prices in order to regularize the price structure.

W. J. Baumol has argued[2] that firms operating under oligopolistic conditions may attempt to maximize sales value rather than profits. The maximization of sales value brings prestige for management, goodwill from the distributive trade, and the possibility of market dominance. Maximizing profits—and particularly short-run profits—may conflict with these aims. This theory is compatible with empirical evidence of indirect competition in price. An expanded volume of sales at ruling prices induced by sales promotion may produce a greater sales revenue than expanded sales volume attained through price reductions.[3]

[1] K. Rothschild, American Economic Association, op. cit., p. 455.

[2] op. cit., 1959, Chapter 3.

[3] ibid., p. 52. 'Now a dollar spent on advertising, if it increases physical volume, must necessarily increase total revenue. But a price reduction is a double-edged sword.'

OLIGOPOLY AND PRICE-LEADERSHIP

In an industry composed of very few firms, varying in size, and in relative efficiencies, uncertainty in relation to price changes may press companies into time-consuming studies of rival response potentials. The desire for peaceful coexistence[1] may become so overwhelming that a price-leader is accepted by the bulk of the industry. The price-leader will formulate price policy secure in the knowledge that rivals will follow his lead. In this manner subjective kinks in the demand schedules of individual companies may be effectively circumvented.

Price-leadership may take many forms, of which the umbrella pattern and the barometric pattern are the most important. The former dominates and dictates price policy, securing the acquiescence of its rivals through respect or fear. The latter can only succeed by its ability to reflect market forces[2] and by convincing others of its ability to interpret and to forecast. The latter form of price-leadership is unlikely to survive rapid changes in market conditions.

Certain economists have argued that the umbrella-type price leader must always be the lowest-cost producer.[3] This is not so. The leader may simply be the largest company, the most financially liquid[4] or the most highly diversified producer. It may, upon occasion, simply be the most aggressive organization. The dominant leader will often tolerate marginal incursions upon its market-share, accepting this as the price for overall stability, especially where it has a large share of the market.[5] The dominant price leader is likely to be influenced in its price fixing more by potential than by existing competition.

The barometric price leader must adopt a far more cautious pricing policy. It may resort to exploratory tactics in order to test rival reactions. Price changes may be announced well in advance of time, and may be cancelled if other firms fail to respond. President Kennedy took advantage of such tactics in 1961 to intimidate American steel companies into

[1] Construed, in the present Russian form, to imply all forms of subversion short of open conflict.

[2] P. Sylos-Labini, *Oligopoly and Technical Progress*, Harvard University Press, 1962, p. 39. 'This means that unless the price fixed by the large firms is an equilibrium price, it will not last.'

[3] e.g. H. Edwards, *Competition and Monopoly in the British Soap Industry*, Oxford, 1962.

[4] It would thus face exhausting price wars with relative equanimity. K. Rothschild, op. cit., p. 459. 'Preparedness for a price war means above all to be able to continue in existence as long as possible in circumstances where price has no relation whatsoever to the realities of a situation, but is used exclusively as a weapon.'

[5] J. M. Clark, 1961, op. cit., p. 384. 'One General Electric official is quoted as saying: "The Company would rather be pushing to expand a 25 per cent share than defending a 50 per cent share."'

non-co-operation with the announced decision of the United States Steel Company to raise steel prices. The risks of non-compliance with a price lead are considerable for a barometric price-leader. Stigler[1] cites an inter-war instance in which the American Tobacco Company raised its prices; the rise was not followed by competitors and the American Tobacco Company rescinded the increase following a severe sales decline. A further sales decline was sustained by the Company for several months thereafter. It may take a long time to recoup goodwill thrown away by one faulty decision. For this reason the lot of the price-leader—especially of the barometric variety—is often unenviable. The barometric price-leader is likely to raise prices with equanimity only in response to a general cost increase affecting all members of the industry. Even under such conditions regard must be paid to potential competition.

INDIVISIBILITIES AND INNOVATION

There is a tendency, in analysing competition under oligopolistic conditions, to ignore or to underestimate the importance of cost differentials between rival firms and to over-emphasize the importance of uncertainty with regard to demand. Differences in unit production costs reflect differences in managerial skills, and in the use made of available resources. In part, however, cost differences between firms reflect discontinuities in the process of industrial development. Technological indivisibilities may be considerable and may affect companies in process of transition from small to large scale. In this way, it is argued, the oligopolistic mechanism may encourage the emergence of privileged companies. In certain cases, indeed, economic indivisibilities may be sufficiently large to obstruct new entry into an industry. It has been suggested that the existence of such obstacles to competition may result in an industrial structure that is congenitally incompatible with competition.[2] Medium and large scale companies may be able to maintain abnormally high levels of profit over lengthy periods without any risk that competition will be fostered.

Theories of this kind place a pessimistic interpretation upon the existence of cost differentials within an industry, and upon the existence of companies of varying size. A more optimistic interpretation should be considered. An important factor related to cost discrepancies between competing companies is to be found in the uneven exploitation of

[1] J. Stigler, AEA, *Readings in Price Theory*, p. 438.

[2] P. Sylos Labini, 1962, op. cit., p. 131. 'Imperfect laws and, generally speaking, artificial elements do not, in modern economies, create but merely buttress oligopolistic market power, which has structural and ultimately technological origins.'

inventions.[1] This unevenness is closely bound up with the accentuated importance of innovation in oligopolistic markets. According to the innovation thesis, the degree of dispersion of costs within an industry 'will depend primarily on the rate at which innovations in technique and production objectives are being made—their frequency and their magnitude—and on the speed with which they are diffused'.[2] Those who lag behind in the innovation process will be under strong compulsion to redress the balance. In this manner, contrary to the suggestion of Sylos Labini, cost differentials may indicate the presence of keen competition.[3]

The gestation period for capital investment may be lengthy in many industries; it is not surprising therefore that competition under oligopoly concentrates upon innovation. This is the facet of competition most likely to be resistant to immediate competitive reaction. Periods of investment activity inevitably overlap, and this may be a partial explanation for efficiency differentials between companies. The lag between product innovation and effective competitive reaction may alter decisively the existing pattern of trade. Innovation may provide the grass roots of competition under oligopolistic conditions.[4]

THE MONOPOLIES COMMISSION AND OLIGOPOLY

A number of the dominant firms examined by the Monopolies Commission were operating under oligopolistic market conditions. In certain respects the Commission has lacked penetration in such inquiries. Its shortcomings were exposed in the cigarette and tobacco inquiry.[5]

At the time of investigation, the Imperial Tobacco Company accounted for 63 per cent of cigarette and tobacco sales in the United Kingdom. Gallaher, its most serious competitor, accounted for a further 30 per cent of the market. However, Imperial Tobacco held a substantial minority shareholding in Gallaher; this holding had been secretly maintained for a number of years. The market structure was therefore a complex form of duopoly.

[1] H. Edwards, 1962, op. cit., p. 68. 'This is no mere random circumstance, but part and parcel of the process—among other reasons because innovation necessarily implies leaders and followers.'

[2] J. Downie, *The Competitive Process*, p. 90.

[3] ibid., p. 95. 'Progress, I have suggested, consists in the creation of cost dispersion, and it is the tendency of cost dispersion to be eliminated which generates progress.'

[4] The introduction of Tide, the first soapless detergent, by Procter and Gamble Ltd in 1950 on the British market was reflected in a dramatic expansion of that company's share of the total soap market. It was not until the mid-1950s that Unilever regained its lost market position.

[5] Report on the Supply of Cigarettes and Tobacco and Cigarette and Tobacco Machinery, 1961. H.C.P. 218.

The Monopolies Commission noted that other cigarette and tobacco manufacturers usually followed Imperial Tobacco's prices without noticeable lag. For a lengthy period Imperial Tobacco had been able to determine the level and structure of its prices in the confidence that it would not have to face serious competition in price. Between 1948 and 1960 Imperial Tobacco had initiated only five general changes in cigarette prices and seven in tobacco prices. Two changes in each category had been occasioned by increases in customs duty; the remainder had been justified on grounds of rising costs of production.

The Monopolies Commission provided little analysis of the process of price determination in the industry; in particular it failed to examine the conditions which had culminated in Gallaher's acceptance of Imperial Tobacco price-leadership. The Commission noted the increasing difficulty of new entry into cigarette and tobacco manufacture; brand promotion was suggested as an important barrier to entry. The Commission made no attempt to relate these factors to the pattern of price determination in the industry. It made no serious attempt to assess the innovative processes in the industry; it failed to examine the impact of brand promotion upon innovation. One commentator has stressed that advertising expenditure could provide the key to the nature of competition in the industry.[1] The Monopolies Commission completely overlooked the point. Failure to relate its extensive range of accumulated data to the critical issues that so clearly emerged in this industry destroyed the value of the inquiry.

A rather better analysis of oligopoly is to be found in the pneumatic tyre report.[2] At the time of investigation, in 1953, new tyre production was in the hands of eleven companies varying in size. The Dunlop Rubber Company was easily the largest single producer in the industry. Three companies were subsidiaries of large United States companies or of continental groups. The largest five companies together accounted for about 90 per cent of the total United Kingdom tyre trade.

The Monopolies Commission recognized the problem of oligopoly as it existed in the tyre trade. Any aggressive price policy on the part of one company would provoke rapid reactions and might culminate in cut-throat competition. In the absence of inter-company consultations, therefore, firms would be very reluctant to allow price competition of this kind to take place. In fact the Dunlop Rubber Company—the largest and most diversified company in the industry—had been accepted as price-leader[3] although its position in this respect was dependent upon the maintenance of a non-aggressive policy. The Commission felt that

[1] B. S. Yamey, *Modern Law Review*, 1961, p. 750.

[2] Report on the Supply and Export of Pneumatic Tyres, 1955, H.C.P. 133.

[3] An example of size and diversification rather than low-cost production providing market dominance.

in such a delicately-balanced industry price competition might be avoided with a minimum amount of formal consultation and that in the absence of dramatic alterations in the structure of the industry it was highly improbable that keen price competition could develop between tyre producers. Nevertheless, in condemning the consultations of the Tyre Manufacturers' Conference[1] the Commission emphasized the possibility that high-cost producers might be pressed somewhat harder into improving their efficiency in the absence of the price discussions. The Commission was influenced in reaching its decision by the knowledge that wide cost differentials existed between members of the Tyre Manufacturers' Conference.

A similar type of industrial structure was examined in the rubber footwear inquiry. Once again the Dunlop Rubber Company dominated the industry. In 1954 eight members of the Rubber Footwear Manufacturers' Association produced about 66 per cent of rubber boots and 50 per cent of canvas footwear sold in the United Kingdom. The Dunlop Group was easily the largest producer of both products. The Association argued that uniform prices resulted from perfect competition, a nonsense argument in the light of fewness of competitors, keen brand attachment, and product differentiation. The Association argued that Dunlop, generally a low-cost producer, was a natural price-leader.

The Monopolies Commission discovered that Dunlop was a high-cost producer. In the absence of consultations and price agreements the Commission felt that price differentials would emerge in the industry. The Dunlop Rubber Company would then be placed under pressure to lower its prices from time to time in anticipation of price changes by its competitors, or in competitive reaction to rival price reductions. A closer relationship would develop between individual unit production costs and prices of companies in rubber footwear production than had existed at the time of the inquiry. This latter development would serve the public interest.

The Monopolies Commission has not been impressive, upon the whole, in its handling of oligopoly inquiries. The Commission has tended to neglect an examination of such critical inter-relationships as those between advertising and potential competition, between brand promotion and industrial concentration, and between price rigidity and indirect forms of price competition. Failure to analyse such issues detracts from the value of the Commission's reports, and casts doubt upon the validity of its conclusions and recommendations.

[1] op. cit., 1955, p. 114. 'They clearly afford the opportunity for strong pressure to be brought to bear on a manufacturer who wishes to pursue a more independent price policy to dissuade him from doing so, and, though this pressure may not always be successful, it sometimes is.'

Chapter Twelve

THE DOMINANT FIRM AND THE COMPETITIVE PROCESS

A study of the competitive process is equally essential to an understanding of the activities of dominant firms as it is in the case of trade associations. In each case the sources of competition tend to be identical. Nevertheless, they are sufficiently different in their application as to warrant individual analysis. The Monopolies Commission always devotes a considerable proportion of its dominant firm reports to a detailed study of the competitive process in the relevant reference field.

COMPETITION WITHIN THE FIRM

It is a misconception that large companies provide united and single-minded approaches to the problems facing them. Rivalries and internal conflict commonly arise within companies as they do within all strata of human society. Where the company represents an amalgamation of a number of formerly independent units the opportunity for internal stress is considerable. Internal stress is perhaps most likely when plants are separated geographically, and retain considerable marketing independence and local goodwill. In such cases rigorous centralized control over pricing policy, investment determination, quality of production, delivery dates, and research expenditures may be necessary to limit the extent of inter-plant competition. Rigorous controls from the centre may conflict with the need to retain enterprise and initiative at plant level. A conflict of interests may then arise.

Large companies may decide that centralization of policy can be obtained only at the expense of high unit production costs and low operational flexibility. Conscious policies of decentralization may therefore be implemented. Decentralization—implying delegated authority with commensurate responsibility—may expose a company to keen inter-plant competition. If the decentralization policy involves more than lip-service, central management will have to convince each plant manager of the value of its desired policies; threats from head office simply nullify decentralization. Undesired inter-plant competition may be tolerated as an acceptable price for flexibility and branch initiative.

A number of dominant firms have actively encouraged individual branches or plants to compete in certain fields with each other.[1] The central organization in such instances would normally insist upon general price control,[2] supervision of investment expenditure and perhaps supervision of advertising allocations. On the other hand the branches may be encouraged to compete with each other on delivery dates, sales promotion, product quality, and perhaps in innovation.

Inter-plant competition was consciously tolerated in the cigarette and tobacco industry. The Imperial Tobacco Company had been created by an amalgamation of a number of competitive units which had enjoyed a long tradition of independence and individuality. Each branch had been anxious to retain as much independence as possible. This desire had been accepted or tolerated by the parent company. At the time of investigation, although the number of branches had been reduced, the Imperial Tobacco Company was still organized basically as it had been in 1901—a number of semi-autonomous units, varying greatly in size and relative importance.

Imperial Tobacco justified its branch system as combining the advantages of large scale production with those of keen internal competition. It felt that the existing structure 'reinforces the effects of outside competition in stimulating progressive increases in efficiency of manufacture and marketing and in ensuring a constant search for products which will best the requirements of the public'.[3] The company recognized that this policy entailed a willingness to close down the less successful branches. Indeed, it pointed to recent decisions regarding branch closures, and its desire to eliminate all but the four most successful branches.

The Monopolies Commission was far less enthusiastic about the success of inter-branch competition within Imperial Tobacco. There was certainly considerable branch freedom in advertising expenditure and brand promotion; but the Commission noted that until 1954 Imperial had been under no strong compulsion to reorganize its original branch structure, even though certain branches were highly unprofitable.[4] While admitting that the system provided incentives for inefficient branches to reduce costs, the Commission felt that the stimulus towards branch elimination since 1954 had stemmed less from inter-branch competition than from the emergence of Gallaher as a powerful

[1] Hedley and Unilever in the soap and detergent industry are excellent examples.

[2] Freedom to negotiate 'special discounts' may be left for decision at plant level.

[3] op. cit., 1961, p. 188.

[4] Relative branch importance had altered considerably, viz. the rapid development of the 'Player' branch at Nottingham.

competitor. The Commission's inquiry itself may also have speeded up reorganization.[1]

The cigarette and tobacco inquiry is the only instance to date in which the Commission has paid attention to arguments concerning inter-branch rivalry within a dominant firm. The Commission noted the potential advantages of inter-branch competition; the Commission showed an awareness of its tenuous and limited importance as an influence upon the Company's policy. Companies may be wary of relying too heavily upon the argument that inter-branch competition is an active constraint upon their policies. The argument could be used as fodder for a conclusion favouring the disintegration of the organization into autonomous units.

COMPETITION FROM INDEPENDENT REFERENCE GOOD SUPPLIERS

This is the most obvious aspect of the competitive process in relation to dominant firms. The Monopolies Commission has always devoted time to consideration of its effectiveness in safeguarding the public from the abuse of market power. The ability of independent competition to protect the public from high prices and inefficiency will depend in part upon the proportion of total sales accounted for by such competitors. It will also depend upon the speed with which successful market penetration on the part of independents can be consolidated by the implementation of capital investment programmes. Additionally it will depend on the success or failure of measures imposed by the dominant firm to eliminate independent competition. United States antitrust authorities have been criticized for relying too heavily upon the existence of competitors and too little upon competition.

The existence of many firms in a referred industry is no indication of effective competition. A tradition of apathy and co-operation may place no pressure upon the dominant firm. On the other hand a few determined companies may galvanize a formerly complacent and apathetic dominant firm into improving its economic performance.[2]

The Monopolies Commission was very concerned by the lack of independent competition in the oxygen and dissolved acetylene industry.[3] At the time of investigation, the British Oxygen Company accounted for 98 per cent of the total United Kingdom market. The Commission concluded that substantial economies of large scale pro-

[1] The investigation of the British Match Corporation indicated a minor degree of inter-branch competition. The Monopolies Commission did not comment on its implications.

[2] See J. M. Clark, 1961, op. cit., p. 95. 'If the major firms held an umbrella over the industry's market and held it too high, the small mavericks in the industry might in the aggregate become the controlling factor.'

[3] Report on the Supply of Industrial and Medical Gases, 1956. H.C.P. 13.

duction encouraged national or regional monopolization of supplies. Evidence was produced of national dominance by one firm in France, and regional dominance in Holland. At the same time evidence was unearthed of consciously predatory practices designed by the British Oxygen Company to eliminate independent competition.

A limited amount of independent competition existed in the dissolved acetylene industry; certain consumers possessed acetylene generating plant and produced their own gas. The British Oxygen Company stressed that customer production was uneconomic and impracticable, owing to difficulties of sludge disposal, and the need for expensive safety precautions. In addition, dissolved acetylene could be carried in cylinders whereas generated acetylene could not. The Commission concluded that British Oxygen's monopoly was virtually unchallenged. There were serious dangers in such dominance by an organization which had 'not been content to rely on its advantages of scale and experience but has continued for many years to pursue a policy of suppressing and restricting competition'.[1]

The Imperial Tobacco Company had dominated the United Kingdom cigarette and tobacco industry throughout the first half of the twentieth century. In 1903, following the elimination of active American competition, its share of the domestic market had been almost 50 per cent; by 1920 this had risen to more than 70 per cent and, with the exception of the coupon trading period in the 1930s, had remained at this level until the 1950s when Imperial Tobacco began to lose part of its markets to Gallaher. In 1959 the Imperial Tobacco Company's market share amounted to 63½ per cent, Gallaher's share having risen to nearly 30 per cent. This figure was larger than that of any individual competitor of Imperial Tobacco throughout the latter's history.

The Monopolies Commission noted the beneficial impact of Gallaher's competition upon the performance of Imperial Tobacco. In particular, Imperial Tobacco had been jolted into undertaking a major reorganization of its branch structure; a number of unprofitable brands had been eliminated. The Commission placed great importance upon the competition from Gallaher. Indeed, the Commission recommended that Imperial Tobacco should sell its shareholding in Gallaher to eliminate all risk of interference in the latter's competitive policy. Active competition from Gallaher must be maintained even at the risk of allowing American control of the Company.[2]

The Monopolies Commission was satisfied with the competition faced by Molins in the cigarette machinery industry. Molins was responsible for 55 per cent of sales and had benefited from financial aid

[1] Report on the Supply of Industrial and Medical Gases, 1956. H.C.P. 13, p. 100.

[2] The Government disagreed with this interpretation.

provided by its two major shareholders, the Imperial Tobacco Company and the British-American Tobacco Company. Nevertheless, Molins had attained its dominant position, in the face of powerful international competition, primarily as a result of superior inventiveness and a superb record of technical development. Its high profits had been earned under competitive conditions; its market dominance could only be safeguarded by future enterprise and efficiency. The Commission felt that active competition provided a complete safeguard for the public interest.

The Commission has paid considerable attention to evidence of competition in industries dominated by one supplier. It has shown some willingness to condone the activities of dominant firms where independent producers have safeguarded the interests of the general public.

COMPETITION FROM NON-REFERENCE GOOD SUPPLIERS

Dominant firms may be subjected to keen competition from suppliers of non-reference goods, especially in industries subject to technical change. The British Match Corporation argued that matches faced competition from cigarette lighters and other forms of battery-powered lighting equipment. There was little evidence that this competition was effective. On the other hand the Monopolies Commission noted the existence of active competition between the main nitrogenous fertilizers[1] supplied by Imperial Chemical Industries[2] and the compound fertilizers[3] produced by Fisons. In general, British farmers were divided sharply over the merits of the two kinds of fertilizers; a number combined nitrogenous fertilizers for healthy growth with phosphorus for hastened maturity; nevertheless, at the margin, competition was effective. This affected the pricing policies of the two companies:

> It appears to us that ICI, whose main endeavour in the fertilizer field for the past forty years has been to expand the demand for nitrogen, has in recent years adjusted its prices somewhat in favour of the farmer buying sulphate for straight use, while Fisons, which has no substantial interest in selling straight sulphate, tries to readjust the balance by means of the bogey system which has the effect of providing a smaller margin of profit on compounds with a higher ammonium sulphate content and correspondingly higher margin on others.[4]

The Monopolies Commission concluded that the tendency to apply an increasing proportion of chemical fertilizers in the form of granular compounds was economical; any policy favouring the straight applica-

[1] Report on the Supply of Chemical Fertilizers, 1959. H.C.P. 267.
[2] Ammonium sulphate, nitro chalk, sodium nitrate and ammonium nitrate.
[3] Together with calcium superphosphate.
[4] op. cit., 1959, p. 215.

tion of fertilizers was open to criticism. Nevertheless, there appeared to be sound agronomic arguments, especially in the case of grass land husbandry, against condemnation of the differential price structure. There had been a strong trend over the years towards the use of compounds; this had not been impeded by the pricing policy of Imperial Chemical Industries.

There have been instances, however, where the Monopolies Commission has considered itself unable to obtain evidence from non-reference good suppliers relating to their importance as competitors of dominant firms under inquiry. It has felt, evidently, that such action would conflict with the nature of its reference. This interpretation has resulted, upon occasion, in an excessively narrow interpretation of the competitive process within an industry. In particular this is true of the inquiry into the supply of electrical equipment for mechanically-propelled land vehicles, where failure to examine the nature of competition from non-electrical equipment largely invalidated the conclusions that were drawn.

COMPETITION FROM OVERSEAS SOURCES

Competition from imported goods may provide an acceptable safeguard for the public against inefficient or exploitative activities of dominant domestic companies. Such competition may not always be deemed to operate in the public interest. In particular, where the imported goods account for a substantial outlay of foreign currencies, and where the employment implications in this country of successful overseas competition are considered severe, the British Government may decide to protect the dominant British producer from such competition. Tariffs and import quotas may be imposed upon offending supplies. Dominant firms may be able to shelter behind the British balance of payments.

Perhaps the most important instance of privately-organized import protection for a dominant firm was discovered in the match inquiry. The British Match Corporation was protected from domestic competition by scale economies and by the lack of market expansion for match supplies. The Monopolies Commission noted that the British Match Corporation was a high cost match producer, yet could earn high profits. It would be unwise, however, to encourage independent producers to undertake match production since excess capacity would result from such action.

The Monopolies Commission examined the network of agreements which limited competition from the Swedish Match Company in the British market. The Commission feared that major modifications of the agreements would drive the latter company into a full-scale competitive onslaught on the British market. If this occurred Swedish Match would certainly dominate. The Commission therefore recommended that this competition should be sacrificed and that the British Match Corporation should be subjected to Government supervision.

In industries imports played little or no part[1] in restraining the operations of dominant firms. In the chemical fertilizer industry the majority of reference products used in the United Kingdom were domestically manufactured, although imported materials were incorporated in the products. Straight potassic fertilizers were an exception, being wholly imported. The Dunlop Rubber Company experienced competition from imports in rubber footwear and pneumatic tyres. In both instances, however, Dunlop was party to restrictive arrangements aimed at reducing the volume of competitive imports on the British market. In general the Commission has placed little faith in the ability of imports to act as a public safeguard.

THE ROLE OF POTENTIAL COMPETITION

Dominant firms are rarely in a position to disregard the activation of potential competition when operating a high price policy. Established firms are fettered by the need to pay keen regard to the risk of attracting new entrants.[2] Additionally such companies must heed the danger of encouraging entry by earning reasonable profits on excessively high levels of costs. In this manner, potential competition may play a similar role to that of actual competition in limiting abuse of dominant positions.[3] Dominant firms will tend to bear in mind a subjective price ceiling; at prices above this ceiling they will expect new entry. Prices may rise above the ceiling. Companies may pay greater attention to reaping short-term profit at the expense of the longer run, especially where uncertainty is high and a function of time. New entry may be occasioned by errors of judgment in estimating the no-entry price ceiling, or by rash entry on the part of outside firms, who may fail to make prudent consideration of the cost-price implications. The concept of no-entry price ceiling is at best a rough guide both for established firms and for potential entrants. Companies will tend to determine the no-entry price ceiling by reference to their own average costs of production. In many instances how-

[1] Imported cigarettes and tobacco accounted for 0·2 per cent of total domestic sales, and all oxygen, dissolved acetylene, and propane supplies were home produced.

[2] H. Edwards, 1960, op. cit., p. 69. 'It is this awareness of the threat of new competition if prices are set too high which governs the equilibrium tendency of the system . . . the dominant objective of the entrepreneur in setting his price is, typically, to forestall the emergence of such new competition.'

[3] B. L. Johns, *Journal of Industrial Economics*, November 1962, p. 49. 'In so far as business firms take account of the strength of potential competition, prices in industrial markets will be lower (and output greater) than if the threat of entry were ignored.'

ever this is a poor measuring rod. Barriers to entry may involve new entrants in relatively higher unit production costs. In these circumstances existing firms may earn high profits without inducing entry. On the other hand, where potential entrants have lower average cost schedules than the established firm, entry may be induced in the face of low profit experience in the industry. Average production cost is not always a useful guide where product differentiation is important. Potential entrants may feel that their high unit costs are compensated for by superior quality in production; they may consider that their products will command sufficient goodwill to render production profitable.

Perhaps the most important form of potential competition in the post-war period has emanated from large companies operating in other industries, possibly utilizing the same raw materials, or similar techniques and skills. Such companies have displayed considerable willingness to enter industries offering high profit inducements or good prospects of rapid market penetration. Barriers to entry in the shape of technical knowledge, finance, goodwill, and scale are usually lower for large existing companies than for newly-constructed entrants. It is apparent that dominant firms take anxious note of this possibility in setting their price-output targets. Dominant firms are most susceptible to potential competition in industries characterized by a high level of technological change. Research and development results may produce competition from unexpected sources. Potential competition, reflecting threatened innovation, is probably the most highly feared of all.

Mr Downie put forward an interesting—though unconvincing—thesis regarding such diversification.[1] He argued that concentration within an industry occurred under the stimulus of widely differing levels of efficiency between competitive firms. Once the concentration movement had been effected, and efficiency differentials had been eliminated, the companies remaining would have little inducement to increase their market shares. Instead they would look outwards 'to seek other industries where the dispersion of efficiency is wide, the average rate of growth is high, and a few large efficient firms have not yet secured a dominant position'.[2] Mr Downie, therefore, concluded that migration, however reluctant,[3] was a one-way traffic from the concentrated to the less concentrated industry.

Unfortunately, perhaps, Mr Downie's contention is at odds with the facts. There is little evidence to show that concentration standardizes

[1] *The Competitive Process*, op. cit.

[2] ibid., p. 106.

[3] ibid., p. 105. 'It is more realistic . . . to think of the firm, not as eagerly scanning the horizon for a chance to break into new fields, but as forced reluctantly from its accustomed matrix by the increasing difficulty of further growth there.'

unit production costs throughout the relevant industry. Many large companies admit to considerable variation in unit costs between branches and/or between plants. The Imperial Tobacco Company was criticized severely by the Monopolies Commission for the variations it had tolerated in branch efficiencies. The British Match Corporation had been criticized earlier on a similar ground. The Monopolies Commission encountered a similar situation with reference to the fertilizer plants of Imperial Chemical Industries. There is no reason to suppose that dominant firms owe their position to efficient production and marketing. There is considerable evidence that dominance has been buttressed for lengthy periods by the maintenance of barriers to new entry and by predatory incursion upon the markets of existing competitors.

The process of diversification in postwar Britain has been stimulated by different reasons than those relied upon by Mr Downie. Three factors in particular have contributed to diversification on the part of British companies. The first is the substantial improvements in financial information relating to companies. The Companies Act 1948 had demanded the publication of company accounts in considerably greater detail than previously. Shareholders and companies were provided with considerable information in this manner. At the same time the growth of institutional investment provided for broadened access to financial information. Most institutional investors hold wide portfolios, giving access to information from a number of companies. Financial information is an important raw material for potential diversification, be it through take-over bids or through the purchase of new plant and equipment.

The study and development of management as a science has provided a second spur to diversification. Management has been provided with finely adjusted tools for decision-taking purposes.[1] The increased dispersion of management knowledge has been reflected in a widened range of management efficiencies; skilled management has been encouraged to bid for companies managed shoddily. This was one motive in the Imperial Chemical Industries abortive bid for Courtaulds.

Inflation, and fiscal efforts to reduce its pace, have provided the third stimulus towards diversification. The take-over bid has been the mechanism through which diversification has been encouraged. Under inflationary conditions company profits tend to rise owing to stock appreciation and a widening cost base upon which percentage margin additions are made when calculating prices. The value of assets[2] may rise fairly rapidly in periods of inflation. Governments have been concerned to win trade union co-operation for wage restraint, and to this end they

[1] E. G. Linear, programming, theory of games, discounted-cash-flow, and critical path techniques.

[2] The present value of future earnings streams discounted at the appropriate (subjective) interest rate.

have devised various techniques for limiting dividend payments. The devices have ranged from outright requests for dividend restraint to the imposition of a higher rate of profits tax upon distributed than upon retained profits. At the same time management, fearing the loss of control that could result from new issues, has tended to finance expansion by ploughed-back profits rather than by new issues based on high dividend payments.[1]

Unfortunately, the investing public is far more concerned with yield than with cover when developing an investment portfolio. The result is that growth-conscious firms, paring dividends to the barest minimum, have been exposed to take-over bids on the ground that their real asset values are grossly underestimated by the market. This development has been exacerbated by Government requests for temporary dividend restraint,[2] or by the imposition of differential profits taxes favouring plough-back and dividend restraint.[3]

The Monopolies Commission has always most carefully assessed the possibility of new firms entering an industry dominated by one or more companies. In certain instances it has concluded that new entry was unlikely. This was so in the cigarettes and tobacco industry. The Commission noted the reduction that had occurred in the number of manufacturers; in part this could be explained by economies of large-scale production, especially by the onerous capital commitment required for plant and stocks of leaf, but also required for financing the duty payable on tobacco leaf from when it left bond until receipt of payment several weeks after sale. Nevertheless, small producers could exist on an economic basis if they were able to rely upon a steady demand for their products. In recent years public taste had been increasingly concentrated on a few proprietary brands of cigarettes. This type of demand could not be built up or sustained without heavy and continued advertising expenditure. An imposing barrier to new entry had thus developed. The Commission hoped that the increasing consumption of filter-tipped cigarettes would increase the variety of popular brands. It concluded that the industry was certain to remain in the hands of a very few firms.

A similarly depressing picture for potential entrants was exposed in the Commission's inquiry into industrial and medical gases. The Commission unearthed a complex network of activities adopted by British Oxygen Company to forestall new entrants. Activities spanned full-line forcing, the use of fighting brands, control over the provision of oxygen plant, and a national pricing system. The Commission correctly forecast a greater potential for competition in the supply of the new-style ton-

[1] Ploughed-back profits account for about 60 per cent of net investment funds in UK.

[2] e.g. Selwyn Lloyd in 1961.

[3] The Corporation Tax introduced in April 1965 has this effect.

nage oxygen which provided the possibility of backward integration by large oxygen consumers. In addition it felt that potential competition might be activated by a removal of certain predatory practices operated by the British Oxygen Company.

Potential competition was more important in the chemical fertilizer industry. Imperial Chemical Industries and Fisons were both competing marginally in each other's major field of supply. Fisons appears to have been under the impression, during the years 1944–54, that there was a tacit understanding that neither would further encroach upon the other's market without giving notice and discussing the matter. Imperial Chemical Industries had been under no such impression. The Commission considered that the misunderstanding had not come to light 'because for some ten years each was preoccupied with the postwar problems in its own field'.[1]

The Monopolies Commission felt that the history of the relations between Fisons and ICI did not 'suggest either that any kind of live-and-let-live policy has contributed to the achievement or maintenance of ICI's monopoly position in nitrogenous fertilizers, or that ICI has abused its power in this field with a view to keeping Fisons out of it'.[2] Indeed, it recognized that Fisons, itself the weaker of the two companies, had been acutely conscious of its inability to dictate to ICI how far the latter should enter into compound manufacture. Potential competition had been a serious factor for consideration in Fisons' pricing strategies.

The Monopolies Commission has shown the utmost respect for the regulatory powers of potential competition. Its recommendations have been designed, consistently, to eliminate practices resulting in high entry barriers. The Commission appears to have underestimated the possibility of entry from large firms in different industries, perhaps through successful take over bids. In industries subjected to technological change or to rapid market expansion diversified entry may be realistic. In industries where scale economies are great, the pace of market expansion low or negative and technical progress low, the impact of potential competition may be slight.[3] Under such conditions there may be justification for opening up the British market to competitive imports. The decision of the British Government to encourage match importation from Russia and Poland has forced the British Match Corporation to tighten up its efficiency and indeed to diversify its production.

[1] op. cit., 1959, p. 200.

[2] ibid., p. 201.

[3] British Match Corporation was protected on these grounds from potential competition.

COMPETITION FROM THE STATE

It has never been the policy of the British Government to organize and to finance State competition in industries dominated by one company, even when the competitive checks of the capitalist system have failed completely. State holdings in road haulage[1] and steel[2] have occurred more by chance than by design. Lack of State competition in Britain contrasts with the policy of the French Government which has incorporated public enterprise into the capitalist system with considerable success. The Labour Party has displayed periodic interest in this kind of State participation, but has not committed itself publicly to such action.

State participation in industries dominated by private enterprise companies should not be accompanied by commercial privileges. State capital must be provided at ruling market rates, State firms should not be allowed to accumulate deficits carried by the Exchequer, and they should be provided with no privileged access to economic or political information relevant to their decision-making. Under such limitations, the State corporation might usefully be created to compete with dominant firms where the public interest has been abused.

In practice, State sponsored competition has been rejected by the Monopolies Commission as a means of regulating the abuses of dominant firms. Price supervision and controls, divestiture of assets, and the elimination by Government of the more obvious abuses have been favoured instead. In large part, this is a reflection of public opinion and of Government attitudes in this country. After 1951 public opinion veered away from further nationalization. The Monopolies Commission could scarcely expect to convince a Conservative Government of the need for State sponsored competition.

PUBLICITY AND THE COMPETITIVE PROCESS

All the inter-war period reports on industrial organization and policy stressed the value of publicity as a check against abuse of a dominant market position. Indeed a number of reports indicated that adequate publicity would provide a fully effective safeguard for the general public.

The post-1945 industrial reports recognized the need for further checks upon dominance; this requirement found its expression in the Acts of 1948, 1953, and 1956. The Acts provided for publicity through publication of the Reports of the Monopolies Commission.[3] HM

[1] British Road Services.

[2] Richard, Thomas and Baldwins.

[3] Some of the early Reports retailed at as little as 3s 6d; a recent Report sells at 22s 6d a copy.

Stationery Office must be criticized for underestimating the demand for copies of Monopolies Commission reports. However, adequate Press and television coverage has provided a wide dissemination of the Commission's conclusions, if not the reasoning upon which they are based.[1]

Most large companies express concern about the maintenance or improvement of their public images. In this respect publicity, or fear of publicity, may prevent gross profiteering and other serious abuses of market dominance.

THE MANAGERIAL REVOLUTION AND THE COMPETITIVE PROCESS

An increasing dispersion of stock ownership, the extensive institutionalization of investment, and a rapid development of the proxy machinery, have served in recent years to weaken shareholder control over corporate enterprise. In large companies effective control tends to be concentrated upon senior management which may own a very small fraction of the total voting stock.

To the extent that management owns shares in the company it manages there is an incentive to obtain maximum profits. Often the shares so held are relatively unimportant and profit incentives weak. Of course senior management must concern itself with profits to a limited extent. Capital must be serviced, and funds must be retained or obtained from the capital market for required investment programmes. In addition, the risk of take-over bids has forced management to watch closely the stock market valuation of their assets. Nevertheless, managerial salaries are usually correlated more closely with company turnover than with company profit. Moreover, the political importance of management is a function more of company size than of company profitability.

In order to breach the widening gulf between the interests of shareholders and of management in large companies, various schemes have been adopted to canalize management self-interest into the drive for profit. Cash bonuses rising with profits as a ratio of sales or of capital employed have been introduced by some companies. The effectiveness of such bonuses has been reduced by high marginal rates of income tax. Increasing emphasis in recent years has been placed instead upon stock purchase options as a profit-incentive. Management may react keenly to such an incentive to raise stock market prices above the purchase-price option with which they have been provided.

> In the stock option, the executive has an interest in the future earnings of the company which he obtained without any cost and without

[1] The Monopolies Commission has insisted upon full publicity for all subsidiary interests of dominant firms. Dunlop's distributive interests were disclosed, as well as Imperial Tobacco's interest in Gallaher, and Lucas's subsidiary interests.

taking any risk and the tax provisions give him a way to cash in on the value of this interest as a low-taxed capital gain and not as high-taxed income.[1]

Stock options may be useful for senior management. For middle-management there are other, more suitable, types of bonus. Specific task standards may be established by senior management, and bonuses may be provided for task fulfilment. Careful selection of task standards, and appropriate bonus provisions, may stimulate middle management to activity designed to raise profit performance.

Nevertheless, the managerial revolution has certainly weakened the profit drive; bonuses provide an imperfect spur to management action. Yet the Monopolies Commission rarely considered the implications of this for the public interest. Actions and not motives are, of course, the critical yardstick of company performance. But motive may go far towards explaining action, and this is critical for the formulation of realistic recommendations.

[1] G. Means, *Pricing Power and the Public Interest*, 1962, p. 283.

Chapter Thirteen

THE DOMINANT FIRM AND BARRIERS TO INDEPENDENT COMPETITION

It is always difficult to distinguish between fair competitive measures resorted to by dominant bodies and those restrictive and predatory practices designed to forestall entry and to eliminate existing rivals. It is more difficult to make this distinction in relation to actions of dominant firms than in relation to trade associations. The dominant firm operates independently, and to its own ends. These ends may be difficult to comprehend from outside. Trade association practices are joint practices, and intent to damage others, if it exists, is easier to discern. By the nature of things, it is also easier to eliminate the undesirable practices of a trade association than of a dominant firm.

PRODUCTION DIFFERENTIATION AND THE PUBLIC INTEREST

Dominant Firm Advertising

Advertising and sales promotion may serve a useful role in the preservation of market dominance in industries characterized by product differentiation, whilst at the same time it may enhance the operation of the competitive process. Once again the observer is faced with a largely unresolved paradox.

Companies may resort to sales promotion as a means of penetrating rival markets and of consolidating a market foothold. They may anticipate a general broadening of the total market. In addition advertising establishes brand names; this may encourage innovation by providing for higher plasticity of consumer expenditure within a known company's product range. It is possible to argue that advertising is essential to technological advance and to economic expansion in consumer-orientated economies.

On the other hand there is no doubt that large-scale advertising raises entry barriers by reducing expenditure plasticity towards new products of unknown companies, and by forcing such firms into heavy advertising outlays. Small-scale competitors may find it difficult under such conditions to maintain their existing market shares, let alone to penetrate the market of the dominant firm. Heavy advertising expenditure by a dominant firm may be so effective that market concentration is further fostered. In this sense advertising may be as much a cause as an effect of oligopoly.

The Monopolies Commission appears to be uncertain of the importance of advertising as an impediment to competition. In one inquiry at least[1] advertising may have provided the key to the structure and performance of component firms. The Monopolies Commission has briefly referred to advertising as an issue, but has made no attempt to analyse its fundamental importance. This attitude was especially evident in the cigarettes and tobacco inquiry.

The industry was dominated by the Imperial Tobacco Company. The only other company of importance was Gallagher, a company in which the Imperial Tobacco Company had secretly maintained a substantial equity holding.[2] In analysing the prospects for new entry into the industry the Commission noted that competitors far smaller than the two giants could operate economically if they were able to rely upon a steady demand for their products. It pointed out, however, that public taste had become concentrated upon a few proprietary brands, and that this type of demand could be established solely by sustained and heavy expenditure upon advertising. The Commission noted, apparently without undue concern, that experience over the past twenty-five years indicated increasing difficulty on the part of medium and small-sized manufacturers who could not maintain a steady level of business without a quite disproportionate expenditure on brand promotion.

Despite the encouraging expansion of Gallaher, and the growing market for filter-tipped cigarettes,[3] the Commission concluded that the bulk of the cigarette trade was likely to remain concentrated in the hands of a very few firms. It made no further reference to advertising expenditure.

The Monopolies Commission should have produced a much closer analysis of the impact of advertising upon the nature of demand within the industry; it should have examined the relationship between advertising and innovation, between advertising and cigarette prices, and between advertising and unit production costs. In omitting such analysis the Commission rendered a satisfactory analysis of the cigarette trade well nigh impossible.[4]

[1] Cigarettes and Tobacco.

[2] Together, the two companies accounted for more than 90 per cent of UK supplies of cigarettes and tobacco.

[3] Which might increase the range of cigarette brands available.

[4] B. S. Yamey, *Modern Law Review*, November 1961, p. 753. 'One gains the impression that advertising and sales promotion provide the key to the structure

Patent Policies

Legislation in the United Kingdom allows for patenting of inventions under specified conditions and for specified periods.[1] This policy, admittedly monopolistic in the narrow and short-run sense, is justified on the ground that it stimulates investment in research, development, and innovation. The patent system does involve risks, however, in industries dominated by one large company, especially where the rate of technological development is low. Under these conditions the patented control of designs and processes may provide important product differentiation advantages for dominant firms. The risk is reduced in rapidly developing industries, where processes and designs are constantly superceded and rendered economically obsolete. Indeed, many firms do not patent under such conditions, but rely upon the time lag between innovation and counter-innovation for the achievement of quasi-rents. Where the gestation period is lengthy quasi-rents may be reaped for many years.

The British Oxygen Company had a long history of patent acquisitions when examined by the Monopolies Commission. In particular, the British Oxygen Company had acquired a number of gas suppliers primarily to obtain their patent rights. The Company claimed, nevertheless, that patent rights acquired in the course of its development had not been critical in the sense that they closed the field to others who might have desired to engage commercially in the production of oxygen. The Linde and Claude patents had expired in 1916 leaving the oxygen production process by fractionation of liquefied air available to all firms; the important Heylandt patents had all expired by 1943. 'It has been open to anyone to produce and distribute liquid oxygen for nearly twenty years, and it has been open to anyone to manufacture, use or sell gaseous oxygen plant for the past forty years without risk of patent infringement.'[2]

The British Oxygen Company had pursued a policy of acquiring patent rights from overseas companies for exploitation in the United Kingdom. The Commission implied that such activities had reduced the research and development effort of the Company. British Oxygen had pursued with success a policy of controlling oxygen plant in order to maintain market dominance in oxygen supply. This policy was contrary to the public interest. Existing legislation did not provide any effective means of preventing this, since British Oxygen operated largely as a licensee under foreign patents.

---

of the industry and competitive behaviour in it—an impression which is confirmed by detailed analyses of the industry in the United States. Yet in the report there is no systematic discussion of the implications of advertising in the industry.'

[1] Supra, Chapter 9.

[2] op. cit., 1956, p. 75.

The British Match Corporation had long been subjected to the suspicion that it had immobilized re-ignitable match production techniques. The Corporation informed the Monopolies Commission that it was not its policy to protect either new machinery or improvements in existing processes by means of patents. It preferred to rely upon the exchange of information between itself and Swedish Match provided for in the Trading Agreement. Attempts at developing and innovating re-ignitable matches[1] and double-headed matches[2] had underlined intractable commercial problems.

The Monopolies Commission has encountered very few instances of market dominance protected by patents. Where such a situation exists the solution is not simple. The Patent Act, 1949, encourages a limited protection system for companies producing new developments. It allows companies to assign patents to whosoever they may wish. There is no available legislation as yet to prevent large companies from acquiring companies which hold important patents. The Oxygen inquiry itself is evidence of the Commission's dilemma when faced by patent action of this kind on the part of large firms. There is no simple solution to this problem; it is difficult to eliminate the undesirable elements of patent legislation without damaging the incentive towards innovation.

Access to Favoured Distributive Channels

The ability of a dominant supplier to prevent its competitors from obtaining unfettered access to distributive outlets may provide it with significant product differentiation advantages. This problem is peculiar to market dominance conditions. Where supply conditions are keenly competitive close arrangements between individual producers and retailers, and even forward integration by suppliers into distribution, arouses little public unease. Indeed, in many instances such developments are publicly encouraged, and consumer benefits in the form of lower prices are self-evident.

Where an industry is dominated by one supplier, however, the relationships between this company and its distributive outlets become a matter of public concern. The Monopolies Commission has carefully analysed all links between dominant firms and their distributors. The links have appeared in three main forms.

(i) *Display Arrangements* between manufacturer and retailers are particularly important where the product is subject to impulse buying. Advertising through media such as the Press and television may be

[1] op. cit., 1953, p. 50. 'A former Chairman of Brymay and of BMC described the re-ignitable match as "an interesting but unpractical scientific toy, quite valueless as an article of commerce".'

[2] The United Kingdom patent for such processes had lapsed in 1950.

fruitful but a relatively high proportion of sales may be effected by thrusting the product upon the potential buyer at the moment of decision. It is not uncommon, under these circumstances, for a dominant producer to enter into arrangements with distributors for the prominent display of his products. This may seriously hinder attempts by competitive suppliers to increase their market penetration even where they adopt large-scale national advertising campaigns.

Such an arrangement was encountered by the Monopolies Commission in the cigarette and tobacco industry. The Imperial Tobacco Company paid a bonus to all retailers who agreed to make available to its products 50 per cent of the slots in their automatic machines and to provide certain window space for Imperial's advertising. The obligations in this latter connection were not defined; the Commission found that representatives of the Imperial Tobacco Company were instructed to interpret this as being not less than 50 per cent of each type of display or advertisement in quantity or quality, both inside and outside the premises.

Imperial Tobacco contended that this practice induced distributors to stock, and to promote the sales of, its products and to ensure that the company was given a reasonable share of such 'point-of-sale' display as was devoted to tobacco goods. In practice, the display proportion required by the Company had been lower than its share of the domestic tobacco trade. A sample survey undertaken in 1958 indicated that the average proportion of display provided for Imperial Tobacco's goods by traders signatory to the bonus agreement was 67 per cent; that provided by non-signatory traders was 56 per cent. Thus the proportion stipulated for bonus purposes was less than that which traders had provided voluntarily to Imperial Tobacco products.

Imperial Tobacco's bonus payments amounted to one-twentieth of the retail margin on cigarettes. Other manufacturers allowed a roughly equivalent bonus, ensuring that the retailer was not penalized for retailing more of their products and less of Imperial's. Any manufacturer could purchase the right to predominant display by offering a distributor a bonus equivalent to that he would sacrifice by abandoning his agreement with Imperial Tobacco.

The Monopolies Commission agreed that the display space allocated to Imperial Tobacco products measured by quantity was certainly no greater and might well be less than the proportion of trade accounted for by the Company. Nevertheless, the value of the display could not be assessed solely by reference to the proportion of space occupied. The Commission interpreted the agreement to mean that Imperial products should have preference in 'centre displays'; in this way Imperial effectively ensured that more than one half of the value of the signatory distributor's display would accrue to itself. The Commission could not decide whether the real advertising value afforded to Imperial was greater or less than the proportion of trade accounted for by the Company.

The Commission was concerned by Imperial Tobacco's failure to make pro-rata display payments dependent upon the display facilities offered. The Company paid for a proportion of the display, thereby ensuring that no competitor could obtain a better display in any shop accepting its bonus payments. The division of display facilities over the best part of the distributive trade had been rigidified in this manner.

The Commission pointed out that Imperial Tobacco's competitors had offered similar bonuses in order to compete with Imperial. Any firm which bought a predominant share of the display by compensating the distributor for the loss of the Imperial bonus would 'in effect be making an extra payment for facilities which Imperial obtains by allowing no more than the equivalent of the normal trade terms allowed by other manufacturers'.[1] It might be required to compensate the distributor over a considerable period. Such a situation could only arise in an industry dominated by one Company or by a powerful trade association.

The Commission was concerned to prevent a further diminution of competition in the cigarettes and tobacco industry. It felt that the bonus system operated by Imperial Tobacco was restrictive of competition. In condemning the scheme the Commission further recommended that any bonus or allowance in future granted to distributors should be related solely to the latter's turnover in the products of the manufacturer. There should be no association between bonuses and display facilities, and no agreement between any manufacturer and distributor to the effect that if the distributor advertised a competing product he should also advertise the products of that company.

(ii) *Exclusive Dealing and Full-line Forcing* is the second form in which privileged access to distributors may be obtained by dominant suppliers. Where a dominant firm enters into exclusive dealing contracts with a significant proportion of the distributive trade there is a serious danger that existing competitors and/or potential competition will be hampered or eliminated, perhaps to the detriment of the consumer.

Exclusive dealing arrangements were practised by the Amalgamated Dental Company Ltd's Group which accounted for 35·7 per cent of domestic sales of dental goods in 1948. The Amalgamated Dental Group had entered into agreements with two of the largest dealers in dental goods in the country, the Dental Manufacturing Company and S.S. White Company, relating to the supplier of burs. The agreements fettered the freedom of the two dealers to stock burs from other suppliers.[2]

[1] op. cit., 1961, p. 202.

[2] The A.D. Group was the only bur manufacturer in the United Kingdom.

The Agreements had been successful in preventing dealers from stocking the increasing volume of imports of Swedish burs.

The Group argued that its agreements had guaranteed long production runs, and had provided significant scale economies. In fact, the quantities of burs covered by the agreements—fewer than one million —represented only a very small part of the Group's total annual output of burs. In addition the Commission felt that normal quantity rebates encouraged large purchasers to bulk their orders for burs. The agreements reinforced the Amalgamated Dental Group's monopoly in bur production by hampering the sale of other burs through the depots of two large dealers. The Commission recommended that the A.D. Group should reconsider these arrangements in the light of its Report.

The Monopolies Commission encountered an interesting form of exclusive dealing in its investigation of the British Oxygen Company. The British Oxygen Company supplied and freely maintained oxygen equipment to a number of purchasers. Purchasers were required to use the equipment only in conjunction with gases supplied by the British Oxygen Company. More extensively, signatories were required to purchase their total requirements of specified gases from the Company unless they obtained express authorization to the contrary.

The British Oxygen Company pointed out that it normally installed and maintained such apparatus completely free of charge; it could not reasonably be expected to allow such apparatus to be used for the gas supplies of competing companies. It would not in practice enforce the requirement that a consumer should take his total gas supplies from British Oxygen. In fact, however, the Commission found that most consumers did not question the clause.

The Commission did not object to the requirement that the Company's apparatus should be limited to its own gas; but it felt that the remainder of the agreement was unfair. The wide limitations could only be aimed at maintaining British Oxygen's monopoly position and in this way operated against the public interest. The Commission urged that British Oxygen should allow the customer to choose between buying and maintaining the apparatus himself, or hiring the apparatus from British Oxygen and maintaining it himself, or accepting the Company's offer to provide and maintain it free of charge. If he should choose to buy or hire the apparatus, he should be able to do so at reasonable prices and should be able to purchase gas from British Oxygen on reasonable terms without committing himself against buying gas from other sources. If on the other hand the customer selected free installation and maintenance, he might reasonably be required to take from British Oxygen some minimum quantity of gas which would justify the costs of installation and maintenance; he might be required additionally to use the Company's apparatus for its gas alone. But he should not be compelled to take from British Oxygen his total gas requirements if they exceeded the minimum specified quantity.

The Monopolies Commission encountered a limited form of exclusive dealing in the electrical equipment for mechanically-propelled land vehicles inquiry. Lucas had arranged a 'Preferential Spares Discount Agreement' with certain distributors, predominantly at the wholesale level. Favourable discount terms were offered in return for an undertaking to purchase spares exclusively from Lucas, both for resale purposes and for use in repairs.

Lucas argued that the system safeguarded both the goodwill of the company and the interests of the consumer by preventing the use of unsatisfactory spares. Lucas emphasized that the arrangement in no way prevented distributors from dealing in complete component supplies of rival manufacturers. The Monopolies Commission accepted these arguments, and concluded that the arrangement did not operate against the public interest.

(iii) *Ownership of Distributive Outlets* by dominant firms may forestall effective competition especially where such ownership covers a significant proportion of the distributive trade. Forward integration may create little concern in a highly competitive industry, but the market dominance of an integrating company must carry a serious danger of eliminating or weakening competition. The Monopolies Commission examined distributive holdings of dominant firms with considerable caution and suspicion.

The Commission noted that the Dunlop Rubber Company had entered the distributive sector of the pneumatic tyre industry during the inter-war years. It had done so partly to obtain first-hand knowledge of its competitors' marketing techniques, partly in anticipation of a similar move on the part of its competitors. At the time of investigation the Dunlop Rubber Company controlled about 20 per cent of tyre distribution in the United Kingdom,[1] with obvious dangers for the public interest. Moreover, the Company had pursued a policy of concealing its distribution interests from competitive suppliers and other tyre distributors. Dunlop had considered secrecy to be necessary to prevent loss of business. The Dunlop distributive companies had not been used to provide exclusive or even primary outlets for Dunlop tyres. In 1951 53 per cent of their sales had represented other manufacturers' tyres and remoulds. It was possible that if the distributors had been identified as Dunlop subsidiaries their sales of other manufacturers' goods would have been lower. On the other hand the Commission pointed out that if Dunlop continued to increase its distributive interests unknown to other

[1] The Company accounted for well over one-third of total pneumatic tyre supplies in the UK.

manufacturers the latter might ultimately be dependent upon Dunlop subsidiaries for a large part of their outlets.

The Monopolies Commission was not unimpressed by the argument that Dunlop's distributing arrangements had amounted to a legitimate expedient to maintain the Company's competitive position, and that their competitors had been equally free to acquire such secret interests. On balance, the Commission could not say that Dunlop's holdings or the secrecy with which they had been operated had in fact operated in a manner contrary to the public interest. In the absence of evidence suggesting further extension of such holdings by Dunlop the Commission was unable to say that they might be expected to become undesirable.

The Imperial Tobacco Company had acquired control over certain distributing firms in the tobacco industry, namely Sinclair, Bewlay and Finlay. Imperial Tobacco had no effective control over the great majority of distributive channels. There was no evidence whatsoever to indicate that Imperial Tobacco had ever desired to obtain such control or that it was likely in the future to regard its holdings as a nucleus for a more comprehensive distributive system. There had been no complaints from other manufacturers alleging discrimination against their products on the part of any of the three controlled concerns. Indeed for many years Imperial Tobacco had sustained losses on its investment in Bewlay, considering that its high-class sites and sales service provided an advertisement for the tobacco trade in general. The Monopolies Commission considered that the ownership of these three firms had no material effect upon the public interest. Imperial Tobacco had not in fact disclosed its holding of Finlay and the Commission argued that there was no compelling reason for withholding disclosure. The Commission felt it was desirable that the full extent of the interest of a monopoly supplier in the industry concerned should be known.

Joseph Lucas Ltd had not publicly acknowledged its ownership of certain subsidiaries. It argued that the Robert Guthrie Group had been acquired to obtain an unbiased reaction to the sale of Lucas equipment and that this purpose would be defeated if its ownership should ever be disclosed. Similar considerations applied to its control of Cox and Company. Risks, on the other hand, had been acquired in the 1920s to obtain an assured supply of cable made to Lucas's specifications from a source not controlled by the cable ring.

The Monopolies Commission was not satisfied by these arguments. It concluded that Lucas's failure to disclose its subsidiaries operated against the public interest. In this conclusion the Monopolies Commission was fortified by the recommendation of the Jenkins Committee[1] that ownership of all subsidiary companies should be disclosed.

The Monopolies Commission has never adopted a doctrinaire attitude

[1] Report of The Company Law Committee, Cmnd. 1749, para. 380 (g).

towards control by dominant firms of distributive outlets. It has been unwilling to allow such holdings to be held secretly but has not considered it necessary to date to recommend divestiture of assets. Once again the Commission has been forced to walk the economic tightrope which separates justifiable commercial freedom from the unfair exercise of market power.

DOMINANT FIRM COST ADVANTAGES AND THE PUBLIC INTEREST

Dominant firms may be able to reap cost advantages over rival companies, not by reason of superior efficiency, but by reason of their market dominance. Such cost advantages may at once furnish the fruit of their power and a shield against competitive tilts at their market dominance. Cost advantages of this kind may stem from patent control, control over outlets, factor control and control over investment finance. Patent control and control over distributive outlets will not be further discussed.

Control over Factors of Production

The degree of advantage provided by such power is dependent upon the extent and effectiveness of the control as well as upon the lack of satisfactory substitutes. The control may be enhanced by the imposition of tariffs and quantitative restrictions upon imported substitutes. Short-run controls may be extended or eliminated in the longer-run by innovation. Chance plays an important role in such latter developments. But chance may be aided by the patenting policy of the dominant firm.

Factor control may be the result of market dominance rather than the cause; indeed factor control may be the result of aggressive efficiency. Whatever its source, however, factor control provides the basis for market expansion and for the elimination of independent competition in a manner which runs counter to the public interest. Factor control of this kind may sap the power of the competitive process to stimulate the slothful and to penalize the inefficient. The Monopolies Commission has treated such control with suspicion and with circumspection.

The British Match Corporation had acquired control of certain companies which dealt in chemicals used in match production. It had charged its competitors as much as 77 per cent more than its own subsidiaries for the use of these materials. This discrimination was not approved by the Monopolies Commission.

Far more important, however, were the detailed agreements concerning match-producing machinery entered into by the British Match Corporation and Swedish Match, the main producer of such machinery. There were no important patents relating to match-making machinery. The basic machines possessed an extremely lengthy economic life; the regular market demand related to ancillary machines, improvements, and spare parts. The total world demand for match-making machinery was subject to fluctuations and it would not be easy for any concern to exist by the production of such machinery alone. Under these conditions the machinery produced by Swedish Match was generally acknowledged to be the best in Europe. The British Match Corporation had arranged with Swedish Match for the full exchange of technical information and had obtained favourable terms when purchasing machinery. Swedish Match was precluded from supplying machinery, both to independent match manufacturers in the UK and to suppliers in BMC's overseas markets. There were no substantial independent manufacturers of specialized match-making machinery in the United Kingdom. Independent manufacturers existed overseas but the Commission could not obtain the necessary information to evaluate their efficiency in comparison with Swedish Match. BMC had indicated that Swedish machinery was superior to any other and had placed great importance upon its continued access to supplies.

The Monopolies Commission criticized these arrangements, pointing out that in effect, if not in intent, the system had obstructed independent competition in the British match industry. The Commission accepted the British Match Corporation's offer to release Swedish Match from its undertaking not to manufacture match-making machinery in the British Isles.

A similar instance confronted the Monopolies Commission during its investigation of industrial and medical gases. The British Oxygen Company controlled the provision of oxygen equipment to competing suppliers. By acquisition or by agreement the Company controlled the commercial policies of four out of the five firms producing oxygen plant in the United Kingdom. Butterly Ltd was the only manufacturer of oxygen plant, both independent of British Oxygen and able in practice to compete in the supply of plant. The British Oxygen Company justified its position on the ground that for many years there had been little or no demand for customer oxygen plant because its own supplies of oxygen had been so cheap. This situation had been transformed of late by the development of tonnage oxygen plants.[1] British Oxygen claimed that oxygen plant could be supplied in the United Kingdom by five independent companies.

The Commission was convinced that British Oxygen had attempted to maintain its monopoly position in the oxygen industry by controlling plant supplies. However, its ability to do so had been reduced by the competition offered by Butterly; the development of tonnage plant had made it commercially possible for large users to produce

[1] These provided large consumers with the opportunity to produce their own oxygen on an economic scale, especially the large steel companies.

oxygen for their own consumption. The Monopolies Commission concluded that British Oxygen's control of oxygen plant had been misused and it recommended that the situation should be remedied. In determining the appropriate remedy, however, the Commission encountered difficulties. Existing legislation was ineffective. The British Oxygen Company had operated largely as a licensee under foreign patents, and as sole agent for the sale in the United Kingdom of machinery which might have been used by its competitors for oxygen production. The Commission finally concluded that competition from Butterly provided a limited safeguard for the public but there were serious dangers in the form of control exercised by the British Oxygen Company.

Where the control exercised over supplies of plant and machinery was limited and where the use of such powers had been moderate the Commission was not prepared to condemn the situation. Such was the case relating to supplies of cigarette-making machinery.

The Imperial Tobacco Company and the British-American Tobacco Company each held 25 per cent of the shares of Molins, the most successful and most efficient producer of cigarette machinery in the United Kingdom. The two companies had jointly provided financial assistance to Molins during its early development. In return the two companies had claimed the right to the exclusive use of all new machines produced by Molins, a right which Imperial Tobacco had exercised extensively until 1945 and thereafter less freely until 1957. During the greater part of that period, however, Molins had not occupied the pre-eminent position in machinery production obtaining at the time of investigation. There was no evidence that any of Imperial Tobacco's competitors had been seriously hindered by inability to purchase machinery from Molins.[1]

Under the agreement negotiated with Molins in 1957 Imperial Tobacco and the British-American Tobacco Company were allowed a sixty day trial for any new machine produced by Molins. In addition they were given safeguards relating to the prices they should pay for Molins' machinery and spares.[2] Molins had undertaken not to supply any machine to Imperial Tobacco's competitors until the trial was completed. No similar undertaking was made with BAT. In practice this afforded Imperial a slight advantage, but Molins supplied machinery to Imperial's competitors quite equitably following the trial period.

The Monopolies Commission felt that considerable advantages were

[1] op. cit., 1961, p. 209. 'It would have been a different matter if the Companies had persisted in maintaining all their advantages long after Molins had established itself as the leading manufacturer of these machines.'

[2] The price provisions merely confirmed the two firms' rights to exercise their bargaining powers.

afforded to Molins' customers by the testing of new machines under working conditions. The advantages obtained by Imperial Tobacco were unlikely to exceed those afforded to any purchaser buying on a larger scale than its competitors. The Commission refused to condemn the arrangement under such circumstances.

Favoured Access to Investment Finance

It has been suggested that favoured access to investment capital provides dominant firms with a significant cost advantage over their competitors. Where a large company earns high profit rates on capital employed and ploughs back heavily it may be willing to accept a lower rate of interest than outside investors because of increased knowledge of and confidence in its policies. Action of this kind has been common since World War Two, and may be criticized as an avoidance of the 'market test' for investment proposals.

In addition, however, large well-known companies often win the confidence of the investing public in a way that the less well-known cannot. The cautious investor is unlikely to invest in small companies, especially where the dominant firm can hamper, even eliminate, them at will. Investment capital under these conditions may be forthcoming at higher interest rates for the small than for the large company, if indeed it is available to the former at all.[1] In the case of the private limited company inability to use the Stock Exchange, together with restrictions placed upon the transferability of its shares, may further impair its access to investment funds. A gap still remains in the British capital market with relation to the provision of long-term finance to small companies.

The small company may be shackled by lack of finance for expansion; this is not usually the case for large established companies intent upon diversifying into markets dominated by large firms wherever profit expectations warrant such action. The reports of the Monopolies Commission bear witness to the importance of this source of competition. The Monopolies Commission did not concern itself with the possibility that a dominant firm might shelter from competition through its privileged access to investment finance. Perhaps it was influenced in its neglect by knowledge of diversification potential. It is more likely, however, that the omission was the result of less plausible reasoning.

ECONOMIES OF SCALE AND THE PUBLIC INTEREST

Trade associations subjected to Monopolies Commission inquiry were able to reap scale economies more commonly in the fields of finance,

[1] Costs per unit of raised capital are likely to be higher for small companies due to indivisibilities in prospectus expenses, brokerage charges, underwriting expenses, and the like.

marketing and risk-taking than in technique of production and in management. Scale economies in the latter fields were commonly sacrificed by the member companies' determination to preserve a modicum of independence from the trade association. This impediment was less frequently encountered in the case of dominant firms.

The ability of the dominant firm to reap scale economies in certain industries inevitably weakened the competitive process. The limited extent of a given market might obliterate effective competition where scale economies were sufficiently large as to warrant the existence of one company alone. The damage effected to the competitive process in such circumstances would be dependent upon the nature of available substitutes, and upon the pace of the innovative process.

There is a danger, however, that excessive attention may be placed upon the scale argument in relation to market dominance. It is possible that large companies may encounter decreasing returns to scale, and find that their dominance is threatened by the existence of smaller and more efficient companies. Scale diseconomies of this kind may manifest themselves through the management function. Increasing problems of co-ordination, planning and control may result from an expansion in the scale of activities. Where this problem develops in serious proportions the company in question may be required to forego technical economies of scale in order to decentralize the management function.

Economists have been somewhat guilty of mis-interpretation in relation to scale diseconomies. Scale diseconomies have sometimes been assumed when what in fact existed were diseconomies of growth. Higher unit production costs may be less the result of a larger scale of activity than of the pace of growth of the firm. The internal problems that result from a high growth rate have been expertly analysed by Mr Robin Marris:

> Almost by definition the planning and execution of expansion is the least routine of administrative acts: organization must be created where none existed before, recruits must be found, new tasks undertaken and new delegation-patterns developed. It is axiomatic that such planning can only be undertaken by existing members. If an organization is to remain efficient, it cannot possibly expand at an indefinitely rapid rate merely by infinitely rapid recruitments.[1]

Even where scale economies provide a background for market dominance an investigating body must proceed with caution. The existence of low unit production costs may then be more a function of economies of dominance than of size. Marketing economies, in particular, may be obtained by the exercise of monopsonistic purchasing powers, to the

[1] R. Marris, *The Economic Theory of Managerial Capitalism*, Macmillan, 1964, p. 114.

detriment of raw material suppliers. It may be very difficult to distinguish between cost advantages resulting from the size of the dominant firm and those resulting from its dominance. Yet the distinction is crucial for any assessment of the public interest.

The Monopolies Commission concluded that there were substantial economies of scale in match production, and that such economies impeded the development of independent competition in the British match industry. The British Match Corporation was thereby sheltered from outside aggression. The Monopolies Commission ascertained that almost all match producing countries faced the same situation; it concluded that independents had little chance of establishing a firm challenge to the British Match Corporation. The Monopolies Commission was convinced that any such development would be undesirable, since it would result in substantial excess capacity in domestic match production. Other measures had to be designed to constrain the activities of the British company.

The Monopolies Commission concluded that there were substantial scale reasons for market dominance in the supply of electrical equipment to the motor industry. The opportunity to take advantage of scale economies had not materialized until the standardization developments in motor car assembly had been effected in the 1920s. With the expansion and concentration of the motor industry, leading component makers had developed large-scale production techniques, and had achieved appropriate scale economies. In particular, Lucas had seized its opportunity by persuading the motor industry to avail itself of cost reductions resulting from standardization. The Commission concluded that the dominance achieved by Lucas had resulted from the exploitation of scale economies; this policy had greatly benefited the motor industry.

Chloride Ltd, on the other hand, was criticized by the Monopolies Commission for slowness in obtaining reductions in cost by rationalization and simplification of the production and distribution processes.

The existence of scale economies in industries sheltered from technical change may create a serious problem for monopoly policy.[1] Dominant firms may shelter for extended periods behind their scale advantages; meanwhile costs and prices may rise through sloth and/or market exploitation. Under such conditions some form of detailed public supervision may be required, especially where the past record of the Company is suspect. The 1948 Act provided no satisfactory powers for price supervision. Current legislation will relieve this omission.

Scale economies may be less of an impediment to competition in rapidly expanding markets, especially where market expansion is accompanied by product innovation. Under these conditions the dominant firm may be compelled to preserve its efficiency and flexibility in

[1] The British match industry was a useful example.

order to avert market incursion by others. Dominant firms may incur excess capacity in order to discourage new entry and to prevent rapidly rising short-run marginal costs at times when market expansion outpaces the completion of new productive capacity.

The Monopolies Commission has rarely provided a satisfactory analysis of scale impediments to competition. Its poor analysis in this field stems directly from its inadequate examination of economic efficiency in relation to the dominant firm, and its lack of interest in comparable overseas companies.

DIRECT MEASURES IN RESTRAINT OF COMPETITION AND THE PUBLIC INTEREST

Selective Price Cutting

The Monopolies Commission encountered few instances in which dominant firms indulged in price cutting on a selective basis. Selective price cutting may be used to limit the effectiveness of the competitive process. Large companies may subsidize the losses arising from such action in one section of the market by the profits they earn in other sections or indeed from their sales in other markets. Selective price cutting may be viewed simply as one aspect of competition, in which one company is pressed into matching a rival's lower prices. In the hands of the dominant firm, however, the motives may prove more sinister; it is not surprising that the Monopolies Commission has been opposed in principle to such activities.

The most interesting instance of selective price cutting occurred in the industrial and medical gases industry. The British Oxygen Company had acquired ownership of 'British Industrial Gases' and had established 'Industrial Gases' in Scotland. It operated both companies as ostensibly independent competitors.

An independent firm, Saturn Oxygen Company,[1] had established a plant in Glasgow in 1938. The subsidiary of the British Oxygen Company had commenced production in Glasgow in the following year. British Oxygen admitted that its subsidiary had reduced prices to the point of competition. It denied ever selling at prices below unit production costs. Saturn Industrial Gases Ltd pointed out, however, that the action of the British Oxygen subsidiary company had compelled it to terminate the production of oxygen and acetylene in Glasgow as from 1949. The Monopolies Commission was satisfied that the British Oxygen Company had used its subsidiary as a secret fighting company, and that this action had been contrary to the public interest. The Commission recommended that British Oxygen should refrain from further activities of this kind.

[1] Now Saturn Industrial Gases Limited.

The Monopolies Commission did not condemn selective price cutting as adopted by Lucas in the supply of electrical equipment for motor vehicles. Lucas had lowered its prices selectively in order to meet competition from AC-Delco in the production of ignition coils. In this instance the Commission was convinced that Lucas' action had been exercised with restraint and as an acceptable competitive reaction:

> Although it may be difficult at times—particularly when one party is much more powerful than the other—to distinguish between price differentiation that intensifies competition and that which is intended to suppress competition, we do not consider that Lucas can be said to have abused its position in this respect.[1]

Once again the Monopolies Commission had been required to exercise its delicate tight-rope act in the area between fair and unfair competitive action.

Import Arrangements

Dominant firms are often protected from imported substitutes by tariff protection afforded by the British Government. A number of dominant firms have extended such protection by means of private arrangement. In the course of the chemical fertilizers inquiry the Monopolies Commission encountered a dominant importing company, Potash Ltd, collectively owned by potash suppliers located in France and Western Germany, who exported potash to the United Kingdom. Potash Ltd was unable to supply the Monopolies Commission with financial data which had not been disclosed to it by its overseas owners. The company emphasized that it always sought to purchase supplies as cheaply as possible and to hold prices at the lowest level possible. It welcomed increasing potash supplies from Eastern Europe as competition which would strengthen its negotiating power *vis-à-vis* its suppliers. Potash Ltd claimed that its dominant position had prevented the development of a less efficient competitive distribution system, and had enabled it to place a disinterested advisory service at the disposal of British farmers.

The Commission agreed that a competitive distribution system would operate at higher unit costs than the system established by Potash Ltd. Nevertheless, the Commission could not establish whether existing potash prices were reasonable in relation to costs. It welcomed the development of competitive supplies of potash from Eastern Europe. The Commission concluded that it was undesirable that a monopoly supplier should operate as part of an international organization designed to eliminate competition.[2] The Commission recommended that potash imports from Canada, the USA, and the USSR, should be stimulated. In

[1] op. cit., 1963, p. 381.

[2] Mr Barnes disagreed in a minority Addendum to the Report.

addition it urged the Government to confer with Imperial Chemical Industries and Fisons—the principal potash purchasers—regarding the development of the strongest possible bargaining position against Potash Ltd.[1]

The Commission was extremely critical of the import protection established by the British Match Corporation; the detailed import agreement with Swedish Match involved penalties for exceeding quota allocations on the British market. The Commission concluded that the Agreement had contributed to unduly high profits and prices in match production. Yet the Commission refused to recommend a termination of the Trading Agreements for fear of the powerful competitive position of the Swedish Company. In place of such recommendation, the Commission suggested that the Government might supervise the prices, costs, and profits of the British Match Corporation and that the Government might take steps to stimulate competitive imports.[2]

The Commission has shown a consistent concern at any rigidity of supply fostered by import arrangements. It has encountered difficulties in formulating its recommendations. It is extremely difficult to evaluate the consequences of a change in arrangements affecting international trade. The number of variables is bewilderingly great and the Government, as well as the Monopolies Commission, has been uncertain regarding the most appropriate solutions.

Acquisition of Competitive Suppliers

When a dominant company acquires control of a competitor, its aims are often ambiguous. In part it may be concerned to safeguard its market dominance, in part it may simply be concerned to rationalize the industry, and to obtain significant economies of large-scale operation. In part it may simply wish to acquire a highly profitable company at a price not fully reflecting the present value of the organization.

The cigarette and tobacco inquiry drew the Monopolies Commission's attention to such a situation. The Imperial Tobacco Company had secretly purchased a controlling interest in Gallaher Ltd in 1932. At that time the latter had been a small private company producing cigarettes for the domestic market. The purchase of control in Gallaher Ltd had been motivated by fear of the company passing into the hands of the American Tobacco Company which had made a determined effort to enter the British Market. Imperial Tobacco's interest in Gallaher Ltd had ceased to be a majority one in 1946; but prior to that date Imperial

[1] Fisons and ICI in fact refused to co-operate in this field, partly one imagines for fear of appearing before the Restrictive Practices Court.

[2] This was a majority conclusion. Three Commissioners suggested that the Government might establish a purchasing agency to promote competition in imported matches.

Tobacco had quite clearly 'carried out so far as the home market is concerned its undertaking not to interfere in any way with the management of Gallaher's business'.[1] At the time of the inquiry Imperial Tobacco held 42½ per cent of Gallaher's issued equity capital.

The Monopolies Commission was concerned by this shareholding, since Imperial Tobacco accounted for 63·4 per cent and Gallaher for 29·3 per cent of total domestic sales of cigarettes and tobacco. The Commission agreed that Imperial Tobacco would prefer to maintain its own sales rather than to obtain such possible higher return from its investment as a loss of trade to Gallaher might produce; yet the Commission felt that if Imperial Tobacco had to lose trade it would prefer to do so to Gallaher than to any other competitor. The Commission considered that 'the situation of an investor whose commercial interests in an independent trader may conflict with the interests of the company whose shares he holds might well become untenable'.[2] The Commission condemned the secrecy which had surrounded the holding, and suggested that all holdings on the part of a dominant firm in any industry should be disclosed publicly in the absence of truly compelling reasons. The Commission recommended that the continuance of Imperial Tobacco's investment in Gallaher operated and might be expected to operate against the public interest. The Commission recommended that Imperial Tobacco should divest itself of its shareholding in Gallaher. No powers had been provided for Government enforcement of this recommendation by the 1948 Act.

The Commission has criticized other dominant firms for acquisitions designed to promote market dominance. The British Oxygen Company was criticized for its consistent policy of taking over producers of oxygen and dissolved acetylene, and as an organization that had not 'been content to rely on its advantages of scale and experience but has continued for many years to pursue a policy of suppressing and restricting competition'.[3] The Commission admitted that scale arguments had played a part in this development.

On the other hand, the Monopolies Commission accepted that the acquisition policy of both Lucas and Chloride in the electrical equipment field had been motivated, primarily, by the need to rationalize and to obtain extra capacity quickly in the face of a rapidly expanding market.

The Wall Paper Manufacturers Ltd[4] argued that their acquisitions of competitors could not prevent competition both from expanding domestic competitors and from overseas manufacturers. The Commission accepted that paint provided a degree of competition, but pointed out that suppliers of imported wallpaper had to surmount a customs duty of 20 per cent. In 1962 existing independent competition in Britain

[1] op. cit., 1961, p. 185. [2] ibid., p. 192. [3] op. cit., 1956, p. 100.

[4] Report on the Supply of Wallpaper, January 21, 1964. H.C.P. 59.

accounted for 16 per cent of the market. WPM was a price leader and the only serious potential danger to its security was the entry of Imperial Chemical Industries into wallpaper production.

Although the mills of WPM competed internally in design and service the Commission regarded this as no substitute for external competition. Scale economies were limited in wallpaper supply and could not explain WPM's persistent acquisition of competitors. The Monopolies Commission recommended that the WPM should not in future acquire interests in undertakings engaged in the manufacture of wallpaper without obtaining the prior consent of the Board of Trade.

The Commission has not found the task of assessing the consequences of expansion by acquisition a simple one. It condemned the secrecy in which certain holdings were maintained but it preserved a flexible and pragmatic attitude regarding the public impact of acquisitions. The Commission considered it necessary to make a recommendation on one occasion which was unenforceable under the 1948 Act.[1] Increased powers provided by current legislation are urgently needed to allow the Board of Trade to implement recommendations that assets should be divested. The 1948 legislation was drafted with trade associations in mind and the statutory powers provided are inadequate for dealing with the dominant firm.

[1] Divestiture of assets.

Chapter Fourteen

DOMINANT FIRM ACTIVITIES AND THE PUBLIC INTEREST

The Monopolies Commission always undertakes a detailed assessment of the nature of competition in dealing with dominant firm references. Effective competition has been welcomed, as a rule, by the Commission as providing a constraint upon the abuse of market dominance. A study of the competitive process is not, however, the limit of the Monopolies Commission's task. The Monopolies Commission has always considered that it should assess the commercial activities of the dominant firm. Such a task is by no means simple. Economics provides little assistance to the Commission in relation to many commercial activities, either through lack of available tools of analysis or through lack of agreement among interpreters of the discipline. Many of the problems are exposed in the forthcoming analysis. The Monopolies Commission has concentrated upon six facets of dominant firm activity:

1. Price Discrimination;
2. Resale Price Maintenance;
3. Distribution Techniques;
4. Standardization of Product;
5. Research, Development and Innovation;
6. Export Activity.

THE DOMINANT FIRM AND PRICE DISCRIMINATION

Price discrimination relates, strictly, to the sale of a single commodity at several prices. In practice, however, the concept may be given wider application. The distinction between a producer who sells a single product at different prices and a producer who sells different products in varying markets at different percentages of profit is a distinction of degree only and scarcely one of principle.

A widening of the concept of price discrimination extends considerably the number of instances encountered. For price discrimination is possible only where the markets supplied are separated in some way and where the costs of transferring the commodity from the cheaper to the dearer market exceed the price differential between the markets. For this reason, price discrimination is most commonly encountered in its limited form, in service trades and in industries characterized by a wide geographical market and high transport costs. A firm may have the power not only to discriminate between customer classes, in such cases, but additionally to determine the constituency of each class. Indeed, it may be able to discriminate between separate quantities of a given product supplied to individual customers. Block tariff and two-part tariffs of the latter variety are commonly employed by public utilities.[1]

Price discrimination is profitable when point elasticity of demand differs in each market at the output position determined by the equation of marginal revenue in each market with the marginal cost of producing total output. If demand is of equal point elasticity in each market the most profitable price would be that determined by the simple equation of marginal cost and marginal revenue and would result in a single price. In certain instances, demand in one market may be dependent upon the price that is charged in another market. First-week and second-week theatre tickets are so interrelated. This involves special problems in pricing policy.

Where price discrimination is both possible and profitable output will be reduced and price raised in the market with the low point elasticity of demand; output will be raised and price lowered in the market with high demand elasticity. Whether or not total output will be expanded as a result of price discrimination will depend on the precise nature of the two demand schedules. If the demand schedule in the lower price market is more concave to the origin than that in the higher price market total output will be greater than under a single price system.[2] Where price discrimination results in a different total output than would result from a single price system this may affect the level of the firm's marginal cost. A rising marginal cost schedule will tend to diminish the increase in output that might otherwise arise through price discrimination. Nevertheless, Mrs Robinson concluded that 'on the whole it is more likely that the introduction of price discrimination will increase output than that it will reduce it'.[3]

Mrs Robinson argued that price discrimination was clearly justified in cases where no output would be produced at all in its absence, but

[1] See A. Gabor, 'A Note on Block Tariffs', *Review of Economic Studies*, 1956—see also R. Houghton, 'Consumer's Surplus and Discriminating Monopoly', *Review of Economic Studies*, 1959.

[2] J. Robinson, *The Economics of Imperfect Competition*, Macmillan, 1933, p. 190.

[3] ibid., p. 194.

where its use served to render production profitable. She argued on the basis that the average revenue of the monopolist could not be in excess of the average utility of consumers. This argument is commonly accepted. Yet its validity is dependent upon certain rarely specified assumptions. In particular the thesis is suspect where the discriminatory tactics of one company succeed at the expense of companies prevented from discriminating in return. I. M. D. Little has argued that the British gas industry competed at such a disadvantage with electricity in the early postwar period.[1] Where this occurs it is well-nigh impossible to estimate whether the gainers—if they so wished—could compensate the losers. Similar complexities limit the validity of vindicating price discrimination in cases where it facilitates the reaping of internal scale economies.

Since a degree of market dominance is a prerequisite for price discrimination it is not surprising that the Monopolies Commission has examined the price structure of dominant firms investigated under the 1948 legislation. In general, the Commission has been hostile towards price discrimination. This attitude was clearly in evidence in the British Oxygen Company inquiry. The Commission considered that the price structure of any dominant supplier should be designed to avoid unfairness between different customers. The British Oxygen Company's pricing system did not measure up to this requirement. The Company had made no attempt to base its prices upon the actual supply costs to specified categories of customer; it had merely attempted to obtain a reasonable overall return on capital employed. The British Oxygen Company informed the Commission of its several vain attempts to formulate a system of prices based upon costs. It produced no satisfactory evidence to explain its failure. The Commission recommended that new price scales should be drawn up for customers of British Oxygen and that customers should be grouped according to the method of supply,[2] and according to the quantity of gas taken. Regard should be had, in fixing prices, to the average cost of supplying each class of consumer. The price lists should be published and should be applied without discrimination to all customers within the relevant classification. Only in extremely special instances should British Oxygen negotiate terms outside the scale.[3]

The Monopolies Commission displayed a parallel dislike of price discrimination as applied by the dominant suppliers of electrical equipment for motor vehicles. The price charged in the initial equipment

[1] *The Price of Fuel*, 1953.

[2] Whether by pipeline, as liquid, or as gas in cylinders.

[3] ibid., p. 99. 'e.g. where a firm was embarking upon some new process which, if commercially successful, might ultimately result in a large increase in the consumption of gas.'

market was considerably below that charged for replacement supplies. In part the price differentials were justified on average cost differences. Initial equipment was supplied in bulk without individual packing direct to the vehicle manufacturers, whereas replacements were sold in individual packs to the general public through a chain of distributors. Nevertheless, the rate of profit on sales had been substantially higher for replacements than for initial equipment. This was indicative of price discrimination.

The manufacturers asserted that the price differentials had developed through fear of the powerful initial equipment buyers, some of whom were only too ready to undertake the manufacture of their own components if prices rose above an acceptable level. Joseph Lucas (Industries) Ltd argued that the system was fair to all concerned since customers paying high prices for replacements would obtain the benefit of low initial equipment supplies when buying the vehicle in which they were attached. This thesis was supported by Chloride, Smiths and Champion.

The Monopolies Commission read a more sinister interpretation into the price discrimination system. It considered that the system had been used to maintain market dominance, and in particular to minimize the opportunities for competitors to obtain a footing in the initial equipment market. The volume of future demand for replacements was largely dependent upon the volume of sales of initial equipment, so that replacement prices could to some extent be arbitrarily fixed. The Commission regarded price discrimination, under such conditions, as objectionable in principle and against the public interest.[1]

The Commission was more sympathetic towards price discrimination as practised in the chemical fertilizer industry. The three dominant suppliers, Imperial Chemical Industries, Fisons, and Potash, had adopted differing systems. Fisons provided compounders with special discounts which were not related to cost savings, with the intention of encouraging compounders to buy home-produced superphosphate. Potash Ltd operated a special price scale for bulk-purchases of muriate of potash, applicable mainly to compounders. The Company argued that rebates were intended in large part to counteract competition from East Germany rather than to reflect cost savings.

The Monopolies Commission accepted both systems. It pointed out that Fisons was scarcely dominant in superphosphate supplies, and that the commodity was subject to secular decline. Most of the larger compounders in any case produced their own superphosphates. The Monopolies Commission actively welcomed Potash's reaction to East German competition.

[1] This should be compared with the conclusion of the Committee on Radio Valves in the early postwar period, Chapter 1.

Imperial Chemical Industries had long pursued a policy designed to expand the demand for nitrogen. To this effect the company had adjusted its prices somewhat in favour of the farmer buying sulphate for straight application. This had pressed Fisons into allowing a smaller profit margin on compounds with a high ammonium sulphate content than it obtained on other products.

The Commission accepted the system on special pleading grounds for agriculture. Whilst recognizing that ICI's policy had encouraged relatively uneconomic kinds of fertilizer application the Monopolies Commission believed there were sound agronomic reasons, particularly in grassland husbandry, for accepting the differential price structure. There was no evidence that the trend towards compounds had been impeded and the Commission refused to condemn ICI's price discrimination.

The Monopolies Commission has encountered a number of instances of price discrimination over distance, where dominant firms supplied reference goods from several plants located in different regions. Problems arose, inevitably, regarding the distinction in price between fringe custom and proximate custom and between custom located near low cost plant and custom located near high cost plant.

The Commission examined the problem of national or regional pricing systems in the British Oxygen Company inquiry. The British Oxygen Company supplied gases from several plants adopting a national price scheme which resulted in identical prices in each of the eight districts supplied.

A regional pricing system would have benefited customers located advantageously in terms of cost, to the detriment of less well-placed customers. Production costs might differ regionally due to the scale of supply plant, the degree of utilization of the plant, the local costs of labour, power, and raw materials, and the skill of management responsible for the plants.

Where plant unit production costs vary considerably a national price system may encourage an uneconomic employment of resources. It was true that oxygen prices were relatively unimportant as a factor determining the location of oxygen-using plant, even for steel plants using tonnage oxygen. Nevertheless, a regional pricing system for oxygen, by exposing plant inefficiencies where they existed, might encourage large-scale consumers of gases in high-cost districts to install their own tonnage plant. The British Oxygen Company would be exposed in such regions to potential or active competition.

On the other hand regional pricing systems were difficult and costly to administer. The need for detailed regional costing data and for flexible pricing might raise administrative costs and thereby the prices charged to oxygen consumers. In addition outlying consumers would undoubtedly suffer under a regional scheme; customers located on district boundaries might be charged inconsistent prices dependent upon boundary lines; this might create ill-will.

The Monopolies Commission accepted the British Oxygen Company's defence of its national price system both for oxygen and for dissolved acetylene. It may well be that the Commission was swayed by the problems of short-term reallocation that would result from so significant a change in pricing structure. Whether its decision was correct in the longer term is debatable.

The decision between a national pricing system and a regional pricing system is by no means easy or clear. There are economic and social arguments that favour either system. The welfare model upon which price discrimination is usually condemned is of doubtful validity under dynamic conditions. Recent developments in the sphere of spatial competition have not resolved the dilemma of the Monopolies Commission. The Commission, of course, has been compelled to formulate conclusions relating to the desirability of national pricing systems which involve price discrimination. Its decisions have scarcely been substantiated by convincing analysis. This weakness is merely a reflection of the lack of guidance as yet provided by economics and other social sciences in this field of market dominance.

A separate aspect of spatial discrimination relates to the decision between delivered and ex-works pricing systems. The problem was encountered in the chemical fertilizer industry. The fertilizer prices of Fisons and Imperial Chemical Industries included delivery to the nearest station, and did not vary with the cost of marine freight. Fisons quoted ex-works prices, exceptionally, to compounders of triple superphosphates; and in Scotland the majority of its supplies were quoted ex-works for compounders. In Northern Ireland, the majority of its fertilizer prices were quoted ex-works, ex-port, or free-on-rail.

Imperial Chemical Industries was fully satisfied with its delivered pricing system, basing its conclusions on grounds of administrative simplicity. Fisons, on the other hand, had informed the Monopolies Commission that it was contemplating a change to ex-works pricing. It had indicated, however, the considerable problems that would result from a change of this kind. Consumers would be discontented if they were forced to pay the cost of long hauls, and the Company would have to decide whether to quote a uniform ex-works price or prices related to the unit production costs of particular works. In the latter event the pattern of production, and the location of new factories might well be affected. Fisons argued that its existing system helped to subsidize remote consumers—often marginal farmers—and that this corresponded with Government policy. Both companies excused ex-works pricing in Scotland and Northern Ireland on grounds of local tradition.

The Commission, by majority decision, refused to recommend a change in pricing policy. It did not wish to disrupt arrangements which appeared on the whole to satisfy both suppliers and consumers and of which the Government Departments concerned had long been aware without raising any objection. Professor G. C. Allen, however, in a succinct addendum to the Report, condemned the majority conclusion. He urged the need to awaken Parliament to the true costs of subsidizing marginal farming and to this end he condemned the existing system as involving 'a hidden subsidy made possible by the monopoly suppliers' practice of charging uniform delivered prices'.[1] He stressed the importance of ex-works pricing in encouraging a better economic location of new fertilizer factories.

Price discrimination, in its various forms, has provided a problem of interpretation for the Monopolies Commission. Welfare economics provides no firm, realistic guidance on this matter. Social justice has, therefore, been the most important criterion adopted. Any decision to condemn price discrimination must follow conscientious and careful analysis of its implications for the dominant firm. Even where price discrimination clearly impedes independent competition the dilemma is unresolved. Market dominance may imply the need for self-restraint. But when self-restraint extends to connivance at its own destruction the public interest is not necessarily satisfied: 'The firm that does not discriminate in its pricing policy, or differentiate in its product line, or invade new markets, dies in the competitive struggle—and business management does not commit suicide.'[2]

THE DOMINANT FIRM AND RESALE PRICE MAINTENANCE

The Monopolies Commission has always paid careful attention to resale price maintenance as practised by dominant firms. The Monopolies Commission has not concerned itself with the specific requirements of resale price maintenance legislation within the United Kingdom. The Commission has adopted a pragmatic approach towards the practice as encountered in varying reference industries. It was prepared to condemn individual resale price maintenance during a period when this was generally enforceable by legal process. There is no reason to suppose that it will be influenced in future inquiries by criteria established in 1964 by the Conservative Government's legislation on resale price maintenance. The Monopolies Commission may well consider that resale price maintenance acceptable to the Restrictive Practices Court was nevertheless undesirable from its own viewpoint. The 1964 legislation

[1] op. cit., 1959, p. 229.

[2] Eli Clemens, 'American Economic Society', *Readings in Industrial Organization and Public Policy*, R. D. Irwin Inc, 1958, p. 274.

will undoubtedly reduce the number of resale price maintenance practices that are encountered by the Monopolies Commission.

The first inquiry in which the Monopolies Commission felt called upon to discuss resale price maintenance enforced by individual action was that into the pneumatic tyre industry. Resale prices had been collectively enforced in this industry, but the Monopolies Commission had condemned this practice. The Commission subsequently considered whether the individual enforcement of resale prices might be tolerated within the pneumatic tyre industry. The pneumatic tyre industry was oligopolistic in structure, and subject to price leadership on the part of the Dunlop Rubber Company. Identical or near-identical tyre prices obtained at the manufacturing level, and the Monopolies Commission could see little possibility of transforming this situation. Individual resale price maintenance would almost certainly result in identical retail prices for pneumatic tyres. In the absence of resale price maintenance, the Commission felt that price competition might develop on a limited scale among tyre traders and this might eventually induce price competition at the manufacturing stage, especially when the price discussions of the Tyre Manufacturers' Conference had been terminated.[1] The Monopolies Commission condemned individual resale price maintenance by a majority vote only. Four Commissioners defended the practice from the viewpoint of the tyre trade, stressing the need for high quality service and for the provision of an adequate service in remote areas. The inaction of the Government in relation to this issue implied its acceptance of the minority viewpoint.

The Monopolies Commission was more united in its condemnation of resale price maintenance as operated by the electrical equipment suppliers for mechanically-propelled land vehicles on the replacement market. The practice applied to practically the entire replacement trade in reference goods. The suppliers defended the practice on the grounds that service standards were dependent upon guaranteed markets, that resale price maintenance had prevented over-charging, and had prevented concentration in the distributive trade.

The Monopolies Commission noted that a certain—and perhaps growing—proportion of users had no reason to demand service from the distributor. Many users were fully able to identify and to fit their required components, but were obliged to pay for services they did not require. The average motorist was unlikely to shop for the cheapest component he could find, irrespective of its suitability for his particular purpose. In the circumstances of the trade, some reorganization of the distribution might well be necessary; the abolition of fixed resale prices might aid the elimination of inefficient distributors. Small distri-

[1] In view of the considerable degree of forward integration into distribution effected by Dunlop, the conclusion appears a little optimistic.

butors would scarcely lose custom if they maintained an efficient service. The risk of over-charging in the absence of fixed resale prices might become a problem; but the danger existed already since the distributor's services were usually required, and subject to a separate charge, for fitting the purchased component.

The Monopolies Commission concluded that termination of resale price maintenance would expose distributors of replacement electrical equipment to competition in price. The impact of such competition would be felt not only on distributive profits, but also upon manufacturers' prices since hard-pressed distributors would exert buying pressure upon the suppliers. The Commission was confident that one result would be a reduction in the existing price discrimination imposed by suppliers on initial equipment and replacement supplies.[1]

The Commission was equally firm in condemning resale price maintenance in the wallpaper industry. The principal manufacturer was the Wall Paper Manufacturers Ltd, together with its manufacturing subsidiaries. The WPM Group defended resale price maintenance as being necessary to preserve a technique of distribution—through pattern book merchants and decorators—of which a section of the public still desired to avail itself. Without resale price maintenance, the Group believed there would be a lower standard of service, a decline in the trade in better class wallpapers, and a termination of the pattern book system of distribution.

The WPM Group itself was not convinced that decorators performed a service commensurate with the margin they were allowed. The Commission could see no reason why the general wallpaper trade should support and preserve the decorator distributive system. The latter system was a declining section of the trade. The purchase of wallpaper through retail shops was growing in importance, and one-fifth of these sales consisted of the Group's price maintained pattern book ways. There was no reason to expect a decline in the provision of better-class wallpapers. Abolition of fixed retail prices would put pressure upon distributive cost reductions,[2] and ultimately upon retail prices not only in pattern book ways, but throughout the wallpaper trade. The Commission was influenced in its condemnation of individual resale price maintenance by the fact that it was practised by the monopoly supplier and by no other supplier, that it was applied only to one-half of the monopoly suppliers' products with a view to supporting a particular

[1] The moral impact of this recommendation appears to have had little effect upon Champion. *Financial Times*, January 30, 1964, p. 8. 'It is understood that other letters demanding the restoration of fixed prices have been received from . . . the Champion Sparking Plug Company.'

[2] The retail prices of wallpaper was about two-and-a-half times the manufacturers' net selling prices. This was high in comparison with most trades.

method of trading, and that some of the goods to which it was applied were supplied through other channels.

In the light of its attitude in other dominant firm inquiries it is perhaps surprising that the Commission condoned individual resale price maintenance in the cigarette and tobacco industry. At the time of the inquiry both the Imperial Tobacco Company and Gallaher Ltd prescribed and enforced the resale prices of their respective products at every stage of supply. The Imperial Tobacco Company contended that the practice safeguarded distributors from loss-leader sales of cigarettes, encouraged distributors to stock and to sell their supplies, and provided the general public with standard price goods from a large number of buying points. In addition resale price maintenance reduced manufacturers' risks in allowing credit to distributors. These advantages had to be measured against the detriment that resale price maintenance prevented distributors from pricing with reference to their individual unit costs.

In the cigarette and tobacco industry the Commission decided in favour of resale price maintenance. It pointed out that distributors' margins accounted for an abnormally low percentage of retail price,[1] and that price reductions would only be small. Successful price cutting would reduce the number of retail outlets, and this might outweigh any advantages in the form of slightly reduced prices. The Commission was alarmed at the possibility of loss-leader selling in cigarettes and tobacco. In particular popular brands might be exposed to such practices, perhaps to the benefit of the Imperial Tobacco Company and Gallaher, but to the detriment of the remainder of the industry. Finally, if distributors began to default as debtors and credit facilities were withdrawn, gross margins would have to be raised so that distributors could obtain less advantageous credit elsewhere. For these reasons, the Monopolies Commission refused to condemn resale price maintenance in the cigarette and tobacco industry.

This conclusion was strongly criticized in a minority addendum. Professor G. C. Allen attacked the 'narrow margins' argument, pointing out that reasonable average margins took no account of the dispersion of margins. He criticized the unwillingness of the Commission to allow a reduction to take place in retail outlets:

> If resale price maintenance were abolished the number of retail outlets and the structure of the distributive trade in cigarettes would come to depend on the preferences of consumers as expressed in the way they chose to spend their money, and not, as at present, on the manufacturers' dictate which frustrates their freedom of choice in one important respect.[2]

[1] This argument was dubious since excise duty formed a heavy proportion of cigarette and tobacco costs in Britain.

[2] op. cit., 1961, p. 214.

Professor G. C. Allen was alarmed at the rigidity imposed upon the distributive system by resale price maintenance in cigarettes and tobacco. He was not disturbed at the prospect of loss-leader selling in the industry, and emphasized the danger of preserving restrictive practices in order to present the elimination of a fringe of independent companies. In this respect he received unequivocal support from a protagonist for the abolition of resale price maintenance:

> But should one restraint on competitive pricing be justified because it might serve incidentally to prevent an increase in the degree of concentration in an already highly concentrated industry? In so far as the public interest can be equated with the consumer interest, the answer, I suggest, is clear: where price competition at the manufacturing stage is not likely to be significant, price competition at the distribution stage offers advantages to the consumers which would outweigh the risks associated with a slightly higher degree of concentration.[1]

Professor G. C. Allen proceeded to scotch the notion that distributors of cigarettes and tobacco would become poor credit risks in the absence of resale price maintenance. He pointed out that the credit position of the more successful distributors would improve as that of the less successful worsened under effective price competition of the distributive level. There would be a painful transition period for high-cost distributors but this should scarce be allowed to stand in the way of an advantageous development within the trade: 'If improvements in the ordering of economic affairs were to be successfully resisted whenever it could be shown that their first impact would have disagreeable consequences for a minority of high-cost traders, then little material progress would be possible.'[2]

Professor G. C. Allen's criticism of the Monopolies Commission with respect to its decision on resale price maintenance in the cigarette and tobacco industry was pertinent and logical. In itself it did not constitute a complete condemnation of the majority decision. Too often, where critical economic decisions are taken, the Monopolies Commission may be criticized for an inadequate examination of the situation. This criticism may be levelled at its handling of resale price maintenance. Information should have been obtained from a wide range of distributors relating to their rate of return on capital and on sales in cigarettes and tobacco; measures of average and dispersion should have been made for varying types of retail outlet and for varying geographical regions. The Commission made little systematic attempt to obtain such data. In its absence, a largely unconvincing decision on the issue was to be expected.

[1] B. S. Yamey, *Modern Law Review*, November 1961, p. 756.
[2] op. cit., 1961, p. 216.

The Monopolies Commission conclusions relating to individual resale price maintenance have occurred, in many instances, at critical political points in time. The condemnation of individual resale price maintenance in pneumatic tyres embarrassed a Government engaged at that time in providing for the enforcement of resale prices by legal process. The condemnation of the practice in electrical equipment supplies for mechanically-propelled land vehicles and in wallpaper provided timely support for a Government concerned with legislating to limit the ability of companies to maintain resale prices.

The hostility normally displayed by the Monopolies Commission towards resale price maintenance has met with the pleasure of many economists. Few economists have ranged themselves in favour of the practice. Nevertheless, reservations must exist concerning the process by which these conclusions have been derived. Too often, the condemnation has been preceded merely by a brief, theoretical analysis of the practice and its economic consequences. There has been a reluctance to clothe the analytical framework with relevant empirical information. The Commission is open to serious criticism on this account. Sound decisions obtained by unsound investigations will not carry the respect of those intimately concerned in the inquiry.

DOMINANT FIRMS AND THE PROCESS OF DISTRIBUTION

The Monopolies Commission, not content with an examination of the production methods of dominant firms, normally examines the channels through which they distribute their products.

The distribution process was examined in some detail by the Commission in the chemical fertilizer inquiry. Imperial Chemical Industries did not deal directly with farmers but sold its products to compounders, agricultural merchants and co-operative societies; Fisons Ltd sold a small proportion of its products directly to farmers through its subsidiary company, George Hadfield and Company Ltd, but in general its practice was similar to that of Imperial Chemical Industries. The Monopolies Commission noted that such distributive methods were common among fertilizer manufacturers apart from those who were themselves agricultural merchants.

The system of selling through merchants was strongly defended by both companies. They pointed out that the farmers' demand for fertilizers was highly seasonal and that it would therefore be wasteful to create an organization for the sole purpose of selling fertilizers to them. While existing merchants provided cheap and efficient distribution for fertilizers, there could be no justification for establishing alternative systems.

The Commission estimated that agricultural merchants of most fertilizer products operated on a margin of 5 per cent to cover both expenses and profit. In some cases the margin was considerably less. The Commission concluded that it was unlikely that Imperial Chemical Industries or Fisons could achieve substantial economies in distribution by selling direct to farmers.

The Monopolies Commission examined the case for allowing better terms to farmers who purchased fertilizers on a large scale than to those who purchased on a small scale. It had been suggested that such a development might be facilitated by direct buying from the manufacturers. The Commission discovered that certain merchants had been prepared to make small allowances on large orders, although the narrow margins on which the merchants operated provided little room for such allowances. The Commission felt that the farmer would have a better opportunity to strike a bargain with his merchant, who would be interested in winning his custom for other goods, than he would with a manufacturer whose sole business was to sell fertilizers.

In contrast with the situation encountered in the fertilizer industry, the Monopolies Commission discovered that the Imperial Tobacco Company had for some years pursued a policy of direct trading particularly with large cigarette and tobacco retailers. The Commission pointed out that in a fully competitive market each manufacturer would be under compulsion to seek the correct economic balance between sale to retailers and sale through wholesalers as a means of minimizing his costs. In the tobacco trade, the Commission was convinced that competitive pressures existed. The Imperial Tobacco Company—and probably most of its competitors—regarded some part of the cost of retailer accounts as a sales promotion cost rather than as an indispensible distributive cost.

The Commission found nothing unusual or improper in this attitude. However, it noted the danger, in an industry characterized by non-price competition and substantial sales promotion, that the entire industry might adopt selling techniques reflecting a high-cost distributive system. The Commission discovered that Gallaher Ltd had been at least as active as the Imperial Tobacco Company in encouraging direct trading. It had not collected evidence which might demonstrate that direct trading was inconsistent with low cost distribution.

Nationally distributed brands of batteries for motor vehicles were sold by the manufacturers to a number of 'Service Agents' each of whom handled one brand only. Retailers wishing to stock a number of brands were forced to buy each brand from a different agent. The system was defended on the ground that agents effected the filling and first charge of the batteries, and that they must enjoy, therefore, a more intimate relationship with the manufacturer than that of a normal distributor. In addition, many agents replated and repaired batteries, and assembled rebuilt batteries to the manufacturer's specifications. The Monopolies Commission was not convinced that exclusive dealing was a necessary price to pay for this kind of service. On the other hand, a manufacturer might reasonably object to providing technical training at some cost to himself which might be used subsequently to the advantage of his competitors. On balance, the Monopolies Commission decided to condone the exclusive dealing arrangements between battery supplier and distributors.

In its examination of the distributive processes adopted by dominant firms, the Commission has been eager to discover whether they extended market dominance, and if so in what manner. In the absence of such evidence the Monopolies Commission has not been keen to comment adversely upon distributive processes. It has paid superficial attention to the need for an efficient and pertinent distributive system. It may be faulted for its failure to undertake a thorough-going investigation and to assemble criteria whereby the distributive system might be evaluated.

THE DOMINANT FIRM AND PRODUCT STANDARDIZATION

The Monopolies Commission has examined the record of dominant firms in the promotion of product standardization; on a few occasions it has praised firms for the cost reductions they have achieved by such policies. In particular Joseph Lucas Ltd was praised for its contribution to the standardization of electrical equipment for motor vehicles. Lucas had emphasized that product standardization did not imply a stagnation in the Company's development policies. The Commission foresaw little danger of over-standardization in the trade, provided that the motor vehicle industry itself remained competitive. The degree of standardization that could be achieved was limited by the design variations of the vehicle makers.

The Commission was far less satisfied by the progress of the Chloride Electrical Storage Company Ltd in standardizing battery supplies. Chloride had maintained two separate, comprehensive ranges of automative batteries, 'Exide' and 'Dagenite'. There appeared to be little technical significance in the maintenance of two brands. Chloride's unit production costs were higher than would have resulted from concentrating production upon one brand. The factories had sacrificed scale economies in order to preserve a choice of brands.

The Imperial Tobacco Company was criticized by the Commission for its policy prior to 1954 of maintaining an unduly wide range of cigarettes and tobacco brands.[1] The Commission blamed this practice upon the lack of effective competition in the industry. Since 1954 when

[1] 'In 1938 Imperial was selling 191 cigarette brands and 596 tobacco brands. By 1960 the figures had been reduced to fifty-seven and 183 respectively.'

Gallaher Ltd had emerged as a major competitor, the Imperial Tobacco Company had reduced the number of its brands. In 1957 about 91 per cent of the Company's cigarettes sales were accounted for by four brands. The Commission did not criticize the existing policy of the Imperial Tobacco Company in relation to product standardization.

The Monopolies Commission has commented somewhat superficially upon the standardization policies of dominant firms. Lack of detailed technical and financial information has weakened its ability to speak from conviction save in the most obvious instances. Once again the need for an efficiency audit is underlined if the Commission is to produce authoritative and convincing conclusions.

THE DOMINANT FIRM AND RESEARCH, DEVELOPMENT AND INNOVATION

Many economists would rate the advantages of large-scale research programmes high among their reasons for encouraging industrial concentration. In their enthusiasm for the opportunities created by market concentration they tend to underestimate the weakening in the stimulus to undertake research induced by sheltered market conditions. The quiet life may be very seductive.

Dominant firms examined by the Commission have usually produced under conditions of oligopoly. Oligopolistic industries may bear a special inducement towards research as a form of competition in conditions of company inter-awareness. Oligopoly is frequently referred to as 'the royal road to technical progress'. Examples are frequently quoted in substantiation of this thesis from technologically dynamic industries such as chemicals, petroleum, aviation and electrical engineering, all of which devote relatively large amounts of resources to research.

On the other hand, recent investigations indicate that suggestions of this kind are too sweeping and too general, and stem from insufficient information. The steel industry,[1] classically and historically oligopolistic, has a very poor research record. The two leading inventions in the steel industry, continuous hot-strip rolling and continuous casting, were scarcely the fruits of oligopolistic competition. The former was the work of a small-scale entrant and was developed by the smaller American steel firms, whilst the latter was largely the work of a single German inventor. The United States Steel Corporation is frequently described as a technical follower.

It is important to examine the kind of research conducted by dominant and large-scale firms. Recent surveys of American industry indicate that firms concentrate heavily upon research programmes promising a very rapid pay-off. In 1958 a McGraw-Hill survey established that 39

[1] J. Jewkes, *et alia*, 1958, op. cit., p. 169.

per cent of large United States firms expected research expenditure to pay off in less than three years; another 52 per cent expected it to pay off in three to five years, and only 9 per cent expected the pay off to be longer than six years.[1]

Since most major inventions take longer than three years to prepare for commercial exploitation, the short pay-off expectation indicates that even applied research in most industrial laboratories is geared towards improvements or minor variations upon extant products and processes. Many would argue that the growth of industrial expenditure upon research and development has to a considerable extent been motivated by the search for another means of achieving product differentiation. Minor product developments are likely to be subject to a high rate of obsolescence, placing a strong stimulus towards rapid pay-off investment.

Many large firms play no part in the major pioneering work on new inventions. Many maintain their competitive position by absorbing smaller ones that have already made substantial technical and commercial progress and possess the men and the know-how, and occasionally the patents. Caution must be exercised in attributing advantages to the dominant firm in research. The Monopolies Commission has wisely adopted a pragmatic approach.

The rapidly rising costs of development programmes in many industries have underlined the advantages of large, dominant firms operating in secure markets, and able to take a long-run view of investment expenditures. On the other hand, competition may be a desirable goad to rapid development, especially where it is estimated that quasi-rents will be available for a limited period for the successful firm. Development under competitive conditions may involve overlapping effort and waste. Nevertheless, it may offer swifter success and on occasion it may make the difference between success and complete failure. The dominant firm, confident in its ability to control and/or to eliminate competition, may become sluggish in its development programmes. A. A. Bright illustrated how the General Electric Company, dominant in the field of artificial lighting, lagged in the development of fluorescent lighting. The emergence of competition from pioneers in fluorescent lighting during the inter-war period galvanized the General Electric Company into a competitive reaction; it quickly asserted its predominance in the fluorescent lighting field.

Many large firms freely admit that they receive many more promising suggestions than they could possibly afford to develop. Where pressures favour the selection of quick pay-off projects, the opportunity for fundamental development may be remote. Many new firms have entered in-

[1] P. Hamberg, 'Invention in the Industrial Research Laboratory', *Journal of Political Economy*, April 1963, p. 99.

dustries for the sole purpose of exploiting ideas discarded by established firms. Dominant firms may impede such important developments.

Once again, the evidence is inconclusive. There is an obvious clash between potential and incentive.[1] The Monopolies Commission has wisely refrained from dogmatism, recognizing that industrial structure itself plays only a limited role in the determination of research and development activities. The training and attitude of management, the historical tradition of the industry, its commercial prospects, and consumer reactions to innovation may outweigh any impact from the industrial structure under examination.

The Monopolies Commission has examined the research and development activities of dominant firms in every reference save that relating to the supply of wallpaper. It has been influenced in its recommendations by the level and pattern of research and development expenditure of those concerned.

For over seventy years the British Oxygen Company had been the principal producer and supplier of oxygen in the United Kingdom. At the time of investigation it was the principal supplier of dissolved acetylene. The Company claimed a good record in research and development, contending that it had contributed to the development of the Brin oxygen process, to the early work on hydrogen liquefaction and to the safe storage of acetylene in cylinders. It pointed out that it had been the first to introduce the mild steel cylinder in 1886 and that its cylinders had become recognized models throughout the world.

The Company admitted that it had played no part in such fundamental developments as the air liquefaction process of Claude and Linde. It had pursued instead of policy of international linkage, thus avoiding the extremely high levels of expenditure upon gas separation problems. It had adopted liquid gas developments so vigorously that it had outstripped foreign competitors with the result that its prices were the lowest in the world. Following World War Two the Company appears to have become more interested in research. A Research and Development Department was established in 1945, and in 1948 a Director was appointed to represent this aspect of the Company's operations. At the time of investigation the Department had a staff of 400 trained researchers; in 1954 £230,000[2] had been allocated for work on the three reference gases. The Company admitted that it had paid more attention to development work than to basic research but pointed to an increasing emphasis upon basic work through the years.

[1] J. M. Clark, 1961, op. cit., p. 201. 'The relatively small firm, if it makes a cost-reducing innovation at all, has a larger interest in using part of the resulting economies in ways that will increase its total sales volume because . . . its cross-elasticity of demand is greater.'

[2] This amounted to roughly 2½ per cent of turnover.

The Monopolies Commission emphasized the responsibility placed upon the British Oxygen Company for research and development in the industry. The Commission commented somewhat tartly that almost all the important new processes had been developed initially overseas and that the Company's role had been that of acquiring patent rights or licences for UK exploitation. Rapid technical advances were still being made in the USA and in Western Germany. The Commission did not explicitly criticize the inadequacy of British Oxygen Company's research effort, although it stressed the importance that it attached to a substantial research effort by the Company. This is the closest the Commission has come to an outright criticism of the research activities of a dominant firm.

On the other hand the Commission was fully satisfied with the research and development activities of the Dunlop Rubber Company both in the pneumatic tyre and in the rubber footwear industry. The Company had played an important part in the development of the original pneumatic tyre. Following this, it had been first in the field with many new products, including aeroplane tyres in 1910, bullet-proof tyres in 1917, giant pneumatic tyres in 1921, and tubeless tyres of natural rubber in 1953. It had taken the lead in introducing non-skid tread patterns and special treads for use in mud, snow, and other abnormal conditions. It had been equally enterprising in developing tyre materials. It had been the first to use carbon black in the tyre thread in 1904, and to experiment in the use of rayon instead of cotton for the casing in 1921. More recently the Dunlop Rubber Company had pioneered research on synthetic rubber. A large experimental plant had been constructed at Fort Dunlop.

In the rubber footwear industry the Dunlop Rubber Company had pioneered methods of applying liquid latex in making seamless rubber boots. At the time of investigation it was the only British producer to use the technique. In addition it had developed improved self-ventilating proofed cotton for canvas footwear, Dunlopillo insoling and arch supports, and a variety of hard-wearing soling compounds, including a micro-cellular material used both by the Company itself and increasingly by other manufacturers.

The Commission appeared to be highly satisfied by Dunlop's research, development, and innovation activities, and was influenced by this in deciding that the Company had acted in accordance with the public interest in both industries, despite its being a high-cost producer.

The Monopolies Commission has placed great importance upon the willingness of dominant firms to conduct research and development. It has perhaps been unduly interested in expenditure rather than in results although in certain instances the two are closely correlated. It is not easy to produce a solution for a lack of interest in research. The Government has no powers to enforce research expenditure. It is by no means certain that research by order would be successful. The Government could use the threat of tariff reductions to increase research expenditure. Equally, it could provide tax concessions for firms conducting specified research programmes. The problem of stimulating research in the dominant firm is highly complex, and requires a detailed technical and market knowledge of the industry under examination.

DOMINANT FIRMS AND EXPORTS

When assessing the activities and performance of a dominant firm it would seem important to examine its effectiveness in export markets. The United Kingdom is highly dependent upon its ability to produce for export in order to import essential food and raw materials, as well as consumer and producer manufactured goods demanded by its citizens.

However, the Monopolies Commission, in the absence of an outright export reference, has rarely been willing to examine this important aspect of the firm's activities. This omission must be considered as one of the major weaknesses in the approach of the Monopolies Commission—a weakness incidentally that appears to have passed without adverse comment.

The Monopolies Commission did make a passing reference to Molins' performance in the export markets for cigarette and tobacco machinery. Molins had earned its high profits in the face of formidable competition in world markets. Under such conditions the Commission felt unable to consider its home operations in isolation. The Commission was highly satisfied with the performance and success of Molins and believed that this was likely to continue.

During the chemical fertilizer investigation, the Commission noted, apparently without undue concern, that Imperial Chemical Industries had supplied the domestic market from time to time only at the expense of the export market. This had occurred during periods when the market for chemical fertilizers was expanding rapidly. The domestic market had been served in preference to overseas markets at the express request of the British Government.

These two references to the export performance of dominant firms are, in the absence of specific references, isolated instances of interest displayed by the Commission. This indicates a very narrow interpretation of the economic factors concerned. It is of critical importance to the public interest that a firm fails to penetrate foreign markets sufficiently to obtain economies of scale in production which might be passed on to the domestic consumer in the form of lower prices or better quality production. Again, it would seem important to find out whether a firm's sluggish enterprise on the domestic market is resulting in lost export orders and falling foreign earnings. The Monopolies Commission should re-examine its attitude towards this aspect of its domestic references.

Armed with a specific export reference, the Monopolies Commission usually carries out comprehensive surveys of the export performance of firms involved. The pneumatic tyre inquiry provided an interesting insight into the Commission's interpretation of an export reference. At the time of examination, there were eleven tyre manufacturing companies together with three other companies which in practice subcontracted the manufacture of tyres to other companies. The Dunlop Rubber Company was easily the largest British tyre manufacturer, accounting for two-thirds of the production of original equipment tyres and rather less than one-half of the production of giant tyres. On the domestic market the Dunlop Rubber Company operated as price leader, and it naturally assumed this role in the export market. In 1952 Dunlop had accounted for 34 per cent of the total exports of the industry. Dunlop expounded to the Commission its long-standing policy of developing overseas markets, primarily by establishing overseas sales offices followed by subsidiary factories. This had helped the company to expand sales in areas where protective tariffs and national sentiment both ran high. In addition it had resulted in savings in freight costs. Dunlop pointed out that since 1920 the main competition faced by the company in export markets came from firms domiciled in the USA.

The Commission could find no evidence of market-sharing arrangements between Dunlop and its overseas competitors. However, following difficulties experienced during the 1920s, both Dunlop and the American manufacturers had considered it advisable to consult informally with each other through the Rubber Export Association of America, before making changes in export prices. The Association was legal in America under the Webb-Pomerene Act[1] which enables American exporters to co-operate in export trade in order to improve export performance.

The consultation system had resulted in a common world price level for tyres of varying qualities, except in markets where the prices were determined by local manufacture. Dunlop had operated in these negotiations as spokesman for non-US tyre manufacturers. The other British manufacturers had been notified of price changes decided upon at the meetings of the Association. In general the ceiling for export prices[2] determined by negotiation had been the wholesale domestic price level in either the British or the American market, whichever chanced to be the lower.

[1] It had been formed in 1918. [2] Priced f.o.b.

The Monopolies Commission could find no serious criticism of the British tyre industry's export performance. Tyre exports in 1953 had been larger in number than those for any other country. In particular they were greater both in quantity and in quality than they had been before the war. The Dunlop Rubber Company had accounted for roughly one third of all export sales.

The Commission found no indication that the price arrangements had prevented British manufacturers, in particular Dunlop, from increasing their share of world markets. The Commission was unable to assess the competitive position of Dunlop, in relation to its major international rivals. The largest American producers operated from a home base many times larger than that of Dunlop's. These firms would be in an extremely strong position, if they so wished, to lower their export prices below the domestic market levels in order to increase their share of world tyre sales. Dunlop, relying more heavily upon tyre exports, and operating from a much smaller domestic base, might be unable to compete against such action.

Under these circumstances, the Commission considered that a price war in world markets would not be in the interests of the United Kingdom and that any determined effort on the part of Dunlop to increase its export sales by a substantial lowering of export prices might well lead to such a price war. Dunlop had stressed that the rubber industry was on the threshold of important developments, particularly in relation to synthetic rubber, and that any alteration in the existing international arrangements at that time could seriously damage British interests. The Commission accepted this contention and tentatively expressed willingness to allow the arrangements to continue.

The Commission was concerned lest Dunlop's position as export price leader should have detrimental effects upon the export performance of other British tyre manufacturers. In the event it concluded that advantages involved in the market expansion of rival British producers would be counterbalanced by a reduction in Dunlop's international bargaining position. There is a risk in such a conclusion of permanently blessing the existing pattern of tyre production for export. The Commission, however, appears to have placed great weight upon the weak bargaining power of the smaller British manufacturers, and upon the danger that they might jeopardize the prices negotiated by Dunlop with the American firms. It concluded that export price leadership by Dunlop operated in the public interest at that stage of the development of the industry.

The other major export reference involved the British match making industry. The British Match Corporation had entered into an agreement with Swedish Match dividing world markets between the two firms. The British Match Corporation was prevented by this agreement from exporting or setting up manufacture in a large number of important markets throughout the world; in return it had been conceded the sole right to manufacture and sell matches in Canada and Brazil, and had been accorded considerable protection from competition by Swedish Match in other territories.

The Commission considered that these market sharing arrangements, as much as any natural advantages possessed by Swedish Match, had been instrumental in manoeuvring the British Match Corporation into a position where it clearly considered that on balance it would lose from competition in world markets with Swedish Match. The Commission reluctantly accepted the interpretation of the Company. There was little possibility of increasing the export earnings of the British Match Corporation by eliminating the international agreement. The British Company was heavily dependent upon the Swedish company for machinery supplies and suffered in any unit cost comparison with Swedish Match. The Commission felt compelled to recommend retention of the Agreement and suggested detailed Government surveillance of the industry.

Except in inquiries fortified by a specific export reference, the Commission has been as unenterprising in the export field with dominant firms as it was with trade associations. It is admittedly more difficult to obtain information relating to export performance. Nevertheless, the failure of the Commission to relate export performance to domestic performance signifies a serious misinterpretation of its task.

CONCLUSION

This chapter has outlined a number of important economic issues which have concerned the Monopolies Commission during its dominant firm inquiries. The Commission has interpreted the available data for the most part in a sound if somewhat unenterprising manner. There are too many instances, however, where the Monopolies Commission has displayed a lack of interest in the collection of detailed technical and financial information relating to its fields of inquiry. The lack of a highly-qualified staff briefed in an appropriate manner is continuously reflected in the failure to obtain relevant information upon which the Monopolies Commifsion might formulate convincing and well-based conclusions.

Chapter Fifteen

THE DOMINANT FIRM AND PUBLIC POLICY

The Monopolies Commission was empowered to examine reference industries dominated by single companies from its establishment in 1948. In practice, however, the early references were concentrated upon the activities of trade associations; the problems relating to the dominant firm were deferred for later examination. The inquiry into the supply of matches was the only specific dominant firm inquiry launched in the early years of the Commission's operations. Legislation in 1956 provided for the creation of a Restrictive Practices Court, and for the judicial review by this court of certain types of restrictive trading agreement. The scope of the Monopolies Commission was correspondingly curtailed.

The Monopolies Commission was freed, by this legislation, to concentrate upon dominant firm inquiries. Its ability to do so was, unfortunately, abbreviated by the decision of the Conservative Government to reduce the size of the Commission. It would appear that the reduction in the Commission's size was accompanied by a reduction in its status not only in the eyes of the Government, but also in the eyes of the informed public. The limelight was switched from the work of the Monopolies Commission to that of its judicial colleague, the Restrictive Practices Court. It is only in recent years that the delegation of political responsibility involved in the transfer of decisions relating to market dominance from the Government of the day to the judiciary has caused concern:

> The disguising of economic policy issues as judicial ones, when they have customarily been settled as political issues, may well prove to have been an unfortunate constitutional development.[1]

In the event, between 1956 and 1962 the work of the Monopolies Commission was considered irrelevant both by the Government and the general public. During this period very few reports were completed by the Monopolies Commission, and those that were completed were not

[1] R. B. Stevens and B. S. Yamey, *The Restrictive Practices Court*, Weidenfeld & Nicolson, 1965, p. 153.

supported by Government action. The willingness of the Government to resist the recommendations of the Commission at this time did not go unnoticed by those subjected to investigation. By 1962 it appeared that the work of the Monopolies Commission had been thoroughly discredited. Commentators were pressing strongly for the establishment of a Monopolies Court, on the pattern of the Restrictive Practices Court, and the life-span of the Commission appeared to be strictly limited.

A fortuitous chain of events, headed by the abortive bid by Imperial Chemical Industries for control of Courtaulds, revived the interest of politicians and economists in the activities of dominant firms. The Monopolies Commission began to regain the public attention that had been lost in 1956. Comparisons commenced between the nature of the Monopolies Commission in the United Kingdom and that of the machinery for the examination of market dominance established in the European Economic Community. Political interest was aroused in relation to the supervision of market concentration by administrative techniques. First, the Conservative Government foresaw the need to extend the scope and the size of the Monopolies Commission; subsequently the newly-elected Labour Government proceeded with a Bill to this end. The problems encountered by the Commission in relation to the supervision and control of the dominant firm arouse considerably greater public concern today than was the case a few years ago.

An analysis of the Monopolies Commission's inquiries into dominant firm activities reveals problems of greater complexity than those encountered in trade association inquiries. The restrictive agreements of trade associations provided the Monopolies Commission with focal points around which the inquiry might be concentrated. The agreements themselves indicated prima facie evidence of an intent to restrict competition. The critical issues of the inquiry were usually bound up in these agreements. But the critical issues of a dominant firm inquiry are rarely so apparent. The activities of dominant firms differ in kind from the activites of any company only by nature of the firm's dominance in the reference market. The determination of prices and of investment, the choice between alternative systems of distribution and the attitude adopted towards the export trade, are of public concern by reason of the firm's dominance. If the decisions of the firm are condemned by the Commission alternatives must be provided. This was not so in relation to trade associations.

The difficulty in locating the critical issues, and the complications involved in assessing dominant firm performance, warrant a more intensive and exhaustive inquiry than has been provided by the Monopolies Commission in response to dominant firm references. The Commission has been handicapped in part by lack of skilled staff, but it cannot claim complete exemption from blame. Members of the Commission have displayed minimal interest in effecting detailed efficiency investigations into those branches of dominant firms responsible for the supply of reference goods. It is unlikely that a satisfactory analysis of the dominant firm can be undertaken in the absence of such an inquiry. Too often, the Monopolies Commission has been compelled, by lack of information, to shield behind the cloak of doctrinaire analysis. Upon occasion, indeed, the Monopolies Commission's analysis smacks of subsequent justification for preconceived conclusions. This impression must be eliminated in future inquiries. The respect in which the Monopolies Commission is held rests upon its ability to justify its conclusions before a critical audience.

PART V

STATISTICAL MEASURES OF ECONOMIC PERFORMANCE

Ignorance is the curse of God,
Knowledge the wing wherewith we fly to heaven.

W. Shakespeare, *Henry VI*, 3, III, 3

Chapter Sixteen

UNIT PRODUCTION COSTS AND PRICES

Earlier chapters have attempted to analyse the attitude of the Monopolies Commission towards the activities and performance of trade associations and dominant firms. Little attention was paid in the course of such analysis towards the statistical measures of economic performance relevant to such inquiries. The deferment of such analysis does not imply that the Monopolies Commission considered its financial and statistical examination as a secondary part of the inquiry. It is the purpose of Part V of this book to examine critically and in detail the quality of the Commission's work in this field.

The Monopolies Commission has usually devoted a considerable proportion of space in its reports to a study of costs and prices. This is a convenient starting point for an assessment of its financial and statistical investigations.

TRADE ASSOCIATION INQUIRIES AND THE SPREAD OF PRODUCTION COSTS

The spread of unit production costs between members of a price fixing trade association must be determined by any body interested in assessing the activities of such an organization. The spread of costs is important for the trade association itself. The wider the spread of costs the greater the degree of stress that is likely between member firms at price fixing sessions, especially when demand conditions deteriorate. Under difficult trading conditions the more efficient, lower cost, companies may be subjected to considerable temptation to undercut trade association prices designed for the protection of less efficient companies. A trade association composed of companies varying widely in productive efficiency almost always suffers from instability. It is particularly vulnerable when faced with violent fluctuations in the level of demand, and where its control over the output of individual companies is limited.

The spread of production costs within a trade association should not be viewed statically. The relative efficiency of individual members may alter radically with the passage of time, especially where technical development is not subjected to centralized control:

> Such variations in realized unit costs arise in part from differences in managerial skill operating essentially the same productive apparatus; but more importantly they arise dynamically from the uneven exploitation of developments in productive technique. What is important is that this is no mere random circumstance, but part and parcel of the process—among other reasons because innovation necessarily implies leaders and followers.[1]

In many industries, too, the level of unit production costs varies sharply with the level of activity. The short-run average cost curve of the company often takes the form of a U shape. Unit production costs may then be relatively high both for companies experiencing a temporary reduction in the level of their activity and for those working on sharply rising marginal cost schedules to satisfy a sudden expansion in the demand for their products. A spread of costs due simply to differences in the level of activity may be short-lived, and will impose little stress upon the trade association.

The outside investigator may find difficulty in obtaining comparative data with which to evaluate the spread of unit production costs within an association. Few trade associations insist upon the adoption by members of uniform costing systems. Yet an outsider is particularly reliant upon the data provided by member firms. Lack of uniformity in costing may create major problems of measurement in the case of multi-product companies faced with making an arbitrary allocation of joint overhead costs. Nevertheless, the Monopolies Commission felt itself compelled to heed information relating to the spread of costs even when the available data lacked uniformity of preparation.

The Monopolies Commission prized information on production costs as providing a critical guide to the public interest implications of trade association activities. Where the spread of costs was considerable and there was no evidence that high cost units were subjected to commercial pressures, the Monopolies Commission was always suspicious. It feared that low cost companies might earn unduly high profits and that the trade association agreements might prevent rationalization in production, to the detriment of the consumer. The Monopolies Commission always treated evidence of a wide spread of costs as prima facie evidence of the need for price competition within the reference industry. The Commission paid insufficient attention to dynamic changes in relative production costs. It paid no attention at all to the importance of the level

[1] H. Edwards, *Competition and Monopoly in the British Soap Industry*, 1960, p. 68.

of company activity in relation to its production costs. The information compiled by the Commission indicated a wide spread of costs between producers in many of the industries that were examined.

The Linoleum Manufacturers' Association furnished the Monopolies Commission with cost data relating to eight of its principal products. The information was of limited value since it had not been prepared on a uniform basis, but it suggested that a wide spread of costs existed between members of the association:

TABLE 5

*Linoleum Products—Pence per Square Yard**

	June 1953			*June 1954*		
Product	*Highest cost per unit*	*Lowest cost per unit*	*Weighted Average cost per unit*	*Highest cost per unit*	*Lowest cost per unit*	*Weighted Average cost per unit*
1st Sheet Marble (3·20 mm.)	109·5	88·31	97·09	89·13	78·60	83·14
'A' plain brown (3·20 mm.)	92·38	77·23	84·99	80·94	65·95	71·52
Inlaid 3rd (2·00 mm.)	86·55	61·73	68·89	n.a.	n.a.	n.a.
No. 3 Printed (1·40 mm.)	44·98	39·89	42·68	42·24	35·67	38·56

* The data provided has been selected from costing information supplied by the Monopolies Commission, 1956, op. cit., p. 38.

The available information denoted a wide cost spread between members of the Association. The Association claimed that the divergences were not significant since the relative efficiency of individual firms varied from one year to another. The Monopolies Commission was unable to substantiate this contention. It noted that in June 1953, December 1953, and June 1954, the same firm had experienced the lowest unit production costs for three out of the seven items costed. The Commission concluded that a wide spread of costs existed, and had existed for some time, between members of the Linoleum Manufacturers' Association. The cost evidence was substantiated by data which indicated a wide spread in the rate of profit earned on individual products by member firms. The Commission believed, in the absence of common prices, that low-cost producers in each linoleum line would expand their market share, and provide lower prices to the consumer. This conclusion was reached without explicit reference to the structure of short-run and long-run supply schedules in linoleum production. Clearly, the Commission's conclusion would be invalidated if short-run expansion of sales were penalized by steep rises in marginal cost and if long-run scale expansion resulted in diseconomies.

The Monopolies Commission recommended that a supervised system of minimum prices for linoleum should replace the common price scheme. It insisted that a uniform costing system should be installed by the association and that unit cost data should be furnished periodically to an independent accountant who might circularize financial data without disclosing the individual identities of participant firms.

The Commission obtained costing data—relating to December 1954—for certain general items produced by members of the Rubber Footwear Manufacturers' Association. Four companies provided cost data, including the Dunlop Rubber Company. These companies accounted for over 90 per cent of RFMA sales of rubber boots.

TABLE 6

Rubber Footwear Costs—December 1954*

Description	*No. of Samples*	*Range of Costs Pence per Pair*
Men's industrial knee boots	4	180–216
Women's industrial knee boots	3	132–168
Industrial three-quarter boots	3	270–330
Misses' wellington boots	3	90–109
Boys' dull wellington boots	3	119–151
Men's white duplex sports shoes	3	82–93

* This information was provided by the Monopolies Commission, 1956, op. cit., p. 57.

The Commission noted the existence of considerable quality variations between manufacturers' products subjected to the common price system. In particular, the Dunlop Rubber Company was the only company to subject its boots to a latex dipping process. Clearly, differences in the level of unit costs did not necessarily reflect differences in the efficiency of supply. The Commission noted that one manufacturer had been the lowest cost producer in each of the five lines of rubber boots costed, and that the Dunlop Rubber Company had been the highest cost producer in two of those lines. Indeed, Dunlop's costs were considerably above those of the lowest cost producer in four out of the five costed lines. This enabled the Commission to refute the Association's contention that the price-leader had always been a low cost producer.

A wide spread of unit production costs between members of the associations existed in practically every aspect of electric cable production. The unit production costs of the largest cable maker, British

Insulated Callender's Cables, were not among the five lowest for any of the six types of mains cable or the seven types of rubber cable costed. The company's unit costs were among the three lowest for a number of types of covered conductor. In only one such instance had more than four members submitted costs.

The Commission was especially concerned in the cable industry by the very wide spread of conversion costs. The Commission concluded that such wide cost divergences in the production of identical goods indicated that prices might be too high even if the average profits earned by the associations were reasonable.

In a number of inquiries the Monopolies Commission was unable to obtain satisfactory costing data for reference goods production. Calico printing was a case in point. The minimum price system was not based upon the use of costing data. It was impossible to obtain representative costs for individual lines and styles, owing to the great diversity in printing work, and the lack of standardization. Costing difficulties were increased where companies operated in a number of fields, and were faced with the allocation of joint overheads upon arbitrary principles.

TRADE ASSOCIATIONS AND UNIFORM COSTING SYSTEMS

Trade associations which operate price fixing arrangements determined in part by reference to costing data usually emphasize the importance of member companies applying a uniform system of cost calculation. In the absence of a uniform costing system, differences between the production costs of members may reflect no more than a variation in attitudes towards joint cost allocations, in the allowances provided for asset depreciation, in the provision for bad debts and such like.

Clearly, the need for uniformity in costing reaches critical proportions where the price fixing arrangements of a trade association span a range of products. Lack of uniformity in costing under these conditions may raise doubts within the association concerning the equality of margins allowed on each of the different product lines. Companies may consider that unfairly wide margins have developed through inadequate costing on a number of products; there may be a rapid expansion in the level of member production in these fields, unwarranted by true market forces. In cases where rapid expansion of this kind is frustrated in the short run by the existence of inflexible plant and equipment, and the lengthy gestation period for capital investment, companies within the trade association may press successfully for a relative rise in those product margins which appear to be least satisfactory. Alternatively quality debasement may develop within the 'low-margin' product lines.

It is true that the introduction of uniform costing will not solve this problem automatically. The allocation system for joint overheads is always arbitrary. Nevertheless, members may respect an arbitrary costing system derived through group debate or imposed by an independent accounting section. It may be necessary to make provision for re-negotiation of such a system following technical changes and innovation which affect association production.

It would be unwise, however, to assume that price systems are incapable of effective operation in the absence of a uniform costing system. Price levels which have been accepted for long periods by trade association members may be subject to remarkably little instability even under conditions of depression or of violent demand fluctuations. Indeed, it may be possible to operate a price system with considerable success in the total absence of a costing system, especially where the association is composed of few firms. Mutual interawareness of the risks involved in initiating price reductions may then prevent the emergence of price competition. Where the association is dominated by one producer in each production line, there may be little use for uniform costing. The dominant member of the association may operate the only systematic costing system, and be fully capable of convincing other members of the wisdom of its price-policy.[1] Price stability might exist for long periods under such circumstances, particularly if the dominant firm was regarded as a low-cost producer.[2]

Uniformity of costing has not been the concern of trade associations alone. The Monopolies Commission placed considerable importance upon the public interest implications of price fixing in the absence of uniform costing. In general, the Commission was willing to condone price systems only where a close, and clearly-defined, relationship between the prices and unit production costs of efficient members placed consistent pressure on high-cost firms to improve their production methods. Uniformity of costing was considered to be important for the fulfilment of such an objective. The Commission endorsed a common price system operated by the Electric Lamp Manufacturers' Association,[3] and a Recommended Minimum Price System in calico printing, in the absence of uniform costing systems. These proved to be the only exceptions to a general principle.

Price fixing trade associations in the copper semis industry experienced difficulties in obtaining satisfactory costing data from member firms. The product range of members was wide, and existing costing systems were unsatisfactory. The associations contended that members

[1] The Calico Printers' Association was almost in this position in the Federation of Calico Printers.

[2] In some cases this regard may be misplaced. Dunlop Rubber Company was mistakenly considered to be a low-cost producer in the pneumatic tyre and rubber footwear industries.

[3] The prices were fixed jointly by Associated Electrical Industries and the General Electric Company.

had sought to improve their costing techniques. The Monopolies Commission sharply criticized the existing system:

> In our opinion the individual costs which are averaged are themselves unsatisfactory and further the prices fixed by the associations do not in fact bear any close relation to that unsatisfactory average. It follows that the relationship between the price which an individual member is required to charge for particular goods and his own costs of producing those goods is remote.[1]

The Commission felt that narrower profit margins might have encouraged member firms to ascertain costs more accurately. It was not unaware that efforts had been made to improve the costing methods—but it considered that the difficulties experienced in this respect provided a cogent argument for eliminating the common price systems.[2]

The Linoleum Manufacturers' Association had not established its prices in the light of detailed costing information supplied by member firms. The Association received details of the weighted unit production costs of the more important linoleum products from an Independent Accounting Section. This system had been criticized severely by the Working Party on Linoleum in its 1947 Report, which had recommended the establishment of a uniform costing system including detailed classifications of terms, processes, and expenditure. It had suggested that all firms should be required to furnish such data to an Independent Accountant, who would collate and circularize the material without disclosing the results of any individual member. The Committee recommended that the Association should make use of such costing information when determining its prices.

The Linoleum Manufacturers' Association had decided against introducing a uniform costing system, partly because it would have involved a complete reorganization of members' existing systems, partly through the fear of disclosing individual production techniques. Each member continued to compute costs, including the allocation of overheads, in its traditional manner.

The Monopolies Commission recommended that a limited form of minimum price fixing should be allowed for association members. It stressed, however, that reliable costing information should be available to the Association. The Commission could find no insuperable difficulty in collecting detailed costing data without disclosing the identity of individual firms. It felt that the Association should take note, when fixing prices, not only of average costs, but of the dispersion around the average. In particular the costs of the lowest-cost producer should be known.

The Commission was almost always disturbed by the absence of

[1] op. cit., 1955, p. 95.

[2] A very similar conclusion was drawn in the BEAMA inquiry, op. cit., p. 253.

uniform costing within a price fixing association, suspecting that high profit levels had rendered unit cost calculations irrelevant or that the product was not suited to a group price fixing system at all. Clear evidence was required of compensating public advantages before a price system was condoned in these circumstances.

TRADE ASSOCIATIONS AND THE PROCESS OF PRICE LEVEL DETERMINATION

The Monopolies Commission examined most circumspectly the manner in which trade associations fixed their prices, noting the costing data provided and the relationships existing between price and cost. It was rarely completely satisfied by the systems it encountered.

The electric lamp inquiry produced an instance of price determination on the part of the two largest electric lamp producing companies. The General Electric Company and Associated Electrical Industries always took the initiative in proposing changes in the retail prices of Association lamps. The companies consulted each other, and exchanged information relating to lamp factory costs. Subsequent upon these discussions a third company, Siemens Limited,[1] would be consulted. A compromise proposal would then be placed before the Council of the Association. The proposal was usually accepted.

The Electric Lamp Manufacturers' Association contended that this system allowed prices to be determined by the yardsticks of the two largest and most experienced companies and that high-cost producers were in no way protected. No manufacturer was a low-cost producer throughout its production range.

The costing systems of GEC and AEI did not enable the ascertainment and comparison of selling and administrative costs for individual types of lamp; the two companies had never contemplated a fixed relationship between costs and prices. Certainly during pre-war years the dominating principle in price fixing had been 'what the market would bear'. During 1951 and 1952 the Commission found few instances of firms which had incurred losses on any category of goods covered by the price agreements. The Commission concluded that losses of any kind were unlikely in the absence of depression, since high-cost units would then be forced to leave the industry.

Price fixing without reference to costing data occurred in relation to sand and gravel supplies in Central Scotland.[2] The West Association had drawn up the initial price list by reference to long-term market

[1] Following the publication of the report of the Commission Siemens Ltd was amalgamated into the AEI Group.

[2] Report on the Supply of Sand and Gravel in Central Scotland, March 1956, H.C.P. 222.

conditions. Regard had been paid to the need to win trade from competing materials. No systematic attempt had been made to relate prices to production costs. Thereafter, prices had been altered from time to time to reflect cost changes. On each occasion market conditions had been examined in some detail. The Association had no costing data at its disposal and no individual unit costs were disclosed during price discussions. The unsystematic manner in which prices had been altered supported the view that they were maintained at unduly high levels. The Commission was convinced that the Association had exploited its dominant position in Central Scotland.

The Metal Window Association was one of the few organizations examined by the Commission which fixed prices on detailed principles closely related to a costing system. Between April 1946 and June 1952 non-statutory price control had been enforced for specified window and door supplies. The Ministry of Works had conducted cost investigations of selected Association members, and had accepted prices on a weighted average cost plus one-ninth. This allowed a 10 per cent profit on selling price. Following the termination of the price controls the MWA had aimed at achieving a similar profit margin. The Association had adopted a costing procedure known as the Hope Formula, by which the weighted unit costs of the three largest producers were averaged; the weighted costs of any other producer with lower unit costs than the lowest of these were also included in the average. A 10 per cent divergence between the lowest and highest costs of such a group was the maximum accepted in averaging. The MWA contended that the Hope Formula limited the impact of high cost production upon the level of association prices.

The Monopolies Commission compared the actual weighted average costs of the Association members with those resulting from the Hope Formula. The difference in fact was very small:

TABLE 7

METAL WINDOWS PRODUCTION

Unit Costs—Actual and Hope Formula
d. per unit

Item No.	*No. of members providing costs*	*Lowest cost*	*Highest cost*	*Hope Formula*	*Actual Weighted A.C.*
1	9	140·3	216·0	145·7	149·4
20	8	222·7	238·6	228·7	229·8
30	5	523·8	586·9	537·6	539·4
40	5	519·5	576·7	532·3	533·8
50	6	176·8	216·9	183·2	186·6
100	4	762·0	836·3	823·8	823·8
120	7	555·9	606·8	568·0	570·3
164	3	917·0	969·1	949·4	954·3

The spread of costs within the Association was not inconsiderable, taking into account the fact that steel bars represented one-third of total costs, and that these were purchased at uniform cost. In almost every instance the cost spread for labour costs was 80 per cent or more; the range for general overheads was even wider. In addition, cost data had only been obtained from nine members. The Commission concluded that the spread was substantial, although less wide than for other industries where comparable data was available. Evidence suggested that the cost spread was diminishing.

The Crittall Manufacturing Company—the lowest-cost producer in the industry—played an important part in price fixing under the Hope Formula. The Commission concluded that whilst this situation existed, and provided that the profit margin was not altered, adequate pressure would be placed upon high costs producers to improve their efficiency. The Commission was concerned by the technique whereby unit costs of Association members were determined on a notional 80 per cent level of activity. Any notional level below this would operate against the public interest by raising artificially the unit production costs of member firms. The Commission considered that the submission of price schedules to an independent body would provide a useful safeguard for the general public.

THE LEVEL OF TRADE ASSOCIATION PRICES

The Monopolies Commission examined the level of prices established and maintained by trade associations. The relationship between price and average unit production costs was analysed, and the movement of prices through time was occasionally compared with Board of Trade general price indices. The Commission canvassed the opinion of important purchasers and interested Government departments concerning the level of trade association prices. It did not, however, of its own initiative, seek out comparative overseas data on price levels. The difficulties of using such data are not inconsiderable, but the apparent lack of willingness to attempt the task may be criticized. Useful information may be gleaned from a carefully compiled international comparison.

The Federation of Calico Printers placed before the Commission the results of a survey made by the Fédération Internationale des Imprimeurs sur Tissus in 1952 of the *prix en vigueur* in the United Kingdom and seven European countries for thirty-seven selected designs or styles. The British Federation construed *prix en vigueur* as meaning current prices. The Federation claimed 'no more than that this independent analysis indicates fairly conclusively that British printing prices in general are lower than European prices in general'.[1] The Commission accepted this

[1] op. cit., 1951, p. 48.

interpretation, but provided little indication in its Report concerning the importance attached to the comparison.

The Electric Lamp Manufacturers' Association produced for the Monopolies Commission a table of comparative retail selling prices for a number of types of general service filament lamps in various countries in 1939 and 1951. An abbreviated list relating to 25-watt lamps is provided in Table 8.

TABLE 8

25-watt Lamp Prices—International Comparisons

Country	*Voltage*	1939 *d.*	1951 *d.*
UK	200–260	18·0	15·0
Switzerland	200–260	12·5	24·0
France	200–260	10·0	22·0
Germany	200–260	14·0	21·0
USA	100–130	7·6	11·2
	200–260	11·7	15·5
Canada	100–130	10·0	15·0
	200–260	18·0	19·5

According to the information provided, British lamp prices had been among the highest in the world in 1939, but by 1951 had become the lowest outside the United States of America. The Commission concluded that the pre-war prices had been unduly high in relation to costs, whereas those in 1951 were, on average, moderate. Nevertheless, the Commission recommended that the Government should review prices from time to time.

Upon occasion, the Commission has compared trade association price changes with price index changes for important raw materials. Such a comparison was made in the Linoleum inquiry. The Commission discovered that the prices of the Linoleum Manufacturers' Association amounted to two and a half times their pre-war level. On the other hand linseed oil, the principal raw material, cost about £110 per ton compared with £28 in 1939; wages in the industry were on average three and a half times the 1938 level. The Commission could see no reason, therefore, 'to reject the view expressed to us both by the larger of the independent manufacturers and also by a considerable body of retailers, local authorities and large commercial users that the LMA's prices are reasonable'.[1] Similarly a study in the rubber footwear industry showed that price rises had remained markedly below the Board of Trade general wholesale price index. Rubber footwear prices had risen less since 1949 than tyre prices and the prices of rubber goods generally. On the other hand they had risen faster than the prices of leather footwear.

[1] op. cit., 1956, p. 56.

The Hard Fibre Cordage Federation justified its prices as resulting from the same basis of formulation as had been adopted during the war for purposes of Government maximum price control. Since the prices had been acceptable to Government, the Federation felt they must now be considered reasonable. The Commission rejected this plea, pointing out that Government price controls had been imposed and maintained as 'a rough and ready means of retarding inflation during and immediately after the war';[1] there could be no justification for regarding methods used to calculate such maximum prices as being suitable in other circumstances, and still less for adopting the prices so calculated as minima.

The Commission's information[2] did not indicate unreasonable cordage prices in relation to costs. But the Commission was far from convinced that prices fixed by the methods adopted would always bear the same relation to average costs as existed at that time. This uncertainty was important in encouraging the Commission to condemn the minimum price system.

The Monopolies Commission did not make a very satisfactory contribution towards the assessment of domestic price fixing agreements by reference to comparative price data. The Commission adopted a largely passive attitude towards the accumulation of data, and displayed little interest in such material as came its way. A much more active accumulation and a more critical analysis of comparative prices might well have reduced the doctrinaire element apparent in the Commission's reports.

DOMINANT FIRM UNIT PRODUCTION COSTS

One useful measure of the economic efficiency of a dominant firm is a comparison between its level of unit production costs and those of competing companies, both at home and overseas. The reliability of this comparison should not be exaggerated. In many industries unit production costs vary considerably with the level of plant capacity[3] achieved, and with the scale upon which production is undertaken. An unfavourable comparison of costs from the viewpoint of the dominant firm may merely reflect a difference in the level of capacity activity achieved during the relevant period or, in the specific case of overseas competitors, it may reflect the larger scale upon which such latter companies are able to produce. In the domestic market, the dominant firm may suffer in cost comparisons from its willingness to undertake indispensable but indivisible expenditures from which rivals reap free advantage. Overseas competitors may be faced with cheaper raw material costs, cheaper

[1] op. cit., p. 77.

[2] Much of which was provided by the manufacturers.

[3] The possibility of shift production casts ambiguity over the entire concept of capacity, economic or technical.

labour, or greater Government tax assistance than is provided to the dominant firm in this country. Under such conditions it might be extremely unfair to criticize the British company for its relatively high production costs.

Most dominant firms are multi-product organizations. This poses the problem of allocating joint overhead costs between reference and non-reference production. There may be sound commercial reasons why the dominant firm has allocated its overheads unduly heavily into the reference field, especially where its remaining production is subjected to intense competition. Most inter-firm comparisons of the type under discussion are further bedevilled by the existence of production differentiation within the reference industry. There may be no satisfactory formula whereby the impact of product differentiation could be eliminated from the cost data provided by competing companies. The dominant firm might then be unfairly penalized for high cost production which is truly a reflection of a product of superior quality to those of its competitors.

Incomparability of cost data would not always work to the disadvantage of the dominant firm. Relatively low unit production costs may reflect an inefficient exploitation of substantial scale economies on the part of the dominant firm. Its rivals may be unable to achieve an equivalent scale of production. Low production costs may be an indication of monopsonistic purchasing power exercised by the dominant firm in its dealings with suppliers. It may reflect a difference in approach to the provision for capital depreciation during periods of rising prices. Clearly, cost data must be used with great care for evaluating the relative efficiencies of dominant firms and their rivals in specified reference fields.

The Monopolies Commission has examined the unit production costs of dominant firms in the majority of its inquiries. It has rarely compared such data with relevant data relating to overseas competitors. It has considered such comparisons unreliable, and in any event it lacks powers to demand such information from overseas companies. The Commission has occasionally referred in its report to comparative cost data compiled by independent investigating bodies. On no occasion has it been prepared to place complete faith in the results of such a comparison. In the domestic market, the Commission has experienced difficulty in obtaining comparable data due to the shortage of competing units. In place of inter-firm cost comparisons the Commission has made inter-plant cost comparisons within the dominant firm; inter-plant cost data has been used to evaluate the success of the dominant firm in rationalization of production. The attempts have rarely proved very satisfactory.

The Commission undertook an inter-plant comparison of the British Match Corporation. Its three largest plants—Brymay, Moreland and Masters—had retained much of their independence following their merger. They continued to produce their distinctive match brands. In the absence of significant independent competition in the United Kingdom, the Commission investigated the comparative production costs of the three branches. The total production costs per gross of domestic sales incurred by the three manufacturers formed the following pattern:

TABLE 9

*Total Match Costs per Gross**

Year	*Brymay*	*Moreland*	*Masters*
	d.	*d.*	*d.*
1936	36·33	28·19	35·92
1937	36·67	28·03	37·62
1938	37·07	29·23	37·50
1947	53·43	46·93	50·75
1948	55·40	47·41	52·06
1949	59·99	44·80	51·82
1950	62·45	49·02	52·27

* See op. cit., 1953, Table VIII, p. 72.

Brymay's unit production costs had been considerably higher than those of Moreland and higher than those of Masters throughout the postwar period. The discrepancy applied both to manufacturing costs and to overheads. Nevertheless, at the time of investigation Brymay was responsible for more than 50 per cent of the industry's output, and its costs alone were reviewed in connection with the fixing of statutory maximum prices.

Brymay, it is true, incurred costs not common to the other manufacturers, such as advertising, the administration of a co-partnership scheme, and the design of book match covers. Advertising expenditure amounted to $1\frac{1}{2}d.$ per gross. The Corporation admitted, also, that product variations accounted for part of the cost differences. In 1948 no costing system had existed which accurately indicated the extent of such differences. The Commission estimated that, after allowing for all such cost differences, Brymay's manufacturing costs were still about $5\frac{1}{2}d.$ per gross higher than those of Moreland.

The Commission concluded that there was no evidence of a consistent attempt at concentrating production on the lowest cost factories,[1] 'except to the extent that in the years following the war they happen to have been situated in areas where labour was more readily available than elsewhere'.[2] On the other hand manufacturing and distribution costs had risen little between 1939 and 1950, and this was an achievement of some merit. The Commission concluded that there was scope for the reduc-

[1] Indeed BMC had only recently installed a costing system.

[2] op. cit., 1953, p. 86.

tion of costs by BMC, and it indicated means by which small cost savings might be transmitted to the consumer.[1]

It is interesting to note that the costs of one independent match producer before the war had exceeded and those of another had undercut those of BMC. Following the war Anglia, Nemco, and UMI had been the highest cost producers. Economies of large scale production were not inconsiderable in match production.

The Commission was somewhat less perturbed by the discovery of unit cost differentials between Imperial Chemical Industries' ammonium sulphate factories at Billingham and Prudhoe:

TABLE 10

*Ammonium Sulphate—Costs per Ton**

	ICI		*Nitrogen*
Year	*Billingham*	*Prudhoe*	*Fertilizers*
1951–2	8·80	10·08†	11·25
1952–3	9·00	10·89	11·55
1953–4	9·60	10·88	11·14
1954–5	10·53	12·15	11·59
1955–6	11·73	13·32	12·14

* op. cit., 1959, p. 147. The figures are quoted ex works, exclusive of bagging, selling expenses and outward carriage.

† Prudhoe was Government controlled until November 21, 1954.

The Monopolies Commission examined closely the difference in costs between Billingham and Prudhoe for 1955–6. It concluded that the cost of making ammonia was lower at the latter factory. Neither factory was self-sufficient in ammonia production and Prudhoe had to purchase a larger proportion of supplies at substantially higher cost per ton than that paid by Billingham. In addition Anhydrite was mined at Billingham whereas Prudhoe had to purchase outside supplies. The cost of making, packing and handling ammonium sulphate at Billingham was lower than at Prudhoe. The Commission was satisfied that the cost discrepancy did not operate against the public interest. In part, the Commission was influenced by the fact that four large by-product producers of ammonium sulphate out of five examined[2] had higher unit production costs than either factory of Imperial Chemical Industries during 1955–6. The costs of these organizations included no ammonia costs at all. The figures could not therefore be treated as being completely comparable.

[1] The Monopolies Commission was equally critical of the manner in which The Imperial Tobacco Company had maintained inefficient and unprofitable branches for long periods. The advent of keen competition from Gallaher had toughened Imperial's internal policy.

[2] Three Gas Boards and two steel companies. The costs did not include a credit for the notional saving in the disposal cost of ammonia.

The Commission closely examined the unit production costs of the British Oxygen Company for 1952 and 1953; it concentrated upon eleven of the fourteen factories producing liquid oxygen and thirty of the thirty-six factories compressing oxygen. The average costs for liquid oxygen ranged from 5*s.* 2*d.* to 7*s.* 1*d.* per 1,000 cubic feet, the weighted average being 5*s.* 11*d.* For liquid oxygen the cost of electricity amounted to about 50 per cent of total works cost. The amount of electricity required for the production of 1,000 cubic feet of oxygen varied between factories, being influenced by the type, size, age, and condition of the plant, the level of output and the resulting load factors, and the local atmospheric pressure. In the case of compressed oxygen, costs ranged from 11*s.* 7*d.* to 24*s.* 9*d.* per 1,000 feet with a weighted average of 15*s.* In this section factories using their own oxygen had an advantage on grounds of transport costs. In addition, the use of bought-in electrolytic oxygen appeared to result in low costs to some of the factories using it.

In addition, the Commission compared the average costs of the British Oxygen Company with those of Saturn Ltd on their trading in propane and Pyrogas respectively for 1953. It found that at the works cost stage and for delivery Saturn's average cost per pound was somewhat the lower. This advantage was more than offset by Saturn's higher selling expenses and general overheads. This latter difference per unit could be directly attributed to the larger turnover of the British Oxygen Company.

The British Oxygen Company strongly denied any laxity in its surveillance of production costs. Regular meetings of all works engineers were held at which the costs and results for each factory were scrutinized and keen comparisons were made between the different factories. The Commission, whilst accepting that certain economies could be effected, could find no evidence to base a general finding that BOC's costs were too high.

The Commission always proceeds with caution in analysing the unit production costs of dominant firms. Upon occasion, it has compared such costs with those of British competitors or with those of overseas suppliers; this approach has rarely proved satisfactory. The Commission can only compare the unit production costs of plants owned by dominant firms where such firms are multi-plant. It has been highly suspicious of wide inter-plant cost differentials where the industry has a background of slow technical development. Where technical development is rapid it is inevitable that certain plant and equipment will be relatively high cost; the gestation period of new investment may be lengthy. It would not normally be considered economic to scrap existing equipment if the average variable cost of producing a given output did not exceed the average total cost of producing the same output with new equipment. It is no easy matter to determine the date of replacement of existing capital equipment. It is a little unfair to punish such errors harshly from an ex post vantage point.

THE LEVEL OF DOMINANT FIRM PRICES

The problems of assessing the public interest implications of dominant firm price levels are similar in nature to those examined in relation to the trade association. The Monopolies Commission has encountered considerable difficulty in evaluating prices. The Monopolies Commission examined comparative price level data occasionally, but never with great success. Lack of comparability between the British firm and overseas producers in prices was evident in chemical fertilizer production; Fisons Ltd was the British firm whose prices were in question. The Commission noted that 'according to the answer given to a question in the House of Commons on July 4, 1957, the price of superphosphates, per ton of nutrient, in the United Kingdom appeared to have been appreciably higher in the year 1955–6 than the prices in certain other Western European countries'.[1]

Fisons contended that the quoted figures were non-comparable, and to prove this commissioned the Economist Intelligence Unit to make a survey of selling prices and production costs of single superphosphate in Western Europe. Despite a general reluctance on the part of overseas suppliers to disclose full details of production costs the Unit was able to formulate certain broad conclusions. The Unit emphasized the important differences in the nature of the products, but produced the financial data displayed in Table II regarding Fisons and Western European producers.[2]

The Commission noted the lack of comparability in the data provided. The prices related to materials of different water soluble P_2O_5 content. Some of the products were bagged, others were not. The terms of delivery differed, some being ex works and others delivered nearest station. In some countries Government subsidies were paid to manufacturers, and had been deducted from the prices. In some, prices were subject to Government surveillance, and manufacturers complained of uneconomic profit margins.

From the information supplied, the Monopolies Commission decided that Fison's relatively high prices reflected high material and distribution costs. These costs were largely outside the Company's control. The high cost of sulphuric acid was due in large measure to the Company's practice of using its most efficient acid plants to produce triple super-

[1] op. cit., 1959, p. 138.

[2] The figures are extracted from data provided on p. 182 and 183 of the Commission's Report.

TABLE 11

COST PER METRIC TON

Single Superphosphate

	Continental Producers £	*Fisons* £
1. Landed cost of Phosphate Rock	5 5 0— 6 15 0	6 13 0
2. Sulphuric Acid	2 5 0— 6 0 0	8 11 0
3. Raw Materials per metric ton of Single Superphosphate	4 10 0— 6 10 0	7 7 0
4. Distribution Costs	2 0 0— 4 5 0	3 11 0
5. Manufacturing Cost plus Profits	3 5 0— 5 5 0	3 15 0*
6. Prices	10 9 0—15 0 0	14 13 0†

* It was stated that this figure was a significant item largely reflecting the efficiency of plant utilization and administration.

† In the case of three out of the four lowest prices obtained by the Unit it was said that they were fixed at levels which manufacturers complained were too low to give an adequate profit.

phosphate. Fisons argued that single superphosphate was obsolescent for straight application in the United Kingdom. Therefore the comparison with other countries, where straight single superphosphate was still the staple phosphatic fertilizer, was not a fair one. The Commission accepted this argument, and agreed that the data shed a favourable light upon Fisons' plant efficiency and administration. The available evidence refuted the criticism levelled at Fisons relating to its selling prices for single superphosphate.

The British Oxygen Company attempted to justify its price levels for oxygen and dissolved acetylene by reference to index number comparisons with well-known official indices:[1]

TABLE 12

	1938	1954
1. Board of Trade Index of Wholesale Prices	100	327
2. London and Cambridge Economic Service: Index of Retail Prices	100	236
3. British Oxygen Company Industrial Cylinder Oxygen Prices	100	143
4. BOC Liquid Oxygen Prices	100	94
5. BOC Dissolved Acetylene Prices	100	144

British Oxygen pointed out the comparatively slow rate of growth of its own price levels in comparison with the official indices of representative 'baskets' of commodities. The Company firmly contended that an increase in competition would increase rather than lower prices, by encouraging an inefficient duplication of resources with inevitable excess capacity. The Monopolies Commission was dissatisfied with this con-

[1] op. cit., 1959, p. 81.

tention. It accepted the argument that BOC's costs were not unduly high, but decided that profit on capital employed had been excessive. The Commission concluded that the prices charged by the British Oxygen Company for oxygen and dissolved acetylene were unduly high. It recommended that steps should be taken to prevent the Company from charging prices which produced such unreasonable profits; a regular review should be effected by the Board of Trade of all information relating to prices, costs, and profits, capital employed and other essential matters.[1]

The process of comparing price levels and price changes of dominant firm products with domestic or overseas data is complex and dangerous. The Monopolies Commission has not placed much faith in such comparisons in practice. It has only attempted this kind of comparison seriously when provided with access to independent or dominant firm-sponsored data. The Commission must be chastised for a lack of initiative in the pioneering of such studies. The Commission should surely operate as an active agent in the search for information, and not as a passive receptacle for information provided fortuitously by interested parties and independent organizations.

[1] ibid., p. 101. 'There is no power at present under Section 10 of the Monopolies and Restrictive Practices Act, 1948, or, as far as we are aware, otherwise, to enforce arrangements such as these. It is not for us to express a view on the question whether legislation would prove to be necessary in practice . . .'

Chapter Seventeen

THE CALCULATION OF RATE OF RETURN ON CAPITAL AS A PUBLIC INTEREST INDICATOR

The Monopolies Commission always attempts an appraisal of the price level established by dominant organizations. The Commission has considered a measurement of rate of return on capital to represent the most valid criterion in assessing the public interest implications of price levels. Criticisms have been levelled at the Commission in relation to the particular manner in which it has calculated rate of return on capital. This chapter outlines the several approaches which may be adopted, and appraises the form of calculation adopted by the Monopolies Commission. The appraisal is limited to the calculation of rate of return on capital as an aid to policy conclusions in the field of market dominance.

FORWARD ESTIMATES OF COMPANY PROFITABILITY

Net Present Value[1]

This is the classic method of assessing the profitability of capital employed by a company. The present value, P, of any project is found by discounting at the relevant cost of capital all future net cash flows to their present value equivalent:

$$P=\sum_{i=I}^{i=n}\frac{Ai}{(I+r)}i$$

where, Σ the summation symbol indicates that the numbers are to be added up, i=the number of years in which net cash flows are expected, and r=the rate of interest used to discount the future net cash flows. The net present value of the project is then found by subtracting the

[1] A detailed analysis is provided by A. J. Merrett and A. Sykes, *The Finance and Analysis of Capital Projects*, Longmans, 1963, p. 34 ff.

capital outlay C of initiating the project from the gross present value P. Thus the net present value $=(P—C)$.

$$\text{N.P.V.}=\sum_{i=I}^{i=n}\frac{Ai}{(I+r)i}—C$$

The net present value approach does not result in a rate of return on capital ratio at all. A positive net present value implies that the capital resources of the company will be raised by the sum indicated immediately it undertakes the investment project, assuming that the net cash flows and the interest rate have been computed with accuracy. It would be feasible for the Monopolies Commission to undertake such an assessment, basing its conclusions on expected dominant firm prices, the lifetime of the project, and the relevant interest rate by which the future net cash flows might be discounted. The Commission might then wish to establish a maximum net present value/initial capital outlay ratio by which to judge the economic performance of a dominant firm. Such a task would be monumental; it would involve the Commission in making forecasts of future prices, demand conditions, interest rates and the like. An outside body could never expect to obtain the confidence of industry in such forecasts. The net present value approach to evaluation of market performance could not be used effectively in the supervision of dominant firm activity.

Yield

The yield method of assessing economic performance did not develop until the late nineteenth century, 'but it has an impressive pedigree including both Fisher and Keynes among its exponents'.[1] The yield on an investment is defined as that rate of interest which discounts future net cash flows of any project into equality with its capital cost. The yield rate of interest results in a zero net present value. The yield is the solution r to the following equation:

$$\text{C}=\sum_{i=I}^{i=n}\frac{Ai}{(I+r)}i$$

where the symbols are as previously defined.[2]

It is clear that the yield assessed in this way corresponds more closely than net present value to the conventional accounting rate of return on capital. Its greater familiarity among the lay public would make it more acceptable than net present value in the evaluation of dominant firm performance. The Monopolies Commission might wish to establish a ceiling yield against which the yields of dominant firms might be compared. This measure would take account of the time pattern of future

[1] Merrett and Sykes, op. cit., p. 36. [2] ibid., p. 36.

net cash flows; and could be adjusted quite simply for risk, especially where risk was considered to be partly a function of time. The measure would relate to future rather than to past economic performance.

The advantage of the yield approach over conventional rate of return on capital measurements underlines its practical weakness as an aid to the supervision of market dominance. Any attempt to anticipate future economic performance is fraught with difficulty. Reliance upon future anticipations alone would surely expose the Commission to industrial criticism and to a fall in public confidence in the validity of its conclusions. An assessment of historical data is not always a satisfactory guide to future performance, but it does meet with public acceptance. The Monopolies Commission, perhaps wisely, has sacrificed the more relevant for the simpler and more acceptable approach.

Take-over Bid Valuations

Assets recently acquired by dominant firms through successful take-over bids might be valued on the basis of this bid. Where acquisitions have occurred frequently this might span a considerable proportion of the capital employed by a dominant firm. Unfortunately, this measure is irrelevant in assessing the performance of dominant firms. Insofar as the take-over bid reflected the net present value of future net cash flows it would capitalize quasi rents accruing to market dominance. But, in any event, the bid is unlikely to reflect the full net present value. Stock Exchange share prices tend to undervalue company assets in inflationary periods, especially when companies restrain dividend payments in order to finance expansion internally. The take-over bidder may offer a price mid-way between real asset values and Stock Exchange valuation. Once the bid has been made speculation may undermine any objectivity that formerly existed. The take-over bid would cover a limited proportion of dominant firm capital. It should not be used at all as a means of measuring the capital employed by dominant firms.

HISTORICAL MEASURES OF CAPITAL EMPLOYED

Stock Exchange Valuations

A few economists have suggested that Stock Exchange share valuations offer an objective and impartial measure of capital employed, and that such measurements are preferable to any other: 'The Stock Exchange might be less informed than the expert investigator on the internal organization of the firm, but in its forecasting of the future it will allow for intangibles, which expert opinion would ignore because they defy strict actuarial treatment.'[1]

[1] J. K. Eastham, *Compensation Term for Nationalized Industry*, Manchester School, 1948, p. 30.

Stock Exchange valuations have been used on a number of occasions by Labour Governments in assessing the compensation payable to shareholders in companies that are to be nationalized. Such valuations have been criticized but less for the technique adopted than in relation to the valuation date selected.[1]

In fact, of course, the Stock Exchange is not an impartial judge of future economic performance. The actual share transactions on the Exchange represent under normal circumstances merely a small proportion of total shares issued. The valuation, if objective, would be relevant for an assessment of capital employed only if the marginal transfers reflected accurately the market valuation of the total stock of a company's shares. Few would argue, however, that the Stock Exchange provides an objective valuation. For many customers, the Stock Exchange provides a useful vehicle for speculation. Its function is more closely related to that of a casino than to that of an objective evaluator of economic worth. Professional investors are more concerned with movements in confidence than with estimates of longer-term profitability:

> This battle of wits . . . does not even require gulls among the public to feed the maws of the professional; —it can be played by professionals amongst themselves. . . . For it is, so to speak, a game of Snap, of Old Maid, of Musical Chairs—a pastime in which he is victor who says Snap neither too soon nor too late, who passes the Old Maid to his neighbour before the game is over, and who secures a chair for himself when the music stops.[2]

In addition, investors tend to pay rather more attention to dividend payments than to cover in assessing the profitability of their share portfolio. Inflation and dividend restraint, particularly during the 1950s, has culminated in the under-valuation of capital employed on the Stock Exchange. Companies might complain with some justice that their efforts to assist the Government in the establishment of an incomes policy were being manipulated against them by a Monopolies Commission which relied upon Stock Exchange valuations of capital employed.

In any event, the Stock Exchange valuation of capital employed is scarcely relevant for an assessment of market performance on the part of dominant firms. Any quasi rents earned as a result of market dominance would presumably be reflected in the valuation of capital employed. The Monopolies Commission requires a measure of capital employed capable of exposing the quasi rents accruing to market dominance. Any measure which contains circularity of analysis must be avoided.

[1] See W. Robson, *Nationalized Industry and Public Ownership*, p. 279–80. Also H. Wilson, 'Paying for the Railways', *New Statesman*, March 5, 1960, p. 321–2.

[2] J. M. Keynes, *General Theory of Employment, Interest and Money*, p. 156.

Original Cost Valuation

The conventional accountant regards himself as the conserver of the money capital entrusted to his supervision. He must ensure that sufficient depreciation charges have been made by the time that existing assets are scrapped to meet the original moneys outlayed upon such assets. To this end, estimates must be made of the expected economic life of such assets and a depreciation system must be superimposed upon it. Traditionally, accountants have been predisposed towards straight-line or reducing balance systems of depreciation; the actual time-pattern of asset depreciation is barely considered.

The valuation of assets by reference to original cost less accumulated depreciation allowances is least ambiguous in times of stable prices and limited technical change. Under such conditions there may be no difference between an original cost valuation and a reproduction cost valuation. But this is clearly untrue in times of rising prices.

Inventory valuations represent a problem in inflationary conditions. A rise in inventory prices reflects a windfall gain to companies carrying them. The accountant usually refuses to feature this gain in company accounts until it is realized. Inventories are valued at cost or market value, whichever chances to be the lower.

Fixed assets are valued on the basis of original cost. This system of valuation receives legal approval in this country. It carries the technical advantage of administrative simplicity. In times of rising prices it is economically unsatisfactory, for it preserves neither the general purchasing power of shareholders' initial capital outlays nor the funds required to reproduce existing capacity.

As an aid to assessing the performance of dominant firms the computation of capital employed by reference to original cost less accumulated depreciation allowances is unsatisfactory in periods of price changes. It is true that the measure avoids capitalization of quasi-rents. But it does not represent a realistic current valuation of existing assets. The Monopolies Commission cannot escape criticism for its ready acceptance of this system of asset valuation.

Original Cost Valuation with General Purchasing Power Adjustment

Many critics of the original cost system advocate the adjustment of such valuations by reference to an index of general purchasing power. They are particularly concerned by the apparent willingness of accountants to ignore changes in the purchasing power of money: 'Accountants typically measure in terms of dollars of different purchasing power. . . . The current dollar and the past dollar, that is, are dollars of different value, but to the accountant either one is just one dollar.'[1]

An attempt at adjusting asset valuations and depreciation allowances

[1] J. Bain, *Industrial Organization*, p. 379.

for changes in the general price level presupposes the availability of a suitable index. Such an index is by no means conceptually simple to produce. The weights selected for incorporated commodities will influence the movement of the general index; frequent weight changes which reflect market changes may mar the temporal comparability of the index. In any event, the determination of index weights may involve value judgments:

> Can an index be framed which will give the right significance to all commodities for all people? Clearly not—the importance of price changes depends on how you spend your money.[1]

Once the weight problem has been resolved attention focuses upon the index number problem. A choice must be made between the Laspehre and the Paasche index, i.e. between base-weighted and current-weighted index evaluation. The movement of the index will be conditioned by the choice that is made. There is no guidance from economic theory or statistical theory available to assist in the choice.

Finally, there is a choice between an index of general retail price movements and an index of wholesale prices. Conceptually the latter is more relevant for asset value determination but the former may be based upon more comprehensive and accurate information. During periods of rapid change in market conditions the two indices may display disparate movement.

The general purchasing power adjustment to asset values may not be required for accumulated depreciation allowances which have been held in the form of a share portfolio. But where there is doubt concerning the current purchasing power of such allowances the position should be examined. The general purchasing power adjustments will produce asset valuations which maintain the real value of historical money outlays. It scores well on grounds of administrative convenience since national indices are available both for retail prices and for wholesale prices.

Reproduction Cost Valuation

The existence of general price stability does not mean that relative prices remain constant. The price of specific assets may rise or fall substantially. In such circumstances original cost valuations, with or without general purchasing power adjustment, will not provide an accurate measure of the reproduction cost of capital equipment. A reproduction cost valuation would reflect the current cost of replacing existing capital capacity. A number of companies have introduced reproduction cost depreciation allowances. Philips of the Netherlands provides a well-known example of reproduction cost valuation based upon the use of specific index numbers.[2]

[1] R. S. Edwards in W. T. Baxter (Ed.), *Studies in Accounting*, p. 293.
[2] A. Goudeket, *Journal of Accountancy*, July 1960.

The reproduction cost valuation corresponds most closely to the current value of existing capital employed by a company. As such, it is conceptually superior to other measures in the assessment of company performance. The practical problems of valuation are not inconsiderable. In particular technical change and quality adjustments may mar any comparison between existing assets and their potential replacements. The extent to which technical improvement may affect asset comparisons was clearly outlined by Gardiner Means in his study of price determination in the United States steel industry.[1] The productive capacity of an 'equivalent' replacement asset may far exceed that of the asset which is to be replaced. It may be difficult to provide for differences in productive capacity:

> Just what is it that is to be reproduced? Is it the physical plant and equipment so that one estimates the cost of building as nearly as possible identical plants regardless of improvements in design and materials that have occurred since the existing plants were acquired? Or is it the service performed which is to be 'reproduced'?[2]

Where a reproduction cost revaluation of assets is undertaken it is necessary to choose between the prices at which a firm may purchase the replacement assets and the prices of which it may sell its own capital equipment. If the market is imperfect—as will often be the case—the prices may differ considerably. In practice, convenience demands that buying price to the firm should be adopted. In many cases the market for sales of capital equipment is non-existent or highly imperfect. The price obtainable may be a function of the time period within which the sale should be effected.

The Monopolies Commission examines rate of return on capital within the context of a single industry. The measurement of capital employed should be based, therefore, upon specific reproduction cost of assets. Unfortunately, the Commission has always rejected this measure.

THE MONOPOLIES COMMISSION AND ORIGINAL COST VALUATION

The Monopolies Commission has rejected the reproduction cost valuation of capital employed by dominant organizations. The Commission has favoured, in place of this measure, an original cost basis for valuing capital employed. It has justified this approach on the ground that comparable data is available for a wide range of industrial activity. Yet, even within the context of original cost asset valuation, the Commission's approach has lacked consistency.

Capital employed by members of the Association of Dental Manu-

[1] *Pricing Power and the Public Interest*, 1962, Chapters V and VI.
[2] G. Means, ibid., p. 100.

facturers and Traders was computed by taking an average of the net assets at the beginning and end of the period concerned, at values shown in the companies' balance sheets. Member companies had always used original cost data for balance sheet purposes. Yet the Commission was more guarded in examining Balance Sheet asset valuations put forward by members of the Electric Lamp Manufacturers' Association. The Commission computed capital employed by members at the terminal accounting dates of relevant years, 'and it is the amount of net assets, comprising the cost of fixed assets less, in appropriate cases, wear and tear allowances (as allowed for income tax but excluding initial allowances)'.[1] The inconsistency of computation is striking. The Commission did not justify its change of approach.

A more detailed attempt at evaluating capital employed was made in the dominant firm inquiry which concerned the British Match Corporation. The value of assets was taken at balance sheet valuations except for (a) plant and machinery, where assets were valued at cost less depreciation at Inland Revenue wear and tear rates and (b) land and buildings where the value was taken at twenty-five times the net annual value for Schedule A income tax purposes. In nearly all cases this was higher than balance sheet values.

In the chemical fertilizer inquiry the Commission was unable to obtain sufficient data for original cost asset valuation; but it still favoured such an approach. The Commission decided therefore to commence from original cost values of capital employed but to allow depreciation charges at replacement cost rates.

Many of the Associations and Companies investigated by the Commission complained bitterly of its reference to original cost measures of capital and depreciation allowances in times of rising prices. In periods of rising prices this approach undervalued capital employed and overvalued profits. The under-valuation of capital employed might be substantial. The Electric Lamp Manufacturers' Association estimated that fixed assets valued at current replacement prices would amount to roughly two and a half times the value at original cost. In addition, depreciation allowances at Inland Revenue rates undervalued the actual cost to members through asset depreciation. The Association did not provide alternative calculations.

The British Match Corporation suggested that buildings, plant and machinery should be valued at current new replacement value. It recommended, alternatively, that the full original cost of assets should be accepted, where necessary, by treating written-down balance sheet values as being equal to one half of their original cost. Notional figures of this kind were presented go the Commission. For the year 1950 this reduced Brymay's rate of return on capital from 17 per cent computed

[1] op. cit., p. 73.

by the Commission to 6 per cent and/or 11 per cent respectively. The Commission published the figures but relied upon its own computations.

The British Oxygen Company argued that replacement cost measures of capital employed should be used by the Commission. The Company produced its own computations, using price indices to revalue the Commission's original cost measurements. In 1954, the Company's computation provided a rate of return on capital of 16 per cent as contrasted with the Commission's estimate of 22 per cent. The British Oxygen Company pointed out that asset prices were rising rapidly and provision must be made for replacement. It reminded the Commission that when the iron and steel industry had been subjected to government price controls, the Iron and Steel Corporation of Great Britain had adopted the basis of current replacement values for its 1952 accounts; on that basis the Corporation had earned a rate of profit on capital employed of 17 per cent. The Monopolies Commission stood by its own figures.

The Commission has provided full publicity for alternative computations put forward by investigated concerns. It has never wavered from its own acceptance of original cost material. In this respect the Commission has been seriously at error. The difficulty of comparing reproduction cost valuations with outside data is admittedly great. Reliance upon irrelevant information is no solution. Reproduction cost computations must be adopted. The evolution of a series of case studies may serve to provide a basis for future comparisons.

THE PROCESS OF REPRODUCTION COST VALUATION OF CAPITAL EMPLOYED

Technical Inquiry

The Monopolies Commission may find difficulty in effecting reproduction cost valuations of assets which are seldom purchased, especially when technical change has intervened between the initial purchase date and the date of the Commission's inquiry. Under such conditions, the thorough technical inquiry recommended in Chapter Five would be of considerable assistance. Skilled quantity surveyors might be employed to value land and buildings. A combined investigation by production engineers, accountants and economists might assist in the valuation of plant and equipment. The Commission has relied excessively on the calculations of outside bodies. It should be prepared to take the initiative where the provision of material is not fully satisfactory. The Commission's scope might have to be extended to allow it to enter industrial premises.

Fire Insurance Policies

It is prudent commercial practice to insure plant, machinery and other destructible assets against fire. Land may not be insured in this manner because it is less subject to destruction. Fire insurance policies are often taken out to cover the replacement value of the asset as new.[1] In such cases the value of the actual assets employed would be lower than the fire insurance valuations. It is common for fire insurance policies to cover the installation charges of assets. This would be acceptable for Monopolies Commission purposes.

The Commission would have to take care lest assets were over-valued for insurance purposes. Most insurance companies protect themselves against such action by contracting to replace destroyed with equivalent assets irrespective of the valuation covered by the insurance premiums. Dominant firms may be tempted to over-value assets for fire insurance to deceive the Monopolies Commission, if it was known that the Commission used this technique of valuation. The possibility is remote but the technical inquiry would prevent the more blatant forms of such deceit from being employed successfully.

Fire insurance valuations are subjected to careful analysis by companies at infrequent intervals. Various kinds of interim adjustment are made between major reviews. This again emphasizes the requirement of a cautious and pragmatic approach by the Commission. The fire insurance policy is at best a check upon other measures. It could scarcely be deployed on an extensive scale.

Net Annual Value of Land and Buildings

The Monopolies Commission has made use of Net Annual Value estimates adopted by the Inland Revenue as the basis for Schedule A income-tax assessments. It has capitalized this sum by multiplying the NAV twenty-five times. The realized value has normally been in excess of balance sheet valuations. Net Annual Value was assessed by the Land Valuation Office. The Monopolies Commission was unwise to adopt such a measure. The valuation was infrequent and probably inaccurate; there were always complaints about the inequitable impacts of the assessment. In any event the abolition of Schedule A taxation has now rendered the measure of historical interest only.

Capitalized Rateable Value

The value placed upon buildings for local authority rating purposes has been suggested as a measure of capital employed, if it is capitalized. This measure is an extremely poor index, inadequately computed from assessments of rentable value, and varying from area to area without good reason; it is disliked by many firms who claim an adverse bias against industry. The measure, imperfect as it is, could not apply at all to machinery and other such assets.

[1] L. R. Amey (in an unpublished PhD thesis) used this technique to evaluate capital employed in two companies.

Second-hand Market and Suppliers' Cost Data

Where fixed assets of the kind under review are traded regularly the Commission should be able to accumulate revaluation data from trade journals and transaction accounts. Where technical change has been low for a lengthy period suppliers of new equipment would be able to provide present replacement cost of new assets.[1] Suitable depreciation provisions could then be calculated. Where quality changes are significant the comparison is dangerous. The technical inquiry should then be used to provide a basis for comparison. In deciding whether to undertake a fully-comprehensive valuation the Commission must weigh accuracy against time; a compromise solution is inevitable.

Specific Index Numbers

It may not be possible, for certain kinds of asset, to obtain objective measures of the reproduction cost of capital employed. In such instances resort to specific index number revaluations is justified. The index must be based on price movements for the class of asset in question. The index may be marred by quality changes and of course it will be subject to the usual index number problem. Nevertheless, a judicious use of specific index numbers is undoubtedly preferable to an uncritical acceptance of original cost balance sheet figures. It is preferable, also, to an automatic acceptance of revalued data provided by reference companies: 'Visions are called forth of the era between 1918 and 1934 when corporations frequently wrote up or wrote down the value of fixed assets on the balance sheet by some arbitrary amount and altered depreciation charges accordingly.'[2]

RATE OF RETURN ON CAPITAL: OMISSIONS AND INCLUSIONS FOR MARKET DOMINANCE

Capital Employed

A number of problems arise in calculating capital employed for the purpose of assessing the economic performance of dominant organizations.

Allocation of Capital in Multi-product Firms: The very great majority of the Commission's inquiries have involved firms producing non-reference as well as reference goods. A number of the inquiries have spanned a range of goods and the Commission has attempted to allocate each

[1] Edwards and Bell, *The Theory and Measurement of Business Income*, p. 185. 'Some types of fixed assets are marketed continuously as new products and are subject to little technical change. The current purchase price of such assets new, at the end of the period, may be obtained in the same way as current purchase price of raw materials, by a telephone call or by arrangement for a year-end statement from the selling company.'

[2] Edwards and Bell, ibid., p. 185.

company's capital between individual reference goods. Certain capital assets are directly related to individual goods: these create no problem. Others are in joint use for several products and an allocation system must be selected. The various accounting techniques used for this purpose are conceptually unsatisfactory. Those allocating by reference to direct cost ratios are extremely poor; those referring to the time factor—machine hour rate or labour hour rate—are superior but arbitrary.

It is clearly naïve for the Monopolies Commission to accept a reference firm's own allocation system for capital.[1] The risk that an unduly heavy capital allocation may be made to the reference good field is clear. Such action would lower the profit/capital ratio in the reference field, perhaps to the firm's ultimate advantage. Companies which target price for similar returns on different products may cheat by allocating capital heavily to the sector where market dominance is greatest. The capital allocation may preserve a semblance of identical rates of return on capital employed in different sectors, prolonging the myth of the 'just price'.

The Monopolies Commission, whilst treating the allocation of capital with suspicion, has refrained in general from introducing its own allocation system in place of those of the reference firms. The Commission's poor technical knowledge of the reference firm is an impediment in this respect. The Commission limited its calculation of capital employed to the five largest producers of pneumatic tyres, since for other producers 'a realistic assessment would have been difficult, because allocation of capital between tyres and other products was impracticable'.[2] A similar situation occurred in the rubber footwear industry where capital employed in the referred sector could not be segregated for three of the six producers examined.

In certain inquiries the Monopolies Commission settled for a compromise solution. It refrained from any attempt at allocation of capital between different products in the copper semis industry. Its figures for capital employed were aggregates for all reference goods. In response to similar problems relating to sand and gravel supplies in Central Scotland the Commission decided to assume that sand and gravel haulage provided the same rate of profit or loss as other haulage transactions.

The Commission clashed with the British Insulin Manufacturers over their allocation of capital employed in insulin production. The manufacturers contended that capital was turned over once a year. The Commission concluded that this was unrealistically low. The Commission was unable to produce a more acceptable allocation system. The Chloride Electrical Storage Company Ltd rejected the Commission's allocation

[1] It often accepted the firms' allocations in early inquiries. The more recent inquiries relating to rate of return on capital show a more healthy suspicion of such allocations. [2] op. cit., p. 95.

of capital employed both as between the different sections of the group's business in reference batteries, and as between reference production and other production. Chloride attempted, instead, to evaluate the capital saving that would be achieved by the elimination of one section of its businesses compared with the relevant profit reduction. Chloride nevertheless admitted that the profitability of its automotive replacement business was much higher than that of its automotive initial equipment business. The Champion Sparking Plug Company criticized the Commission for allocating too heavy a proportion of capital to export sales. Champion argued that if export business were lost there would be little reduction in its capital commitments. Capital should be re-allocated so that only the marginal savings, achieved in the absence of exports, would be allocated to exports. After making certain additional changes Champion's estimated rate of return on capital in the UK for 1958 was 28·7 per cent as compared with the Commission's figure of 57·8 per cent. The Commission was unimpressed, pointing out that export trade was an integral part of Champion's business and could not be considered in any sense as marginal. This latest Report displays a desirable increase in the independence of approach adopted by the Monopolies Commission. It is to be hoped that this is indicative of a more determined attitude in this important aspect of inquiry and analysis.[1] The detailed efficiency audit recommended earlier would further strengthen the independence and reliability of the Commission's approach.

Trade Investments: Where referred companies hold investments in fields other than those referred to the Commission, it is quite clear that such assets must be excluded from capital employed. Should the rate of return on such investments differ from that on capital employed in the reference field, the inclusion of the former would distort the final ratio.[2]

The problem may not always be simple to solve. A firm may hold its working capital in the form of short-term bills or other marketable securities. Silberston and Solomons argue that such securities should be excluded from capital employed.[3] This conclusion is incorrect since it would distinguish unfairly in favour of the firm which carried its working

[1] One still feels that the diversified firm has more opportunity to deceive the Commission than its more specialized counterpart. An efficiency audit would do much towardsr edressing the balance.

[2] Suppose that Firm X employed £10,000 of capital in producing Good Y which obtained £1,000 profit. It holds £2,000 investments in another industry earning £50 in the year concerned. Inclusion of such investments would reduce the rate of return on capital from 10 per cent to 8·75 per cent.

[3] 'The Rate of Return on Capital Employed', *Economic Journal*, 1952, p. 791. 'The first firm is not using its reserves in the business whilst they are in the form of securities.'

capital in the form of bank deposits. The criterion for inclusion must be whether the assets are primarily held for operational purposes in the reference field. The line must be drawn with the utmost caution. The distinction between temporarily unemployed and redundant 'assets' is a fine one indeed.

The Monopolies Commission excluded trade investments from its figures of capital employed. The exclusions appear to have been of importance in calico printing and electrical equipment supplies to motor vehicles. The Commission does not appear to have noted the danger of discriminating in favour of firm's holding large cash reserves.

Goodwill: Many firms carry substantial figures on the asset sides of their balance sheets under the heading of goodwill. Goodwill usually represents an intangible asset relating to prospective quasi-rents. Upon occasion the figure represents payments made, in purchasing an organization, in excess of the reproduction cost valuation of the physical assets. Some firms are content to leave goodwill as a permanent feature of the balance sheet. Others write down its balance sheet valuation by making annual deductions from gross revenue, thereby reducing profit.

It is absolutely essential that the Monopolies Commission should accept neither the inclusion of goodwill in capital employed, nor the reduction of profits for the purpose of eliminating goodwill. To do so involves fatal circularity of reasoning which will render the ratio of profit to capital employed meaningless for market dominance inquiries.[1] Goodwill provides a reflection in asset valuation, of the 'monopoly' profits that should be isolated. Where the goodwill figure is clearly expressed the Monopolies Commission is presented with little difficulty. In certain cases, however, goodwill is incorporated in a disguised form on the balance sheet through inflation of tangible asset values. This danger underlines the need for caution in the valuation of company assets by the Commission. It further strengthens the need for a detailed 'efficiency' audit of investigated firms. Internal asset valuations may fully incorporate the present value of prospective quasi-rents. In general, however, the problem of goodwill is practical. There is little disagreement regarding the need to eliminate it for market dominance inquiries.

Problems arise in the case of firms that have recently acquired other companies by paying an amount in excess of the reproduction cost of assets in exchange for the goodwill of those acquired. Elimination of goodwill under such circumstances results in the firm having a lower capital employed value for Commission purposes than in fact was

[1] Silberston and Solomons, op. cit., p. 785. 'The value of goodwill will include the present value of the monopoly element in expected future profits. To give a "reasonable" return on capital, including goodwill, would be to perpetuate the very monopoly profits which it is sought to control.'

expended. Incorporation of goodwill perpetuates monopoly profits. In such cases goodwill should be excluded from capital employed. Reproduction costs of assets is the relevant measuring rod. The take-over price is a bygone, and irrelevant for future commercial policy. The Commission must isolate the quasi-rent element of profit, if this is feasible. To do so goodwill must be rejected.

Hired and Rented Assets

Conventionally, the rental or hire of loaned assets appears as a deduction from revenue in the profit and loss account.[1] The assets do not then feature in the balance sheet as capital employed by the firm. Where the interest payment on the hired asset differs from the rate of return on capital for the entire organization the exclusion of such assets from capital employed is unsuitable for Monopolies Commission analysis. The Commission is interested in the entire physical assets employed in the reference field. Whether the assets are hired or owned is immaterial. For sake of consistency the Commission should capitalize hired assets and eliminate the interest charged against revenue.[2] Reproduction costs valuations should be obtained for hired assets, if necessary by reference to the various techniques outlined in this chapter.

In practice the Monopolies Commission has not capitalized rented assets. It has relied upon revenue reductions. This practice involved conceptual inconsistency and should be revised.

Initial Losses: When firms enter untested markets or establish themselves in new geographical areas they may be prepared to accept lengthy gestation periods during which losses may be sustained. Some firms argue that initial losses should be capitalized for Monopolies Commission purposes since such losses are in the nature of further investment. In practice, however, there is little to commend such action. Initial losses may be taken into account by reference to profit on capital employed ratios spanning a number of years; this is preferable to capitalizing the sum into perpetuity. The problem is scarcely significant for dominant firms since the majority enjoy well-established market positions and a

[1] L. Taylor Harrington, 'Using "Return on Capital" as a Measure of Success'. Manchester Statistical Society, March 8, 1961, p. 16. 'Normally the use of these will enter into the calculation of return on capital through the cost side of the ratios (i.e. reducing profits) but it may be felt desirable to include their value in assets employed instead of charging their hire as a cost.'

[2] Silberston and Solomons, op. cit., p. 793. 'It is true that in comparing the results of otherwise identical firms, one of which rents property and one of which does not, this treatment would give different rates of return unless rent paid as a percentage of the capital value of rented buildings were the same as the rate of profit on owned assets, or unless this capital value were negligible in amount.'

balanced asset age-structure. Save in periods of exceptional change, dominant firms are unlikely to experience widely-fluctuating profit on capital employed as a result of initial losses. Imperial Chemical Industries pointed out that for many years it had incurred losses on its domestic and export fertilizer business. It was not until 1947 that these earlier losses had been offset by profits. The company submitted that its investment in fertilizer manufacture, considered over the entire period, had yielded an inadequate profit. The Commission considered the hazards of the early years in its assessment of Imperial Chemical Industries' current rate of return on capital employed. The Commission concluded that the initial losses had been fully offset and that current policy should be examined on its merits.

Redundant Assets: Changing conditions of supply and demand may render a formerly useful asset redundant in its present occupation. Particularly where such assets have a very low opportunity cost, they may remain as figures on the asset side of the balance sheet for lengthy periods; alternatively, they may be written-down as charges against revenue. Redundant assets should be eliminated from capital employed for Monopolies Commission analysis and charges made against gross revenue should be added back. The Monopolies Commission is interested in capital employed; it should not place a premium upon the retention of unemployed assets.

The task of defining a redundant asset is not simple.[1] Some would argue that assets are redundant when the average total cost of producing a given output by the use of new equipment is less than the average variable cost by the use of existing equipment. One may not wish to press the point so far, but at some point an effective efficiency audit would enable the Commission to declare assets redundant.

The Monopolies Commission, during its inquiry into the metal windows industry, pointed out that certain property owned by Crittall had been excluded from its calculation of capital employed. The property consisted of dwelling houses, of which nearly 80 per cent were occupied by existing or past employees of the Company. The net incomes from these houses had been deducted from profit. At present the Commission usually lacks the requisite information for such action. Legislation might be required providing for Commission access to factory premises for it to make such decisions. Once again the recommended efficiency audit would serve a useful purpose by subjecting capital employed to a detailed scrutiny.

[1] Silberston and Solomons, op. cit., p. 798. 'Of course, what is a redundant asset depends to a great extent on the efficiency with which assets are used. An inefficient producer might need two machines to do what an efficient producer could do with one.'

Abortive Development Expenditure: Some industries[1] are characterized by the risk that expensive investment will bring no return whatsoever. Capital employed in such industries may have no opportunity cost. Where investment proves abortive many economists would write it off as a bygone that should not influence future policy. Firms, on the contrary, may wish to retain the book-value of such investment in order to broaden the capital base and to put high profit earnings on successful capital into perspective. In principle abortive expenditures should not feature in capital employed; sensible reference to a risk factor will prevent an unjust assessment of rate of return on successfully employed capital.

Risk Capital v. Debt Capital: Companies obtain finance for investment in various forms: equity capital, preference capital, debenture loans, bank advances and the like. It is suggested, occasionally, that various forms of such capital should be excluded from capital employed for Monopolies Commission purposes.[2] In particular, it has been urged that the return to risk capital is the correct measure of a dominant firm's operations, and that trade credit, bank overdrafts, and debenture stock at least should be eliminated; some would even eliminate fixed interest preference stock.

These suggestions indicate a lack of understanding of the purpose of Monopolies Commission inquiries. The Commission is concerned with the operations of a specified bundle of assets and with the rate of return earned on those assets. The distribution of gains is a separate issue and the Commission has never yet examined this aspect of a firm's activity. To do so would in the eyes of many constitute an intolerable interference in the affairs of private enterprise. The Commission must continue to examine the total employed assets of the firm; it should not concern itself unduly with the liability structure of the Company. Where necessary interest deductions charged to gross revenue against liabilities should be added back to gross revenue for the determination of profit.

The Monopolies Commission has always added back to profit interest payments on borrowed money and all forms of taxation payments. This is consistent with its inclusion of interest bearing assets in the measure of capital employed.

Profit Earned

The close inter-relationship between profit and capital employed has become apparent in the analysis of the latter part of the ratio. The

[1] e.g. oil-mining, gold-digging, water-divining.

[2] Account may be taken, when applying the risk factor, of the uses to which capital is put. This occurred in the cigarettes and tobacco inquiry.

Monopolies Commission clearly defined its interpretation of profit in its earliest report which related to the supply of dental goods:

> Excess of net sales plus any other trading receipts over costs of production and general operating expenses which include depreciation (but not initial allowances), amortization of leases, 'net Schedule A' values for owner-occupiers (in lieu of rent) and all forms of directors' remuneration, but not any taxation on profits (EPT NDC, profits tax or income tax), interest on borrowed money (e.g. debenture or bank loan interest) or transfers to general reserve.[1]

A number of unresolved problems of computation should be examined.

Proprietors' Remuneration and Salaries: The Monopolies Commission has been somewhat lax in allowing firms to deduct the salaries of directors and senior management from gross revenue at their own rates. High 'profits' may be obscured in medium-sized or small firms by high 'salary' remuneration for such officials. The risk is particularly apparent in director-controlled companies; the Inland Revenue has devised strict rules for taxation purposes in such companies. The Commission should take care to deduct salaries based upon opportunity-cost when formulating the profit figures of dominant firms. Salaries paid to 'sleeping partners' should be eliminated completely in profit assessment.

Wages: The Monopolies Commission has displayed weakness in its unquestioning acceptance of wage deductions allocated by firms against gross revenue. Dominant firms may expend monopoly 'profits' in the provision of wages and fringe benefits in excess of market levels. This possibility should certainly be examined and any excess of a significant magnitude should be added back to profit. The pattern of profit recipients is irrelevant in measuring the rate of return on capital. But profit distribution is more relevant when examining the public interest implications of rate of return on capital.

Sales Promotion Expenditure: Many firms consider sales promotion as one form of investment, and would like to see it capitalized for measurement purposes. The Commission has treated such expenditure as an allowable deduction from revenue.[2] The Commission's general attitude is acceptable although greater circumspection is required regarding details. The Commission should attempt an asssesment of the role of

[1] Report on the Supply of Dental Goods, p. 138.

[2] It has not been careful to prevent undue allocation of expenses to the reference sector where diversified companies are involved.

advertising, adding back to profit expenditure considered to be wasteful. This suggestion is proferred somewhat tentatively, with recognition of practical difficulties involved. Fear that dominant firms will squander quasi-rents on advertising in an attempt to perpetuate quasi-rents motivates the request for care.

Research and Development Expenditure: Research and development expenditure is a form of investment and a powerful case may be made for its capitalization. Practical difficulties in so doing, however, are considerable. The choice of the rate of interest used to capitalize research expenditures would be arbitrary. There would be need to constantly re-examine the capitalized figure to eliminate redundancy. On balance, the Commission's approach in deducting research and development expenditure from gross revenue is preferable. There is a risk that expenditure upon research and development may have been misdirected; this is difficult to assess ex post and impossible ex ante. Judgments of this kind should be undertaken separately, and the full amount should be allowed against profit.[1]

Profits and Economic Efficiency: Earlier analysis was directed at the danger that high unit costs might result in a low rate of return on capital. The Commission has tried to assess the performance of investigated companies in comparison with that of domestic and overseas competitors. There are numerous pitfalls and problems in such a financial comparison. A full scale technical and financial investigation would support this aspect of the Commission's task. In the light of this audit costs clearly attributable to sloth and inefficiency should be added back to profits for rate of return on capital measurements. The Commission has never attempted this in practice.

RATE OF RETURN ON CAPITAL—THE IRON AND STEEL BOARD APPROACH

In 1953 the Iron and Steel Board was charged with the responsibility for supervising the prices charged for steel products. It was additionally provided with permissive powers to determine maximum prices for home sales by producers of iron and steel products. In the discharge of its responsibilities the Board at first applied the same principles as its predecessors at the Ministry of Supply. Maximum prices were based on the operating costs of representative producers—excluding after 1954

[1] The danger arises in diversified companies that research expenditure may be heavily allocated to the reference sector. The Commission was concerned at this possibility among the electrical equipment supplies to motor vehicle assemblies. A technical inquiry would protect against such an occurrence.

a band of the highest cost producers—together with a standard margin for depreciation and profit.

With the passage of time, however, the Board became increasingly doubtful of this approach. The Board decided that its pricing system should be designed to encourage capital development in the steel industry. To this end, prices should take account of the operating and capital costs of hypothetical new plants, incorporating the most modern new techniques and operating at a high level of efficiency. The operating costs of a new plant were usually below those of older plants; but these cost savings scarcely compensated for the higher capital charges of modern plant in the absence of revolutionary changes in technique. Thus the Board's gradual shift from average historic cost pricing to new plant cost pricing resulted in rather higher maximum prices in 1957 for certain steel products than would otherwise have resulted. Its experiment in the field of price determination indicated a willingness to take note of economic analysis.

It would not be easy for the Monopolies Commission to follow the example of the Iron and Steel Board in determining the capital employed and the operating costs of dominant firms that are relevant to its exercise. A lack of detailed and long-standing experience of the industry in question would handicap the Commission in achieving so complex an exercise. Even the full use of an efficiency audit would be suspect in relation to an objective of this nature. But the Iron and Steel Board has provided a willingness to experiment in modern techniques of analysis which is singularly lacking in the case of the Monopolies Commission. The Commission has remained steadfastly loyal to irrelevant measures which provide a mere semblance of consistency. The Commission does not measure like with like; its shifting standard is the worse for providing an appearance of impartiality. At least, the adoption of reproduction cost techniques would provide a series of comparative studies, in time, based upon genuinely consistent and relevant principles.

Chapter Eighteen

RATE OF RETURN ON CAPITAL AND THE PUBLIC INTEREST

The Monopolies Commission has analysed the rate of return on capital employed in the majority of supply, processing and export fields referred for investigation by the Board of Trade. The previous chapter critically discussed the measure adopted by the Commission to this end. It was argued that conceptual inadequacies reduced the value of the measure as a public interest indicator. Recommendations were made with the design of improving its usefulness.

It is by no means simple, however, to make use of rate of return on capital, however relevantly computed, as a yardstick whereby the economic performance of dominant firms may be historically evaluated. It is yet more difficult to adjust the historical measure for predictive purposes. This chapter attempts to outline the problems involved and to assess the approach adopted by the Monopolies Commission.

SELECTION OF THE PUBLIC INTEREST YARDSTICK

The Monopolies Commission, apparently, did not establish any formal standard for the evaluation of rate of return on capital employed by trade associations in the early reference fields. Instead, it seems to have relied upon rules of thumb. In any event, the Commission was more often concerned with examining the spread of costs between members of associations than with comparing the average rate of return on capital achieved by trade association members with an external standard. Rudimentary comparisons were made in a few inquiries between the association's average rate of return on capital and the average achieved by independent suppliers. Little importance appears to have been attached to such measures.

The British Electrical and Allied Machinery Association was faced by a Monopolies Commission comparison of its rate of return on capital with an industrial standard. It was the only occasion on which trade associations were so dealt with. The Groups investigated suggested that their average rate of return on capital should be compared and measured against the profits earned by three groups of industries in 1952. The figures provided related to groups listed in the Actuaries Investment Index current in 1951–2. The Index related to the profits of five companies in the motor vehicle industry, twelve in electrical manufacturing and thirteen in a miscellaneous group. The respective rates of profit on capital employed for these groups were 22 per cent, 20 per cent and 21 per cent.[1]

The Monopolies Commission rejected the suggested standard on the ground of its limited scope. The attempt of the trade association to formulate a rate of return on capital yardstick may have impressed the Monopolies Commission. In any event, the Commission decided, for the first time—and the only occasion involving a trade association—to compare the rate of return on capital employed in the reference field by trade association members with an outside standard. To this end, the Monopolies Commission selected the measure of rate of return on capital published by *The Economist* newspaper. This measure related to some 2,000 public companies in manufacturing and non-manufacturing industry. The Commission considered this measure to be superior to those suggested by BEAMA. The selected yardstick was largely retained by the Commission for use in subsequent dominant firm inquiries. Certain important adjustments were made to the data published by *The Economist* newspaper:

> It was assumed that the profits shown in the accounts published in the first three-quarters of any calendar year would have been earned mainly in the preceding calendar year; figures from accounts published in the fourth quarter, which were thought likely to relate approximately equally to the previous year and to the year in which they were published, were omitted from our calculations. Capital employed was calculated by taking the total assets, excluding outside investments and goodwill items but including cash balances, and deducting therefrom current liabilities and provisions. Profit yields were based on the published profits (i) before deduction of tax, (ii) before payment of interest (which was estimated in accordance with current interest rates) on loans and overdrafts, and (iii) after deducting one-half of the non-recurring profits to eliminate the tax element therein and other non-trading items. Thus capital employed was represented not only by share capital but by all forms of borrowing (including debentures and bank overdrafts) and by capital and revenue reserves (including provision for future taxation); and the profit ratios represented the yield, before tax, on that capital. Although we found

[1] For further details, see op. cit., 1957, p. 251.

it convenient to start from the data assembled by *The Economist* the method of computation was our own.[1]

The Commission was always self-effacing about its selected yardstick. It recognized quite clearly that no precise comparison was possible between its accepted standard and the rate of return on capital computed for dominant firms operating in reference fields. On the other hand, the Commission believed that the basis of computation adopted by its own accounting team corresponded more closely with this measure than with any other then available. The Commission was most anxious that comparisons should be limited to rate of return on original cost capital.[2] It was suspicious of reproduction cost calculations.

A number of dominant firms submitted their own suggestions regarding rate of return on capital statistics most suited for comparative purposes. The British Oxygen Company pointed out that the Iron and Steel Corporation of Great Britain—during the period of direct Government price control over iron and steel products—had adopted a current replacement value basis for its accounts (1952); on that basis the rate of return on capital employed in iron and steel had amounted to 17 per cent. The British Oxygen Company argued that, since a publicly-controlled industry had been allowed to earn 17 per cent on a replacement basis, it was unfair to criticize one of its suppliers for making a similar rate of return on capital. The Monopolies Commission rejected the thesis.

The Imperial Tobacco Company submitted a calculation of rate of return on capital for 3,000 public companies quoted on the United Kingdom Stock Exchanges. The calculation had first emerged in a book entitled 'Company Income and Finance 1949–53' issued for private circulation by the National Institute of Economic and Social Research. It was kept up to date, subsequently, by the Board of Trade. The results were published in *Economic Trends*.[3]

The figures in *Economic Trends* were assembled by grouping individual accounts whose financial years ended within each fiscal year and describing the aggregates so obtained as relating to the calendar year ended within the fiscal year. The figures in *Economic Trends* were arrived at after excluding as far as possible companies which operated primarily overseas. The statistics were subjected to a more detailed analysis than were those of *The Economist* newspaper. On the other hand the relevant data provided by *The Economist* was available considerably earlier than that published in *Economic Trends*.

[1] Report on the Supply of Cigarettes and Tobacco and of Cigarette and Tobacco Machinery, H.C.P. 218, July 1961, Appendix 6, p. 223.

[2] See Report on the Supply of Certain Industrial and Medical Gases, H.C.P. December 13, 1956.

[3] See *Board of Trade Journal*, December 7, 1962, for further details.

The Imperial Tobacco Company excluded from its calculation of rate of return on capital for manufacturing industry all cash balances and tax reserve certificates. The company argued that cash should be excluded from capital employed since most of it was temporarily unemployed capital on call or short-term deposit. For the period in question the Commission considered that industry as a whole had been carrying an unusually large amount of cash, part of which had been surplus. For this reason, the Commission's own measure had over-stated capital employed during the period whilst the Imperial Tobacco Company's measure had under-stated capital employed. The Commission admitted, additionally, that profit ratios would have been greater if it had been possible to readjust the data to a uniform original cost basis. It had insufficient information to make this adjustment. The methods adopted could only be viewed as broad indicators of the rate of return on capital earned by manufacturing industry.

Joseph Lucas (Industries) Ltd asked that its results should be compared with those of the motor vehicle and motor component and accessory industries subject to similar risks and fluctuations as itself. The company produced figures from *Economic Trends* relating to component makers and motor manufacturers. The Commission rejected this standard in deciding whether Lucas had earned excessively high profits.

The Commission itself never expressed full satisfaction with any general measure of the rate of return on capital earned by manufacturing industry.[1] This is not surpising. It may be possible, for analytical purposes, to talk in terms of normal profit, especially when discussing freely competitive industries from the viewpoint of the long-run. In the modern industrial economy such a concept is less valuable. Rate of return on capital averaged for manufacturing industry in general reflects a consolidation of varying degrees of imperfection. It cannot be presumed to approximate the mythical competitive norm.

The economist would examine the industry under review to estimate that minimum rate of return which would attract required new investment. In seeking out this long-run rate, the economist would not reject short-term 'disequilibrium' rates entirely. But in any case, the required minimum rate of return in the long-run sense may vary from time to time. An autonomous movement in the aggregate consumption schedule may affect the required rate. A government attempt to promote a long-term faster rate of growth may have an effect upon interest rates for a considerable period of time. Government manipulation of short-term interest rates may influence long rates. At best the required rate of return on capital will oscillate. The Commission has tended to evade the complexity of this issue, in recent years at least, by referring to the figures published by *The Economist* relating to 2,000 public companies. This

[1] See Table 13 for details.

TABLE 13

Measures Suggested and Accepted for Rate of Return on Capital Comparisons*

	1952	1953	1954	1955	1956	1957	1958	1959	1960	1961	1962
The Economist Figures for Manufacturing* Industry. Reorganized.	15·4	16·6	17·2	17·3	16·5	15·4	14·1	15·7	15·5	13·2	
Economic Trends figures:* Monopolies Commission Selection	17·1	17·6	18·2	18·0	16·4	15·5	14·2	15·3	15·8	13·2	
Economic Trends: Imperial Tobacco Company Selection	19·4	20·2	20·9	20·4	18·0	16·7	—	—	—	—	
Economic Trends: Vehicles	—	—	26·0	25·6	18·0	15·0	16·6	19·4	19·0	10·7	
Economic Trends: Component Makers	—	—	27·1	23·9	19·4	18·6	19·3	19·7	17·8	13·2	
Motor Manufacturers: Lucas	—	—	34·0	27·3	15·4	12·0	19·5	22·9	22·8	9·7	
Motorcycles and Aircraft: Economist	—	—	26·9	23·0	17·7	16·1	16·3	24·1	18·5	12·2	

measure in recent years has oscillated between 15 to 16 per cent. Exceptionally, in 1961, it fell to 13·2 per cent. The Commission has not used this measure inflexibly. It has always examined the relevance of special pleading.

HIGH RATE OF RETURN ON CAPITAL—MISCALCULATION OF MARKET FORCES

High rates of return on capital may occur, occasionally, through miscalculation of market forces rather than through designed exploitation policy of dominant firms. One should not underestimate the problems faced by firms and associations when pricing for a target return. Price decisions involve imperfect assumptions regarding competitive reactions and market penetration. They involve, perhaps, assumptions concerning Government fiscal and monetary policy that may prove to be completely misguided. They involve assumptions concerning the impact of brand promotion that may not be exactly fulfilled in practice. The problem is considerable in relation to long-term strategy. It is intractable in the short-run and when dealing with selected ranges of a company's products. On the other hand, evidence of a continuous over-attainment of target rate of return on capital must be treated with acute suspicion. Even in an expanding market it is possible to readjust future plans in the light of past performance.

The three largest manufacturers of acrylic teeth[1] had obtained rates of return on capital for 1948 of 116 per cent, 95 per cent and 57 per cent. In part, this reflected, undoubtedly, the increased turnover which resulted from National Health Service legislation. Turnover in 1948 had been four times greater than it had been in 1947 for two of the three producers. In 1949 the manufacturers had made substantial price reductions. The price reductions had been offset, however, by cost economies related to vastly increased turnover, and the net profit rates had remained at levels similar to those for 1948. Here was an excellent example of a market expanding more quickly than suppliers anticipated; the result was a high rate of return on capital which remained in the face of rectifying action. The Commission, nevertheless, commented adversely upon the profit levels obtained by the manufacturers concerned.

Fisons Ltd had aimed at obtaining a rate of return on capital valued on an historical cost basis of about 20 per cent. The average rate of return realized in recent years had been somewhat higher, due in the main to the high rate of 29·3 per cent which had been achieved in 1955–6. Fisons argued that this had been largely due to an unexpected increase in sales, and regarded 1955–6 as being abnormal. The Company

[1] Report on the Supply of Dental Goods, 1950.

admitted playing for safety when budgeting, in view of its heavy capital commitments. The Monopolies Commission was unimpressed by the argument that Fisons had underestimated demand and it recommended that Fisons should budget for a lower rate of profit in future. It would appear that the miscalculation argument carries little weight with the Commission regarding future pricing policies in the absence of truly abnormal developments in the reference market.[1] This view is probably more justified in industries dominated by one firm than in the case of trade associations unless the latter maintain rigorous centralized control over the investment policies of member companies.

HIGH RATE OF RETURN ON CAPITAL—THE EXPORT MARKET

The public interest guidance drafted into the 1948 Act strongly implied a nationalistic approach to the impact of market dominance. This would imply that a high rate of return may be acceptable if dependent upon high profits earned in overseas trade. The Monopolies Commission is scarcely likely to pay open homage to such a thesis, and if it did so the Board of Trade would delete the reference for fear of damaging international relationships. Nevertheless, there is a strong case for suspecting that the Commission implicitly accepted the thesis in the cigarette machinery inquiry. The eight year average rate of return on capital earned by Molins had been 36·2 per cent on an historical cost basis. Molins argued that only 24 per cent of its total trade was accounted for by the home market. If export prices were higher than domestic prices, sales resistance might develop overseas, perhaps culminating in a trade embargo. In fact, a higher level of profit had been earned on exports than on home market sales during most of the period covered by the investigation. The Commission concluded that Molins' high rate of return on capital had not damaged the public interest. Although the Commission explicitly stressed the existence of competition and Molins' pre-eminence in the field of innovation, there is no doubt that it was following the dictate of the 1948 Act that British firms should not be condemned for exploitation of an overseas market.[2] The Act appears to make no distinction in this respect between advanced and under-developed economies. The Commission has faithfully reflected the intention of the Act.

[1] Lucas argued its highest rates of profit were obtained in the earlier years examined when market conditions were abnormal. It pointed to a sharp downward trend in more recent years.

[2] op. cit., p. 211. 'Although exports, as such, are not within our terms of reference we cannot but have some regard to the inter-dependence of Molins' home and export business and to the benefits which the latter brings to the national economy.'

HIGH RATE OF RETURN ON CAPITAL—REWARD FOR INNOVATION AND ECONOMIC EFFICIENCY

Many economists argue that quasi-rents earned as a result of successful economic performance and innovation by dominant firms should not be condemned. The quasi-rents may indeed be a justifiable reward for enterprise.[1] An earlier chapter suggested, in fact, that competition among the few, especially in technically progressive industries, may centre on the innovative process. In such conditions quasi-rents may be a necessary sacrifice for innovation.

> In some cases, however, it is so successful as to yield profits far above what is necessary in order to induce the corresponding investment. These cases then provide the baits that lure capital on to untried trails. Their presence explains in part how it is possible for so large a section of the capitalistic world to work for nothing.[2]

Dominant firms which claim the right to a high rate of return on capital on the ground of innovative performance must be prepared to substantiate their claims. In this respect evidence indicating a high research outlay is irrelevant. Such expenditures, in any case, have been set off against gross revenue in the assessment of profit.

The Champion Sparking Plug Company contended that its rate of return on capital had been achieved in the teeth of competition and that its profit level was a success indicator. Profit, it asserted, was earned on the 'top slice' of turnover; if it was high the Company should not be criticized. The Monopolies Commission agreed that the Champion Sparking Plug Company was efficient and that part of its profit reflected such efficiency. But between 1953 and 1960 Champion's rate of return on capital in sparking plug production had ranged between 47·5 per cent and 62·2 per cent. The average rate of return had amounted to 57 per cent. The Monopolies Commission decided that the prime reason for this high rate of return was to be found in Champion's domination of the plug initial equipment market. This domination had placed the Company in the position of price leader for sparking plugs. The Monopolies Commission condemned the high rate of return achieved by the Company during the review period.

Few companies have resorted to this defence of high rates of return on capital when examined by the Monopolies Commission. Most companies have avoided all arguments which might admit that rate of return was high. This reluctance reflects a pessimistic interpretation of the

[1] J. Bain, *Industrial Organization*, 1959, p. 376. 'The general argument for "rewards to innovation" as a justifiable type of excess profits seems valid, but there are difficulties in deciding just how much of such reward is needed.'

[2] J. Schumpeter, *Capitalism, Socialism and Democracy*, p. 90.

Commission's attitude towards the quasi-rents of innovation. This interpretation is not entirely justified by available evidence. The thesis was invoked with some success in the cigarette machinery inquiry. Molins convinced the Commission that its high rate of return had been earned through superior technical ability in a highly competitive market and that it depended 'for its livelihood on its ability to remain ahead of its competitors in inventiveness and in practical application of inventions'.[1] The Commission was influenced by this argument in making a favourable judgment on Molins' achieved rate of return. It is somewhat surprising that more dominant firms have not attempted to justify high profit levels on the ground of innovation resulting from research and development expenditures.

The Commission has failed to achieve convincing conclusions on contentions that efficiency of organization might justify short-term quasi-rents. The Commission might have more to say with regard to this issue if it introduced full-scale efficiency audits.

HIGH RATE OF RETURN ON CAPITAL—A PLATFORM FOR INVESTMENT

It is sometimes suggested that premium profits are justified because they provide the capital resources necessary for expansion and for research and development. Firms proudly emphasize the high percentage of profit ploughed back into industrial expansion and renovation. Retained earnings—despite heavy company taxation—have accounted for 60 per cent of private investment in Britain since the war.

Many firms in rapidly growing industries require finance for net investment and prefer to obtain such finance through plough-back. In part, this preference may be fostered by a desire for economy. It costs stock exchange listed companies of large size about \$2·60[2] per hundred dollars of capital to raise finance through open sale of common stock. It may be even more expensive to offer existing shareholders a rights issue at a discount than to sell in the open market. These costs are eliminated if capital is obtained by retaining company earnings. In part, however, use of retained earnings is favoured through fear of loss of control if large bundles of equities were floated in the market. Faced with the risk of weakened control, a company may prefer to expand less rapidly. 'It is in such a situation that the firm feels that its own net earnings must provide the major part of its growth, in addition to dividends sufficient to satisfy its existing stockholders, when sweetened by the prospect of long-run growth in the value and earnings of the equity securities.'[3] Under such conditions funds for expansion may be considered as part

[1] op. cit., p. 211. [2] G. Means, 1962, op. cit., p. 269.
[3] J. M. Clark, 1961, op. cit., p. 378.

of the full-cost which firms attempt to recover. Where this is offset by a very low cash dividend it may be merely a matter of the form in which returns are taken. 'But if powerful firms add it to a liberal rate of cash dividend on investment, it may represent a target return raised by monopoloidal power.'[1]

In any case, it is doubtful whether the retained earnings argument could justify the maintenance of high rates of return. The system involves charging present consumers prices designed to supply a volume of capital which will provide shareholders with future earning benefits.[2] The system is even less justifiable when part only of the high profit is retained as capital and the remainder is distributed to shareholders in the form of dividends. Consistently high rates of return on capital may disrupt industrial relations and culminate in bitterly-pressed wage-increase claims, especially where high dividends are paid.

There are further economic weaknesses in the retained earnings justification for high rate of return on capital. There is of course economy in the system in its avoidance of having recourse to the capital market. On the other hand, this evasion of contact with the capital market implies avoidance of the market test for prospective investment programmes. This may result—especially where a company is prepared to expand only within well-tried fields—in a costly misallocation of investment and in a rigidification of existing production techniques. The high-profit company will be able to obtain capital for lowly-ranked investment projects; the low-profit or the newly-established company may be unable to obtain funds for comparatively highly-ranked propositions. The worst abuses of such developments might be prevented by State taxation incentives to distribution of profit; this would stimulate companies into use of the New Issue market.[3] Such action would aid the newly-established firm to obtain finance capital.[4]

The British Oxygen Company, in justifying its rate of return on capital, pointed out that the resources needed for development in industrial and medical gases were very great. When fresh capital was required from the investing public the British Oxygen Company needed to be in a position 'to provide a certain measure of capital extension from reserves'.[5] The Commission noted that between 1945 and 1951 the

[1] J. M. Clark, 1961, op. cit., p. 378.

[2] G. Means, 1962, op. cit., p. 269. 'If the customers are overcharged to supply capital and given an equivalent amount of stock to represent their interest, this might be reasonable.'

[3] The Merchant Banks would no doubt agree with this suggestion.

[4] J. Bain, 1959, op. cit., p. 378. 'The fact that excess profits are reinvested in expansion or in research and innovation does not justify them; the alternative of lower profits plus "outside" financing should accomplish at least equally desirable investment behaviour.'

[5] op. cit., 1956, p. 84.

British Oxygen Company had paid a dividend of 20 per cent on its ordinary capital and in the latter year had made a bonus issue equal to 50 per cent of its existing ordinary stock. From 1952 to 1954 the dividend had been 15 per cent and in 1954 this had amounted to about 5 per cent on capital employed measured on a historical cost basis. In 1955 British Oxygen had raised £8 million in new capital by offering £1 units for 50*s*., which at the rate of dividend of 15 per cent would provide shareholders with 6 per cent on initial outlay. The Commission estimated therefore that British Oxygen would require between 5–6 per cent return on capital employed to maintain dividends at the existing level. To give shareholders 6 per cent on their initial outlay required a profit before taxation of 9 per cent. A substantial part of BOC's profits would remain after giving this return to shareholders. The Commission rejected the Company's defence.

Fisons indicated that it tended to play for safety when budgeting on account of its heavy capital commitments. The Company pointed out that it was operating in an expanding market. In order to maintain its market share the company was forced to expand its productive capacity. A considerable amount of capital had in fact been invested since 1945 in additional productive capacity at Immingham, Stanford-le-Hope, and in its Research Department. The Company therefore required a level of profits 'adequate not only to provide a reasonable return to the public on the Ordinary capital in issue, but also to appropriate to reserve as a very minimum requirement an annual retention equivalent to the dividend distributed'.[1] Between 1945 and 1957, Fisons had raised £19½ million in new capital from the market, and had retained £4½ million in undistributed profit. Fisons argued that new investors would have been unwilling to provide the full £19½ million if the Company had not achieved so fine a record in supplementing such funds with retained earnings.

The Monopolies Commission agreed with Fisons that sufficient funds were required to replace existing assets as and when required. The Commission concluded that such funds would not be fully provided by an original cost depreciation system and that some retained earnings would be required by a provident organization. In fact, Fisons' retained earnings had substantially exceeded the required level, and had made a contribution towards expansion finance. The Monopolies Commission was not prepared to condemn this out of hand. It could see no wrong in companies financing expansion in this manner under keenly competitive conditions, especially where the market was growing rapidly. But in Fisons' case the industry was scarcely competitive. A monopoly supplier pursuing such a policy might be criticized on the ground that both its

[1] op. cit., 1959, p. 184. 'Its profit levels, the company says, are designed to give a position or platform from which it can finance expansion and modernization by attracting investment.'

price and its investment decisions would escape the market test: 'In exerting his market power in this way, he not only forces the consumer to pay prices higher than are reasonably justified by costs, but he also secures a disproportionate share of the new capital available for investment.'

Fisons was substantially sheltered from competition by Government tariff protection, and from internal market vagaries by Government subsidies. The Monopolies Commission, in these circumstances, was not prepared to allow the retained earnings thesis as a justification for Fisons' relatively high rate of return on capital. Its condemnation applied irrespective of the use made by Fisons of its retained earnings; indeed, the Commission rejected the justification by Fisons that the funds had been used to reduce its dependence upon Imperial Chemical Industries for supplies of nitrogen. The Commission recommended that Fisons should follow in future a pricing policy resulting in a lower rate of return on capital than had been budgeted in recent years.

It would appear that the Monopolies Commission underestimated the inter-dependence between past profit performance and the ability to raise capital on the new issue market. Potential shareholders may attach greater importance to distributed profit than to total company earnings, when determining or extending their investment portfolios. High dividends paid by a dominant firm out of high total profits may enable that company to avoid the market test for future capital formation more thoroughly than by retaining profit for expansion. Uninformed investors rely heavily upon past performance as a guide to future potential. The Monopolies Commission, by recommending a reduction in Fisons' rate of return on capital, implicitly recommended that the Company should be penalized in its resort to the new issue market as well as in its reliance upon retained earnings. It is doubtful whether the Commission was aware of this.

HIGH RATE OF RETURN ON CAPITAL—RISK AND UNCERTAINTY

A number of companies investigated by the Monopolies Commission have attempted to justify achieved rates of return on capital on the ground of risk. The Restrictive Practices Court, also, has been involved in similar discussion and, in one instance, was guilty of undistinguished logic in reaching its conclusions.[1]

Forward estimates of company profitability—in contrast to historical reviews—are always uncertain. They are based upon expected future net cash flows over an estimated lifetime of the relevant project. The rate of interest used to discount future net cash flows is itself only an estimation. The data is subject to uncertainty, whether actuarially

[1] In re Cement Makers' Federation Agreement—Reports of Restrictive Practices Cases, Volume 2, p. 241 ff.

assessible or not. There can be no doubt that certain companies find it less easy to predict accurately their future profit expectations than others. Most economists would accept that an outcome of known magnitude is preferable, *ceteris paribus*, to an uncertain or fluctuating outcome of a similar estimated magnitude. This is the essence of the high risk thesis. The implication is that investment projects subject to high risk should offer the prospect of a rather higher rate of return on capital than projects with a more clearly determined future earning pattern.

Many companies rely upon this thesis as a justification for high rates of return on capital earned over a lengthy time-period. In this form the argument is invalid; the thesis is based upon *ex ante* expectations. When all companies within a given industry earn persistently high rates of return on capital it is difficult to label the industry as a high-risk investment sector. The potential shareholder—relying upon past performance as a guide to future performance—would scarcely feel that his capital was at risk in the sense relevant to this discussion.

Any company which relies upon the high risk justification for a high rate of return on capital must surely furnish evidence of fluctuations through time in its own performance, or of fluctuations in its success over its referred product range, or fluctuations at selected points in time between competing companies' economic performances. Exceptionally, a high risk investment project may be undertaken by a historically low risk company, and a risk premium may be justified on that basis, as an *ex post* reward for its successful launching. But such instances should be examined circumspectly in the case of dominant firms.

The Monopolies Commission should not necessarily provide *carte blanche* to dominant firms in high risk industries with respect to their rates of return on capital. The Commission might conclude, conceivably, that risk rewards were themselves unduly high. A systematic over-estimation of risk within an industry may so restrict the volume of investment that the excess profit of successful companies outweighed the losses of unsuccessful companies. In such conditions, anybody concerned with the evaluation and supervision of rate of return on capital might consider intervention to be justified.

The British Oxygen Company argued that in budgeting for a particular rate of return on capital in favourable trading conditions regard had to be paid to the risk of future trade recessions. The Company's advisers were doubtful whether sufficient allowances had been made against such an occurrence. But the Monopolies Commission remained unimpressed by the high risk argument as it related to industrial and medical gases. The British Oxygen Company was dominant in the referred field and was unfettered by competition from effective substitutes. Its position was closely parallel to that of the recognized public utility concerns prior to their nationalization. The sole risk element related to the operations of British Oxygen was that involved in fluctuations in the national level of industrial activity. The Commission therefore concluded that British Oxygen was a low-risk firm and did not need to earn the same return on capital as a company producing under more competitive conditions. BOC's profits had been 'unjustifiably high for an almost complete monopoly facing a limited financial risk'.[1] This conclusion was rejected by two Commissioners in a minority addendum to the Report.

Imperial Chemical Industries and Fisons invoked the high risk defence for their respective rates of return on capital in chemical fertilizer production. Imperial Chemical Industries contended that the fertilizer nitrogen business was more hazardous than average heavy manufacturing industry in Britain, since it required a large investment in physical assets, and tied up working capital over long periods. Fisons argued that the chemical industry, generally, expected a rather higher return on capital employed than the average realized by manufacturing industry as a whole, on account of high development costs and the rapid rate of obsolescence.

The Commission was impressed by the high degree of risk faced by Imperial Chemical Industries over many years on its home and export fertilizer business. However, for the past twenty years the business had been profitable, and could not be considered unduly hazardous. The Commission was unwilling to condemn the Company's rate of return on capital at that time. Nevertheless, it underlined the danger to the public interest involved in profit levels above the average for manufacturing industry earned in a subsidized market such as chemical fertilizers. In rejecting the high risk argument for the industry the Commission concluded that Fisons had obtained, and budgeted for, an excessively high rate of return on capital.

The Champion Sparking Plug Company had earned an average rate of profit, 1953–60, of 57 per cent on capital employed. Champion pointed out that the specialized nature of its business implied a greater degree of risk than those of certain other component makers. The Monopolies Commission accepted this argument and agreed that a rate of profit higher than the normal might, therefore, be justified. On the other hand, it thought it unlikely that the parent company, given its world-wide interests, would allow a situation to develop in which plugs were rendered obsolete, without providing itself with alternative sources of production. The Commission felt that Champion's position as price-leader in the sparking plug industry provided the Company with considerable freedom in deciding upon its price and profit levels.

Champion emphasized, however, that it was on the point of losing a considerable proportion of its initial equipment business. Part of the

[1] op. cit., 1956, p. 96.

loss would go to an old-established competitor, but the loss was due in the main to the decision of the Ford Motor Company to equip its vehicles with Autolite plugs which would be produced by a Ford subsidiary in the United Kingdom. The British Motor Corporation would shortly be Champion's sole remaining customer among the Big Five motor car assemblers. Champion has been pressed into quoting lower prices for initial equipment.

This development provided support for Champion's argument relating to the risk of potential competition. The Commission could not determine whether Champion had suffered only a temporary set-back or whether this was the beginning of a very different division of sparking plug business. On balance, the Commission decided to rely on its conclusions upon evidence of past performance; it concluded that the high profits obtained by the Champion Sparking Plug Company were contrary to the public interest.

The Monopolies Commission rejected the high risk argument put forward by Joseph Lucas (Industries) Ltd. Despite postwar fluctuations in the prosperity of the motor industry there had been rapid expansion in recent years. This expansion might be expected to continue, and provided some protection for Lucas against market vagaries. At the same time, Lucas was cushioned against the impact of a short-term recession in the initial equipment market by its interest in the more stable replacement market. In such circumstances Lucas could not substantiate its claim to be the subject of high risk production. In the same inquiry, the Chloride Electrical Storage Company invoked the high risk defence for its budgeted rate of return on capital. The Monopolies Commission again rejected the argument, but did not condemn the Company's achieved rate of return on capital.

The Monopolies Commission has not been very impressed by the high risk defence of high rates of return in reference fields. It has rightly demanded evidence of fluctuations in the rate earned by a dominant firm through time and/or variations in rates as between firms at any point in time. As a general rule, it has assumed that market dominance would serve to reduce risk. In this respect the Commission can scarcely be faulted.

RATE OF RETURN ON CAPITAL AND TRADE ASSOCIATION INQUIRIES

The analysis of rate of return on capital has largely been concentrated upon dominant firm inquiries. This reflects the attitude of the Monopolies Commission. Trade association inquiries seldom involved a detailed study of factors influencing the rate of return on capital achieved by parties to the agreements under examination.

It is unwise of any investigating body to consider the average rate of return earned by trade association members without paying due regard to the nature and extent of the dispersion. A wide spread of rates earned may indicate a degree of instability. Further analysis is then necessary relating to the dynamics of the association and existing restrictions upon the ability of members to achieve a relative expansion in market share.

The copper semis inquiry involved a consideration of these issues. The average level of profit achieved by association members had been comfortable but not unreasonable. There was a wide spread in the rates of return of individual members, and the profits of certain manufacturers and of certain sections had been high. The Commission felt, therefore, that the general level of association prices, despite the restraint imposed by various forms of competition, was unduly high. This situation was contrary to the public interest.

The three main groups of the British Electrical and Allied Manufacturers' Association[1] defended average rates of return on capital of 19 per cent, 28 per cent and 22 per cent respectively. These figures were based on historical cost accounting techniques. The Commission compared these rates unfavourably with those of manufacturing industry in general. It demonstrated the wide variation in the profits of different groups. The manufacturers retorted that the differences were transient, and that the common price system stimulated competition in technical matters. In the race to improve efficiency, it was inevitable that different manufacturers should achieve success at different times. However, the Commission demonstrated that profit differentials were often long-standing and that changes in relative efficiencies were not rapid.

The Monopolies Commission was always impressed by evidence of low profits coupled with a narrow spread of profit rates within an association. This situation obtained in the linoleum industry. The Linoleum Manufacturers' Association in 1954 had earned on average 11½ per cent on capital employed. In view of the sellers' market this could not be considered excessive. The spread of profit in 1954 between the four largest manufacturers within the Association was only 8 per cent to 15·6 per cent. Whilst profit margins on different lines of linoleum had varied widely in recent years, the average profits of the Linoleum Manufacturers' Association had been moderate.

The Commission was also impressed where the largest producer was both low-cost and earning reasonable profits. This situation obtained in the Metal Windows industry. The Metal Windows Association had earned an average of 12·4 per cent on capital employed in 1954–5. Crittall Ltd accounted for nearly one half of the domestic sales of the Association and had earned 20·9 per cent on capital employed. Crittall Ltd was the lowest-cost member and ruling prices had placed

[1] Steam plant for land use, other plant, small motors and generators.

considerable pressure on the margins of high-cost members. The Commission condoned the Association's price agreement.

CONCLUSIONS

The Monopolies Commission has paid considerable attention to rate of return on capital, particularly in dominant firm inquiries. Table 14 indicates the Commission's approach to rate of return on capital and the dominant firm.

TABLE 14

Rate of Return on Capital Employed—Reference Fields

Firm	*Years*	*Historical Cost Valuation per cent*	*Figures for Manufacturing Industry* The Economist *per cent*	*Replacement Cost Valuation* per cent*	*Contrary Decision*	*Favourable Decision*
The British Oxygen Company	1952–4	23—24	16·4	16½—17	Yes	—
Imperial Chemical Industries	1955–6	17·3	16·9	11·1	—	Yes
Fisons	1956–7	21·6	16·0	13·8	Yes	—
Imperial Tobacco Company	1957	11·8	15·4	—	—	Yes
Lucas class (i)		26·9	15—17	—	Yes	—
Lucas other	1954–61	21·8	Approx.	—	—	Yes†
Champion	1954–60	57·0	15—17	—	Yes	—
Smiths	1955–61	12·2	15—17	—	—	Yes
Chloride	1954–60	21·2	15—17	—	—	Yes†

* Various measures are used in formulating these figures.
† The acceptance was uncertain and tentative.

By and large, the Monopolies Commission had been guided by *The Economist* newspaper's figures for manufacturing industry in deciding whether rates of return on capital employed are acceptable or contrary to the public interest. This yard-stick is in no sense an indication of the competitive norm, at least in the sense that this concept is usually understood by economists. Many firms included in the measure are scarcely operating under conditions of free competition; the sample of firms referred to may well be biased by an over-representation of large companies; and private limited companies are entirely excluded from the analysis. In addition, the measure is largely irrelevant in periods of moving prices because it employs predominantly historical cost measurement techniques. The Commission itself has publicly admitted the imperfection of its measuring rod, but has always insisted that it is the best available. To date it has used the figures with considerable caution, erring on the side of generosity to the firm under examination. It has been little influenced by special pleading for high profits save where the profits have been earned on the export market and/or under highly competitive conditions.

The Commission's approach marks a significant withdrawal from the nineteenth century emphasis upon commercial freedom. The Commission has recommended that high profit levels should be lowered. Government implementation of such recommendations involved specific and direct interference in the affairs of the industrial sector.

Interference in the pricing policy of dominant firms bears certain dangers. A reduction in the price level of a dominant firm may increase the rate of return on capital employed if the relevant point elasticities of supply and demand follow certain patterns. The problem of a high rate of return might then prove difficult to solve save through discriminatory company taxation. On the other hand, reduced prices might result in long delivery dates and rationing with the inevitable risk of resource misallocation, black market operations, and weaknesses in the signalling system. This may be a poor substitute for high profit pricing by dominant firms. Once again, enforced profit reductions may deter new competition and fortify the market dominance of the referred firm; this is by no means automatically desirable. If certain sectors are subjected to price control and others are not the implications for investment allocation may be serious. In particular competitive industries as defined under the 1948 Act may receive an excess of investible funds, to the detriment of dominant firms. The profit-drive may provide a mainspring to efficiency and technical progress. Excessive intervention may result in economic stagnation—scarcely the foremost purpose of the Monopolies Commission inquiries. Finally, the problem arises of Government intervention which results in sub-normal profits. Under such conditions the shareholders of the dominant firm might rightly demand Government recompense. If this should be guaranteed, the entire rationale of the private enterprise system of industrial organization would be in question. Profit control involves complexities often evaded by those pressing for Government intervention. The Commission itself may well be accused of failing to analyse the full consequences of its recommendations.

These difficulties should not be taken as evidence for an outright rejection of profit control. Competitive imperfections may make some form of direct control imperative. But there are social costs in profit control which should be weighed against the social benefits in formulating recommendations for Government action. The economic consequences of profit control may often, on balance, be beneficial. Intellectual honesty demands a more intensive study of its implications than has hitherto been made by the Monopolies Commission.

PART VI

GOVERNMENT ACTION: ECONOMIC CONSEQUENCES

The times have been,
That, when the brains were out, the man would die,
And there an end; but now they rise again,
With twenty mortal murders on their crowns,
And push us from our stools;

W. Shakespeare, *Macbeth*, III, iv, 78

Chapter Nineteen

THE IMPLEMENTATION OF MONOPOLIES COMMISSION RECOMMENDATIONS

The Monopolies Commission is a purely advisory body. Its reports carry no legislative authority, and its interest in a reference field terminates upon the submission of its report to the Board of Trade or other relevant Government department. Where necessary the Government department concerned may contact the Commission to clarify ambiguities arising from the submitted report.

The Board of Trade scrutinizes each report in order to determine whether sections should be deleted on the ground that their publication would be detrimental to the public interest. The Board of Trade will meet the relevant companies for assistance in this task. A number of companies have commented tartly about the Board's reticence in relation to the contents of the reports during such discussions:

> Excisions from the Report are permitted if publication of certain matter ought to be excluded on the grounds of public interest. Industry is, however, put at a very great disadvantage when applying to the Board of Trade for excisions to be made on these grounds, because it is not entitled to see the Report before publication. It is accordingly extremely difficult, without knowing the full context in which any particular passages are included, to know just how far (in the public interest) excisions should be requested.

The Board of Trade pleads Parliamentary Privilege in refusing to disclose the contents of Monopolies Commission reports. No doubt the Board provides broad indications in suitable circumstances, especially where export markets are concerned. Nevertheless, the entire process of consultation is clumsy and somewhat artificial. There is little justification for refusing interested parties a preview of the Report. If necessary, amending legislation could be drafted to this effect.

The Board of Trade does not always provide detailed reasons for excisions. This is not surprising since excisions may involve delicate politico-economic issues. In a recent publication the Board of Trade commented in some detail upon excisions allowed from the Commission's Report:[1]

> In accordance with (a) of the proviso to Section 9 of the Monopolies and Restrictive Practices (Inquiry and Control) Act, 1948, the Board of Trade have omitted from the Report as laid before Parliament certain details the publication of which would in their opinion be contrary to the public interest.
>
> These details comprise the actual prices charged to vehicle manufacturers for certain items of initial equipment (or, in one case, replacement equipment), and certain discounts which would have enabled such prices to be calculated. Sales figures for certain batteries have also been omitted.[2]

The Board of Trade has exercised considerable care, in the making of such excisions, to ensure that important information should not be completely withdrawn from the general public. Such an occurrence was feared occasionally and provision was made accordingly:

> The omission of some detail on prices has meant that the precise extent of the differences between the initial equipment prices and retail prices of the equipment in question is no longer apparent. The initial equipment prices that have been omitted ranged from about one-twelfth to about one-half of the retail price. Most of them fell between one-quarter and two-fifths of the retail price.[3]

The Board of Trade was always loth to allow excisions from the chapter providing conclusions on the public interest and the Commission's recommendations.

The average period elapsing between the Commission's signature upon, and Government publication of, reports has been fairly brief, approximately three months. Upon occasion the time-lag has been lengthy; the match industry report was delayed at this stage for seven months, presumably while the Board of Trade scrutinized details of the British Match Corporation's international agreements. On the other hand, extremely speedy publication is possible for reports favourable to Government policy. The wallpaper report, with its condemnation of individual resale price maintenance, was published within five weeks of arriving at the Board of Trade.[4] Variations in printing pressure at Her Majesty's Stationery Office have been blamed for time-lags between report and publication. The impression is given that Monopolies Com-

[1] Report on the Supply of Electrical Equipment to Mechanically Propelled Land Vehicles, 1963. H.C.P. 21. [2] ibid., p. iii. [3] ibid., p. iii.

[4] Edward Heath, MP, was then pressing forward legislation designed to limit the scope of individual resale price maintenance, and the report received wide publicity.

mission reports are not considered as printing priorities, at least under normal conditions.

GOVERNMENT ACTION UPON MONOPOLIES COMMISSION REPORTS

The Government is in no way committed to enforce the recommendations of the Commission following an industry investigation. The relevant Government department usually discusses the contents of the report with interested organizations and, having formulated its policy, negotiates with such organizations regarding the most suitable action. The Government usually provides little public indication of its reaction to a report until it announces its policy decision.

Some variation in the length of time necesary for Government to formulate policy, to select the most suitable plan of action, and to make appropriate arrangements, whether by Statutory Order or by voluntary undertaking, is inevitable. Cases are bound to vary in complexity both in relation to the critical issues and in relation to Government action. Such variations inevitably influence the time period between signing the Report and Government action.

In practice, however, many cases have been subjected to unnecessary delay. The average period between publication and action in the twelve cases in which action to date has issued has been fourteen months. This in itself indicates a lengthy time-lag, but the average conceals specific instances in which delay has been unjustifiably great. The period between publication of the cables report and action announced by the Board of Trade was twenty-five months. In this instance interminable disagreements between the Government and trade associations culminated in a threat by the former to draft a Statutory Order. This threat elicited a grudging but speedy undertaking from the trade associations. A similar period of delay followed the publication of the chemical fertilizers report, although in this instance Fisons had anticipated Government action by reducing the prices of certain of its fertilizer products. A period of eighteen months was allowed to elapse between publication of the dental goods report and subsequent Government action. (This under a Labour Government!)

The most conspicuous time-lag of all was that of two years between the publication of the 'follow-up' report into imported timber and subsequent Government legislation. The delay in this instance was notably reprehensible since the report exposed non-compliance, by the hardwood and softwood sections of the Timber Trade Federation, with regard to their voluntary undertakings. Immediate and ruthless legislation was required in this instance. The Government forfeited public respect by its demonstration of a lack of political courage. The time-lag between the publication of the initial report upon imported timber and the eventual Statutory Order was all but seven years! An unconvincing attempt was made by the Board of Trade to explain the delay that had occurred:

> The issue facing the Board was a complicated one. It could be resolved either by way of an Order or by some less formal method, such as further undertakings by the Trade. There were of necessity prolonged discussions with the Trade and, as a result of these, we were able to satisfy ourselves that the best way to proceed was by way of an Order.[1]

On the other hand, action in a few instances has been comparatively swift. Despite hostility on the part of the Timber Trade Federation, the threat of an Order resulted in a voluntary undertaking, following the first report on the industry, within six months. Similarly, the Government swiftly accepted the recommendation of the Monopolies Commission concerning building supplies in Greater London and extracted a voluntary undertaking within five months of the report's publication.

In general, there can be little doubt that the time-lags involved have partially resulted from a lack of sense of urgency, both from the trade organizations involved, and from the Government. It is most important that action upon Monopolies Commission reports should be taken in as speedy a manner as is compatible with fairness and efficiency. Investment decisions may be severely damaged by spineless procrastinations. The reputation of the Commission is scarcely enhanced by recurrent Governmental delay in acting upon its recommendations.

STATUTORY ORDER OR VOLUNTARY UNDERTAKING

The Government may enforce a recommendation of the Monopolies Commission, if it so wishes, and if the recommendation is covered by Section 10 of the 1948 Act, by statutory order. Such an order may not be made within less than three months from the date on which the report was laid before Parliament.[2] The statutory order enables the Government to legislate without having recourse to the full procedure of ordinary legislation. Contravention of such an order would constitute a civil offence. Remedies could be sought either by Government itself or by private citizens harmed by the contravention.

If the Government wishes to take action by statutory order, and the chosen action is contrary to the Commission's findings, it would first be necessary to reverse the Commission's findings by obtaining a suitable

[1] Proceedings in the House of Common, July 6, 1960, col. 652. The Parliamentary Secretary—The Board of Trade.

[2] This restriction applies only to the case where a House of Commons resolution has been passed. (Section 10(1)(e)(11) of the 1948 Act.)

resolution in the House of Commons. This could then be followed by the normal Section 10 procedure.[1]

The statutory order is not, of course, the only form of action open to the Government consequent upon a Monopolies Commission report. The 1948 Act did not preclude the relevant Government department from taking such informal action as might seem satisfactory. In practice the great majority of reports have been dealt with upon such an informal basis. The Act provided that where the Government extracted voluntary undertakings the Monopolies Commission might be directed to make a follow-up investigation to ascertain to what extent the undertaking had been honoured. To date, only one such reference has been made.[2]

The Advantages of a Statutory Order

Action by order results in immediate legal commitment upon the trade association or company specified therein. Infringement of an Order would result in the following procedure:

> The drill now under an Order is that we should apply to the Court of Chancery for an injunction to prevent an arrangement or agreement which the Order specifies to be unlawful from being carried out. We should support this by a body of evidence which tended to show that such an arrangement had been arrived at. If the injunction were obtained and this practice still continued, we should apply for an Order for committal for contempt of court, the evidence being similar to that in the previous application to the Court of Chancery.[3]

In addition to such Government action individual persons who felt that they had been harmed by the infringement could bring an action through civil processes for an injunction and/or a suit for damages. Thus an Order supplies a secondary public safeguard should the Government department involved be tardy in making use of the legal processes available.

Disadvantages of an Order

In making an Order there are certain practical difficulties and dangers. If the wording of an Order is ambiguous or inaccurate, actions could be brought by private citizens, and might be upheld by the courts, even though the infringing activities were fully acceptable to the Government which had drafted the Order. Thus a great responsibility is placed upon the shoulders of those responsible for drafting the order. The making of the Dental Goods Order in 1951 by the Labour Government focused

[1] The Monopolies and Mergers Act, 1965, op. cit., repeated this section of the 1948 Act. The new legislation simplifies and streamlines the procedure for making an Order, and extends the scope for such action.

[2] The Section 12 Report on the imported timber industry.

[3] 'Proceedings in the House of Common', July 6, 1960—Mr Rodgers.

public attention upon the problems of drafting a relatively straightforward order. The Labour Government was compelled to withdraw one draft from the House for reorganization on the ground of serious ambiguity. The draft which was finally approved was subjected to considerable criticism in the House of Commons on the grounds that it still contained a dangerous element of ambiguity.[1] Similar problems were encountered during the making of the Imported Timber Order in 1960.

A second disadvantage of operating through an Order is the rigidity of the process in the face of changes in Government attitude or in the material circumstances facing the organization concerned. A considerable time-period may elapse before the Order can be withdrawn. During the period in which the Order subsists, the trade association or firm infringing a direction now considered by the Government to be inappropriate would risk successful civil suits by private citizens. Freedom of movement and interpretation are thus to some extent sacrificed by the use of an Order.

Thirdly, the drafting and preparation of an Order, and the ability to find Parliamentary time for obtaining the necessary Resolutions, imply delays in imposing the wishes of Government upon the firm or trade association concerned. The very long delay involved in the implementation of an Order relating to the imported timber trade was blamed upon drafting problems.[2] Thus procedure by Order may militate against swift justice.

The Preferences of Industry

In the great majority of cases trade associations and companies involved in inquiries have been highly critical of the conclusions of the Monopolies Commission. They have been critical, therefore, of Government action designed to enforce the conclusions of the Commission. Yet in almost every instance trade associations and firms have elected, in the last analysis, to make voluntary undertakings with a determined Government rather than to allow themselves to be subjected to a Statutory Order. The calico printers were antipathetic to Government action on the lines recommended by the Report, but the Government faced them with the alternative of an Order. The Federation quickly consented to the required undertaking. The cable industry held out against making an undertaking for almost two years. Within weeks of being threatened

[1] 'Proceedings in the House of Commons', June 20, 1951, col. 646. Mr Linstead. 'The last thing that the Association has to say is that this Order, in spite of the fact that it has had to be withdrawn at least once, to be looked at again by the lawyers, is still obscure.'

[2] Proceedings in the House of Lords, July 14, 1960, col. 295. Lord Ebbisham. 'The Federation, finally, in April 1959 indicated that they would prefer matters to run their course and to let the Board of Trade make an Order. All subsequent delay was stated to be due to the legal complications in the drafting of that Order.'

by an Order the two trade associations supplied the required undertakings to Government. The Timber Trade Federation carried out at stormy resistance to Government action on the lines of the 1953 report of the Commission; faced by the alternative of an Order an undertaking was swiftly made to the Government. The Association of Dental Manufacturers and Traders was subjected to a statutory order covering certain recommendations made by the Monopolies Commission. The association protested that it would much have preferred to enter into a voluntary undertaking with the Labour Government. These selected instances demonstrate the extent to which trade associations and firms have been prepared to modify their opposition rather than to force the Government to act through legislation. The only instance on record of an association that appears to have welcomed an Order is that of the Timber Trade Federation following the Section 12 report of the Monopolies Commission which was published in 1958.[1] In general, trade associations and firms appear to prefer the undertaking to the Order primarily on the grounds of the former's flexibility. An undertaking may easily be withdrawn with the consent of the relevant government department, if material conditions should change. For instance, the British Oxygen Company was recently released from certain of its undertakings to the Government which related to tonnage oxygen supplies.

Sections of the Timber Trade Federation of the United Kingdom agreed to accept a voluntary undertaking in 1954, rather than submit to an Order. In recommending the abrogation of the agreements, required by the undertaking, the special committee of the Timber Trade Federation had borne in mind that 'it was a very difficult matter to secure the revocation of an Order once made'.[2] This argument was further developed by the President of the TTF who stated that 'if the Trade took no action in the matter, the Government certainly would, and if this resulted in an Order in Council, the terms might be more onerous still. In this connection it should be remembered that an Order could only be annulled by Parliamentary action, but if the Trade surrendered the Agreements and Undertakings of its own accord as recommended by the Commission, it would preserve its mobility of action and its right to raise the question again, without having the millstone of an Order round its neck.'[3]

These arguments emphasize the predominant factors which encourage organizations to submit to voluntary undertakings. In addition—though this would never be expressed publicly—certain trade associations or

[1] 'Proceedings in the House of Commons', July 6, 1960, col. 652. Mr Rodgers. Parliamentary Secretary to the Board of Trade. 'A happy result of this is that the trade recognizes the necessity for this step and that we can count on its co-operation. I am now firmly convinced that the Order will not be broken.'

[2] Report on whether and to what extent the Recommendations of the Commission has been complied with at p. 7. [3] ibid., p. 7.

companies may conclude that a voluntary undertaking could be more safely dishonoured than a Statutory Order.

THE NATURE OF GOVERNMENT ACTION

The Monopolies Commission had completed twenty-seven inquiries by June 1965. One inquiry awaited publication. One report concerned a Section 15 reference and resulted in general legislation in the form of the Restrictive Trade Practices Act, 1956. As a result of this general legislation, the Government decided against implementing the recommendations of the Monopolies Commission in nine reference fields. The restrictive agreements concerned were subject to registration with the Registrar of Restrictive Trading Agreements and were open to review before the Restrictive Practices Court: A few trade associations were bitterly disappointed by this decision:

> By the time that the Commission's Report was published the Restrictive Practices Act, 1956, had come into force, and thus the Board of Trade had no option but to refer the industry to the Registrar . . . and the Agreements then under review had to be registered, under the new legislation. The industry had to commence its task once again, and decide whether or not to defend its arrangements before the Court, which meant the preparation of many cases to see whether it was possible to satisfy the criteria in Clause 21 (i) of the Act. Subsequently, having determined which Agreements to defend, their full defence had to be prepared and the work entailed in this is enormous.

The Government has intervened, therefore, in one way and another, in sixteen of the references completed by the Commission. One of these followed a Section 12 inquiry. Evidence of the degree of acceptance by the Government of the Commission's findings is less conclusive, therefore, than it might seem by superficial reference to the twenty-six published reports.

In two reference fields only did the Government implement its conclusions by way of Statutory Order. The first report produced by the Commission, relating to the supply of dental goods, recommended, by a majority decision, that certain Collective Discrimination techniques adopted by the Association should be made unlawful by Statutory Order. The Commission felt that the remaining recommendations made in the report could best be implemented by voluntary negotiations with the Association.

This was the only report subjected to a policy decision of a Labour Government. The Government decided to implement in full the recommendations of the Monopolies Commission. Using the powers provided by Section 10 of the 1948 Act, the Minister of Health and the Secretary of State for Scotland, as competent authorities, made the Monopolies and Restrictive Practices (Dental Goods) Order, 1951—S.I. No. 1200—on July 2, 1951. The Order became operational on July 30 and rendered exclusive dealing arrangements unlawful insofar as they were intended, or likely, to have the effect of restricting entry into the trade or were used to enforce resale prices. The remainder of the criticisms of the Commission were left to be dealt with by the industry itself. An undertaking was extracted from the Association of Dental Manufacturers and Traders that rules and regulations would be revised to this effect.

The second instance in which an Order was used to implement the policy of the Government occurred in the imported timber trade, following a breach of the voluntary undertakings entered into with Government by the hardwood and softwood sections of the Timber Trade Federation. This time a Conservative Government made the order following a lengthy period of discussion and negotiation with the imported timber trade.

In all other reference fields the Government proceeded by means of discussion and eventual extraction of 'voluntary' undertakings from the associations and firms involved. An earlier section has outlined the manner in which the Government extracted the required undertakings. In general, it appears to have suited the mood of both industry and the Conservative Government to implement policy, where possible, by co-operation rather than by legislated order. The Labour Party from time to time has displayed some restlessness over this preference, but when in office itself it has always indicated that it was prepared to work through voluntary channels.[1] There is little difference in the attitudes of the major political parties in relation to this issue.

GOVERNMENT ACTION AND TRADE ASSOCIATION PRACTICES

The relevant Government department is under no legal compulsion to implement the recommendations of the Monopolies Commission. Many sceptics of the 1948 legislation contended that this would be the Achilles heel of British monopoly control. The dangers inherent in a permissive situation should never be underestimated. But criticism of this kind in relation to governmental action prior to the 1956 legislation can scarcely be substantiated. The majority of Monopolies Commission recommendations relating to trade associations were implemented by the Government through voluntary undertakings.

The Government was prepared to implement practically all the major recommendations of the Commission relating to trade associations.

[1] Notably, of course, in the dental goods case. At the change of Government in 1951, the Labour Board of Trade was busy negotiating over rainwater goods and electric lamps. No action had then been declared.

Common and Minimum Price Agreements

The Government, in general, followed closely the recommendations of the Commission relating to price agreements. A useful example is afforded by reference to the cable making industry. The common price systems of the various sections of the Cable Makers' Association and the Covered Conductors Association had been criticized keenly by the Monopolies Commission. On May 20, 1954, the Minister of Supply announced general acceptance of the Commission's findings.

The Minister extracted an undertaking from the Cable Makers' Association to the effect that it should submit data on costs for the supply of cable to the British Electricity Authority as long as its price systems were maintained. The Minister refused to implement the recommendation that prices to other cable buyers should be based upon a published relationship with those charged to the British Electricity Authority. Such action would have contravened established Government practice of maintaining secrecy for prices negotiated by nationalized industries. In place of publication, the Government required evidence from time to time that prices were reasonable for private enterprise purchasers.

The Minister accepted the recommendations that common prices in rubber cable and covered conductors should be terminated and, if the parties so desired, should be replaced by minimum price schemes offering reasonable profits to the lowest cost producer of each type of cable. Cost and profit data should be submitted to the appropriate Government department. In place of terminating price agreements for telephone cable supplied to purchasers other than the General Post Office, the Government required an assurance that prices so charged should bear a satisfactory relationship to those charged to the General Post Office. Thus, in this industry both instances of non-acceptance of recommendations by the Government occurred in minority sections of the market and the Government provided alternative safeguards for the consumers involved.

In fact, the Cable Makers' Association and the Covered Conductors Association both decided to establish the permitted minimum price systems. Shortly after the inception of the system the National Coal Board requested and obtained an investigation of the minimum prices selected for certain kinds of cable supplied by the CMA.[1] This investigation culminated in a downward adjustment in the profit factors used in the computation of minimum prices.[2] In the following year, 1958, the Board of Trade allowed the Rubber and Thermoplastic Cable Makers' Association to introduce a simplified procedure for the computation of minimum prices.

[1] Annual Report of the Board of Trade for year ended 1956.

[2] ibid., year ended December 31, 1957.

The minimum price system enforced by the Federation of Calico Printers was condemned by the Monopolies Commission. The Commission proposed that a system of recommended minimum prices without sanctions might be allowed in the industry. On November 15, 1955, the Board of Trade announced that an undertaking to this effect had been extracted from the Federation. The Federation adopted a recommended minimum price system and a scale of recommended engraving rental charges.

The price system operated by the British Insulin Manufacturers was accepted by the Monopolies Commission with the proviso that the Government should regularly supervise insulin prices and profits. The Departments principally concerned conducted periodic surveys of the prices and profits and costs of the British Insulin Manufacturers and concluded in June 1959 that they were fair and reasonable. In 1961 the Ministry of Health decided to undertake a second inquiry into insulin costs and profits. This investigation was completed in 1962.[1]

Collective Tendering Agreements

The London Builders' Conference furnished the sole instance of a collective tendering system subjected to Government action. The Monopolies Commission strongly criticized the Conference's tendering system in which the Chairman was able to make various kinds of alteration in the initial tenders of members before they were passed on to those requesting the tender. The Government moved swiftly on the recommendations of the Report, and persuaded the Conference to abandon its activities from December 21, 1954. The Minister of Works stressed the need to eliminate similar activities operative in other areas. To this effect the Government announced that in future 'firms will not be included on any list of approved Government contractors for new buildings if in tendering for such work they follow the practices criticized by the Commission. The firms already on the lists are being asked to confirm that they wish to remain there and accept this condition. . . . The attention of the associations of local authorities is being drawn to the Report and to the action taken.'[2] The Government, in this instance, was prepared to act on a wider scale than the Commission's terms of reference would allow it to recommend.

Collective Resale Price Maintenance Agreements

The Government implemented each Commission recommendation favouring the termination of collective resale price maintenance agree-

[1] Annual Report for year ended December 31, 1963, p. 5. 'The Ministry's findings have now been made available. The Ministry have found no reason to intervene in the pricing policies of the manufacturers of insulin.'

[2] Annual Report of the BOT for year ended December 31, 1954.

ments save for those reports which fell within the scope of the 1956 legislation. The attitude both of the Monopolies Commission and of the Government was antipathetic towards this practice. In the dental goods case the Government implemented the Commission's adverse conclusion by means of statutory order. This action had been specifically proposed by the Commission. The Government extracted an undertaking from the Electric Lamp Manufacturers' Association that it would terminate the enforcement of resale price maintenance by means of collective sanctions. This too had been recommended by the Commission.

Market Sharing Agreements

The Commission condemned all market sharing systems except that operated by the British Insulin Manufacturers. In every case where the reference field was dealt with by the Government the recommendations were implemented by means of voluntary undertakings. In this respect undertakings were extracted from trade associations in the electric lamp, electric wires and cables, and the calico printing industries.

Exclusive Dealing and Collective Boycott Agreements

Exclusive dealing and collective boycott agreements were regular features of Monopolies Commission inquiries. The systems were operated for a variety of reasons including the enforcement of resale price maintenance, the support of common or minimum price systems, and even as an end in themselves. In every case the Monopolies Commission recommended that they should be terminated.

In the dental goods case the Government proceeded to render the system unlawful by means of Statutory Order. In the rainwater goods, electric lamps, cables, and imported timber industries the Government extracted voluntary agreements to terminate the system. The imported timber case is worthy of further examination. The Timber Trade Federation had made the voluntary undertaking when faced with the alternative of expressing enforced willingness, or submitting to an order. In so doing, the Federation had deplored the Government's action. Copies of the undertaking were sent by the Government to all members and non-members of the relevant sections of the Federation, the timber trade press was informed, and the resolutions of abrogation were published in the *Timber Trades Journal* and in *Timber and Plywood* during February and March 1954. During 1955, however, certain persons complained that they had been precluded from importing because their names were not on an approved list. The Board of Trade refused to act upon these complaints when questioned in the House of Commons. During 1956 further complaints were received about the inability of consumers to trade directly with agents. As a result, a Section 12 reference was placed before the Monopolies Commission concerning the undertakings of the

Timber Trade Federation. The Report was published in 1958 and concluded that the hardwood and softwood sections of the trade had substituted for abrogated agreements other arrangements of similar effect to the original agreements. The Government negotiated with the Federation from mid-1958 until mid-1960 before announcing the acceptance of the Commission's conclusions. An order was then drafted and legislated, prohibiting the offending practices in hardwood and softwood. The story did not end at this point. In February 1962 the Board of Trade noted that two complaints had been received concerning the activities of the plywood section. The Board announced that the matter was under review. This episode underlines the need for a more vigilant policy than that at present pursued in tracking the effectiveness of voluntary undertakings.

Aggregated Rebate Agreements

Aggregated rebate agreements, comprehensively operated, may serve the same purpose as exclusive dealing arrangements. The Monopolies Commission recommended that the Electric Lamp Manufacturers' Association should terminate its aggregated rebate system. The Government refused to implement the recommendation, deciding 'to reserve judgment on the recommendation . . . in order to give time to ascertain whether or not the continuance of this arrangement will tend to impair the effects of the abolition of exclusive dealing'.[1] In taking this stand the Government was influenced by the importance of aggregated rebate system to the smooth-functioning of the common price scheme accepted by the Commission. In addition, it was felt that abolition of the system would affect adversely the smaller manufacturers within the Association.

In this respect the Government may well have erred. The aggregated rebate system provided a powerful stimulus towards exclusive dealing and weakened the impact of certain other recommendations of the Commission. One firm suggested that 'the failure to implement the Commission's recommendation in this respect made the action taken with regard to exclusive dealing valueless'.[2]

CONCUSIONS

The evidence accumulated from Annual Reports of the Board of Trade indicates a high degree of Government acceptance of Monopolies Commission findings in the trade association inquiries dealt with by the Government. Criticism justifiably centred around the time-period

[1] The Annual Report of the Board of Trade for the year ended December 1952.

[2] P. Gunault and J. Jackson, 1960, op. cit., p. 138.

between publication and action. In part, the time-lag reflected complex negotiations with trade associations intent upon delaying Government action. In part, it reflected a low priority rating for action on the part of the relevant Government department. A vigilant executive could have eliminated the more serious criticisms.

More important, however, is the problem of policing voluntary undertakings. The Government reacted in the imported timber case with a Section 12 reference only following a series of complaints. In many industries damaged parties may be too weak or too afraid to complain. Undertakings may be dishonoured or misinterpreted on a serious scale before Government action is generated. It may well be necessary for one section of the Monopolies Commission to be permanently detailed to police undertakings, and to this end the Commission could be provided with full access to premises, documents, and witnesses. The Commission might be required to make two-yearly reports to the Board of Trade. This recommendation would be of greater relevance for dominant firm inquiries than for trade association inquiries.

GOVERNMENT ACTION AND THE DOMINANT FIRM

The number of dominant firm reports actually subjected to Government action is so far limited, and the issues involved have been complex and varied. Government action is best analysed, therefore, on a reference by reference basis.

The British Match Corporation

The British Match Corporation was involved in a complex network of agreements with its principal European competitor, Swedish Match. The Monopolies Commission, fearing to make recommendations which might lead to a breach of these Agreements, recommended that machinery should be established for regulating the Corporation's activities. In particular, the Government should assume a continuing responsibility for supervision of costs and prices of match producers, importers and distributors. Maximum prices related to the unit costs of the lowest-cost factory should be fixed by the Government both for home produced and imported matches for all stages of distribution. In addition, the Monopolies Commission proposed that subsidiaries of the British Match Corporation should supply materials to all United Kingdom match producers without price discrimination, and that the Corporation's offer to release Swedish Match from its undertaking not to manufacture match-making machinery in the United Kingdom should be accepted. A minority addendum to the Commission's report suggested that the quota agreements might be abolished and that a purchasing agency under Government sponsorship might act as exclusive purchaser either for all matches or for all imported matches. The Government rejected the recommendation for price control over matches:

> I doubt whether the system of strict price control proposed in the Commission's Report would provide an effective remedy. New competitors would be less likely to enter the trade and there would be no stimulus to efficiency, if any gains arising from efficient production were liable to be swept away by Government Order.[1]

The remainder of the Commission's majority proposals were accepted. The President pointed out that he was exploring the possibility of removing certain obstacles to competition in the industry. On March 5, 1954, the Board of Trade announced a successful conclusion to its negotiations. The British Match Corporation and Swedish Match had concluded a New Agreement eliminating the objectionable quota and compensation agreements. In the New Agreement there was no provision either for sharing the United Kingdom market, or for limiting the expansion of United Kingdom manufacturing capacity. At the same time the Agreement preserved United Kingdom overseas interests. Swedish Match would continue to sell machinery to the British Match Corporation on favourable terms and to provide technical information. In future, this latter service would cost BMC £40,000 per annum.[2] The Swedish Company insisted upon the right to end the Agreement at one year's notice. The Government was no doubt as relieved as the British Match Corporation by the co-operative attitude of the Swedish company. The results certainly exceeded the Monopolies Commission's expectations.

The British Oxygen Company

The British Oxygen Company inquiry produced features of great interest in analysing the response of Government to the findings of the Monopolies Commission. The Commission had condemned a wide range of predatory practices which had been employed from time to time by the British Oxygen Company in order to maintain its market dominance in industrial and medical gases. In addition, the majority report of the Commission recommended that the Board of Trade should undertake bi-annual reviews of prices, costs, profits, capital employed and other relevant issues for an effective system of price supervision. The Commission rejected any formal limitation on profits as endangering efficiency incentives. It also rejected, as constituting excessive interference, day-to-day regulation of prices by the Board of Trade. The Commission recognized that there were no powers then available under

[1] The Annual Report of the Board of Trade for year ended March 31, 1953.

[2] *The Economist*, April 10, 1954, p. 138. 'The payment for technical help, while reasonable in itself, is perhaps a reminder that the Swedish company was perfectly satisfied with the old agreements as they stood.'

Section 10 to enforce its proposals.[1] The Commission had also condemned the system of full-line forcing adopted by the Company. Two Commissioners, in a minority addendum, rejected price supervision and recommended instead serious consideration of taking the Company into public ownership and providing a guaranteed return on capital invested. This was a surprisingly radical recommendation in the light of former Monopolies Commission reports.

After a considerable lapse of time, and following lengthy discussions, the Board of Trade announced the conclusion of a voluntary agreement with the British Oxygen Company on March 28, 1958. The Government announced its unwillingness to implement the price supervision recommendation of the Commission. The Government also refused to take the British Oxygen Company into public ownership, or to take action by general legislation to split the Company into a number of competing units. The Board of Trade announced instead a range of undertakings extracted from the Company. The Company had agreed to refrain from acquiring other producers of gases with a view to increasing its monopoly position, and in addition to refrain from using associated companies for local and selective price reductions in order to eliminate competitors. The Company promised that no consumer would be compelled to use its apparatus in order to qualify for its gas supplies. There would be no future attempts to bind customers to British Oxygen gases in order to obtain specified types and quantities. The Company would supply gas-using equipment at reasonable prices and would not require the customer to use its gas in the equipment. Where customers used British Oxygen's gas equipment the Company might require them to use its own gas in such equipment. Further quantities of gas could be obtained from rival suppliers. The Company undertook to make its price scales available publicly for oxygen and dissolved acetylene. Any list price alterations would be published immediately. Gas consumers would be classified for this purpose according to the method of supply and the quantities taken. Price scales would not apply to consumers taking supplies by pipe in tonnage quantities and Government departments and hospitals would negotiate supply prices in the customary manner. The Board agreed that the British Oxygen Company might request a review of price scale undertakings if conditions in the industry materially changed. The Company undertook in addition that all its fixed period contracts should not exceed one year, that consumers should be

[1] *The Economist*, January 5, 1957, p. 59. 'Price control is hardly the most obvious way to restore free competition to any industry. British anti-monopoly legislation makes no provision for the breaking up of any company into competing units (and incidentally none for this special form of discriminating price control). But without some such power to restore competition, rather than to chain monopolies by the leg, it might be as well to disband the reconstituted Monopolies Commission.'

completely free to reject period contracts, and that prices applicable to such contracts should be identical with scales published at the time of contract. Finally, the Company informed the Board of Trade that its plant building resources were at the disposal of all who wished to purchase, and that plant sales would take place independently of gas supplies.

It is perhaps significant that the Board considered it desirable to draw the attention of the British Oxygen Company to the powers conferred in Section 12 of the Act, for referring to the Monopolies Commission follow-up references in relation to voluntary undertakings. This is the only occasion to date where the Board of Trade has considered a warning of this kind to be necessary.

On August 16, 1962, the British Oxygen Company was released from its undertaking to publish price lists in connection with gas sales to industrial users purchasing more than 12,000 cubic feet of gas per annum. Henceforth, the Company was allowed to negotiate prices upon an individual basis, and to engage in contracts spanning any time-period. The British Oxygen Company was held fully to its undertakings in relation to smaller consumers who accounted numerically for 80 per cent of its total customers. Certain aspects of the British Press were opposed to the Government's relaxation:

> Perhaps the Board of Trade freed BOC from its undertakings out of a love of fair play. But it is an odd sort of fair play that gives back to the giant of the industry the power to use a pricing system whose abuses had been specifically condemned in the Monopolies Commission's report. Surely the aim of legislation against monopolies is to reduce the advantage of any monopolist over its smaller competitors? And would it not have been 'fairer', also, to have accepted evidence from the other side?[1]

A number of complaints have been levelled at the British Oxygen Company since the relevant undertakings were relaxed. The Board of Trade has duly noted the complaints. Time will demonstrate whether the generosity of the Board of Trade was, in this instance, misplaced.

The Chemical Fertilizer Industry

The Monopolies Commission completely vindicated the activities of Imperial Chemical Industries in the Report on the Supply of Chemical Fertilizers, published in February 1960. The activities of Fisons and British Slag as dominant suppliers of basic slag were also vindicated. The Commission's only criticism of Potash Ltd was directed at its being part of an international organization designed to eliminate competition. The Commission recommended that alternative overseas sources should be cultivated. In addition, the Government was asked to

[1] *The Economist*, November 17, 1962, p. 698.

discuss with Fisons, Imperial Chemical Industries, and other large buyers the possibility that further measures might be taken to develop a powerful bargaining position with overseas potash producers.

The Commission concluded that Fisons had aimed at a rate of return on capital in the field of superphosphates and compounds that had been excessively high. It recommended that Fisons should adjust its pricing policy to yield a lower rate of profit than had been achieved in recent years. The Commission felt that Fisons could be relied upon to carry out this recommendation. Fisons accordingly proceeded to lower the prices of its products in the offending reference field.

In 1961, the Board of Trade announced that discussions had been held with the major British potash purchasers. The trade considered, however, that the balance of advantage was against closer integration in purchasing. In August 1962, the Board announced that Imperial Chemical Industries and Fisons had provided assurances that they would not seek unreasonable profits from the sectors in which the Commission had found them to be monopoly suppliers. They had undertaken to afford facilities to accountants appointed by the Board to ensure that the assurances were upheld. This undertaking went beyond the recommendations of the Commission and no statutory powers were available to place pressure upon the companies. It remains to surmise about the importance of Government fertilizer subsidies and the bargaining counter thereby afforded to the Board of Trade and the Ministry of Agriculture prior to the Annual Fertilizer Subsidy Review.

The Imperial Tobacco Company

The Monopolies Commission's report on the supply of cigarettes and tobacco was published on July 5, 1961, following a lengthy delay after its despatch of the Report to the Board of Trade. The Monopolies Commission concluded that the substantial shareholding maintained secretly by the Imperial Tobacco Company in its principal competitor, Gallaher Ltd, was contrary to the public interest, and should be eliminated. In addition, the bonus system operated by the Imperial Tobacco Company in exchange for advertising commitments on the part of distributors was condemned. *The Economist* newspaper received the recommendations with evident delight:

> Mr Maudling can now hardly avoid having to lay down some kind of public policy on 'single firm' monopolies. Imperial Tobacco, according to its chairman, Mr Roger Clarke, will not willingly accede to the commission's recommendation that it sells Gallaher stock. . . . On the day the commission's report appeared Gallaher 10*s.* ordinary stock fell by 3*s.* 7½*d.* to 40*s.*[1]

[1] *The Economist*, July 8, 1961, p. 154.

The Board of Trade announced the Government's attitude towards the recommendations of the Commission on December 28, 1961. The Government was not prepared to implement the recommendation that the Imperial Tobacco Company should be divested of its Gallaher stock, but it was prepared to implement the recommendation relating to bonus payments, in this respect applying its policy throughout the cigarette and tobacco industry. The Government's sop did not allay the anger of *The Economist* newspaper: 'In the past the Government has often tinkered with recommendations from the Monopolies Commission. But this is a direct rebuff, which damages the Commission's standing and which could inhibit any future recommendations it may make in the field of monopoly to which the Government has already restricted it.'[1]

In justification for its refusal to implement the divestiture recommendation, the Board of Trade pointed out that competition had intensified in the industry after the Monopolies Commission had made its report. Available data supports this contention. Two weeks prior to the Board of Trade's statement, Gallaher Ltd had decided to enter the gift coupon field by purchasing J. Wix and Sons (Kensitas) on a £13·3 million share exchange deal; this move was designed to strengthen Gallaher's competitive position. Yet the objections of the Imperial Tobacco Company towards gift coupon trading were well known. The share exchange deal between Gallaher Ltd and the American Tobacco Company reduced the percentage shareholding of the Imperial Tobacco Company in Gallaher Ltd from 42·5 per cent to 37 per cent.

The Imperial Tobacco Company, after considerable soul-searching, undertook to refrain from interference in the management of Gallaher. It is with considerable reluctance that any company would surrender all supervision over the affairs of so large a trade investment:

> At the moment Gallaher is an efficiently run business and its shares are a profitable investment for Imperial Tobacco, contributing roughly three points of its net equity earnings of about 40 per cent. But it may not always be in the interests of Imperial Tobacco's shareholders that, as far as Gallaher is concerned, their directors should remain permanently mum. If Gallaher fell on evil days, what then? Would the Imperial Tobacco directors then sit back, content that the degree of competition had diminished?[2]

It is by no means clear why the Government refused to implement the Monopolies Commission's divestment recommendation. In part, the answer may lie in the lack of powers under Section 10 of the 1948 legislation. In part, the answer may lie in the fear that the stock exchange valuation of Gallaher's voting shares might fall as the divestment pro-

[1] *The Economist*, January 6, 1962.
[2] ibid.

ceeded, and that this would provide the American Tobacco Company with an opportunity to make a cheap entry into the British market. Insofar as the latter danger was responsible for the Government decision, the Government was short-sighted. The Imperial Tobacco Company need not have been required to sell Gallaher stock on the open market. A free distribution could have been made by Imperial Tobacco of its Gallaher shares to its existing shareholders. Due accommodation might have been made for any tax complications. Alternatively, the Government itself might have acquired the offending shares at a suitable valuation, refraining if it so wished from interference in management of Gallaher. Yet again, the Government might have prevailed upon the large institutional investors to take up a placing of the stock at a suitable valuation. A useful example of such an operation was afforded in steel denationalization between 1953 and 1960.

It is clear that suitable action was possible. If the Government rejected the Commission's recommendation as ill-conceived further explanation was due. In its absence it must be presumed that the Government was lacking in political backbone:

> If Imperial Tobacco had been forced to sell its shareholding, the marketing of the Gallaher shares would not have been easy. The stock market's relief that this shadow has been removed was measured by the net rise of 2*s*. to 41*s*. in Gallaher. Tax complications may have stood in the way of either a free distribution or the sale of the Gallaher shares; but the Government could surely have provided some accommodation on this point. The easy way out of not doing anything is, moreover, no excuse for rejecting the findings of a competent body designed to examine the working of single-firm monopolies.[1]

CONCLUSIONS AND RECOMMENDATIONS

Section 10 of the 1948 Monopolies and Restrictive Practices (Inquiry and Control) Act was drafted with the trade association in mind. Section 10 provided adequate statutory powers for the Government to eliminate undesirable restrictive agreements and/or practices. But the Board of Trade lacked the power required to implement by statutory order many of the Commission's recommendations relating to dominant firm inquiries. This weakness became apparent following the 1956 Restrictive Trade Practices Act.

Where Section 10 powers proved inadequate the Government might hope to implement recommendations by voluntary undertakings; alternatively, it could also fall back upon the normal legislative procedures. Neither technique was really adequate for all circumstances.

[1] *The Economist*, January 6, 1962.

The Conservative Political Centre, in a report by Lord Poole, criticized the inadequacy of Section 10 under existing conditions: 'The main objection to this situation is constitutional. In effect the Government is forced into the false position of arguing in the House of Commons about the exercise of powers that Parliament has not yet granted. We therefore recommend that the powers granted by Section 10 of the 1948 Act should be extended.'[1]

Lord Poole recommended that Section 10 should be extended to empower the Board of Trade to require regular returns of information in reference fields, to impose restrictions as regards prices, and where appropriate to order divestment of assets. He recommended that the exercise of these powers should be subject to an affirmative resolution of the House of Commons subsequent upon an adverse decision by the Monopolies Commission.

In the light of the Poole Committee findings, the Conservative Government produced a White Paper which outlined proposed legislation in the field of Monopolies, Mergers and Restrictive Practices.[2] The White Paper stated that Section 10 of the 1948 Act should be extended to meet current requirements:

> In the past the firms concerned have usually been willing to comply with the Government's requests in such cases by giving voluntary undertakings. The Government would want to continue to negotiate voluntary undertakings wherever possible, but there should be effective powers in reserve if the object of the legislation is not to be frustrated.[3]

The White Paper specifically mentioned the intention to provide powers to enable the Government to insist upon divestment where the public interest required such action. This indicated a *volte-face* from March 1962 when Sir James Pitman had introduced a Bill to provide the Board of Trade with such powers.[4] The Bill had been unsuccessful.

The Conservative Government had no opportunity to legislate to this end in 1964 before it fell from office. The new Labour Government, however, was also committed to action in the field. The relevant Monopolies and Mergers Bill was presented to the House of Commons by the President of the Board of Trade on March 3, 1965.[5] Clause 3 of the Bill would give to the Board of Trade new powers to make orders subsequent upon a Monopolies Commission report. The Board of Trade would be able to require the publication of price lists, to regulate prices, to

[1] *Monopoly and the Public Interest*, 1963, p. 29.

[2] Cmnd. 2299, March 1964.

[3] ibid., p. 3.

[4] *The Economist*, March 17, 1962, p. 1050. 'Although this Bill has highly respected support, its legislative chances cannot be put very high.'

[5] The Monopolies and Mergers Act, 1965, Eliz. 2 c. 50, at August 5, 1965.

prohibit acquisitions or to impose conditions on acquisition. The Board would also be empowered to provide for the dissolution of monopolies and mergers. Orders dissolving monopolies or mergers would have to be approved in draft by resolution of each House of Parliament. Other orders under the clause would require an affirmative resolution by each House of Parliament. Clause 4 would permit the Board of Trade, on the basis of a Monopolies Commission report, to take action against monopoly situations which were incompatible with a treaty to which the United Kingdom was a party, for example the convention establishing the European Free Trade Association. Orders made under this clause would be subject to annulment in pursuance of a resolution of either House of Parliament.

The proposed extension of Board of Trade power in respect to Monopolies Commission recommendations is highly desirable. The new powers will enable the Board of Trade to negotiate from a position of strength with dominant firms. One word of warning may be pertinent in relation to the divestment powers proposed by the Government. Care should be exercised to ensure that divestment is economically feasible prior to making an order. The United States of America has encountered problems in this area of Government intervention:

> Judge Wyzanski rejected the Government's proposal that the United Shoe Machinery Corporation should be divided into three separate companies. He found that all the company's machines were manufactured at a single plant, so that there would be no practical way of dividing it into viable parts. He complained that the Government had not thought through its proposals and the consequential problems which they would entail. 'A petition of dissolution,' he said, 'should reflect greater attention to practical problems and should involve supporting economic data and prophecies such as are presented in corporate reorganization and public utility dissolution cases!'[1]

Certain critics of the 1948 legislation have argued that the Monopolies Commission should be empowered to enforce its own decisions, or alternatively that the Government should be compelled to implement the findings of the Monopolies Commission. This would eliminate the danger of a weak or uncommitted Government lowering the prestige and authority of the Commission by failure to implement closely-argued recommendations. It would also tend to reduce the lengthy time-lag between the publication of a report and the implementation of its recommendations.

On the other hand, the issues raised by dominant firm reports are often of national, indeed occasionally of international, significance. The Government may scarcely be expected to delegate to a Royal Commis-

[1] A. D. Neale, *The Anti-trust Laws of the USA*, 1960, p. 401.

sion of Inquiry issues of substantial national importance, the consequences of which remain the responsibility of the Government.[1] The American judicial system cannot be upheld as a model in this respect since American anti-trust legislation stems from a political philosophy seriously committed to the supremacy of 'the rule of law'. Britain has never been committed to the same extent to this philosophy.

R. B. Stevens and B. S. Yamey, in a recent publication, criticized the increasing reliance of the Government upon delegated decisions in the field of monopoly control: 'It may be difficult to put a controversial Bill through Parliament, and it may be politically inconvenient to implement the recommendations of a Monopolies Commission report. But if it is so politically controversial, is it desirable for the Minister to hide behind a judge's robe and disclaim any liability for the decision?'[2]

Action taken upon a report of the Monopolies Commission may entail political consequences, and such action is appropriately political. The Government must preserve the right, therefore, to overrule recommendations made by the Monopolies Commission. Nevertheless, the reputation of the Monopolies Commission is dependent upon the support its recommendations receive from the Government. A decision to ignore a recommendation, or to take other action, should not be made lightly. New safeguards should therefore be provided to prevent irresponsible damage to the Monopolies Commission's reputation.

The Government should be required by statute to make a decision upon the recommendations of the Monopolies Commission within nine months of the signing of a report. The action taken might be through voluntary undertaking or through statutory order. Should the Government decide to reject or modify any recommendation of the Commission, however, it should be obliged to submit its decision to an affirmative resolution of the House of Commons. The issue would then be subjected to discussion and irresponsible tampering with recommendations of the Commission would, perhaps, be exposed. From time to time, the Government might be obliged to ask the permission of the House of Commons to refrain from action. It is high time that the Government should recognize that a decision to refrain from action is, nevertheless, a decision, perhaps of considerable political and economic significance.

The Government has always been reluctant to implement Monopolies Commission recommendations by means of Statutory Order. Voluntary agreements are preferred on grounds of speed, flexibility, and

[1] Bow Group, 1963, op. cit., p. 75. 'We do not feel that it would be at all justifiable to allow the Commission to enforce its own decisions. The Government must retain the final power of decision in matters of such economic importance, although it is desirable that it march closely in step with the Commission.'

[2] *The Restrictive Practices Court*, Weidenfeld & Nicolson, 1965, p. 153.

goodwill. But voluntary agreements are only effective if they are fully honoured. Many sceptics of the 1948 Act criticize the lack of policing arrangements for voluntary agreements. The only available machinery in existence is the Section 12 reference to the Monopolies Commission. The slipshod surveillance of voluntary undertakings was criticized by the Sixth Committee on Estimates in 1953:

> Your Committee consider that the effectiveness of the Commission will be prejudiced if it becomes apparent that adherence to voluntary agreements is not subsequently examined. They realize that investigations of the kind provided for in the Act would add to the matters already long awaiting the Commission's attention.

In fact, the Board of Trade has considered itself justified, to date, in making only one Section 12 reference to the Monopolies Commission. The Imported Timber reference enabled the Commission to demonstrate that the softwood and hardwood sections of the Timber Trade Federation had dishonoured their undertakings.

There are problems involved in policing voluntary undertakings. The expenditure of time and effort would be considerable, not only for the Monopolies Commission, but also for the organizations subjected to further inquiries. Nevertheless, there can be little doubt concerning the inadequacy of existing procedures.

At an earlier stage in this chapter it was suggested that the Monopolies Commission might be provided with a section detailed permanently to police voluntary undertakings. The Commission might then be required to furnish two-yearly reports to the Board of Trade regarding voluntary undertakings. In addition, the Board of Trade should provide the Monopolies Commission with a full section 12 reference whenever it has reason to believe that undertakings have been dishonoured. The two-yearly reports of the Monopolies Commission would assist the Board of Trade in its selection of Section 12 references.

The prestige and authority of the Monopolies Commission is dependent in large part upon the strict implementation of its recommendations. Undertakings provided to Government must be policed. The Monopolies Commission, as well as the general public, has the right to expect vigilance to ensure the maintenance of undertakings provided to the Government.

Chapter Twenty

ECONOMIC CONSEQUENCES OF MONOPOLIES COMMISSION REPORTS

It is important to commence on an appropriate note of caution. Economic events are usually exceedingly complex. The complexity multiplies when attempting to isolate causes and to allocate the appropriate weights. A number of companies feel completely unable to comment upon the economic consequences of action taken under the 1948 Act. The Secretary of British Insulated Callender's Cables Ltd neatly explained his position in this respect:

> We feel that to endeavour to answer the series of questions which you have raised would be to enter into a field of controversy upon matters which are inevitably to a large extent based on opinion rather than on fact, and which moreover are subject to the major difficulty of distinguishing between *post hoc* and *propter hoc.*

In the absence of a Section 12 reference to the Monopolies Commission there is no machinery for reviewing the economic consequences of action taken in the light of Monopolies Commission inquiries. In addition, the number of inquiries so far resulting in Government action has been limited. There is far more information now available relating to the economic consequences of 1956 Restrictive Trade Practices Act than to those of the 1948 legislation.

A selected number of case studies are used to assess the significance of developments following upon completion of Monopolies Commission inquiries. For the most part, the short-term consequences appear disappointing. Few trade associations are prepared to admit that important economic consequences have issued from their respective inquiries. Those that do so emphasize the importance of other pressures operative during the critical period. In part, the lack of results is due to the Government's unwillingness to comply fully with the Commission's recommendations; in small part, it may be due to ineffective policing of voluntary agreements. For example, the unwillingness of the Government to condemn aggregated rebates in the electric lamp industry, left an incentive to exclusive dealing between Association members and distributors despite the termination of the exclusive dealing agreements. The hardwood and softwood sections of the Timber Trade Federation destroyed the essence of their undertakings to the Government without exposing themselves to penalties. The pattern of trade in imported timber had scarcely changed by 1960 from that operative at the time of the first Monopolies Commission inquiry.

In part, however, the lack of economic results from action on a Monopolies Commission inquiry may be due to exogenous developments. In a number of industries, a form of price leadership developed, following the abrogation of price agreements;[1] in others, price information agreements reduce the impact of price competition;[2] and in others, apathy and lack of enterprise render the competitive process ineffective.[3] Particularly in oligopolistic industries, a tradition of inter-firm co-operation may provide a secure basis for a price information agreement designed to nullify the impact of Government action. In some cases, industrial concentration[4] following the abrogation of price agreements provided the basis for such systems.

Price information agreements have been subjected to careful scrutiny by the Registrar of Restrictive Trading Agreements. In his second Report, the Registrar emphasized the development of information agreements:

> Not infrequently on the ending of a price agreement the parties enter into an information agreement under which they send to their trade association or to a central agency their price lists or the prices at which they have entered into contracts. Information to be sent may also relate to the quantities of goods sold, the persons or classes of persons to whom they are sold, the discounts allowed and the persons to whom they are allowed, and other terms and conditions of trade which have been accepted. The trade association or other central agency then circulates this information to the parties as promptly, at as frequent intervals, and in as much detail as may be desired.[5]

The rash of such agreements, following early judgments of the Restrictive Practices Court, is indicative of the broader influence of the 1956 than of the 1948 legislation.

The Registrar of Restrictive Trading Agreements noted the relevance of tradition in limiting the development of keen competition. In par-

[1] e.g. electric wires and cables.

[2] e.g. calico printing.

[3] e.g. the dental goods industry: Individual manufacturers, without collusion, refused supplies on trade terms to certain customers in a manner similar to that prior to the Order. In the absence of collusion it was impossible to intervene.

[4] e.g. cables.

[5] Report for the period January 1, 1960–June 30, 1961, Cmnd. 1603, p. 3.

ticular, he pointed out that termination of a price agreement might deter price reductions 'because of the widely held fear that any reductions will lead to "cut-throat competition"'.[1]

Mr J. Heath, following a detailed investigation, concluded that the short-term consequences of terminating price agreements 'do not seem as widespread or as deep as many people expected'.[2] On the other hand, he stressed the importance of the economic climate to such developments. 'With demand generally high, one would not expect the degree of competition between sellers to increase significantly.'[3] This point is borne out by the Registrar of Restrictive Trading Agreements in his third report: 'Usually where there has been any very drastic fall there would seem to be causes, such as a serious fall in demand or the emergence of new competitors which causes might of themselves have led to the termination of the restrictions.'[4]

All the available evidence indicates that the direct and immediate economic impact of Monopolies Commission inquiries has been slight. The impact of the Restrictive Practices Court has been considerably greater. At the same time, the reports of the Monopolies Commission have made little indirect impact upon organizations under no immediate threat of inquiry. This worried the Bow Group in its recent report upon monopolies and mergers:

> We attach great importance to the indirect effects of the Commission's work . . . it is most desirable that industrialists should accept and gradually adopt the Commission's standards of their own volition. But this will only be done if the standards are seen to be reasonably arrived at and likely to be enforced.

Nevertheless, the Monopolies Commission's efforts should not be viewed with complete scepticism. In the longer-term, the Commission may have succeeded in eliminating undesirable practices entailing important consequences for investment and price determination.[5] It may well be that the Commission's work will prove far more impressive in the long-run than it has in the short-run.

THE PROCESS OF CALICO PRINTING—A CASE STUDY

The Monopolies Commission reported on the process of calico printing on April 14, 1954. In its report, the Commission recommended that the compulsory minimum price agreement operated by the Federation of

[1] ibid., p. 2.
[2] J. Heath, Manchester School, May 1961, p. 200.
[3] ibid., p. 200.
[4] Report for the period July 1, 1961–June 30, 1963, Cmnd. 2246, p. 3.
[5] J. Heath, *The Banker*, February 1960, p. 111. 'The indirect effects both on prices and in other ways may be considerably greater, but with a time-lag.'

Calico Printers should be terminated, together with the output sharing agreement and the termination of the redundancy scheme, and the winding-up of Print Trade Reorganization Ltd. The recommendations encountered considerable hostility within the calico printing trade:

> Mr Gardner, the union's president, criticized the recommendations that the pricing system should be ended; and he declared: 'We have no intention of quietly going back to the days of cut-throat competition.' Mr W. L. Heywood, general secretary of the union, later explained that this was the considered view of the union. He may have done so with some slight embarrassment. For Mr Heywood is himself a member of the Monopolies Commission, though he did not sign the report on calico printing.[1]

A lengthy period of negotiation ensued between the Government and the Federation of Calico Printers, during which the Federation strenuously defended its market sharing (breakwater) scheme. The tardiness of the Government was noted by the press with a modicum of sympathy:

> The only case where the Government clearly has been dilatory is that Mr Thorneycroft has sat for the last nine months on the Calico Printers' report. This report threw a lurid light on the tangle of restrictive practices in Lancashire's declining cotton industry; it is a very hot political potato in that part of the world. In view of the attitude of the trade unions, it is a fair guess that Labour politicians themselves would have been just as dilatory. . . .[2]

An increase in surplus capacity in calico printing during 1955 stiffened the intransigence of the Federation; the Board of Trade was pressed, finally, into threatening Section 10 legislation in order to extract the required undertaking from the Federation during November 1955.[3] In the event, the Federation agreed to terminate its output sharing agreement, and its minimum price agreement. But the Federation reserved the right to produce a list of recommended minimum prices, trading terms, and engraving rental scales. These lists implied no obligation upon members. The redundancy scheme was allowed to run its course until 1959. But the Federation pointed out the uselessness of this scheme in the absence of finance, either from the industry or from the Exchequer. Speaking for the Federation, Mr Copley pointed out that 'the Board can hardly be expected to rubber-stamp the Commission's

[1] *The Economist*, May 29, 1954, p. 735.

[2] *The Economist*, February 5, 1955, p. 433.

[3] *The Economist*, February 19, 1955, p. 684. 'The Federation of Calico Printers commented bitterly that it was yielding only to a threat . . . to make such arrangements in calico printing "and in that trade alone" illegal by statutory order.'

view that an agreement which the Board certified in 1949 to be "in the national interest" became "against the public interest" four years later'.[1] In 1949 the industry's redundancy scheme had received the blessing of the Finance Corporation for Industry.[2]

The Federation took advantage of its right to institute a recommended minimum price system, following the termination of the obligatory agreements. All available evidence suggests that the undertaking with the Government was honoured in the spirit as well as the letter. The recommended minimum price system, in due course, became subject to registration under 1956 legislation. On March 21, 1956, the Federation suggested to the Board of Trade that their price scheme, accepted by the Board, could not be considered registrable. They requested confirmation of this assumption. The Board of Trade pointed out that the mere fact of Government action subsequent upon a Monopolies Commission inquiry did not release the Federation from its obligation to register. 'If these cases were excepted from registration, it would mean that the criteria applied to them would be different from those which will be applied by the Restrictive Practices Court to all other arrangements falling within the scope of the Bill.' The recommended minimum price scheme was accordingly registered at the appropriate time. The Engraving rental scheme—renamed the Design Licensing Scheme—was registered later following a misunderstanding concerning the scope of the 1956 Act.

During the period of their existence the recommended minimum prices were generally observed by members of the industry. Observance of such prices was facilitated by the whole-hearted support provided by the largest member of the Federation, the Calico Printers' Association. At no time was this company considered to be price leader. The Company had no desire to undertake such a function, and was not, in any event, the largest producer in all types of calico printing. On the other hand, the CPA's views on the level of which the minimum prices should be held were always influential in the trade on account of its highly qualified personnel and comparatively good cost accounting system. At no time did the CPA take advantage of its dominant position during recommended minimum price negotiations.

Perhaps a more important reason for general acceptance of the recommended prices related to the nature of the scheme itself. The minimum price lists had always been regarded as more than a simple pricing scheme. The lists represented a consistent system of price formation.

[1] *The Economist*, December 3, 1955, p. 837.

[2] *The Economist*, December 31, 1955, p. 1173. 'Mr Copley regards the opinion of the Board of Trade in 1949 [in favour of the printers] as sacrosanct and the recent decision as nonsense. Are not second thoughts often best?' Stephen Cawley—ex-director of a calico printing works.

This system appealed to most firms even in the complete absence of obligations. It is important to note that, throughout the history of its price-fixing powers, the Federation had never resorted to sanctions. It had always been able to operate successfully through a discussion system.

It appears, however, that the price paid for obtaining general acceptance of the recommended price system under conditions of excess capacity was a rather lower level of minimum prices than would have been maintained under an obligatory system. The lower price level reduced the temptation to indulge in price cutting. Under the recommended price system it was, in particular, difficult to lift price levels following periods of recession. In an industry such as calico printing where the range of qualities is wide, the opportunity for hidden price cutting is considerable. This appears to have been an occasional feature of the trade.

The Federation decided against defending the recommended price scheme before the Restrictive Practices Court. The recommended scheme was abandoned following a six month trial run for a price information scheme that was not registrable under the 1956 legislation. The price information scheme was run according to 'Cocker' and was intended, once again, to conform strictly with the spirit as well as the letter of the legislation. According to one informant[1] the following procedure was regularly adopted:

> The printers submit two returns—Form 'A' and Form 'B'. Form 'A' is submitted somewhat infrequently and indicates the price formation system the printer is using together with the level of his prices at that time. It is resubmitted following any change in his price formation system. Form 'B' is submitted weekly and states, order by order, the deviation which the printer made from his Form 'A' prices over the relevant trading period.

Excess capacity in calico printing was reduced somewhat as a consequence of the 1959 Cotton Industry Reorganization Act. The calico printing section qualified for assistance to scrap equipment. The minimum figure of $33\frac{1}{3}$ per cent needed to qualify was barely attained. Despite action under the 1959 Act, there is still considerable excess capacity in the industry. The Calico Printers' Association has been buying up a number of printing firms, either openly or secretly, with the object of closing them down. An example of such action was the closure of James Hardcastle which had been a member of the Bleachers' Association. The CPA bought this company's machinery.

In spite of excess capacity, there is little evidence of severe price cutting in the industry. The industry is sufficiently oligopolistic to induce price stability through fear of retaliation. Throughout the postwar

[1] A firm which is a member of the Federation.

period the number of firms in the industry has been limited by scale requirements. A number of firms were eliminated as a result of the Reorganization Scheme. At present, only about twelve firms in the industry really matter, and one of these, the Calico Printers' Association, controls six branches. Available evidence suggests that the CPA has not extended its market share since termination of the price scheme. It has been rationalizing production on an extensive scale.

One result of excess capacity has been the inability to raise prices in the face of cost increases. There is little doubt that had the price agreements been in force printing prices would be considerably higher than they are. This is illustrated by Table 15 relating to dress print prices:

TABLE 15

Calico Dress Print Prices

1957–62

Monthly Average	*Finishing Price in pence per yard*
1957	19·24
1958	20·12
1959	19·99
1960	20·12
1961	20·12
1962	20·50

This table indicates very little price movement during the period under observation. The price increases observable are considerably below general price movements as indicated by the Index of Retail Prices. At the same time there has been a general tendency to provide better service in calico printing. In particular, rapid delivery is of great importance in the trade. Printers have concentrated heavily upon this facet of the competitive process. A difference in delivery dates of only two to three days is often sufficient to win contracts.

In conclusion, it appears that abolition of the price schemes in calico printing was not attended by the disastrous trading conditions that the Federation stressed to be likely in giving evidence before the Monopolies Commission. The price information scheme resulted in lower prices and keener competition than was likely before the Commission's inquiry. This was achieved with a minimum of dislocation in an industry experiencing difficult trading conditions.

THE SUPPLY OF INSULATED ELECTRIC WIRES AND CABLES—A CASE STUDY

As a consequence of the Monopolies Commission's findings, market-sharing schemes, exclusive dealing arrangements and rebate systems were terminated in 1954 by the Cable Makers' Association and the

Covered Conductors Association in accordance with an undertaking made to the Government.[1] The Ministry of Supply allowed the price system operated in mains and supertension cable to continue, subject to detailed surveillance by the British Electricity Authority. In general, however, the common price systems of the Cable Makers' Association were terminated. They were replaced by minimum price systems subject to a review of costs and profits from time to time by the appropriate Government Department. The minimum price schemes were based on the average costs of the lowest cost producer in each type of cable. This had been strongly criticized by members of the associations.[2] In practice, the immediate economic effect of the undertaking was insignificant. The common price systems for mains cable and general wire had been based on the average costs of the five lowest cost firms in each type of cable. The new schemes, in most types of cable, resulted in rather less than a 5 per cent price reduction.[3]

Meanwhile, important changes were taking place in the cable-making industry. The Independent Companies had been protected somewhat from aggressive competition during the Second World War by the system of allocating raw materials. Following the war, the Cable Makers' Association had shown a less aggressive attitude and the Independents had been able to encroach on the Association's market share by offering substantially lower prices. The investment required to enter the industry, especially in the general wire section, was not exceptionally high and a number of Independents which had entered in the late 1930s had consolidated their position during the postwar period.

During the early postwar period thermoplastic cable, a cheaper and more effective product, began to offer serious competition to rubber-covered cable, especially in the general and house-wiring sections of the cable industry. This development served to lower entry barriers in this section,[4] providing an impetus towards new entry. Several members of the Association failed to respond quickly to this development. The Independents took advantage of their tardiness.[5] Entry into the mains cable section was evidently less easy because of difficulties in the supply of suitable high-speed machinery.

The developments in thermoplastic cable created difficulties regarding a readjustment of rubber cable prices, and a delay on the part of

[1] Annual Report of the Board of Trade for year ended December 1954, p. 16.

[2] They pointed out that the lowest cost producer might spend nothing on technical research and development, sales marketing and the like. This would bear heavily upon firms which were technical leaders in the cable industry.

[3] See *The Economist*, February 6, 1960, p. 539.

[4] J. B. Heath, Manchester School, May 1961, p. 196. 'The equipment cost about 10 per cent of the old, and was easier to operate.'

[5] *The Economist*, February 6, 1960, p. 539. 'This gave the independents a big chance which they did not let slip.'

Association members in the scrapping of obsolete capacity. At the same time, domestic sales were becoming increasingly important as overseas development in cable production reduced the British export market. In 1958, just as the shadow of the Restrictive Trade Practices Court began to loom, the Government decided to impose restrictions on the capital expenditure programmes of public authorities, from which almost 50 per cent of the domestic cable business emanated. At this stage there were signs of concealed price cutting within the Associations concerned.

The first clear sign of internal difficulties within the Cable Makers' Association came in 1957 when Crompton Parkinson removed its subsidiary, Derby Cables, from the Association. From 1958 onwards the battle was on in earnest. The two largest companies in the industry, British Insulated Callender's Cables and Associated Electrical Industries, initiated a concentration movement by bidding for other cable manufacturers. Associated Electrical Industries acquired W. T. Henley and London Electric Wire, together with the latter's subsidiary, Liverpool Electric Cable. The Henley and Liverpool cable-making factories were subsequently closed down. Meanwhile, British Insulated Callender's Cables had been rationalizing its operations from 1955, concentrating production at its modernized plant at Erith in Kent. It had purchased Telcon, Scottish Cables, and Metropolitan Electric Cable in anticipation of the coming struggle. It removed the operations of the last-mentioned Company to Erith.[1] Other cable makers were also reorganizing and re-grouping during the late 1950s. In 1959, for instance, Enfield Rolling Mills took over its former holding company, Enfield Cables, and later merged its power cable activities with Standard Telephones and Cables. These rationalization developments took place against a back-cloth of increasing excess capacity in the cable industry.

The pressure of excess capacity weakened the regulatory powers of the trade associations. In 1958 concealed price cutting became a feature of the industry. In November 1958 the members of the Cable Makers' Association formally accepted a price reduction, officially to meet competition from the Independents, but probably also to eliminate secret reductions. In April 1959 the price agreements were formally abandoned and heavy price reductions were effected. In June 1959 British Insulated Callender's Cables initiated a further round of price reductions. Prices had fallen in total by about 20 per cent in the immediate period following the termination of the agreements. Agreements

[1] Directors' Report for BICC for year 1958, p. 28. 'Whilst we may see some further mergers from time to time, many companies in the cable industry will continue as separate concerns. Some of these are admittedly small and specialize in a very limited range of products, but they nevertheless provide overall an active competition.'

covering telephone and supertension cable were not abandoned, but were registered under the 1956 legislation.

At the time when the price agreements were terminated, British Insulated Callender's Cables appears to have made a determined bid to become price leader. Its lead was not followed, partly due to excess capacity but due also to a lack of trust between the former Association members. Many of the smaller producers suspected their larger competitors of cut-throat competition designed to force them out of the industry. In 1959, the Board of Trade received complaints to this effect from a number of small firms in the industry. The Board refused to refer the matter to the Monopolies Commission but promised that it would watch developments carefully.[1]

During the final quarter of 1959 vain discussions took place among the large cable producers in an attempt to produce a price agreement for registration under the 1956 Act. The reduction in profitability of the industry was a compelling but insufficient reason for renewed co-operation. British Insulated Callender's Cables had obtained dangerously low rates of return on turnover during 1958 and 1959:

TABLE 16

BICC: Rate of Return on Turnover 1958–9

	per cent
January–June 1958	7·5
July–December 1958	8·5
January–June 1959	7·6

In November 1959 BICC made a desperate and successful bid for price-leadership in the cables industry. It raised its prices by 7½ per cent for low voltage mains cables, in an industry composed of eleven important competitors. This section of the market accounted for about one third of the £100 million expended annually upon cables in the domestic market. All the producers in the section followed BICC's lead and thereby brought the sharpest phase of the price war to a close.[2] The new price levels within the section were just sufficient to enable the more efficient producers to break even.

It was not until January 1960, however, that BICC attempted to become price leader in the house and general wiring cables section. This section, accounting for a further one-third of British cable expenditure, was far less concentrated than the mains cable section. In January 1960

[1] Annual Report of the Board of Trade for year ended December 31, 1959, p. 3, and December 31, 1960, p. 4.

[2] J. B. Heath, 1961, op. cit., p. 197. 'Through its dominant position, and with skilful timing, BICC established a position of price leadership much stronger than had existed before, and with a substantially lower level of prices.'

there were still more than forty firms making general wire—roughly the same numbers that the Monopolies Commission had found in 1948—and the spread of costs reported by the Commission was as wide as 20–30 per cent. Once again, nevertheless, BICC's bold move was accepted by rival firms, and its price leadership position consolidated.[1]

The remaining one-third of the industry constituted no problem. The agreements covering telephone and super-tension cable had not been abrogated. The termination of the price agreement for covered conductors had coincided with a business boom.

Cable prices began to drift upwards during 1961 and the industry appears to have regained some form of stability, albeit based upon narrower margins than before the termination of the price agreements. Many of the formerly independent firms continued to charge prices slightly below those of the bulk of the industry. Such operations were not popular in the trade. Following the establishment of price leadership, price information agreements were introduced in the mains cable, general wiring, and covered conductor sections of the industry. These are not registrable, at present, under 1956 legislation.

The wave of mergers in the industry began to decline following the establishment of price leadership conditions. Suggestions that cable makers should amalgamate were resisted keenly in many sectors. In part, reluctance to effect further concentration may reflect the fear of Government intervention.[2] In part, it may reflect a more healthy industrial structure and brighter economic prospects.

Mr J. B. Heath[3] argued that the increased concentration of the cable industry had been off-set by easier entry into the thermoplastic cable field. On the other hand, certain cable-makers had been forced to purchase supplies through intermediate producers often owned by backward-integrated cable makers, and this constituted a limited impediment to the competitive process. His inquiries produced no evidence of quality deterioration during the spell of cut-throat competition. Expenditure upon research and development had not been reduced. On the other hand a number of firms 'were postponing investment in the industry until its future became clearer and its prices more profitable.

[1] *The Economist*, February 6, 1960, p. 539. 'It is now their turn to see if they can operate under the system of price leadership that other industries have used for years as an equally comfortable, or politically less unpopular, alternative to price competition.'

[2] *The Economist*, February 6, 1960, p. 539. 'The industry is no doubt conscious, too, that if amalgamation continues to the point where questions of public interest arise, the government could decide to remove or reduce the 17½ per cent tariff on mains cable and take action to limit the operations of the international cartel, the International Cable Development Corporation, whose rules still broadly govern imports of mains cable by this country.'

[3] op. cit., 1961, p. 199.

There was evidence of diversification, both old and new, into products unconnected with cables.'[1]

It is not easy to isolate the direct consequences of the voluntary undertakings for the structure and activities of the cable industry. In particular, the impact of 1956 legislation played an important role in the 1958–60 troubles of the industry. The results of the period indicate the innate resilience and capacity for recovery of companies and sectors subjected to dislocation. This should encourage bold conclusions from future Monopolies Commission inquiries, where the situation merits radical action.

THE SUPPLY OF MATCHES—A CASE STUDY

The Monopolies Commission's report relating to the British Match Corporation was published on May 13, 1953. On June 18th, Mr Thorneycroft indicated his acceptance of the Commission's findings, although he doubted the efficacy of the price control system suggested by the majority of the Commission.

In late July 1953 the Board of Trade concluded an agreement with the USSR Government, whereby in the coming year £500,000 of matches from Russia would be purchased for the British market. There was no indication that this action arose directly from the Monopolies Commission's findings. Nevertheless, it did inject a degree of competition into the British market.[2]

An agreement between the Board of Trade and the British Match Corporation was reached on April 5, 1954. A Revised Trading Agreement was negotiated between the British Match Corporation and Swedish Match, incorporating the substance of the undertakings.[3]

The British Match Corporation was virtually the sole producer of British matches; matches were not subjected to strong competition from competitive substitutes. The Monopolies Commission had commented upon the scale economies apparent in match production. In addition, the match industry was not notably dynamic technologically nor subject to very much innovative competition. With this background, the British Match Corporation constituted perhaps the most sheltered dominant firm examined by the Commission. The Commission was unable to put

[1] J. Heath, op. cit., at p. 199.

[2] *The Economist*, August 1, 1953, p. 347. 'Competitive imports from sources or through importers not associated with the British Match or Swedish Match combines have recently increased; even so, in 1952 they totalled only just over a million gross boxes.'

[3] *The Economist*, April 10, 1954, p. 138. 'Abolition of the quota arrangements, as the Commission's minority observed last year, may not of itself ensure "vigorous competition" between the two major groups; but it leaves other makers or importers wholly free to compete, if they want to.'

forward a convincing solution to problems existing in the supply of matches.

The Government, following its negotiated agreement, consistently encouraged match imports from the 'Iron Curtain' countries. The British Match Corporation became increasingly concerned at competition from this source after 1954. The Company felt that the price level for Socialist matches smacked of export subsidies. In 1956 the British Match Corporation noted that import competition in the match market stemmed from Sweden, Norway, Finland, Russia, Poland, Czechoslovakia, Yugoslavia, Austria, Belgium, Italy and the Netherlands.

Increasing import sales on the British market did not reflect an increase in the total market for matches. From the mid-1950s the British match market had lacked dynamic. It appeared that domestic demand for matches did not expand with population expansion, or with the expansion of cigarette and tobacco sales. The main reason for this seems to have been rapidly developing competition from alternative lighting devices. It is not surprising, under such conditions, that the British Match Corporation complained bitterly about the Government policy of raising match quotas from 'Iron Curtain' countries.[1] Table 17 indicates the increasing pressure imported matches placed upon the British Match Corporation after the Monopolies Commission inquiry had been completed.[2]

TABLE 17

Sales of Matches in the United Kingdom
Millions of customs units (1 *c.u.* = 7,200 *ms*)

	Year ended March 31st									
	1953	1954	1955	1956	1957	1958	1959	1960	1961	1962
British	12·8	12·0	11·7	11·4	11·3	11·1	11·0	10·7	10·0	10·1
Imported	4·8	5·5	5·8	6·2	6·1	6·2	6·2	6·4	6·1	6·0

The British Match Corporation recognized the danger of accentuated competition within a static total market; it was virtually a large single-product company. The Corporation actively commenced a rationalization policy related to its match producing units from 1956. In that year Bryant and May, the largest subsidiary of the Corporation, closed down its Leeds factory. In 1957, Masters closed down its Barking factory. In both instances such action was taken with considerable reluctance, but 'the economic advantages of concentrating the group production in the remaining factories could not be gainsaid'.[3] It is interesting

[1] BMC report and accounts for year ended March 31, 1961. 'We do not believe that any other British Industry making consumer goods has been called upon to suffer proportionately as much as the match industry under the terms of the Anglo-Soviet Trade Agreement.'

[2] Statistics selected from the reports and accounts of the BMC.

[3] BMC report and accounts for year ended March 31, 1957.

to note this encouraging reappraisal of Group policy as a result of greater competition. The Commission had been unhappy about the lack of rationalization within the British Match Corporation.

Meanwhile, the Corporation launched a large investment programme designed to modernize and to re-equip the Bryant and May production units. This was well under way by 1958, and the estimated total cost was in the region of £1½ million. In 1961 the programme had been completed and the Corporation considered its new Glasgow plant to be the most modern and efficient in the world match industry. Any reductions in unit cost of production resulting from this programme were quickly swallowed up by other cost increases. Labour costs rose significantly partly due to a shortening of the basic working week. Profit levels appear to have been somewhat depressed.

In 1956 the Corporation announced its intention to diversify production as a means of counteracting stagnation in the match market.[1] Bryant and May was selected as the most suitable vehicle through which diversification should be effected. The programme became operational in 1957. In May 1957 £500,000 was invested in the Airscrew and Jicwood Company which produced 'man-made timber' under patent together with a range of fans for industrial and domestic uses. In February 1958 a 50 per cent interest was acquired in Prestfibre, a company producing mouldings of special interest to the radio, television, and automobile industries. The Corporation subsequently diversified rapidly, involving itself in a wide range of activities, many connected more or less closely with the timber industry. By March 1963 the British Match Corporation was able to disclose substantial interests in cardboard box production, glues and gelatines, Bengal lights, industrial wire products, fireworks, ticket issuing machines, steel-wool, soap filled pads and scouring cloths and smoke pesticides. In addition, the Corporation held overseas interests in soft drink and milk production, saw-milling and logging, printing, and steel furniture production. This is an impressive range of interests acquired in a remarkably short time-period. Table 18 provides quantitative evidence of the Corporation's diversification programme.[2]

In 1960 tariff reductions within the European Free Trade Association introduced further competitive problems for British Match. The pledged elimination of tariffs on inter-member trade in industrial commodities was bound to sharpen competition in matches from Sweden and Norway. The tariff had amounted to 8*d.* for every 7,200 matches imported, and had been imposed for many years.

[1] BMC sales overseas had remained roughly constant between 1958–62 at about 32·5 million gross boxes.

[2] It is interesting to note that BMC's rate of return on capital was rather higher in matches than in other fields after 1960.

The 10 per cent surcharge imposed by the Chancellor of the Exchequer upon revenue duties in July 1961 adversely affected domestic match sales. Fortunately, the 10 per cent surcharge was removed in the 1962 Budget. At the same time, however, the EFTA tariff was halved. Prospects of British entry into the European Economic Community loomed large, and this implied intensified competition in the British match market. BMC does not appear to have expected many opportunities of competing effectively in European markets. In fact, of course, the British negotiations at Brussels were fruitless, and the expected entry did not take place.

The British Match Corporation became increasingly concerned, in the late 1950s, by the disadvantage it suffered in being dependent upon imported timber, most of which was purchased in Canada. The Corporation decided, in 1962, to initiate a substantial poplar planting programme in Britain, involving a long-term investment of twenty-five to thirty years designed to eliminate the existing cost disadvantages.

TABLE 18

The British Match Corporation: Match and Non-Match Activities 1959–63

			March 31*st*		
BMC	1959	1960	1961	1962	1963
	per cent	*per cent*	*per cent*	*per cent*	*per cent*
Asset Values					
(*Valued in* 1959)					
1. Match industry	85·7	77·8	76·1	75·9	75
2. Other activities	14·3	22·2	23·9	24·1	25
Profit					
(*before tax*)					
1. Match industry	85·4	73·6	80·1	79·8	81·1
2. Other activities	14·6	26·4	19·9	20·2	18·9

THE SUPPLY OF INDUSTRIAL GASES—A CASE STUDY

The Monopolies Commission severely criticized many of the activities of the British Oxygen Company in the industrial and medical gases industry. The Government subsequently extracted voluntary undertakings from the Company relating to many of the Commission's recommendations. It rejected the price supervision recommendation.

The Monopolies Commission emphasized the importance of a major research effort from the British Oxygen Company. The Board of Trade subsequently reiterated the point. The British Oxygen Company strenuously defended its research record, pointing out that at least £500,000 per annum was devoted to research and development in industrial gases and associated plant and equipment. It is interesting to note, however, that in 1958 the Company's operating divisions were given more responsibility for research and development work directly related to their needs. It was intended that this should result in better balance between work on operational problems and research of a more fundamental character which would continue in the central laboratories. In 1959 the Company announced that it had completed arrangements for the production of hydrogen and helium in liquid form. This development was important for many special scientific applications where the ability to reach temperatures near absolute zero—minus 273°C.—was of prime importance. The development of super-insulants resulted in marked reductions in the evaporation loss hitherto experienced in handling and storing at low temperatures hydrogen, helium, and other gases. The Company does appear to have become more research conscious following the Commission's report. Whether it was stimulated into activity by the report or by market factors is impossible to judge from available material.

The years following the Commission's report appear to have been characterized by reductions in profitability in the gases division. In part, this was a reflection of under-activity in many spheres of heavy industry and general engineering. In part, it was caused by a fall in export sales which resulted from increasing import restrictions imposed in a number of countries. From 1958 the British Oxygen Company incurred a series of cost increases, exacerbated by a shortened working week in 1960, during a period in which the price scales announced in 1957 remained unchanged. This development inevitably culminated in narrowed profit margins. Price increases were announced in May 1961 and were actively introduced in October. This helped to improve the profit margins on industrial gases.

During the period under review, fundamental changes were taking place in the nature of the market for industrial gases. Liquid oxygen sales began to level off from 1956, and the growth sector became concentrated upon supplies of tonnage oxygen. Utilization of oxygen on such a large scale warranted the installation of expensive production plant at the point of use. In 1959 the British Oxygen Company announced that its existing tonnage plant capacity for gases of 900 tons per day was to be expanded to 2,200 tons per day under long-term contracts. This development would serve the requirements of the new steel-works and steelwork extensions throughout the United Kingdom. The steel industry had begun to use oxygen experimentally in steel-making processes during the late 1950s. During 1961 and 1962, tonnage oxygen plants commenced production one after another, and the market became highly competitive.[1] Fear of backward integration by steel com-

[1] BOC Directors' Report and Accounts—year ended September 30, 1960. 'There is undoubtedly a tremendous future for oxygen in iron and steel-making, but optimism for this growth prospect should be tempered by an understanding of conditions. It takes several years . . . from the start of planning of such major

panies served to narrow profit margins still further. At the same time consumers of gaseous oxygen were rapidly switching to liquid oxygen, to the detriment of the former sector. The pattern of oxygen supply and its cost structure had changed substantially from that in existence when the Monopolies Commission had examined the industry in 1953–4. On this ground, the British Oxygen Company, early in 1962, approached the Board of Trade requesting an alteration in its undertakings. The Company was duly informed, on August 16, 1962, that in connection with sales to industrial users who purchased more than 12,000 cubic feet of any one gas per annum, it need not publish price scales, it would be allowed to negotiate prices with individual consumers, and it could enter into long-term contracts. The alteration in the nature of the undertakings was announced to the House of Commons on November 13, 1962. The undertakings were not changed regarding other gas consumers. The British Oxygen Company welcomed the change in policy.[1]

The Board of Trade justified its action on two main grounds. The great development of tonnage oxygen capacity in Britain, from 200 tons per day in 1958 to 3,000 tons a day in 1962, had been an important factor. In addition, Air Products Ltd, an American subsidiary company, had firmly established itself as a supplier of liquid and bottled oxygen. Air Products Ltd, of course, was not bound by the undertakings limiting the competitive activities of the British Oxygen Company, and could offer secretly negotiated long-term contracts where it so wished.

Air Products Ltd had been particularly successful in the tonnage oxygen market. It had obtained 20 per cent of the market in this growth sector of the industrial gases industry. In fact, however, the intervention of Air Products had only reduced BOC's market share excluding tonnage oxygen from 98 per cent to 95 per cent.

Air Products Ltd protested strongly to the Board of Trade about the relaxation of the British Oxygen Company's undertakings. It pointed out that the British Oxygen Company could thenceforth retain customers by means of long-term contracts in areas into which competition from Air Products Ltd had not penetrated. Air Products Ltd was then heavily centred in the South, with plants at Cardiff, Ebbw Vale, and Fawley. It would be pressed into speeding up its expansion

installations to their full operation, and the customer may decide that he will purchase and operate his own oxygen plant. The competition . . . in this tonnage oxygen business is as severe as ever.'

[1] BOC Directors' Report and Accounts for year ended September 30, 1962. 'In any case it had become increasingly difficult for us to make full use of various technical advances, for example in passing on to the particular customers affected the benefit of the new method of the supply by pipeline grid. We can now deal with competition whatever form it takes, and can promote alternative technical methods to the best advantage.'

plans in the Midlands and the North by the Board's decision. The Board of Trade appears to have ignored or rejected Air Product's plea for an independent and impartial investigation into the exact nature of competition in the United Kingdom industrial gases industry.

The Board of Trade came under heavy fire from the financial and business press for its action.[1] The comment of Cartel[2] adequately reflects the public reaction to its decision:

> When the barriers to entry into an industry are as formidable as massive investment and an established network of distribution make them for oxygen production, it is shortsighted of the Board of Trade to remove whatever slight restrictions on BOC's commercial activity offer assistance to its sole competitor. Short-term contracts and a knowledge of BOC's prices did give Air Products a market foothold; now BOC will be free to return to the practices the Monopolies Commission condemned. . . . Altogether the BOC story illustrated rather well the weakness of British monopoly legislation, especially its dependence on ministers for strong action. The omission of a divestiture power from the monopoly legislation is also again shown to be a major deficiency. If BOC had been split up in 1956 conditions of entry for new enterprises might well have been less onerous than they are today.

TABLE 19

BOC: Selected Statistics Relating to Annual Price Increases 1939–62*

	per cent
Board of Trade Index of Wholesale Prices	6
Iron and Steel Price Index	5·5
London and Cambridge Economic Service	4·7
Ministry of Labour—Index of Retail Prices: Fuel and Light	5·1
The British Oxygen Company—Average Gaseous Oxygen Prices	2·4
The British Oxygen Company—Average Liquid Oxygen Prices	0·6

* Frequent changes in the basis of compilation of price indices mar their value for long-period comparative purposes.

The Board of Trade received complaints in 1962 concerning the activities of the British Oxygen Company subsequent upon its release from certain undertakings. No reference was made to such complaints in the Annual Report of the Board of Trade for the year ended December 1963 and one must hope that they were ill-founded. The economic consequences of the Commission's inquiry into industrial gases are

[1] *The Economist*, November 17, 1962, p. 698. 'Surely the aim of legislation against monopolies is to reduce the advantage of any monopolist over its small competitors? And would it not have been "fairer", also, to have accepted evidence from the other side?'

[2] January 1963, p. 10.

encouraging; the study demonstrates the ability of the Government to influence market performance. It is to be hoped that the Government will not retract its sanctions too swiftly, in the light of encouraging market developments.

THE SUPPLY OF CIGARETTES AND TOBACCO—A CASE STUDY

The findings of the Monopolies Commission in the cigarette and tobacco inquiry were published by the Board of Trade on July 4, 1961. The Commission recommended the termination of the bonus system operated by the Imperial Tobacco Company and the divestment of the latter's shareholding in Gallaher. From the outset it always seemed more likely that the former than the latter finding would be enforced by the Government. The Imperial Tobacco Company announced at its press conference that 'we have sought to operate it [bonus agreement] fairly and we have reason to know that it is greatly appreciated by many distributors; but we shall, of course, look at it again in the light of the Commission's observations and discuss the matter with the Board of Trade'. Nevertheless, on July 11, 1961, a notice was despatched to bonus customers emphasizing that Imperial's forthcoming bonus payment would be made in the normal way on July 14th, and that the obligations under the Company's bonus agreement remained unchanged. The Company promised that if any change was effected due notice would be provided, and bonus earned under the existing scheme would be paid.

The Board of Trade announced a voluntary undertaking with the Imperial Tobacco Company on December 28, 1961. The Board of Trade did not require the Imperial Tobacco Company to divest itself of its Gallaher shareholding, but extracted instead a promise that Imperial Tobacco would not interfere in the management of Gallaher. In addition, Imperial Tobacco agreed to terminate the system of bonus payments related to advertising and display facilities at customers' premises. This latter undertaking would be effected as soon as was reasonably practicable. The Board of Trade announced its intention to prevent the use of similar schemes by other tobacco manufacturers. The Imperial Tobacco Company agreed to eliminate the bonus system by November 1, 1962. On October 5, 1962, details of the new bonus agreement were submitted to retailers of Imperial Tobacco's products. In 1963 the Board of Trade announced that undertakings had been extracted from members of the Federation of Home and Export Manufacturers concerning bonus agreements.

Imperial Tobacco's share of the cigarette and tobacco market had been declining for a considerable period of time. At the time of the Commission's inquiry, in 1959, it had amounted to 63½ per cent. This had fallen to 60 per cent by January 1962. The market dominance of the

Imperial Tobacco Company had not prevented the market expansion of its main rivals, Gallaher and, to a lesser extent, Rothmans.[1]

Prior to the announced undertaking, J. Wix Ltd had introduced gift coupons to the British cigarette market with 'Kensitas'. The cigarette card was not included in this development. A few days before the undertaking the American Tobacco Company sold J. Wix to Gallaher, thereby increasing its shareholding in the British company, and reducing the proportionate shareholding in Gallaher of the Imperial Tobacco Company.

On February 10, 1962, financial results for Imperial Tobacco revealed that for the year ended October 1961 the Company had halted the recent decline in its trading profits. Profits had been helped by the June increase in cigarette and tobacco prices. This was followed in July by the 10 per cent surcharge on tobacco duties, producing an exceptional stock profit of £1½ million which was transferred directly to reserves. The financial results indicated that Imperial Tobacco was stabilizing its market share at around 60 per cent and that it was 'now staving off the competitive challenge of Gallaher and other cigarette manufacturers more successfully'.[2] One indication of the determination within Imperial Tobacco to compete keenly was the decision to replace the traditional and old-fashioned design on the flat packets of 'Players' with the modern design already used on the flip-top packets. Keen competition in the cigarettes and tobacco industry was always more likely to take place through innovation, quality and advertising than directly through price.

In August 1962 Imperial Tobacco announced its decision to enter the coupon trading field to combat the success of Gallaher with 'Kensitas'. This decision marked a reversal of Imperial Tobacco's traditional aversion to coupon trading, and was undoubtedly pressed upon the company by public response to Gallaher's product. The period in question was conditioned by the public reaction to the linkage of smoking and health hazards. Coupon trading may partly have been a competitive reaction to subsequent falling sales. The Imperial Tobacco Company stressed that there was no relationship between the Monopolies Commission's report and the development of coupon trading.

Imperial Tobacco has argued that the termination of the Bonus Agreement had very little effect either on the pattern of sales promotion in the industry or on the share allocated voluntarily by retailers to display of its own products. There have been a few sporadic instances of manufacturer payment offers for counter displays. These were relatively insignificant.

[1] *The Economist*, January 6, 1962. 'Imperial Tobacco may be a price leader but it does not wield the big stick.'

[2] *The Economist*, February 10, 1962, p. 566.

In recent years, competition has intensified in the cigarettes and tobacco industry owing to a change in the nature of demand. The health/smoking reports of the past few years have not instigated a dramatic decline in smoking. They have accelerated a change in smoking habits, away from non-tipped cigarettes, in favour of tipped cigarettes, pipes and cigars. In 1963, in the United Kingdom, plain cigarette consumption fell from 178·1 million lbs weight to 168·7 million lbs. Tipped cigarette consumption rose from 52·6 million to 69·1 million lbs, while pipe and hand-rolling tobacco sales remained steady at around the 33 million lbs mark. The company best suited to take advantage of the growing popularity of tipped cigarettes is Carreras, with 6 per cent of the UK cigarette market but with 16 per cent of the tipped, against Gallaher's 36 per cent and 37 per cent, and Imperial Tobacco's 57 per cent and 48 per cent respectively.[1]

[1] *The Stock Exchange Gazette*, March 20, 1964, p. 66.

PART VII

CONCLUSIONS AND RECOMMENDATIONS

Laws are generally found to be nets of such a texture as the little creep through, the great break through, and the middle-sized alone are entangled in.

F. Bacon, *On Politics*

Chapter Twenty-one

THE MONOPOLIES COMMISSION AND FUTURE DEVELOPMENTS

At the time of writing, a Bill relating to the British Monopolies Commission is passing through the Houses of Parliament. Further legislation is planned by the Labour Government in the field of monopoly control; the Conservative Party, also, is committed to fresh legislation in this field. A brief review of prospective legislation is therefore required.

THE ADMINISTRATIVE APPROACH TO MARKET DOMINANCE

Earlier chapters examined in some detail the respective merits of the administrative and the judicial solution to problems of market dominance. It has been suggested that the present division of responsibility between the Monopolies Commission and the Restrictive Practices Court may well be satisfactory. Certain authors are cautious about using the judicial solution at all for problems of economic performance: 'A close study of the antitrust cases suggests the conclusion that the realm of economic assessment will be invaded by the courts at their peril, and that effective law will be based, if at all, on a reduction of the issues to facts concerned with collusion and restrictive intent.'[1]

The Conservative Party clearly favours the administrative approach to problems of the dominant firm. Extension of the judicial system of review to this sector was rejected in a Conservative Government White Paper published in March 1964.[2] The White Paper closely followed in this respect the recommendations of the committee chaired by Lord Poole, which had reported in March 1963.[3]

The Conservative Party was convinced that 'the "neutral" and uncommitted approach to monopoly on which present legislation is based remains fundamentally right and they do not propose to introduce into the law any presumption that monopoly or size are in themselves undesirable'.[4]

The Labour Government has not yet displayed its attitude towards

[1] A. D. Neale, *The Antitrust Laws of the USA*, CUP, 1960, p. 503.

[2] Monopolies, Mergers and Restrictive Practices, Cmnd. 2299.

[3] Conservative Political Centre, *Monopoly and the Public Interest*, March 1963.

[4] Cmnd. 2299, p. 1.

the administrative solution to problems of market dominance. The 1965 Bill suggests that Labour thinking is largely in line with that of the Conservative Party on this issue. The Bill is designed to strengthen the role of the Monopolies Commission. There is little likelihood, in the foreseeable future, that the dominant firm will be subjected to the judicial process.

ENLARGEMENT OF THE MONOPOLIES COMMISSION

From the outset, the Monopolies Commission has been criticized for its slowness in completing inquiries into reference fields. In response to such criticism, legislation in 1953 had provided for an enlargement of the Monopolies Commission. The Commission had been empowered to expand the number of references tackled within a given time-period by working in sub-divisions. This privilege has been withdrawn in 1956, and the size of the Monopolies Commission had been reduced. The period 1953 to 1956 provides the most fertile period of the Commission's existence. Its speed of inquiry at that time compared favourably with certain periods in the life of the Restrictive Practices Court:

> Another virtue claimed in 1956 was speed. It was said that this would distinguish the Court from its predecessor, the Monopolies Commission. But even this has become increasingly less obvious. None of the recent cases has lasted for less than thirty days. This means not only heavy expenses, but, inevitably, that very few cases can be disposed of. In 1962 there were three decisions; in 1963 there were six. The wheel has come full circle, for the Monopolies Commission, at its peak, was capable of producing almost the same number of reports.[1]

During the early 1960s the Conservative Government was made increasingly uneasy about its downgrading of the Monopolies Commission since 1956. Problems of the dominant firm were subjected to widespread public discussion. The Monopolies Commission proved extremely slow in inquiring into reference fields. Public pressure mounted for a return to the 1953 position regarding the size of the Commission.

The Conservative White Paper in 1964 proposed to further extend the scope of the Monopolies Commission into mergers and restrictive practices relating to service trades. But in return for this, the Monopolies Commission would be enlarged and would be empowered to work in sub-divisions. The Monopolies and Mergers Bill of the Labour Government provides for this enlargement of the Monopolies Commission.[2]

[1] R. B. Stevens and B. S. Yamey, *The Restrictive Practices Court*, p. 143.

[2] Bill 92, March 3, 1965, Clause 1, Monopolies and Mergers Act, 1965, op. cit. The Act provides that there shall be not less than four nor more than twenty-five members of the Commission; the Board of Trade may increase the maximum by order by statutory instrument.

This legislation has been long overdue. The Commission has been incapacitated since 1956 by its shortage of members.

ALTERATIONS IN THE SCOPE OF THE MONOPOLIES COMMISSION

The Supply of Services

The 1948 legislation had restricted the scope of the Monopolies Commission to the supply, processing, and export of goods. The service trades were largely excluded from the scope of the Commission. During the early 1960s the Conservative Government encountered increasing criticism relating to this omission. Remedial legislation was proposed in the 1964 White Paper. The Government proposed to empower the Monopolies Commission 'to make inquiries in the field of commercial services (in particular, services relating to goods) at the request of the Government where the latter consider this to be necessary in the public interest'.[1] Restrictive practices in the service sector would fall within the scope of the Monopolies Commission, and would be exempt from the obligation to registration and to potential review by the Restrictive Practices Court.

The Labour Government proceeded to meet the proposal of the Conservative Party White Paper in the Monopolies and Mergers Bill of March 1965. Clause 2 would empower the Monopolies Commission to inquire into the supply of services at the reference of the Board of Trade. The relevant conditions for an inquiry would be the same as those for the supply of goods. Services rendered under a contract of service or free of charge, and arrangements relating to pay, conditions of employment, etc., would be excluded from consideration.

Mergers and Take-over Bids

The wave of mergers and take-over bids during the 1950s and the early 1960s inspired considerable unease in political and economic quarters. In particular, it was feared that mergers provided a useful device for evading competition stimulated by the decisions of the Restrictive Practices Court. Action was clearly required: 'The need for remedial legislation here is urgent; and no better precedent could be found than Section 7 of the Clayton Act.'[2]

In February 1963 the Bow Group[3] strongly recommended that mergers should be subjected to public review. The Bow Group was not anxious to submit a large number of mergers and prospective mergers to

[1] Cmnd. 299, op. cit., p. 7.

[2] R. Stevens, 'Experience and Experiment in the Legal Control of Competition in the United Kingdom', *The Yale Law Journal*, Volume 70, No. 6, May 1961, p. 901.

[3] *Monopolies and Mergers*, op. cit.

a Monopolies Commission inquiry. It suggested that only those mergers involving a consideration of over £1 million should be notified to the administration. Each such merger might be notified to the Board of Trade by submission of a prospectus setting out the reasons for it and the public interest considerations involved. This requirement would eliminate a number of mergers clearly inimical to the public interest. The Bow Group anticipated that few cases would actually need to be referred to the Monopolies Commission. Any review would pose serious problems: 'Any thorough investigation will be complex and might last months or even years. If it occurred before a merger it would cause serious delay. . . . It would have to be based on expectations rather than on facts and would probably deter at least some valuable mergers.'[1]

In March 1963 the Bow Group received support for its mergers proposals from the Poole Committee. The Poole Committee emphasized the difficulty in dissolving 'scrambled' mergers, even when this was desirable. It warned that undesirable mergers should, therefore, be eliminated at birth: 'To be effective, policy will have to take a step forward in time and come to grips with mergers threatening to create or accentuate a harmful monopoly situation. The emphasis will have to shift from cure to prevention.'[2]

The Poole Committee recommended that companies should be required to notify the proposed Registrar of Monopolies when contemplating mergers resulting in a combination of net assets exceeding £1·5 million or where one or more of the companies concerned had net assets exceeding £1 million. If the Registrar considered that the proposed merger would result in market dominance he should refer the proposal to the Monopolies Commission. It should be possible to prevent a merger being completed pending investigation by the Commission. Where the Commission gave a provisional clearance to the merger it should not be precluded from subsequently investigating the monopoly which had thereby arisen.

The Conservative White Paper in 1964 proposed action in relation to mergers. The Conservative Government considered that a small minority of mergers might have harmful results. It was desirable that such cases should be investigated: 'For this purpose the Government propose that the new Monopolies Commission should be empowered, at the direction of the Board of Trade, to inquire into any proposed or recently completed merger which would result in a monopoly or would increase the power of an existing monopoly.'[3]

The Government did not anticipate that inquiries of this nature would often be required. Firms contemplating a merger might always

[1] *Monopolies and Mergers*, p. 79.
[2] *Monopoly and the Public Interest*, March 1963, op. cit., p. 14.
[3] Cmnd. 2299, op. cit., p. 4.

consult the Board of Trade about the proposals. Where an inquiry was referred to the Monopolies Commission, the latter's attention would be directed to such considerations as efficiency, technical and technological advance, industrial growth and competitive power in international trade. The Conservative Government rejected the Poole committee recommendation that powers should be sought to hold up proposed mergers while they were examined. It was felt that this could frustrate desirable mergers. The Government would be responsible for taking appropriate action in the light of a Monopolies Commission report. The exercise of proposed powers would be subject to Parliamentary approval.

The Labour Government subsequently introduced a Bill relating to mergers. The Monopolies and Mergers Bill would permit the Board of Trade to refer a merger or a proposed merger to the Monopolies Commission where the merger would lead to or strengthen a monopoly position (as defined) or alternatively where the value of assets taken over would exceed £5 million. As a general rule, a merger might not be referred more than six months after its completion; special provision was made, however, for the case where the completion of a merger was neither published nor notified to the Board of Trade. The Monopolies Commission would be required to report within six months, or in exceptional circumstances within nine months, whether the merger operated or might be expected to operate against the public interest.

Where a reference was made to the Monopolies Commission, the Board of Trade might make temporary 'standstill' orders to prohibit the completion of the merger. These temporary orders would be subject to annulment in pursuance of a resolution of either House of Parliament, and there was provision for automatic expiration. Clearly, however, the Labour Bill extends further than the proposals in the Conservative White Paper.

The Bill makes special provision in relation to newspaper mergers. Board of Trade consent would be required for the transfer of daily or Sunday newspapers, or newspaper assets, to persons already having newspaper interests, if such persons already controlled, or would control through the transfer, daily or Sunday newspapers having an aggregate weekly circulation in the United Kingdom in excess of three million copies. Transfers without consent would be unlawful and void, and would give rise to criminal offences. The Board of Trade would be required to refer the proposed transfer to the Monopolies Commission within one month of applications, except where the newspaper operated at a loss or where the case was one of urgency. The Monopolies Commission would be required to report within the same time limit as for other mergers. It would have regard to the need for accurate presentation of news and free expression of opinion. There would be provision for the appointment of additional members to the Commission for such references.

In certain respects the provisions of the Bill in relation to mergers give rise to anxiety. It is difficult to see how the Commission could produce an authoritative report in the time allotted. Inevitably, speculation would be of paramount importance. Historical data would be largely irrelevant in the majority of inquiries. The Monopolies Commission could easily mar its reputation in other fields by poor work on merger references. It is to be hoped that the existence of legislative powers will deter the less beneficial mergers. It would be a pity to expose the Monopolies Commission to public ridicule.

THE CONSTITUTION AND PROCEDURE OF THE MONOPOLIES COMMISSION

The Conservative Government proposed, in its White Paper, a radical alteration in the scope and the procedure of the Monopolies Commission. The proposals were intended to counter the criticisms of those investigated that the Monopolies Commission combined the functions of judge and prosecutor. The proposals were designed to provide a clearer distinction between the factual investigation stage of the Commission's inquiry and the public interest assessment stage.

The Conservative Government proposed, to this end, to appoint a Registrar of Monopolies who would be responsible for effecting the factual investigation, and for setting out for the Monopolies Commission the questions and issues involved. The Registrar 'would be available to assist the Commission in its task of assessing where the public interest lay by making such further investigation and elucidation as the Commission might find necessary'.[1]

The Registrar would have been responsible for selecting references for inquiry by the Monopolies Commission. Selected references would be subject to approval by the Board of Trade. The Conservative Government considered that the Registrar would be of assistance to the Monopolies Commission, and that his independence would be recognized by industry. He might consult with companies prior to considering the possibility of recommending a Monopolies Commission reference.

The White Paper proposal was not incorporated in the Monopolies and Mergers Bill introduced in March 1965. The Labour Government wished to consider the issue more deeply before introducing further legislation. This omission is most fortunate. For the proposals of the White Paper would damage the administrative approach to market dominance. An administrative inquiry has the advantage over a judicial review of greater informality. Where the issues are complex, informality

[1] Cmnd. 2299, op. cit., p. 2.

may allow for a more searching examination and more relevant and soundly-based conclusions. The White Paper proposals would largely isolate the Monopolies Commission from the factual investigation. Like the Restrictive Practices Court, the Monopolies Commission would base its judgments upon evidence placed before it.

The Registrar of Monopolies could scarcely be considered independent, when he was clearly responsible for selecting references for inquiry and review. By the nature of his occupation he would be pressed into the role of prosecuting counsel—like his counterpart, the Registrar of Restrictive Trading Agreements.

The Monopolies Commission should be retained in its present form, and on an enlarged basis. The Clarification Hearing should be eliminated and should be superseded by a series of informal meetings between the Monopolies Commission and the companies under examination. The formal Public Interest Hearing might then proceed on a more relevant and more satisfying basis.

POWERS TO IMPLEMENT THE RECOMMENDATIONS OF THE MONOPOLIES COMMISSION

Since 1956 the Board of Trade has found itself handicapped, in determining appropriate action on Monopolies Commission reports, by inadequate powers in Section 10 of the 1948 Act. The Conservative White Paper, 1964, recognized this inadequacy and proposed fresh legislation in this field:

> The powers in Section 10 of the Monopolies and Restrictive Practices (Inquiry and Control) Act, 1948, are mainly directed to dealing with restrictive agreements, which formed the main part of the Commission's work before they were transferred to the Restrictive Practices Court in 1956. These powers have not been found suitable for dealing with all those practices of a monopoly which may be shown to be against the public interest.[1]

The Conservative Government proposed, therefore, to recast and to expand the provisions of Section 10. Powers were to be sought to require a dominant firm to divest itself of interests, although it was hoped that such powers would be rarely used.

The Labour Government's Monopolies and Mergers Bill provides for an expansion of Section 10 powers. The Board of Trade would be given additional powers to require the publication of price lists, to regulate prices, to prohibit acquisitions or to impose conditions on acquisition. The Board of Trade would also be empowered to provide for the dissolution of monopolies and mergers. Orders dissolving monopolies or

[1] Cmnd. 2299, op. cit., p. 3.

mergers would have to be approved in draft by resolution of each House of Parliament. Other orders would require affirmative resolutions by each House of Parliament.

Legislation of this nature is urgently required. The Monopolies Commission will carry no authority if those under examination are aware that the Government is unable to implement its recommendations. The statutory powers, themselves, may rarely be used; but they are most helpful in extracting voluntary co-operation from companies subjected to adverse recommendations by the Monopolies Commission.

Appendix One

MEMBERS OF THE MONOPOLIES COMMISSION 1949–64

Name	*Office yrs.*	*Date of Initial Appointment*	*Date of Resignation*	*Capacity*
Sir Archibald Carter	4	February 1, 1949	December 31, 1953	Full-time Chairman
F. T. Saunders	5	February 1, 1949	January 31, 1954	Full-time
Frederick Grant	3½	February 1, 1949	October 1952	Part-time
Gordon Stott, QC	7½	February 1, 1949	October 31, 1956	Part-time
R. E. Yeabsley, CBE	7½	February 1, 1949	October 31, 1956	Part-time
C. N. Gallie	7½	January 1, 1949	October 31, 1956	Part-time
Mrs J. Robinson	3	January 1, 1949	November 1952	Part-time
The Honourable J. Wedgewood	4½	January 1, 1949	July 1953	Part-time
Professor G. C. Allen, CBE	12	November 24, 1950	November 23, 1962	Part-time
I. C. Hill, CBE	12	Early 1951	1963	Part-time
Sir D. A. S. Cairns, QC	2½	January 1, 1954	October 31, 1956	Full-time Chairman
Sir Arnold Plant	3½	May 1953	October 31, 1956	Part-time
Sir Thomas Barnes, GCB, CBE	6	November 1953	December 1959	Part-time
Mr Birch	6	November 1953	September 1959	Part-time
Mr Heywood, OBE	3	November 1953	October 31, 1956	Part-time
Professor Goodhart, KBE, QC	2½	January 1, 1954	October 31, 1956	Part-time
Mr Gifford, OBE	2½	January 1, 1954	October 31, 1956	Part-time
Mr Cullen	2½	January 1, 1954	October 31, 1956	Part-time
Mr Davidson	—	January 20, 1954	—	Part-time
Mr Wrangham, CBE	2½	January 20, 1954	October 31, 1956	Part-time
Mr Archdale	1	February 15, 1955	January 1, 1956	Part-time
Mr R. F. Levy, QC	—	November 1, 1956	—	Full-time Chairman
Andrew Black, CBE	—	December 24, 1956	—	Part-time
Dr L. T. N. Gray	—	November 15, 1956	—	Part-time
Sir Frank Shires	4½	November 13, 1956	May 1961	Part-time
W. E. Jones, CBE	—	September 1959	—	Part-time
A. W. Roskill, QC	—	May 1960	—	Part-time

Sir L. Watkinson, KBE, CB, MC	— March 1961	—	Part-time
C. B. Miller	— October 1961	—	Part-time
Professor T. Barna	— 1962	—	Part-time
P. Walker	— 1963	—	Part-time

Appendix Two

A CASE STUDY OF THE PROCEDURE OF INQUIRY—THE IMPERIAL TOBACCO COMPANY

(GREAT BRITAIN AND IRELAND) LTD

The Monopolies Commission received two references from the Board of Trade on November 29, 1956. The first related to the supply of cigarettes and manufactured cigarette and pipe tobacco in the United Kingdom. The second related to the supply of machinery for the manufacture or packaging of cigarettes or of cigarette and pipe tobacco in the United Kingdom. Imperial Tobacco was directly involved in these references, as the principal supplier of cigarettes and tobacco and the principal purchaser of machinery.

The Executive Committee of the Board of Imperial Tobacco decided to treat the investigation as an important economic and legal matter. It constituted a Monopolies Commission Committee to undertake responsibility for the inquiry, and provided it with considerable delegated authority for this purpose. The Monopolies Commission Committee included one member of the Executive Committee, the Chief Accountant, the Company Solicitor, and the Head of the Economic Section. The Committee was required to provide the Monopolies Commission with the fullest possible assistance. Major documents prepared by the Committee for submission to the Commission were subjected to examination by the Executive Committee.

An initial meeting between the Monopolies Commission and representatives of Imperial Tobacco took place on December 13, 1956. At this meeting the Commission outlined its intended procedure of inquiry, and invited the Company to provide broad details of its organization and commercial policy.

The Commission commenced an examination of the Records and Minutes of the Company in February 1957. Commission staff examined documents dating to the initial formation of the Company, although the inquiry concentrated upon the years 1952–6. The entire operation did not end until January 1958. Meanwhile accountants seconded from the

Board of Trade were proceeding with an independent organized investigation of costs and profits.

On March 18, 1957, the Commission provided Imperial with a large fact-finding questionnaire, covering an extremely wide field. Imperial commenced work on this immediately and submitted detailed answers in three volumes in October 1957. Supplementary questions were subsequently drafted by the Commission between May 1958 and August 1959, many of them involving a great deal of empirical research on the part of the Company.

The Commission provided Imperial with a summary of information and evidence in May 1959 and requested the Company's written comments. Imperial was dissatisfied with certain aspects of the material but decided against a time-consuming reorganization and redrafting of the material. The Company was then invited to a formal Clarification Hearing on June 11 and 12, 1959.

Imperial Tobacco recognized that this factual Hearing must inevitably impinge upon matters relating to the public interest. The Committee therefore examined previous reports of the Commission in some detail, and then held a mock economic inquest in order to prepare answers for questions that might arise in cross-examination.

The Company was not represented by counsel at the Clarification Hearing, although one such representative attended the Hearing for experience prior to the Public Interest Hearing. The atmosphere of the Hearing was formal, and the Commissioners were guarded in respect of public interest issues. The Company obtained little guidance on matters which were likely to become important in the later stages of the inquiry.

On October 22, 1959, Imperial received a Public Interest letter, summarizing the factual findings of the Commission, and providing a detailed list of complaints received from other organizations and persons. The Company was requested to provide written answers to certain broadly defined questions which the Commission might consider to be of importance to the public interest.

Imperial Tobacco responded to this with detailed answers on January 7, 1960. This operation did not involve much empirical research, but it did constitute major complexities of formulation. The Committee was once again responsible for the task. By this stage counsel took an active part.

The Company was invited to a Public Interest Hearing in March 1960, for which it made careful preparations. Counsel played an important part in the organization of material for the Hearing and in the preparation of a Statement of Case. The Hearing was conducted in a formal atmosphere, and the Commission was guarded in its questions, providing little information about its own attitude towards the issues under discussion. The Company was disappointed by the lack of indications from the Commission, at this stage as to the grounds on which certain practices, etc., might be held to be against the public interest.

The Commission made further contact with Imperial on various matters between August and November 1960, including a short discussion in October concerning certain recent developments involving the Company. The Commission did not provide Imperial with any indication of the conclusions it was formulating from the information it had compiled.

On January 6, 1961, Imperial Tobacco was notified that the Report had been signed by the Monopolies Commission and was in the hands of the President of the Board of Trade. The Commission henceforth released the Company from any obligation to inform it of current developments.

The Board of Trade invited representatives of Imperial Tobacco to discuss whether there should be any excisions from the Report before publication. Discussions took place but in the absence of indication of the contents of the Report Imperial found it extremely difficult to discuss possible excisions. Since the Board refused to allow the Company a preview of the Report prior to publication, Imperial was pressed into allocating sections of the Report to separate representatives for reading in order to prepare for a noon press conference three hours after publication.

Classified Bibliography

I STUDIES IN THE THEORY OF MONOPOLISTIC COMPETITION

P. W. Andrews. *Manufacturing Business* (London, Macmillan, 1949).

J. Bain. *Barriers to New Competition* (Cambridge, Mass., Harvard University Press, 1956).

J. Bain. *Industrial Organization* (London and New York, Wiley, 1959).

W. Baumol. *Business Behaviour, Value and Growth* (London, Macmillan, 1959).

A. Phelps Brown and J. Wiseman. *A Course in Applied Economics* (London, Pitman, 1964).

E. Chamberlin. *The Theory of Monopolistic Competition* (Cambridge, Mass., Harvard University Press, 1947).

E. Chamberlin (Ed.). *Monopoly and Competition and Their Regulation* (London, Macmillan, 1954).

J. M. Clark. *Competition as a Dynamic Process* (Brookings, 1961).

H. Edwards. *Competition and Monopoly in the British Soap Industry* (Oxford, University Press, 1962).

W. Fellner. *Competition Among the Few* (New York, Kelley, 1949).

P. Sylos Labini. *Oligopoly and Technical Progress* (Cambridge, Mass., Harvard University Press, 1962).

A. P. Lerner. *The Economics of Control* (New York, Macmillan, 1944).

W. A. Lewis. *Overhead Costs* (Allen and Unwin, London, 1949).

I. M. D. Little. *The Price of Fuel* (Oxford University Press, 1953).

I. M. D. Little. *A Critique of Welfare Economics* (Oxford, University Press, 1950).

R. Marris. *The Economics of Managerial Capitalism* (London, Macmillan, 1964).

G. Means. *Pricing Power and the Public Interest* (New York, Harper & Bros., 1962).

E. Penrose. *The Theory of the Growth of the Firm* (Oxford University Press, 1959).

G. Richardson. *Information and Investment* (Oxford, University Press, 1960).

Sir D. Robertson. *Lectures on Economic Principles* (London, Fontana, 1963).

E. A. G. Robinson. *Monopoly* (London, Nisbet and Cambridge University Press, 1941).

J. Robinson. *The Economics of Imperfect Competition* (London, Macmillan, 1933).

J. Schumpeter. *Capitalism, Socialism and Democracy* (London, Allen & Unwin, 1943).

J. Schumpeter. *A History of Economic Analysis* (London, Allen & Unwin, 1961).

T. Scitovsky. *Welfare and Competition* (London, Allen & Unwin, 1952).

R. Triffin. *Monopolistic Competition and General Equilibrium Theory* (Cambridge, Mass., Harvard University Press, 1941).

P. Wiles. *Price, Cost and Output* (Oxford, University Press, 1956).

II DESCRIPTIVE AND HISTORICAL STUDIES

G. C. Allen. *The Structure of Industry* (London, Longmans, 1961).

G. C. Allen. *British Industries and Their Organization* (London, Longmans, 1959).

American Economic Association. *Readings in Industrial Organization and Policy* (New York, Irwin, 1958).

H. W. Arndt. *The Economic Lessons of the Nineteen-Thirties* (Oxford, University Press, 1944).

D. Burn. *The Structure of British Industry*, Two Volumes (Cambridge, University Press, 1958).

C. F. Carter and B. Williams. *Industry and Technical Progress* (London, Oxford University Press, 1957).

C. F. Carter and B. Williams. *Investment in Innovation* (London, Oxford University Press, 1958.)

P. L. Cook and R. Cohen. *The Effect of Mergers* (London, Allen & Unwin, 1958).

J. H. Dunning and C. J. Thomas. *British Industry* (London, Hutchinson, 1961).

R. S. Edwards and H. Townsend. *Business Enterprise* (London, Macmillan, 1959).

L. Erhard. *Prosperity Through Competition* (London, Thames & Hudson, 1960).

P. Sargent Florence. *The Logic of British and American Industry* (London, Routledge & Kegan Paul, 1958).

P. Sargent Florence. *Ownership, Control and Success of Large Companies* (London, Sweet & Maxwell, 1961).

J. K. Galbraith. *American Capitalism* (London, H. Hamilton, 1952).

J. M. Grove. *Government and Industry in Britain* (London, Longmans, 1962).

J. Jewkes, Sawers and Stillerman. *The Sources of Invention* (London, Macmillan, 1958).

F. H. Knight. *Risk, Uncertainty and Profit* (London School of Economics, 1933).

H. Levy. *Monopoly and Competition* (London, 1911).
H. Levy. *Monopolies, Cartels and Trusts in British Industry* (London, Macmillan, 1927).
W. A. Lewis. *Economic Survey* 1919–39 (London, Allen & Unwin, 1949).
A. Marshall. *Industry and Trade* (London, Macmillan, 1927).
A. C. Pigou. *Aspects of British Economic History* 1918–25 (London, Macmillan, 1947).
H. Wilson. *New Deal for Coal* (London, 1945).
T. Wilson. *Modern Capitalism and Economic Progress* (London, Macmillan, 1950).
A. J. Youngson. *The British Economy* 1920–57 (London, Allen & Unwin, 1960).

III STUDIES IN THE PUBLIC CONTROL OF MONOPOLY

American Economic Association. *Readings in the Social Control of Business* (The Blackiston Company, 1949).
A. Campbell, Ellis and Wilberforce. *Restrictive Trade Practices* (London, Sweet & Maxwell, 1957).
Cheshire and Fifoot. *Contract Law* (London, Butterworths, 1956).
J. M. Clark. *The Social Control of Business* (New York, McGraw-Hill, 1939).
D. Dewey. *Monopoly in Economics and Law*
C. D. Edwards. *Maintaining Competition* (New York, McGraw-Hill, 1949).
W. Friedmann (Ed.). *Antitrust Laws* (London, 1956).
W. Friedmann. *Law and Social Change in Contemporary Britain* (London, Stevens, 1951).
P. Guenault and J. Jackson. *The Control of Monopoly in the UK* (London, Longmans, 1960).
J. Jewkes. *Ordeal by Planning* (London, Macmillan, 1949).
F. Knox. *The Co-operative Movement and Monopoly in Britain* (London, Co-op College, 1957).
W. A. Lewis. *The Principles of Economic Planning* (London, Allen & Unwin, 1949).
D. Lloyd. *Public Policy* (London, 1953).
M. S. Massell. *Competition and Monopoly* (Brookings, 1964).
J. Miller (Ed.). *Competition, Cartels and Their Regulation* (North-Holland PC, 1962).
A. D. Neale. *The Antitrust Laws of the USA* (Cambridge, University Press, 1960).
W. A. Robson. *Nationalized Industry and Public Ownership* (London, Allen & Unwin, 1960).

B. Stevens and B. S. Yamey. *The Restrictive Practices Court* (London, Weidenfeld & Nicolson, 1965).

IV ACCOUNTING AND STATISTICAL STUDIES

L. R. Amey. *Concepts, Measurement and Determinants of Productivity Within the Firm* (unpublished PhD thesis, Nottingham, 1956).

W. T. Baxter (Ed.). *Studies in Accounting.*

The British Institute of Management. *Efficiency Comparisons within Large Organizations* (1962).

J. Dean. *Managerial Economics* (New York, Prentice-Hall, 1959).

E. O. Edwards and Bell. *The Theory and Measurement of Business Income* (California University Press, 1961).

J. Meij (Ed.). *Depreciation and Replacement Policy* (North-Holland PC, 1961).

A. J. Merrett and A. Sykes. *The Finance and Analysis of Investment Projects* (London, Longmans, 1963).

V GOVERNMENT PUBLICATIONS ON MARKET DOMINANCE 1918–65

Report of the Committee on Commercial and Industrial Policy (1918).

Report of the Committee on Trusts (1919).

Report on the Committee of Industry and Trade (1929).

Report of the Sub-Committee on Retail Prices (1920).

Report of the Committee on Restraint of Trade (1930).

The Liberal Report—Britain's Industrial Future (1928).

Employment Policy (Cmnd. 6527–1944).

Report of the Central Price Regulation Committee on Prices of Radio Valves (1946).

Cotton Industry Working Party Report (1946).

Report of the Committee on Cement Costs (1947).

Report of the Committee on the Distribution of Building Materials and Components (1948).

Report of the Royal Commission on the Press (1947–9).

Report of the Committee on Resale Price Maintenance (Cmnd. 796, 1949).

Report of the Royal Commission on the Press (Cmnd. 1811, 1961–2).

The Monopolies and Restrictive Practices (Inquiry and Control) Act, 1948.

The Monopolies and Restrictive Practices Commission Act (1953).

The Restrictive Trade Practices Act (1956).

Monopolies, Mergers and Restrictive Practices (Cmnd. 2299, 1964).

VI REPORTS OF THE BRITISH MONOPOLIES COMMISSION

Report on the Supply of Dental Goods (1950, HCP 18).
Report on the Supply of Cast Iron Rainwater Goods (1951, HCP 136).
Report on the Supply of Electric Lamps (1951, HCP 287).
Report on the Supply of Insulated Electric Wires and Cables (1952, HCP 209).
Report on the Supply of Insulin (1952, HCP 296).
Report on the Supply and Exports of Matches and the Supply of Match-Making Machinery (1953, HCP 161).
Report on the Supply of Imported Timber (1953, HCP 281).
Report on the Process of Calico Printing (1954, HCP 140).
Report on the Supply of Buildings in the Greater London Area (1954, HCP 264).
Report on the Supply and Export of Certain Semi-Manufacturers of Copper and Copper-Based Alloys (1955, HCP 56).
Collective Discrimination: A Report on Exclusive Dealing, Collective Boycotts, Aggregated Rebates and Other Discriminatory Trade Practices (Cmnd. 9504, 1955).
Report on the Supply and Export of Pneumatic Tyres (1955, HCP 133).
Report on the Supply of Sand and Gravel in Central Scotland (1956, HCP 222).
Report on the Supply of Hard Fibre Cordage (1956, HCP 294).
Report on the Supply of Linoleum (1956, HCP 366).
Report on the Supply of Certain Rubber Footwear (1956, HCP 328).
Report on the Supply of Certain Industrial and Medical Gases (1956, HCP 13).
Report on the Supply and Exports of Electrical and Allied Machinery and Plant (1957, HCP 42).
Report on the Supply of Electronic Valves and Cathode Ray Tubes (1956, HCP 16).
Report on the Supply of Tea (1956, HCP 15).
Report on the Supply of Standard Metal Windows and Doors (1956, HCP 14).
Imported Timber: Report on Whether and to What Extent the Recommendation of the Commission has been Complied With (1958, HCP 274).
Report on the Supply of Chemical Fertilizer (1959, HCP 267).
Report on the Supply of Cigarettes and Tobacco and of Cigarette and Tobacco Machinery (1961, HCP 218).
Report on the Supply of Electrical Equipment for Mechanically Propelled Land Vehicles (1963, HCP 21).
Report on the Supply of Wallpaper (1964, HCP 59).

Index

(Authors' references in CAPITALS)

Abortive development expenditure, 298
Acquisitions, 232–4
Administrative approach, 371–2
Advertising, 169–70, 171–2, 215–16
Aggregated rebates, 176–7, 335
Agricultural Marketing Boards, 67
ALLEN, G. C., 112, 241, 245
Allocation of cost, 267
Allocation of overheads, 275
Amalgamated Dental Company, 220–1
American Cotton Yarn Association, 23
American Tobacco Company, 197
American Tobacco Company v. USA, 172
Asquith Coalition Government, 19
Association of Dental Manufacturers and Traders:
  exclusive dealing, 175
  Government Order, 330
  miscalculation of profit, 307
  valuations of assets, 288–9
Associated Electrical Industries, 270

BAIN, J., 171, 181, 309
Barriers to competition, 161–86, 215–34
BAUMOL, W. J., 194–5
BENTHAM, 43
Black Nut and Bolt case, In *re*, 119
Block tariffs, 236
Board of Trade, 51, 54, 56, 57, 61, 62, 63, 66, 67, 323–78
Bonus agreement, 219–20
BOW GROUP, 68, 89, 90, 105, 345, 373–4
British Electrical and Allied Machinery Association:
  countervailing power, 132–3
  exports, 138
  profit, 317
  rate of return on capital, 302–3
  stability of prices, 117–18
British Employers' Confederation, 20
British Insulated Callenders Cables:
  economic consequences of action, 347, 355–7
  spread of costs, 266–7
British Insulin Manufacturers:
  capital allocations, 293
  Government action, 332
  market sharing, 166
  research, 143–4
British Match Corporation:
  asset valuations, 289–90
  economic consequences of action, 358–61
  efficiency, 209
  exports, 255–6
  factor control, 224–5
  Government action, 336–7
  imports, 232
  inter-plant comparisons, 275–7
  market-sharing, 167
  overseas competition, 206–7
  patents, 218
  potential competition, 211
  publication delays, 324
  scale economies, 229
British Oxygen Company:
  acquisitions, 233
  asset valuations, 290
  economic consequences, 361–5
  factor control, 225–6
  full-line forcing, 221–6
  Government action, 337–9
  independent competition, 203–4
  inter-plant comparisons, 278
  patents, 217
  potential competition, 210–11
  price discrimination, 237, 239–40
  price levels, 280–1
  profit, 311–12
  rate of return on capital, 304
  research, 251–2
  risk and uncertainty, 314–15
  selective price cutting, 230

Calico printing, 23–4, 83
Capital—*see* rate of return on
Cast Iron Rainwater Goods:
  countervailing power, 135
  non-reference good competition, 154–5

Cement Makers' Federation, In *re*, 100
Chairman of Monopolies Commission, 53, 55, 57, 59, 76, 104
Champion Sparking Plug Company:
  capital allocations, 294
  efficiency profits, 309
  high risk, 315–16
Chloride Electrical Storage Company:
  capital allocations, 293–4
  price discrimination, 238
  risk and uncertainty, 316
  scale economies, 229
  standardization, 248
CHURCHILL, WINSTON, 21
Cigarettes and Tobacco, Supply of, 73
Clarification Hearing, 84, 89
CLARK, J. M., 113, 251, 310
Coalition Government, 22
Collective boycott, 334–5. *See also* Exclusive dealing
Collective Discrimination, Report on, 70, 86–7, 174
Collective enforcement of resale price maintenance, 333–4. *See also* resale price maintenance
Commercial and Industrial Policy, Committee on, 28
Companies Act, 1948, 209
Competition in price, 109–48
Competitive process, 149–60, 201–14
Complaints, 92–3
Conservative Party and monopoly:
  constitution of Monopolies Commission, 376–7
  inter-war attitudes, 37–8
  mergers, 374
  procedure of Monopolies Commission, 86
  size of Monopolies Commission, 372
  tribunal approach to monopoly, 372
CONSERVATIVE POLITICAL CENTRE, 96, 343, 374
COOK, P. L., 167
Co-operative Movement and competition, 159–60
Co-operative Wholesale Society, 159
Copper-semis, Report on Supply and Export of:
  capital allocations, 293
  concentration, 131
  exports, 138–9
  imports, 183–4
  independent competition, 153
  overseas competition, 155
  potential competition, 157
  price fixing, 124
  quality, 124
  scale economies, 182–3
  uniform costing system, 268–9
Cost:
  costs and prices, 263–81
  spread of costs, 263–7
  uniform costing systems, 267–70
  unit costs, 274–9
Cost of Monopolies Commission Inquiries, 90–2
Cotton Industry (Reorganization) Act, 1939, 24–5
Countervailing power, 132–6
COURNOT-MARSHALL and monopoly, 64
Criteria for market-share assessment, 66
Critical issues in monopoly inquiries, 93–5
Crittall Manufacturing Company, 272, 297, 317
Crofter case, 46–7
CUNLIFFE-LISTER, Sir P., 37

Delays in Government Action, 325–6
Dental Goods Order, 1951, 327
Discount and rebate agreements, 168–9
Display arrangements, 218–220
Distillers Company, 27
Distribution processes, 246–8
Dominant firm cost advantages, 224–7
DOWNIE, J., 208
Dunlop Rubber Company:
  competition, 150
  cost spread, 266
  distribution outlets, 222
  exports, 254–5
  oligopoly, 199–200
  overseas competition, 207
  research, 252
  secret discounts, 168–9
Dyestuffs industry, 18

Economic consequences of Government action, 347–67
Economic efficiency and market dominance, 101–5, 274, 300

ECONOMIC TRENDS, 304–5
ECONOMIST, THE:
  economic consequences of action, 350–1, 354, 357, 358, 364, 366
  Government action, 342, 343
  rate of return on capital, 303, 304, 305, 318
Electrical Equipment for Mechanically Propelled Land Vehicles, Supply of:
  distribution processes, 247–8
  excisions from Report, 324
  exclusive dealing, 222
  non-reference good competition, 206
  price discrimination, 237–8
  resale price maintenance, 242–3
  scale economies, 229
  trade investments, 295
Electric Lamps, Supply of:
  asset valuation, 289
  control over resources, 179
  Co-operative Society competition, 159–60
  economic consequences of action, 347
  exclusive dealing, 176
  Government action, 335
  independent competition, 153
  inter-member competition, 151
  market-sharing agreements, 165–6
  patent agreements, 173–4
  price determination, 270
  price levels, 273
  State competition, 157–8
  uniform costing system, 268
Electric Wires and Cables, Supply of:
  concentration, 130
  countervailing power, 134–5
  economic consequences of action, 353–8
  Government action, 325, 332
  potential competition, 156–7
  spread of costs, 266–7
Employment Policy, White Paper on, 22, 126
ESHER, LORD, 45
Excisions from Monopolies Commission reports, 323–4
Exclusive dealing, 174–6, 220–2, 334–5
Export Groups, 21
Exports, 75, 253–6
External scale economies, 181
Federal Trade Commission, 61, 100
Federation of British Industries, 20, 87
Federation of Calico Printers:
  economic consequences of action, 349–53
  Government action, 328
  market-sharing agreement, 163–5
  price levels, 272–3
  price stability, 114, 123
  quality, 125
  resource control, 179–80
  standardization, 147
  statutory order, 328
  trade investments, 295
  unemployment, 128–9
Fertilizers, Supply of, 205, 206, 253, 325, 339, 340
fforde Committee, 32
Finance Act, 1935, 25
Fire insurance policies, 290–1
First World War, 19, 20, 21
Fisons Ltd:
  distribution processes, 246–7
  Government action, 339–40
  potential competition, 211
  price discrimination, 238–40
  price levels, 279–80
  profit as investment platform, 312–13
  profit miscalculation, 307–8
  risk, 315
Five Counties Scheme, 23
Fixed Percentage Quota, 162
Fixed Quota, 162
FOG, B., 150–1
Franks Committee, 55
Free entry, 157
Free trade policy, 17–18

GABOR, A., 236
GALBRAITH, J. K., 141
Gallaher Ltd, 73, 216, 246
GATT, 137, 184
General Electric Company:
  patents, 174
  price determination, 270
  resource control, 179
  scale economies, 182
GILBERT, C. B. E., 59
Gold Standard, 18, 23
Goodwill, 295–6
Government action, 323–46

Hard Fibre Cordage, Supply of:
  countervailing power, 133
  imports, 184
  market sharing agreements, 163
  price level, 274
  quality agreement, 167–8
  unemployment, 129
HARRINGTON, L. TAYLOR, 296
HEATH, EDWARD, MP, 324
HEATH, J., 349, 354, 356, 358
HM Stationery Office, 212–13, 324
Hired and rented assets, 296
HUNTER, A., 141, 187

Imperial Airways Company, 27
Imperial Chemical Industries, 205–6
  bid for Courtaulds, 209
  distribution processes, 246–7
  exports, 253
  Government action, 339–40
  initial losses, 297
  inter-plant comparisons, 277
  potential competition, 211
  price discrimination, 238–40
    risk, 315
Imperial Tobacco Company:
  acquisitions, 232–3
  advertising, 216
  concentration, 131
  cost of inquiry, 91
  display arrangements, 219–20
  distribution processes, 246
  distributive outlets, 223
  economic consequences of action, 365–7
  efficiency, 209
  exports, 253
  factor control, 226
  Government action, 340–2
  independent competition, 204–5
  interplant competition, 202–3
  oligopoly, 73, 198–9
  rate of return on capital, 304–5
  resale price maintenance, 244–5
  standardization, 248–9
Import agreements, 183–5
Import Duties Act, 1932, 18
Import Duties Advisory Committee, 25
Imported Timber Order, 1960, 328
Imports, 231–2
Independent Competition, 152–4, 203–5
Index numbers, 287–8, 292
Indivisibilities, 197–8
Industry and Trade, Committee on, 28, 29, 30
Initial losses, 296–7
Innovation, 197–8
Inter-Member competition, 149–52
Interplant comparisons, 275–8
Investment finance, 227
Investment platform, 310–13
Iron and Steel Board, 300–1
Iron and Steel Control, 20
Iron and Steel Corporation, 290
Iron and Steel Federation, 25

JEWKES, J., *et alia*, 140, 142, 143, 249

KALDOR, N., 170
KEYNES, J. M., 285
Kinked demand curve, 194–5

Labour Party on monopoly:
  administrative approach to monopoly control, 373
  coal-mining, 24
  inter-war attitudes, 21, 22, 36, 37
  legislation, 17, 72, 80, 372–3, 375–6
  State competition, 157–212
Lausanne Agreement, 183–4
LEWIS, W. A., 77
Liberal Party on monopoly, 34, 35, 36
Linoleum, Supply of:
  exports, 137
  overseas competition, 155
  price stability, 120, 273
  profit, 317
  quality, 124–5, 168
  spread of costs, 265–6
  uniform costing, 269–70
LITTLE, I. M. D., 237
LLOYD GEORGE, 19
London Builders' Conference, 333
LUCAS (J.) LTD:
  distribution, 247–8
  distributive outlets, 223
  exclusive dealing, 222
  price discrimination, 238
  rate of return on capital, 305
  risk, 316
  selective price cutting, 231
  standardization, 248
Lynskey Tribunal, 95

MacDonald, Ramsay, 18, 28
Managerial revolution, 158–9, 213–14

Market-sharing, 161–7, 334
MARRIS, R., 228
Maxwell-Fyfe (Sir David), 69
McKenna Duties, 17
MEANS, G., 214, 288
Melchett, Lord, 25
Mergers, 373–4, 375–6
MERRETT and SYKES, 282–3
Mitchell v. Reynolds (1711), 40–1
Mogul case (1892), 45
Molins Ltd:
  export profits, 308
  independent competition, 204–5
  innovation profits, 310
  machinery trials, 226–7
Monopolies and Restrictive Practices Commission Act, 1953, 53
Monopolies and Restrictive Practices Act, 1948, 51
Monopoly (defined), 64–5
Monopoly and Mergers Bill, 1965, 80
Moving Percentage Quota, 162

National Association of Rope and Twine Merchants, 133
National Economic Development Council, 56–7, 60
National Health Service, 307
National Union of Manufacturers, 20
Net annual value, 291
Net present value, 282–3
New Deal, 23
no-entry price ceiling, 156, 207
Non-reference good competition, 154–5, 205–6
Nordenfelt v. Maxim Nordenfelt Guns (1894), 41

OEEC, 181
Oligopoly, 72–4, 188–9, 193–200
open price filing, 348–52
Opportunity Cost, 90–1
Ottawa Agreement, 1932, 18–19
Overseas competition, 155–6, 206–7
Ownership of outlets, 222–4

Patent Act, 1949, 218
Patents, 172–4, 178, 217–18
Phoebus Agreement, 165–6
Pneumatic Tyres, Supply and Export of, 86, 242, 293
Potash Ltd, 231–2, 339–40
Potential competition, 156–7, 207–11
Price, 109–48, 263–81
  determination, 270–2
  discrimination, 235–41
  leadership, 196–7
  levels, 272–4, 279–81
Price agreements, 109–48
  common, 110
  concentration defence, 130–2
  countervailing power defence, 132–6
  exports defence, 136–9
  investment defence, 121–2
  maximum, 110
  minimum, 110
  quality defence, 123–30
  research and development defence, 139–146
  shopping-around defence, 119–20
    stability, 110–23
  standardization defence, 146–8
  unemployment defence, 126–30
Procedure of Monopolies Commission, 81–105
Procedure of Restrictive Practices Court, 86
Product differentiation, 171–7
Product standardization, 248–9
Profit:
  and efficiency, 309–10
  and exports, 308
  and innovation, 309–10
  and miscalculations, 307–8
  calculations, 298–9
Profiteering Act, 1919, 21, 29
Protection, 18, 19
Public Interest, 71, 72, 101, 302, 307
Public Interest Hearing, 85, 89
Publicity, 158, 212–13

Quality agreements, 167–8

Radcliffe Committee Report, 180
Radio Valves, Report on, 31–2
Rate of return on capital, 282–319
  allocation problems, 292–4
  net present value valuation, 282–3
  original cost valuation, 286–7, 288–90
  rateable value valuation, 291
  redundant assets and, 297
  reproduction cost valuation, 287–8
  Stock Exchange valuation, 284–5
  take-over bid valuation, 284
  trade investments and, 294–5
  yield valuation, 283–4

Registrar of Restrictive Trading Practices, 97–101, 348
Resale price maintenance, 241–6
Resale Prices Act, 1964, 241
Research and development, 249–53, 300
Restraint of trade, 39–44, 47
Restrictive Practices Court, 93, 98–101
Restrictive Trade Practices Act, 1956, 54, 70–1
RICHARDSON, G., 116, 148
Risk and uncertainty, 313–16
ROBINSON, JOAN, 157, 236
ROTHSCHILD, K. W., 194, 195
Royal Commission on the Press, 1947–9, 66–7
Rubber footwear, Supply of:
  capital allocations, 293
  discounts and rebates, 168
  inter-party competition, 152
  oligopoly, 200
  price level, 273
  spread of costs, 266

Safeguarding of Industry Act, 1921, 18
Sales promotion, 169–70, 299–300
Sand and Gravel in Central Scotland, Supply of, 270–1, 293
Saturn Industrial Gases Ltd, 230, 278
Scale economies, 181–3, 227–30. *See also* External scale economies
Scope of the 1948 Act, 61–80
Second World War, 20–2
Secretary to the Monopolies Commission, 74, 75, 104
Section 10 of 1948 Act, 342
Section 12 of 1948 Act, 79, 87–8, 347
Section 15 of 1958 Act, 69–70, 86–7
Select Committee on Estimates, 1953, 53, 55, 58, 61, 83, 89, 91–2, 102–3
Selective price cutting, 185–6, 230–1
Service trades, 373
SILBERSTON and SOLOMONS, 294
Simon Committee, 32, 33, 34, 62
Snowy Mountains contract, 138
Sorrell v. Smith (1925), 46
Spindles Act, 1936, 25
Staff of Monopolies Commission, 57–60
Standard metal windows, Supply of, 146, 154, 185–6, 271–2, 317
State competition, 157–8, 212
Statutory order, 79, 325–30
STEVENS and YAMEY, 345
STIGLER, J., 197
Structure of Monopolies Commission, 51–60
Supply of services, 68, 373
Swedish Match Company, 255, 336–7, 358–61
SYLOS LABINI, P., 196
Symonds, Lord, 95

Technical inquiry, 290
Timber Trade Federation, 87–8
  exclusive dealing, 334–5
  Government action, 325–6, 329, 331, 346
Time period of inquiry, 88–90
THORNEYCROFT, P., MP, 52
Tortious conspiracy, 45–8
Trade association cost advantages, 177–81
Trade Facilities Act, 1921, 27
Trades Union Congress, 87
Trusts, Committee on, 28–30
Two-part tariffs, 236
Tyre Manufacturers' Conference, 74, 168–9, 169–70, 199–200

United States Steel Corporation, 249

Wallpaper, Supply of, 76, 233–4, 243–4, 324
WILSON, H., MP, 52, 69
WILSON, T., 114, 123, 147, 149, 188
Working Party on Cotton Industry, 30
WORSWICK, G. D. N., 120

YAMEY, B., 199, 245

For Product Safety Concerns and Information please contact our EU representative GPSR@taylorandfrancis.com
Taylor & Francis Verlag GmbH, Kaufingerstraße 24, 80331 München, Germany

www.ingramcontent.com/pod-product-compliance
Lightning Source LLC
LaVergne TN
LVHW011108300926
849160LV00008B/306

* 9 7 8 1 1 3 8 8 7 8 6 3 1 *